To Jack O'Reilly
a valued colleague
in advancing the
Order's founding
principles

Carl H. Anderson

THE WAY OF LOVE

Reflections on Pope Benedict XVI's

Encyclical

Deus Caritas Est

Edited by
Livio Melina and Carl A. Anderson

PONTIFICAL JOHN PAUL II INSTITUTE FOR
STUDIES ON
MARRIAGE AND FAMILY

IGNATIUS PRESS   SAN FRANCISCO

Cover art: © *L'Osservatore Romano*

Cover design by Roxanne Mei Lum

English edition © 2006 by The Pontifical John Paul II Institute
for Studies on Marriage and Family
All rights reserved
Published in 2006 Ignatius Press, San Francisco
ISBN 978-1-58617-167-4
ISBN 1-58617-167-4
Library of Congress Control Number 2006924094
Printed in the United States of America ∞

ACKNOWLEDGMENT

The preparation of the texts of this book has been made possible by the Knights of Columbus.

CONTENTS

PREFACE

"I wish in my first Encyclical to speak of the love which God lavishes upon us and which we in turn must share with others" (*DCE* 1). With these words Benedict XVI expresses his fundamental intention in offering this course-setting encyclical to the Church. With this text he situates himself at the heart of the Gospel message and shows how such a message is in no way foreign to man. He has begun an extraordinary path for the Church, a path on which the hungering heart of every man may be refreshed by an encounter with the Good News. In the encounter of *érōs* and *agápē*, in the encounter of desire's initial spark and the divine gift that opens it up to new horizons, human love discovers in the depths of its own origins the fullness for which it constantly yearns. The brilliance of the lived encounter between *érōs* and *agápē* can be seen in the radiant countenance of the one who has experienced such a meeting in his own heart. His happiness becomes grateful joy in light of this unexpected event.

One experiences just such a joyful surprise upon reading Benedict XVI's first encyclical: surprise, due to the chosen subject, which is enormously significant for our society, as well as to the perspectives that shed light where darkness has rendered so many contemporary thinkers effectively blind.

The Pontifical John Paul II Institute for Studies on Marriage and Family, founded twenty-five years ago by a pope who, when he was a young priest, had "learned to love human love", could not receive a text such as this with anything less than joy. From the very beginning the fundamental work of the Institute has been pursuing a deeper understanding of God's intentions for marriage and family. In these twenty-five years various generations of students and professors, following the legacy of John Paul II, have been able to discover and communicate the beauty of the vocation for which all men have been created: the call to love.

With the sensitivity to the greatness of human love passed on by John Paul II, we could not only receive with joy a text in which Pope

9

Benedict "wishes to speak of love", but we could also allow ourselves to be inspired by his teaching. Following this inspiration, we have responded to the gift of the papal encyclical by offering some initial reflections on it. Professors from the Institute's various sessions have wished to express what in their understanding are the main themes of the document, approaching the topics raised by the Holy Father with different theological and philosophical perspectives. Rather than presuming to explain exhaustively the questions raised in the encyclical, this book tries to highlight the meaning and fecundity of the lines of thought suggested by the Pope. The Institute's work over the years has allowed these initial reflections to be offered even in this relatively short time. Readers will also find essential bibliographic references within the various studies that make up this book. These will hopefully allow all to deepen their understanding of the underlying themes and of the penetrating answer offered by Benedict XVI. In this way this book is offered as a path toward a fuller understanding of the profundity and richness of love.

The work that John Paul II gave to the Institute for Studies on Marriage and Family twenty-five years ago continues today to be enormously necessary for the life and mission of the Church in a world that hungers for true love. The Institute's labor is corroborated and supported by the first encyclical from Benedict XVI: Love is first lived in the family, and it is in this context that the person can first mature in love.

As we present to the public this collaborative work, carried out simultaneously in three languages, we must thank many people for their assistance. The labor of translators and writers, accomplished in such a short time, has made it possible for this book to be ready for the celebration of the twenty-fifth anniversary. Very special thanks go to the Knights of Columbus, whose generosity has made the completion of this project possible.

Rome, May 13, 2006
Feast of Our Lady of Fatima
Twenty-Fifth Anniversary of the Founding of the John Paul II Institute

Livio Melina, President
Carl A. Anderson, Vice-President of the American session

Introduction

The Way of Love

Camillo Cardinal Ruini*

We are indebted to Pope Benedict XVI for a great gift: the encyclical *Deus Caritas Est*. The language he uses is so straightforward and captivating that it can be read quickly. However, to understand in depth and absorb thoroughly the richness of his message require careful and prolonged meditation. The theme is, specifically, Christian love, but within it "the themes 'God,' 'Christ' and 'Love' are fused together as the central guide of Christian faith". Precisely so did the Pope himself describe the true purpose of this encyclical at the audience held on January 23 for the Pontifical Council *Cor Unum*. Its strength and attraction lie first in the fact that it takes seriously certain major questions and challenges, which are the fruit of common sense and of the culture in which we live. Straightaway in the opening pages, he singles out the accusation that Christianity and the Church, with their commandments and prohibitions, have poisoned and turned to bitterness the joy of love, the most precious thing in life (see *DCE* 3), and in the remainder of the encyclical he demonstrates how fallacious this accusation is, that the truth of the matter is actually quite the reverse.

Two "very concrete questions about Christian life" are then asked (see *DCE* 16), which the Pope intends to answer in his encyclical. As he himself wrote to the readers of *Famiglia Cristiana*: "Is it possible to love God [without seeing him]? And again, can love be imposed from

* Grand Chancellor of the Pontifical John Paul II Institute for Studies on Marriage and Family.

11

outside?" It is precisely the analysis of this love, *érōs* and *agápē*, in its differentiated and complex but ultimately unitary reality, compared to the biblical image of God and man, especially to "the real novelty of the New Testament", which consists "in the figure of Christ himself, who gives flesh and blood to those concepts—an unprecedented realism" (*DCE* 12), that allows us to see that Christianity does not constitute a world apart, detached from the vital relations fundamental to human existence and parallel or opposed to that primordial human phenomenon which is love, but rather one that accepts the whole person, intervening in the search for love in order to purify it and to reveal new dimensions of it (see *DCE* 7–8).

The theological density of *Deus Caritas Est* emerges most strikingly from the way in which the perturbing (in comparison to what mankind and reasoned research would expect) novelty of the countenance of the Christian God is explained—that God who, upon the death of his Son on the Cross, turns "against himself" for love of mankind (*DCE* 12)—and at the same time the profound continuity between Christian faith in God and the ongoing research of reason and the world of religions (see *DCE* 9–10). This subject, very dear to the theologian Joseph Ratzinger, was magisterially discussed by him in an inaugural lecture at Bonn University, prior to commencing teaching there on June 24, 1959. The lecture was entitled: "The God of Faith and the God of Philosophers".

Equally powerful is the encyclical's anthropological probing, especially with regard to the sensitive issue of the relationship between man and woman, between love and marriage (see *DCE* 11). In fact, this encyclical achieves the felicitous accomplishment of a theology that is radically christological and Christ-centered and is, therefore, both radically theological and anthropological. In his comments on the Vatican II texts, published in 1968 and taken from the *Lexikon für Theologie und Kirche*, Joseph Ratzinger identified *Gaudium et Spes* 22 as providing valuable insight.

In this way the first encyclical of the new pontiff also demonstrates a close link with the Magisterium of his predecessor, in particular with the encyclical *Dives in Misericordia*, through which John Paul II, by combining theocentrism and anthropocentrism, introduced us to the mystery of the love that God the Father has for us in

Jesus Christ, in the salvific force, current, and concrete requirements of the Gospel of Divine Mercy; but also with the six cycles of catechesis on human love that had the effect of an extraordinary renewal, updating and making our approach to this fundamental reality of life and its many implications more robust.

The second part of *Deus Caritas Est* is of a more directly practical nature, concerning the ecclesial exercise of the commandment of love of neighbor, but it has an "intrinsic link" with the first, as Benedict XVI states in the introduction. As the second part unfolds, we see that it is based on two specific statements posited at the beginning. The first of these is that the Church's charity is a manifestation of the trinitarian love of God, who in Christ loves us without measure and with the power of his Spirit transforms us and renders us capable of loving in turn (see *DCE* 19). The second is that, as a consequence, the exercise of love of neighbor is the essential duty of the Church, of every believer in fact, but also of the entire ecclesial community at every level, as is also the proclamation of the Word and the administering of the sacraments (see *DCE* 20–25).

Also in the second part of the encyclical, the Pope tackles an objection that has been brought against the charitable activities of the Church ever since the nineteenth century and that has gained greater ground in recent decades even, to a certain degree, in ecclesial circles: that the poor need justice rather than charity, which only serves to soothe people's consciences and hampers the establishment of justice (see *DCE* 26). The reply to this objection was prepared after a thorough study of the ties between charity and justice, between Church and politics. Benedict XVI makes it quite clear that both the essential link that unites politics with justice and the distinction between State and Church that belongs to the fundamental structure of Christianity, in light of the fact that justice "is both the aim and ... intrinsic criterion of all politics" (*DCE* 28a), are ethical in nature.

Equally clear in those pages of the encyclical is the affirmation that no just ordering of the State can ever render the service of love superfluous. To think the opposite is to imply a materialistic concept that "demeans man and ultimately disregards all that is specifically human" (*DCE* 28b), as a result of which the living, breathing man is sacrificed to the *moloch* of a hypothetical future.

In the face of "incomprehensible and apparently unjustified suffering in the world" (*DCE* 38), charity does not doubt the power and goodness of God. It remains unshakably certain that God is our Father and that he loves us (see *DCE* 37–38). The hymn to charity in the First Letter to the Corinthians (cf. *DCE* 13) is therefore the *Magna Carta* of all ecclesial service. Practical activity will always be insufficient unless it visibly expresses a deep personal sharing in the needs and suffering of others, my being personally present in my gift (see *DCE* 34). With this encyclical the Pope invites us "to experience love and in this way cause the light of God to enter into the world" (*DCE* 39) in the certain knowledge that love is possible, as borne out by the uninterrupted chain of saints who have put this into practice, in particular as shown by Mary who, beneath the Cross of her Son, became the Mother of us all forever (see *DCE* 40–42).

Deus Caritas Est has already been read by large numbers of people around the world. It offers them, in the context of love, a concise, profoundly reasoned presentation of faith in Christ, where God the Creator, who is Intelligence and Love, becomes, in the Son, one of us, loves us, forgives us, and introduces us into his eternal communion of life forever. In this way he points out the path of existence to us, be it personal or social, public or private, to be lived in freedom according to the rule of truth and love, and gives us the strength to proceed honestly down this path. We shall, consequently, be helped considerably by this encyclical in our duties as pastors and evangelizers. The charitable witness and activity of the ecclesial community in particular will benefit greatly from it. The pastoral care of the family as well as the everyday lives of Christian families will be enlightened and encouraged, as they find in it the full and authentic sense of the love that holds them together.

Sharing wholeheartedly in this grand ecclesial vision, the John Paul II Pontifical Institute for Studies on Marriage and Family welcomes with joy the Pope's encyclical. On May 13, 1981, John Paul II entrusted to the Institute the mission of studying God's design for marriage and the family and preparing an "adequate anthropology" that would endeavor to understand and interpret man in his essentially human aspect, in the light of faith and with the help of the human sciences and in close connection with the urgent pastoral needs of the Church. A suitable method would be needed for this: beginning both with divine revelation and the original human experience and enclosing them in a circularity in which they can throw light upon each other.

The John Paul II Institute consequently sees in *Deus Caritas Est* a valuable confirmation of the path followed and an invitation to continue along it, renew it, and study it in depth. Its mission has been reinvigorated by the invitation of Benedict XVI to turn our gaze toward love, the center of Christian faith. On the celebration of its twenty-fifth anniversary, the Institute recalls its founder, the Servant of God Pope John Paul II, with everlasting affection. Through his Magisterium we have been able to learn how much the Christian God loves human love and sets it as the path to be followed so that mankind may arrive at friendship with him.

It is with great joy, therefore, that I present this commentary to you, prepared by the professors of the different departments of the Institute. This text, written by those who devote their time to studying the place of human love in the divine plan, is an initial examination of the papal document. These pages offer the theological context for some of the insights of the document as well as the new horizons that the encyclical opens up for Church's evangelizing mission. They are intended to be a starting point for a renewed reflection on human love that shows how "to experience love and in this way to cause the light of God to enter into the world" (*DCE* 39).

From this point of view, and in the present situation, the Institute's mission becomes both urgent and exciting at one and the same time. "The debasement of human love, the suppression of the authentic capacity for loving, is turning out in our time to be the most suitable and effective weapon to drive God away from men and women, to distance God from the human gaze and heart." Faced as we are by this culture of death it is now more necessary than ever to study through and through the unity of God's design for the individual, for marriage, and for the family, on the basis of an adequate anthropology. Yes! We have to insist upon this: "It is therefore the vocation to love that makes the human person an authentic image of God: man and woman come to resemble God to the extent that they become loving people" (Benedict XVI, addressing the Ecclesial Diocesan Convention of Rome, June 6, 2005).

Love: The Encounter with an Event

Livio Melina[*]

Overture

"Man cannot live without love. He remains a being that is incomprehensible for himself, his life is senseless, if love is not revealed to him, if he does not encounter love, if he does not experience it and make it his own, if he does not participate intimately in it." In *Redemptor Hominis* (*RH* 10), the inaugural encyclical of his pontificate, Pope John Paul II indicated in this way the existential value of love for the human being, that is, the centrality of the experience of love for the destiny of the person. In his first encyclical, Benedict XVI sets out once more from this very same place in order to bring us back to the heart of the Christian message: "Being a Christian is not the result of an ethical choice or a lofty idea, but the encounter with an event, a person, which gives life a new horizon and a decisive direction" (*DCE* 1). It is well known that the first notes of a symphony determine the dominant theme of the rest of the musical conversation. Certainly, a pope who is passionately fond of music is attuned to such logic: Why, then, the choice of this "overture" at the beginning of the new pontificate?

Speaking of the theological vision of Hans Urs von Balthasar, the theologian Joseph Ratzinger affirmed that not only the theological problem, but also the pastoral problem of the Church today is to "arrange for people to encounter the *beauty* of the faith" (Ratzinger 2005: 36; italics added). Christianity is not first of all a doctrine to be studied (*logos*) or an ethics to be applied (*ethos*). It is an event that enthralls with its incomparable beauty because it reveals the love of God that comes to us in Christ.

---

[*] President of the Pontifical John Paul II Institute for Studies on Marriage and Family.

Indeed, this is the event spoken of in John's Gospel: "For God so loved the world that he gave his only-begotten Son, that whoever believes in him should . . . have eternal life" (Jn 3:16). "There is nothing more beautiful than to be surprised by the Gospel, by the encounter with Christ." Thus the duty of the pastor, although it can appear difficult, is indeed in itself beautiful and great, because in reality "it is truly a service to joy, to God's joy, which longs to break into the world" (Homily of the inaugural Mass of the Pontificate, April 24, 2005). Benedict XVI intends, therefore, to bring us back to the living center, to the essence of the Christian message, in order to find in it again the freshness and the simplicity of an event. This event astonishes, opens a new horizon, and gives life a new and decisive direction: a direction that is determined by the discovery of the Love of the Father that comes to us in Jesus.

In all matters, the beginning has an absolutely singular value. The beginning of being a Christian is not an act of our will or a thought of our intelligence. The beginning is not made by us; it is given to us; it is an event that happens. Something new, unforeseen, and unpredictable enters into time, into the event of humanity and of every single person. The astonishment awakened in the encounter is born from the exceptional correspondence that is experienced with the original makeup of man's own heart. While interiorly transformed by the event that has taken place, man discovers at the same time the innate sense of being created by God.

> All that begins has a virtue that is never found again,
> A force, a newness, a freshness as the dawn.
> A youth, an ardor. A surge. An ingenuousness.
> A birth that is never found again.
> The first day is the day most beautiful.
> The first day is perhaps the only beautiful day.
> And baptism is the sacrament of the first day.
>   (Péguy 1978: 28)

Love enters silently and mysteriously into man's life on the holy day of baptism, but it is a human and personal encounter that awakens, or reawakens, this beginning with the same gratuity through a gift of the Spirit. This encounter makes it a human beginning, conscious and free, of a new adventure of faith, hope, and love. St. Augustine teaches us: "Initium ut esset creatus est homo, ante quem nullus fuit" (So that there may be a beginning, man was created, before whom nothing was) (*De civitate Dei* XII, 20, 4). Man is called to create a newness in the world, the very newness of love, precisely in the grateful memory of its origin from the Love of God. Every action that distances itself from this beginning is nothing other than a re-action, which mechanically reproposes the banality of evil (cf. Arendt 2000: 177–78).

Thus, according to the encyclical, the human experience of the encounter, and in a singular way of the encounter of love, becomes the key for grasping the very message of revelation. "The message of love proclaimed to us by the Bible and the Church's Tradition has some points of contact with the common human experience of love" (*DCE* 7). A "virtuous" hermeneutical circle is thus created, in which the experience of human love offers the analogy for understanding the incomprehensible Love of God manifested in Christ, which, remaining all the while the original and transcendent foundation of human love, comes to expression within human love, transforming it profoundly but without ever denying its creaturely structure. The Redeemer is in fact the Creator himself, who brings to fulfillment the initial good of his work of love.

Moreover, the beginning of love, which streams forth from the wound of beauty, cannot remain an aesthetic moment that is exhausted in itself. By its very nature, it is a principle of movement toward fulfillment. "Love is indeed 'ecstasy', ... but [ecstasy] as a journey" (*DCE* 6) toward fulfillment. In the initial event, love has the character of a promise and, by its innate character, moves toward completion. But what is the source, what is the nature, what is the dynamic of such a journey, which is the "journey of love"? Here, then are the milestones that signal the direction of the journey. In order to touch the concrete human reality, the event also bears a human structure, into which it is taken up and integrated.

Love as a Response: The Source of Love

Søren Kierkegaard poses these questions and answers in *The Works of Love* (Kierkegaard 2003: 157): "Where is love born? Where is its origin and font? Where is the place that contains it and from which it emanates? Yes, this place is hidden, that is, it is in hiding. It is a place hidden within man. From this place emanates the life of love, because 'life proceeds from the heart' (Prov 4:23)." The root from which love comes is more profound than its conscious life; it is more intimate and secret than the very desire in which it is manifested. It precedes the conscious motivations of our acts.

In the phenomenology of erotic experience, desire seems to have primacy. We sense ourselves to be needy, lacking, and seeking fulfillment. According to Plato, *érōs* is the offspring of *penia*, which indicates that something is lacking in its origins, which makes us tend ineluctably toward an unknown and intangible fullness. [The Greek word *penia* means poverty or need.] It is also the offspring of *póros*, of a secret wealth. [The Greek word *póros* in general means a pathway or a means of achieving or accomplishing] (*Symp.* 203bff.). Thus begins the drama of desire, which is "a thirst of the soul", according to the definition of St. Augustine (*Enarr. in Ps.* 62:5), which stretches us beyond what we think to desire. Blondel observed that "our desires often hide from us our true desires" (Blondel 1973: 170). What do we truly desire; what is the object of our perennially unsatisfied love? The Latin authors rejoined the term *desiderium* (desire) to *sidera* (the stars): something grand but also unreachable. The Caligula of Albert Camus desired the moon. But not even the moon, now conquered, is enough for the human heart. *Quid animo satis?* (What satisfies the soul?)

Thus, the ambiguity within desire emerges. On one hand, it is the memory and nostalgia of the infinite, the yearning for the stars; on the other hand, it is the restless, ever-unsatisfied retreat toward the finite, incapable of satisfying the thirst of the heart. Entrusted only to desire, love seems to be lost as an unrealizable dream. Nonetheless, desire knows something of what it ineluctably seeks, without being able to realize it. "Amor praecedit desiderium" (love precedes desire), St. Thomas Aquinas affirms, when speaking about the order of the passions among themselves (*STh* I–II, 25, 2). Before the movement toward the beloved, we undergo a passion due to external reality, which influences us and gives rise to desire. In order to desire, it is necessary to love: "desiderium ex amore" (desire from love) (*Contra Gentiles* IV, 54, no. 3926). There is an ontological priority of love over desire and over every other passion, so that love is the first and common root of every action.

Human love, in its appetitive dimension, is always a response to a first love that has been given. What is, then, the initial love? It is not only a natural love, understood as a metaphysical principle of movement of all creatures toward the perfect Good, from whom these originate and whom they naturally love more than themselves (*STh* I, 60, 5). Rather, it is love as a principle of affective movement, stretching out toward union with the object that is loved.

"Since God has first loved us (cf. 1 Jn 4:10), love is now no longer a mere 'command'; it is the response to the gift of love with which God draws near to us" (*DCE* 1). On the cause of our love for God, St. Bernard states that "in seeking the cause by which one must love God, one begins with seeking the merit of God. The main point is that he has first loved us. Therefore, he is worthy to be loved in return, especially if one draws attention to whom he has loved, to whom has been loved, and to how much he has loved" (*De diligendo Deo* I, 1). The source of love precedes us: it is in us, in our greatest depths, but as a gift gratuitously bestowed in our life, which astonishes us and reveals its meaning, which is directed toward a destiny greater than any desire that man could conceive.

The Realism of Love and the Movement of Affectivity

When God commands us to love, he does not impose upon us a commandment that concerns "a feeling which we ourselves are incapable of producing". In fact, "in the gradual unfolding of this encounter, it is clearly revealed that love is not merely a sentiment" (*DCE* 17). Love is a response to an event, which takes place and enters into one's life "first", urging a free and personal embrace. But now we must follow the affective dynamic of love that evokes in the lover a movement toward the full encounter with the beloved: "evokes", that is, calls forth, inviting freedom to that gift of self in which it finds its ultimate truth. In fact, "man, who is the only creature on earth which God willed for itself, cannot fully find himself except through a sincere gift of himself" (*GS* 24).

Scripture itself, read in the Church's tradition, recommends here the analogy of human and divine love. The Song of Songs offers an example of amorous language, taking seeing and hearing as a point of departure from which profound admiration is awakened, the origin of affectivity: "O my dove, in the clefts of the rock, in the covert of the cliff, let me see your face, let me hear your voice, for your voice is sweet, and your face is comely" (Song 2:14). The affective dimension consists in being impacted, through the senses, by characteristics of the object that render it lovable: the comely face and the sweet voice.

Since both poles are necessary for love—the lover (the subject of love) and the beloved (the object perceived as lovable)—it is manifested not only as an impulse, but as an initial affective union. The latter has a twofold character: it is an *intentional* presence of the beloved in the lover, which gives origin to a *dynamism*, insofar as it arises from the attraction that the beloved has awakened and continues to awake in the lover. This very singular dynamic aspect distinguishes the affective moment from a merely speculative type of knowledge of the object. Love's mode of knowing is different from and original to every other sort of knowledge because it arises within a perception of the suitableness [*convenienza*]† of the beloved. However, it is not a selfish point of view, which would reduce the beloved to a horizon of mere interest for the lover. In fact, love is from the beginning *vis unitiva et concretiva* (a power that unites and joins together), according to the formula of Pseudo-Dionysus that is often repeated by Aquinas (Dionysius, *De div. Nom.* 4, 12: *PG* 3, 709d; cf. *STh* I–II, 25, 2).

Love is not satisfied by union with the beloved on the intentional level: in order to be faithful to its intrinsic dynamism, it must seek real union. It is this real union, in fact, that presents itself as suitable (*conveniente*).* Simultaneously, then, the realist character of love becomes evident, which truly tends toward the other and not simply toward the impression that the other has awakened in the subject of the lover. In order to be realized, it must be founded on the objective suitability with the beloved, according to the design of creative wisdom, within which love, too, finds its ultimate meaning.

---

* From *con-venire*—to come together, to come with.

The Person and Love

Benedict XVI reminds us that the event of love is always an encounter with a person. As the encyclical affirms, speaking of the Song of Songs: "The experience of love ... involves a real discovery of the other, moving beyond the selfish character that prevailed earlier" (*DCE* 6). The intentionality of love has a person as its proper end, either another or oneself. "Love is the name of a person", St. Thomas Aquinas affirms (*STh* I, 37, 1). We are able to love the things we desire only in reference to a person whom we love, while it is only a person whom we are able to love for himself.

This singular correlation between love and person was perceived and expounded systematically by the personalism of the last century, which defended, on one side, the irreducible subjective singularity of the person that emerges in love and, on the other side, the originality of the knowledge that love permits and that is qualitatively distinguished from other forms of knowledge.

Love implies, first of all, an approval of the other, of the goodness of his existence, an approval that unites the human act of love with the gaze of the Creator, who sees and approves the goodness of his creatures. Joseph Pieper has expressed this idea in this way: "Loving someone or something means finding him or it ... 'good'. It is a way of turning to him or it and saying: 'It's good that you exist; it's good that you are in this world!'" (Pieper 1997: 163–64).

In the presence of a person, this approval does not stop at the particular qualities of the beloved, which could be found in other persons as well, perhaps even to a greater degree. Instead, it is bound up with human being itself in its unrepeatable uniqueness. Faced with the loss of someone we love, to find consolation in saying, "in the end, I could also find the same beauty, the same intelligence, and the same virtues in some other", would mean never having truly loved that person in his uniqueness, having stopped at the superficial things that selfishly suited us (cf. Crosby 1996: 61–81).

Yet from this admiration is also born a movement of active promotion of the other (cf. Nédoncelle 1957: 15–21), of energetic cooperation so that the other's destiny may be fulfilled. Love thus implies an awakening of our very person in the admiration of the other and in the mutuality of sensing our own person as precious in the eyes of the other. When the will for promotion is mutual, then, it is realized in a shared mission, which renders love visible and expresses it in the world.

The Good as a Mediation of Love

It is not possible to arrive at this point, however, without reference to the truth about the good that is intrinsic to love and that is able to direct our actions, making them adequate for realizing love as an effective promotion of the other and for establishing communion between persons. It is reason that opens this objective dimension, which measures action in its truth, not simply insofar as it is expressive of the subject, but insofar as it is effectively proportionate to the other.

The human act finds its fundamental criterion for moral goodness in being an act of authentic love, which promotes and brings about communion with the other, willing the true good of the other. Here we meet what, according to Thomas, is the specific characteristic of the movement of love, which distinguishes it from all the other motions of the soul (*STh* I–II, 26, 4). In fact, love tends at the same time, not solely toward one, but toward two objects: to the other person with whom one desires to enter into real communion and to the good, which is willed for the other and which constitutes the real, necessary mediation of love in action. "Amare est velle alicui bonum" (cf. *Contra Gentiles* III, 90, no. 2657), to love is to will the good for someone. This is the Thomistic formula that defines the act of love. If the ultimate formal intentionality is directed to the person of the other, it is done so by way of the choice for that which is truly good for that person.

The good of a particular action, which the will elects from the perspective of communion, has its own objective density, independent of the subject, which must be verified by reason in relation to the promotion of the good of the person of the other. The guarantee that it is an authentic love of friendship, in which the intention of the loving subject does not retreat into itself but goes forth from itself (ecstasy), remaining turned toward the friend who is loved in himself, is given by the subordination of the will to the truth about the good that creates communion (cf. Melina 2001: 37–51).

The objectivity of the good, perceived by practical reason within the dynamism of acting, is the condition of authenticity for the sought-after communion, which is dependent upon that which is prior to intention. In the end, obedience to such a truth about the good is a covenant with the intention of love of God's creative wisdom, which is established at the level of moral rationality and of the virtues. It finds its perfection in the inherent naturalness of the friendship with Christ that the Holy Spirit generates in the believer and that comes to be the new law of love. The natural law, which human reason is able to grasp on its own, is in fact the first level of a fullness of the law that has been revealed and fulfilled by Christ, *plenitudo legis*, as St. Ambrose affirms (*In Psalmum CXVIII Expositio*, sermo 18, 37: *PL* 15, 1541, cited in *VS* 15).

The Dynamism of Love

If love is the event of a unique encounter, it is not exhausted in the magic moment of the first self-giving, in the admiring stupor of the suitability that has been discovered with the beloved. Love invites one, rather, to a journey of purification and maturation toward fulfillment and is rooted in the truth about the good that guarantees its authenticity. Although beginning with a feeling, it does not stop at the feeling; rather, it becomes a choice of the will and a concrete task in history in order to establish the communion of persons. Whereas love is perpetual, the state of being enamored, by its very nature, comes to an end and, in order to continue, must be transformed: it must pass from the affective level to the level of the will.

Benedict XVI clearly calls attention to the fact that upon setting out from the encounter, an itinerary of growth and purification of love must develop, bringing the encounter to its fulfillment. In so doing, he warns against a limited aesthetic that would evade the necessity of moral obligation in love. If love does not wish to remain a moment but seeks rather to insert itself into human temporality, into human history and the concreteness of society, it must come to terms with the necessity of patient labor.

Here the moral perspective of love is opened anew, the fate of which is entrusted to freedom (Botturi 2004: 37–64). In fact, the morality of love signifies watching over relation, undertaking a mission beyond emotions. This allows the affirmation of the other in the concreteness of life, in the dimension of time; that is, in fidelity, in maturation, and in the responsibility to bear fruit. Thus it is understandable how love can also be a commandment.

Here, then, is delineated the complete context within which love as "an encounter with an event" is situated (Pèrez-Soba 2001: 345–77). The encounter is preceded by a *presence* that has been given, in which the person experiences a possible promise of fulfillment. This avoids an excessive activism in understanding the encounter and allows an understanding of the human act of love as a response to a prior love, which another directs toward me. The *encounter* is not therefore exhausted in itself; rather, it is the origin of a dynamism that involves personal responsibility from the moment it is perceived as the revelation of a greater richness, hidden as yet, but proclaimed as present.

The promise is an invitation to a journey and to a mission, in order to reach the fullness to which the encounter tends: the *communion* of persons. Thus, freedom is called forth to respond to the encounter with a mission. In communion, the journey's goal, one sees that the end of love is not a simple act of love but requires a mutuality that establishes the other's consent to the gift of love itself and the union of both wills in the shared action.

This analysis of the personal dynamic that sustains human love also allows us to understand, on the supernatural level, the event of the grace of Christ in terms of a personal encounter of friendship. It is only through a gift of the Holy Spirit, present in the personal event, that the encounter with Christ is recognized, generating an attraction capable of involving the person and becoming relevant in life, to the point of determining the horizon and direction of that life (Giussani 1994: 77–98).

"A new commandment I give to you, that you love one another; even as I have loved you, that you also love one another" (Jn 13:34). The primacy of grace in human action is founded on the love of the communion between Christ and the Father. Thus, the perfect Love of the most Holy Trinity, which is the love of communion, through Christ becomes the principle of every human love. Communion is not only the end of acting, the end of a restless desire; rather, it is the original gift, offered to men in the gift of Christ.

Freedom in Love

"If a man offered for love all the wealth of his house, it would be utterly scorned" (Song 8:7). In fact, it is only in freedom that one is able to love. "Freedom is the greatest good that the heavens have given to man", according to the noteworthy phrase of Miguel de Cervantes in *Don Quixote*. But human freedom finds its full meaning in being ordered to love. Only in freedom is one able to love truly, and, on the other hand, one is truly free only when loving.

Human freedom is God's great risk, and it is motivated by his aim of an authentic love from man that cannot, therefore, be required, but only called forth by way of love itself. In the face of man's refusal, the love of God assumes the form of the cross: the ultimate invitation and the ultimate respect for human freedom. The French author Olivier Clément tells of a boy who amused himself by puzzling the curate of his parish with the following dilemma: "You said that God is omnipotent. Now if he is truly omnipotent, could he perhaps create a rock so heavy that he would not be able to lift it?" He confesses that, with the passing of the years, he realized that effectively God had created such a rock so heavy that he himself could not lift it: human freedom. He could not lift it only because his hands were bound in order to respect it. We could add to the story of Clément that the hands of God were not bound; rather, they allowed themselves to be nailed to the Cross. The Cross of Christ is the culmination of love that respects the freedom of the beloved yet continues to call it forth in order to obtain a response.

At the beginning of his encyclical, Benedict XVI speaks of the timeliness and significance of the Christian message of God who is Love, "in a world where the name of God is sometimes associated with vengeance or even a duty of hatred and violence" (*DCE* 1). For some, the very idea of an absolute truth, the very idea of God, would need to be eliminated because it is the bearer of a claim that inevitably generates intolerance. Here is the dramatic challenge of the context in which humanity lives today. On one side, there is "truth" without love, which generates intolerance. On the other side, there is "love" that, in order to exist, renounces truth and its universal claim. Contemplating the Cross of Christ, the summit of love, one sees the liberating nature of Christian truth, which does not impose itself, but humbly proposes itself to the freedom of man, waiting for a response.

The Way of Testimony

Thus one can grasp the way of evangelization that Benedict XVI proposes for the Church today. More than forty years ago the great Swiss theologian Hans Urs von Balthasar said *love alone is credible*, thus posing the question of the very essence of Christianity. The "overture" of this pontificate invites us to gather around this living center, which is neither a doctrine nor an ethic, but an experience to which we must bear witness.

In fact, love can only be witnessed and proposed, never imposed. It is the truth for which we thirst and which, in order to be understood, requires that freedom be open to it. In the context of the growing secularization of the West, and in the encounter with the other world religions, the great challenge of the new evangelization requires, above all else, the possibility of encountering persons who reveal love and who open a path of love in human history with their testimony. The life of testimony, in which human love becomes a visible and perceivable sign, is the privileged place of communication of the love received in the initial event of the encounter with Christ. In fact, "he encounters us ever anew, in the men and women who reflect his presence" (*DCE* 17).

Bibliography

Arendt, H. 2000. *Vita activa: La condizione umana*. Milan: Bompiani. [*The Human Condition*. Chicago: University of Chicago Press, 1958.]

Balthasar, H. U. von. 1982. *Solo l'amore è credibile*. Rome: Borla. [*Love Alone Is Credible*. San Francisco: Ignatius Press, 2004.]

Blondel, M. 1973. *L'Action (1893): Essai d'une critique de la vie et d'une science de la pratique*. Paris: Presses Universitaires de France. [*Action (1893): Essay on a Critique of Life and a Science of Practice*. Notre Dame: University of Notre Dame Press, 1984.]

Botturi, F. 2004. "Etica degli affetti?" In *Affetti e legami*, edited by F. Botturi and C. Vigna. Milan: Vita e Pensiero.

Crosby, J. 1996. *The Selfhood of the Human Person*. Washington, D.C.: Catholic University of America Press.

Giussani, L. 1994. *Tracce d'esperienza cristiana*. In *Opere 1966–1992*, vol. 2. Milan: Jaca Book.

Kierkegaard, S. 2003. *Gli atti dell'amore*. Milan: Bompiani. [*Works of Love: Kierkegaard's Writings*. Vol. 16. Princeton: Princeton University Press, 1998.]

Melina, L. 2001. "Agire per il bene della comunione". In *Cristo e il dinamismo dell'agire*. Rome: Pul-Mursia.

Nédoncelle, M. 1957. *Vers une philosophie de l'amour et de la personne*. Paris: Aubier.

Péguy, C. 1978. *Il portico del mistero della seconda virtù*. Milan: Jaca Book. [*The Portico of the Mystery of the Second Virtue*. Metuchen: Scarecrow Press, 1970.]

Pérez-Soba, J.J. 2001. "Presencia, encuentro y comunión". In *La plenitud del obrar cristiano: Dinámica de la acción y perspectiva teológica de la moral*, edited by L. Melina, J. Noriega, and J.J. Pérez-Soba. Madrid: Palabra.

Pieper, J. 1997. *Faith, Hope, Love*. San Francisco: Ignatius Press.

Ratzinger, J. 2005. *On the Way to Jesus Christ*. San Francisco: Ignatius Press.

The Way of Love in the Church's Mission to the World

*David L. Schindler**

Our task is to reflect on the Church's charitable mission to the world as understood in *Deus Caritas Est*. Given the limits of the present forum, we make no claim of being comprehensive. Rather, our concern will be to highlight the issues most likely to arise in the current circumstances of the West. We begin with a look at Benedict's own overview of *Deus Caritas Est*.

I. The Love that "Moves the Sun and Stars" and Has a Human Face and Human Heart

Pope Benedict presents his new encyclical with Dante's words about the light that is at the same time "the love that moves the sun and the other stars" (*Paradise* 33, 145). This light and love in their unity "are the primordial creative powers that move the universe" (Benedict XVI 2006). Though these words reveal the thought of Aristotle, who "saw in *eros* the power that moves the world", Dante perceives something "completely new and inconceivable for the Greek philosopher": the revelation of God as "trinitarian circle of knowledge and love" (ibid.).

Even more, Dante saw that this trinitarian God of love has a human face and indeed a human heart in Jesus Christ. Dante thus shows the "continuity between Christian faith in God and the search developed by reason and by the world of religions", while at the same time he

---

*Dean and Gagnon Professor of Fundamental Theology, Pontifical John Paul II Institute for Studies on Marriage and Family at The Catholic University of America, Washington, D.C.

shows the novelty of a love that has led God "to take on flesh and
blood, the entire human being" (ibid.). God's *erōs*, in a word, is not
only a "primordial cosmic force"; it is also the "love that created man
and that bows down before him, as the Good Samaritan bent down to
the wounded and robbed man" (ibid.).

Although love has become a much-abused word today, Benedict
insists that we must take it up again and purify it, showing how faith
in this love might become "a vision-understanding that transforms us"
(ibid.). In an age in which "hostility and greed have become super-
powers" (ibid.) and in which religion has been abused "to the point
of deifying hatred", the burden of the encyclical is to show that a
"neutral rationality alone" (ibid.) can no longer protect us; that, on
the contrary, we "need the living God, who loved us even to death"
(ibid.).

Benedict says that the encyclical welds together the subjects "God",
"Christ", and "Love" in order to show the humanity of faith. This is
to be done above all by showing how *erōs* is transformed into *agápē*,
the "love for the other which is no longer self-seeking but becomes
concern for the other, ready to sacrifice for him or her and also open
to the gift of a new human life" (ibid.). This *erōs* that is ordered to the
self-transcendence of *agápē*—that is, in such a way that these two loves
bear an inner unity with each other—is in the first instance manifested "in an indissoluble matrimony between man and woman [that]
finds its form rooted in creation" (ibid.). It is in this relation between
man and woman that we see above all that "man is created for love"
(ibid.). Indeed, the Bible shows us how this spousal love images for us
both God's relation to man and man's relation to God. Above all, we
see in the New Testament how this spousal imagery deepens incon-
ceivably in the incarnate Logos' becoming food for us in the Eucharist, so that we now share truly in his very body and blood. With this
foundation, says Benedict, the encyclical shows that "the essence of
the love of God and neighbor as described in the Bible is ... the
center of Christian existence, the result of faith" (ibid.).

The second part of the encyclical underlines how "the totally personal act" of *agápē* cannot remain something "isolated"; rather, it must
on the contrary "become also an essential act of the Church as community" (ibid.). "It also requires an institutional form which is expressed

in the communal working of the Church" (ibid.). This communal working is more than "a form of social assistance that is casually added to the Church's reality, an initiative that could also be left to others" (ibid.). In its communication of love of neighbor, the Church's charitable activity must "make the living God in some way visible" (ibid.). "In charitable organization, God and Christ must not be foreign words; in reality, they indicate the original source of ecclesial charity" (ibid.). Thus, in a word, "charitable commitment has a meaning that goes well beyond simple philanthropy" (ibid.). God himself moves us "interiorly to relieve misery", and in this way "it is he himself whom we bring to the suffering world" (ibid.).

II. The Relation between Justice and Charity and the Distinctiveness of the Church's Charitable Activity in the World

Benedict says in his presentation of *Deus Caritas Est* that the two parts of the encyclical are well understood only if seen as a whole (ibid.). This unity is evident immediately in Benedict's placing of the Church's mission to charitable activity in the light of the Trinity and of the Father's sending of his Son in the Spirit. The Church's charitable activity, in its most fundamental meaning, is a participation in the missionary love of the Son in anticipation of the gift of the Holy Spirit (*DCE* 19). "The entire activity of the Church is an expression of a love that seeks the integral good of man: It seeks his evangelization through Word and Sacrament, ... and it seeks to promote man in the various arenas of life and human activity. Love is therefore the service that the Church carries out in order to attend constantly to man's sufferings and his needs, including material needs" (*DCE* 19). It is this aspect, "the service of charity", that Benedict proposes to focus on in the second part of *Deus Caritas Est*.

(1) *The sacramental "mysticism" of the Eucharist is social in character.* Union with God entails "union with all those to whom he gives himself. I cannot possess Christ just for myself; I can belong to him only in union with all those who have become, or will become, his own. Communion [thus] draws me out of myself towards ... unity with all Christians. We become

'one body', completely joined in a single existence. Love of God and love of neighbor are now truly united" (*DCE* 14).

The transition Jesus makes to the twofold commandment of love of God and of neighbor "is [thus] not simply a matter of morality—something that could exist apart from and alongside faith in Christ and its sacramental re-actualization. Faith, worship and *ethos* are interwoven as a single reality which takes shape in our encounter with God's *agape*" (*DCE* 14). Hence "the usual contraposition between worship and ethics simply falls apart. 'Worship' itself, Eucharistic communion, includes the reality both of being loved and of loving others in turn. A Eucharist which does not pass over into the concrete practice of love is intrinsically fragmented.... The 'commandment' of love is only possible because it is more than a requirement. Love can be 'commanded' because it has first been given" (*DCE* 14).

"This principle is the starting-point for understanding the great parables of Jesus" (*DCE* 15). For example, the parable of the Good Samaritan teaches us that "anyone who needs me, and whom I can help, is my neighbor. The concept of 'neighbor' is now universalized, yet it remains concrete. Despite being extended to all mankind, it is not reduced to a generic, abstract and undemanding expression of love, but calls for my own practical commitment here and now" (*DCE* 15). Further, we see that Jesus identifies himself with those most in need—the hungry, the thirsty, the stranger, the naked, the sick, and those in prison. In a word, "love of God and love of neighbor have become one: in the least of the brethren we find Jesus himself, and in Jesus we find God" (*DCE* 15).

(2) *The saints and Mary*. It is the saints who above all exhibit the inseparability of the love of God and the love of neighbor. The saints "constantly renewed their capacity for love of neighbor from their encounter with the Eucharistic Lord, and conversely this encounter acquired its realism and depth in their service to others" (*DCE* 18). The double commandment to love God and to love one's neighbor both "live from the love of God who has loved us first" (*DCE* 18).

Benedict says that "prayer, as a means of drawing ever new strength from Christ, is concretely and urgently needed" (*DCE* 36). Citing Mother Teresa on the need for a connection with God in our daily life (*DCE* 36), the Pope stresses "the importance of prayer in the face of the activism and the growing secularism of many Christians engaged in charitable work" (*DCE* 37).

It is Mary above all who reveals the unified meaning of this double commandment and the significance of prayer. In her great words— "My soul magnifies the Lord"—she "expresses her whole program of life: not setting herself at the center, but leaving space for God, who is encountered both in prayer and in service of neighbor—only then does goodness enter the world" (*DCE* 41). "Rather than carrying out her own projects, [Mary] places herself completely at the disposal of God's initiatives" (*DCE* 41). In "her quiet gestures", "in the delicacy with which she recognizes the need of the spouses at Cana and makes it known to Jesus", we see that she is a woman who loves (*DCE* 41).

The saints thus make one thing clear: "Those who draw near to God do not withdraw from men, but rather become truly close to them. In no one do we see this more clearly than in Mary" (*DCE* 42).

(3) *The Church's responsibility for charity.* Love of neighbor, says the Pope, is first of all "a responsibility for each individual member of the faithful, but it is also a responsibility for the entire ecclesial community at every level" (*DCE* 20). This "constitutive relevance" of the love of neighbor in the Church was manifest from the beginning, for example, in the early believers' common possession of goods (Acts 2:44–45).

In time, the Church put this fundamental ecclesial principle into practice through the establishing of the diaconal office (cf. Acts 6:5–6). A group of seven persons was entrusted with the daily distribution to widows and the like. Benedict points out that these persons were not to carry out this task in a purely technical manner (*tantummodo technicum ministerium*). On the contrary, they were to be men "full of the Spirit and of wisdom" (cf. Acts 6:1–6). Which is to say, the concrete social service they were to provide was at the same time "a spiritual service" (*DCE* 21). Benedict discusses several examples of how, in the course of Church history, this charitable service is seen as essential to her "ministry of the sacraments and the preaching of the Gospel" (*DCE* 22).

The foregoing considerations point toward two essential facts: first, "the Church's deepest nature is expressed in her three-fold responsibility: of proclaiming the word of God (*kerygma-martyria*), celebrating the sacraments (*leitourgia*), and exercising the ministry of charity (*diakonia*). These duties presuppose each other and are inseparable" (*DCE* 25a). Second, "the Church is God's family in the world. In this family no one ought to go without the necessities of life. Yet at the same time *caritas-agape* extends beyond the frontiers of the Church" (*DCE* 25b).

We must remain mindful of these two essential facts if we are to understand properly the encyclical's discussion of the central issues of the relation between justice and charity and of the distinctiveness of the Church's charitable-social activity in the world—to which issues we now turn.

(4) *Justice and charity.* The Pope begins his discussion of this issue by noting the objection that has emerged since the nineteenth century with respect to the Church's charitable activity (*DCE* 26). "The poor, it is claimed, do not need charity but justice" (*DCE* 26). "Instead of contributing through individual works of charity to maintain the *status quo*, we need to build a just social order in which all receive their share of the world's goods and no longer have to depend on charity" (*DCE* 26). Benedict acknowledges that there is some truth to this argument but "also much that is mistaken" (*DCE* 26). He emphasizes that "the pursuit of justice must be a fundamental norm of the State and that the aim of a just social order is to guarantee to each person, according to the principle of subsidiarity, his share of the community's goods" (*DCE* 26). He notes that the issue of social justice has taken on a new dimension "with the industrialization of society in the nineteenth century" (*DCE* 26).

Though, admittedly, "the Church's leadership was slow to realize that the issue of the just structuring of society had to be approached in a new way", a growing number of groups, associations, and the like—especially new religious orders—were founded to combat poverty, disease, and the need for better education (*DCE* 27). Then there were the social encyclicals, beginning with Leo XIII (*Rerum Novarum*, 1891) and followed by Pius XI (*Quadragesimo Anno*, 1931) and then later by John XXIII (*Mater et Magistra*, 1961), Paul VI (*Populorum Progressio*, 1967), and the trilogy of social encyclicals by John Paul II (*Laborem Exercens*, 1981; *Sollicitudo Rei Socialis*, 1987; and *Centesimus Annus*, 1991).

In light of the above, and in light further of the complexity of today's situation due at once to the collapse of the collectivist revolution of the twentieth century and to the growth of a globalized economy, Benedict says we need to consider anew the relevance of the Church's social doctrine even beyond the confines of the Church. In so doing, he says, two fundamental points must be considered: (a) that "the just ordering of society and the State is a central responsibility of politics" (*DCE* 28a); and (b) that "love—*caritas*—will always prove necessary, even in the most just society" (*DCE* 28b). In the initial public discussion of *Deus Caritas Est* there has been much commentary on these two principles, and it is therefore important to examine them carefully. How are these principles to be understood, in light of the unity of the encyclical as affirmed by Benedict and in light as well of the changed social situation in the world?

(a) Regarding the statement that the just ordering of society and the State is a matter properly of politics, the Pope begins by affirming as "fundamental to Christianity"

> the distinction between what belongs to Caesar and what belongs to God (cf. Mt 22:21), in other words, the distinction between Church and State, or, as the Second Vatican Council puts it, the autonomy of the temporal sphere [*Gaudium et Spes*, 36]. The State may not impose religion, yet it must guarantee religious freedom.... For her part, the Church ... has a proper independence and is structured on the basis of her faith as a community which the State must recognize. The two spheres are distinct, yet always interrelated. (*DCE* 28)

It is important, especially in light of tendencies in Western liberal societies, to see that the distinction between Church and State affirmed here by *Deus Caritas Est* does not entail embrace of a purely juridical state. That is, justice remains "both the aim and the intrinsic criterion of all politics. Politics is more than a mere mechanism for defining the rules of public life; its origin and goal are found in justice, which by its very nature has to do with ethics" (*DCE* 28). The necessary distinction between Church and State, in other words, does not entail a separation between (moral) truth and the State. The purpose of the

State is not simply a matter of refereeing among various individuals and groups claiming immunity from possible coercion by other individuals or groups. On the contrary, as just stated, it is a matter of the positive pursuit of a justice intrinsically bound up with the ethical good.

Furthermore, recognition of the fact that pursuit of the just ordering of society is properly the function of the State, and not the Church, does not mean that the Church's role in this pursuit is merely negative, or indeed purely "accidental", with respect to her own proper mission. On the contrary, the issue of justice is a matter of practical reason, and this reason needs constant purification, "since it can never be completely free of the danger of a certain ethical blindness caused by the dazzling effect of power and special interests" (DCE 28). It is here, then, says Benedict, that "politics and faith meet" (DCE 28).

> Faith by its specific nature is an encounter with the living God—an encounter opening up new horizons extending beyond the sphere of reason. But it is also a purifying force for reason itself. From God's standpoint, faith liberates reason from its blind spots and therefore helps it to be ever more fully itself. Faith enables reason to do its work more effectively and to see its proper object more clearly. (DCE 28)

On the one hand, then, the Church's social doctrine gives the Church no power over the State: the two must remain institutionally-juridically separate. "The formation of just structures is not directly the duty [statim officium] of the Church, but belongs to the world of politics, the sphere of the autonomous use of reason [ad ambitum scilicet rationis sui ipsius consciae]" (DCE 29). On the other hand, this social doctrine aims "to help purify reason and to contribute, here and now, to the acknowledgment and attainment of what is just" (DCE 28a). "The Church has an indirect duty [officium intermedium] here, in that she is called to contribute to the purification of reason and to the reawakening of those moral forces without which just structures are neither established nor prove effective in the long run" (DCE 29).

It is helpful to note here the significance of Vatican II's communio ecclesiology, which, while essentially including the institutional (Petrine) dimension of the Church in fidelity to Vatican I (cf. CDF, Some

Aspects of the Church Understood as Communion), nevertheless draws out the distinct meaning of the Church as a communion of christological-eucharistic love. This ecclesiology helps to clarify further the crucial distinction being made by *Deus Caritas Est*: although the institutions of Church and State each have their own proper end, reason—the reason shared by all human beings—retains its ultimate finality in the love whose sacrament is the Church. "The Church's social teaching argues on the basis of reason and natural law, namely, on the basis of what is in accord with the nature of every human being" (*DCE* 28a). It is not the responsibility of the Church—that is, the Church *qua* formal-juridical institution—"to make this teaching prevail in political life" (*DCE* 28a). But this does not mean that she can or should "remain on the sidelines in the fight for justice. She has to play her part through rational argument, and she has to reawaken the spiritual energy without which justice, which always demands sacrifice, cannot prevail and prosper" (*DCE* 28a).

Deus Caritas Est's assigning the just ordering of society properly to the State thus implies no withdrawal whatsoever of the Church from a commitment to social justice—a commitment, for example, to the elimination of "structures of sin" in the sense developed by John Paul II (*SRS* 37; *CA* 38; *EV* 12; cf. also *Dominum et Vivificantem* 56). The issue, rather, concerns the manner in which this commitment is to be executed. The pertinent point is that, consistent with Vatican II's ecclesiology of *communio*, *Deus Caritas Est* is insisting that the Church must carry out her commitment to social justice through means that are, not directly juridical-institutional, but on the contrary a matter properly of her missionary communion-love. The commitment to social justice and to the elimination of unjust social structures is to be carried out properly by the Church *qua* communion of saints—a communion first constituted as a *sacramental gift* from God in Christ and which, as such, is not reducible to community in a "sociological-democratic" sense. It is in and through this missionary eucharistic-*communio* love that the Church "form[s] [the] consciences [of the 'People of God'] in political life and ... stimulate[s] greater insight [on their part] into the authentic requirements of justice as well as greater readiness to act accordingly, even when this might involve conflict with situations of personal interest [*etiam cum contrarium est singulorum lucri*]" (*DCE* 28a).

(b) This leads to the second principle emphasized by Benedict: "love—*caritas*—will always prove necessary, even in the most just society. There is no ordering of the State so just that it can eliminate the need for a service of love" (*DCE* 28b). Thus if, in accord with the principle just discussed, Christian faith/love assists rational ethical argument and social justice to be "more fully [themselves]" (*DCE* 28a), we should see that Christian love also goes beyond the justice properly realized by the State. "There will always be suffering which cries out for consolation and help. There will always be loneliness. There will always be situations of material need where help in the form of concrete love of neighbor is indispensable" (*DCE* 28b).

What the suffering person most needs, in other words, is not something that the machinery of the State as such can provide: namely, "loving personal concern" (*DCE* 28b). Indeed, as the great contemporary "saints" of charitable activity today—for example, Mother Teresa, Madeleine Delbrêl (see Delbrêl 2000), Dorothy Day (see Day 1999), and others—have emphasized, the suffering that runs deepest is that caused by the absence of meaning, especially of ultimate meaning. In this they echo the words of *Deus Caritas Est*: "Often the deepest cause of suffering is the very absence of God" (*DCE* 31c). In and through her "saints", the Church "is alive with the love enkindled by the Spirit of Christ", a love that "does not simply offer people material help, but refreshment and care for their souls, something which often is even more necessary than material support" (*DCE* 28b). To deny this is to presuppose an unacceptably "materialist conception of man" (*DCE* 28b).

"The direct duty [*proximum operandi officium*] to work for a just ordering of society", then, falls with the lay faithful who, as citizens of the State, must work for the common good in legislative as well as cultural areas (*DCE* 29). Again, this implies respecting the "legitimate autonomy" (*legitimam autonomiam*) of social life and "cooperating with other citizens according to their respective competences", that is, while recognizing that it "remains true that charity must animate the entire lives [*pervadere vitam*] of the lay faithful and therefore also their political activity, lived as 'social charity'" (*DCE* 29).

As the final phrase here suggests, it is important, apropos of a proper understanding of the relation between justice and charity, to recall again the unity of the two parts of *Deus Caritas Est* as stressed by Benedict. The reason and natural law to which the lay faithful must properly appeal in their efforts to secure justice in the political order bear an inner relation, already *qua* human-natural, to love, a love understood as an *érōs* that cannot but move toward its fulfillment in *agápē*—that cannot be fulfilled *as érōs* outside of a dynamic for transformation toward and in *agápē*. Were this not true, "the essence of Christianity would be detached from the vital relations fundamental to human existence and would become a world apart" (*DCE* 7). Were this not true, Jesus, in his path that "leads through the Cross to the Resurrection", would not portray "the essence of love and indeed of human life" (*DCE* 6). Further, ethos—ethical reason—would not be interwoven with faith and worship "as a single reality which takes shape in our encounter with God's *agape*" (*DCE* 14), as is implied in the Church's reality as sacramental *communio*.

In a word, then, the reason to which the lay faithful are to appeal in their public pursuit of justice is never "neutral" (Benedict XVI 2006). Rather, reason itself is ordered to love (cf. *DCE* 10), a love that has its first and most basic meaning in the created order in marriage and, in the New Testament, in the Eucharist of the incarnate Logos.

It is from within this ever-present dynamic for love and for encounter with the living God in Christ and his Church that the lay faithful are to carry out their proper mission of ethical formation, of purifying reason, and of being ready to act in the pursuit of social justice. To be sure, the very nature of this love itself precludes "what is nowadays considered proselytism" (*DCE* 31c). Christians living this love will "never seek to impose the Church's faith upon others. They realize that a pure and generous love is the best witness to the God in whom they believe and by whom we are driven to love" (*DCE* 31c). "A Christian knows when it is time to speak of God and when it is better to say nothing and to let love alone speak: he knows that God is love (cf. 1 Jn 4:8)" (*DCE* 31c).

In a word: the laity's necessary appeals to reason and the natural law when cooperating with other citizens in politics—appeals, that is, to the "legitimate autonomy" of social life—must not be taken to imply, even for a moment, that the reason of *every human being*, even in modern differentiated societies, is not restless for the Logos, the "primordial reason" who "is at the same time a lover" (*DCE* 10) and who is eucharistically-sacramentally present in the Church. It is this call to love—the call to fulfill human *érōs* in *agápē* in *this* sense—that must suffuse the lives (*pervadere vitam*, cf. *DCE* 29) of the laity here and now and in their common pursuit of public justice with other citizens—that is, even as we know that this call to *agápē*-inspired and -formed justice will never be completely realized in the present life and, in any case, can never be imposed or forced on others.

(5) *The distinctiveness of the Church's charitable activity. Deus Caritas Est* reaffirms John Paul II's insistence (in *SRS*) on "the readiness of the Catholic Church to cooperate with the charitable agencies of [other] Churches and [ecclesial] Communities" (*DCE* 30). *Deus Caritas Est* also affirms the fruitfulness of the "many forms of cooperation between State and Church agencies" that have grown up (*DCE* 30). The increase in diversified organizations devoted to meeting the various human needs, says Benedict, is "due to the fact that the command of love of neighbor is inscribed by the Creator in man's very nature [*a Creatore in ipsa hominis natura est inscriptus*]" (*DCE* 31). But this increase is also the "result of the presence of Christianity in the world"—and thus we see "how the power of Christianity [can] spread well beyond the frontiers of the Christian faith" (*DCE* 31). "For this reason," says Benedict, "it is very important that the Church's charitable activity maintains all of its splendor and does not become just another form of social assistance" (*DCE* 31). And so he asks: "What are the essential elements of Christian and ecclesial charity?" (*DCE* 31). What is it that Christian faith and love "add" to "secular" charitable activity? *Deus Caritas Est* answers with three comments.

(a) First, Christians who engage in social work need to be professionally competent, and this generally implies civil training that is not the peculiar prerogative of Christians. While professional competence and training are "a primary, fundamental requirement", however, they are not of themselves sufficient (*facultas professionalis prima est fundamentalis necessitas, sed sola non sufficit*) (*DCE* 31a). On the contrary, in addition to this necessary professional training, Christian charity workers require also and before all else a "formation of the heart" (*ante omnia, "cordis formatio"*) (*DCE* 31a). "Technically proper care [*cura simpliciter technice apta*]" is not enough (*DCE* 31a). Charitable workers need to be rooted in "that encounter with God in Christ which awakens their love and opens their spirits to others" (*DCE* 31a).

(b) Second, "Christian charitable activity must be independent of parties and ideologies [*factionibus et doctrinis*]. It is not a means of changing the world ideologically [*secundum quandam doctrinam*], and it is not at the service of worldly strategies [*neque adstat in ministerio mundanorum consiliorum*], but it is a way of making present here and now the love which man always needs" (*DCE* 31). *Deus Caritas Est* takes special note in this context of the "various versions of a philosophy of progress" that have dominated the modern age since the nineteenth century, citing in particular Marxism (*DCE* 31b). Such philosophies reject charity because they judge that the exercise of charity obstructs the dynamic for overturning the unjust structures of society, thus thwarting the progress of history.

(c) Third, and as already noted above, charity cannot be understood as a means of what is today considered "proselytism".

> Love is free; it is not practiced as a way of achieving other ends. But this does not mean that charitable activity must somehow leave God and Christ aside. For it is always concerned with the whole man. Often the deepest cause of suffering is the very absence of God. Those who practice charity in the Church's name will never seek to impose the Church's faith upon others. (*DCE* 31c)

In light both of *Deus Caritas Est*'s concern that Christian charity maintain its distinctness as a form of social assistance and, indeed, of dominant tendencies among Christians in Western societies, it is worthwhile to underscore how, in relying necessarily on technical training and professional competence in carrying out his work, the Christian social worker must take care to avoid slipping, however unwittingly, into the activist-secularist mindset that *Deus Caritas Est* decries (*DCE* 37).

Thus, in the texts just cited, *Deus Caritas Est* emphasizes that Christian social work necessarily presupposes professional competence—that is, because and insofar as such competence is a matter of human reason and nature. At the same time the encyclical stresses that "before all else" a "formation of the heart" involving encounter with God in Christ must accompany and penetrate this social work—because and insofar as human reason and nature in their concrete history always stand in need of puri- fication and (re-)formation. A prevalent "ideology" in our time, unspo- ken and largely unconscious, would reduce the sense of this formation to an *intention* that (otherwise) leaves the methods and content of social assistance untouched—so that secular and Christian charitable activities and organizations are then conceived to be more or less identical inso- far as they are engaged in feeding the hungry, caring for AIDS patients, providing loving homes for children, and the like. In such a framework, the specificity of Christian love is conceived largely (albeit often uncon- sciously) "moralistically", as a matter of a goodwill that simply takes over the logic of conventional professional-secular training and methods and puts the latter to a good use—by situating that logic within a new inten- tional horizon. This new intentional horizon is necessary, of course, but it is not yet sufficient.

Deus Caritas Est's position, then, is rather more substantial than this. It is the very activity of social work itself that becomes different upon being assumed by Christians—different, that is, in its inner form and not merely by virtue of an intention that is "superadded". This is seen above all in the "saints" of social work, like Mother Teresa in our own age. Somehow the very "how" and "what" of social work, the very meaning of "competence", in these persons takes on a trans- formed quality, a different sense of time and space and presence. Such saints make clear above all that the whole and every aspect—including all technical aspects—of social work have to do intrinsically with *meaning*—ultimately, the meaning of the human before God that alone can—finally, profoundly—breathe enduring joy into suffering and hope into forsakenness. Only in this way does Christian faith/love become a "vision-understanding that transforms" (Benedict XVI 2006), as dis- tinct from merely a new good intention that continues to presume a conventional technical-secular logic.

This does not at all mean that Christian social charity cannot and should not also take on institutional forms that are not unlike other— secular—social agencies, which would require a distinct sort of "plan- ning, foresight and cooperation with [these] other ... institutions"

(*DCE* 31). The point is that, even in these cases, the formation of the heart demanded of Christians will make a claim affecting not only their intention but the inner order or "rationality" of how they participate in and govern such institutions. Christian workers in these institutions will realize that, to be "workers of . . . justice, [they] must be [themselves] workers who are *being made just* by contact with him who is justice itself: Jesus of Nazareth"; that "the place of this encounter is the Church, nowhere more powerfully present than in her sacraments and liturgy" (Ratzinger 2005). Christian workers will realize that their institutions must be concerned for justice when issues and problems arise that the broader culture "no longer sees as bound up with human dignity, like protecting the right to life of every human being from conception to natural death, or when the Church confesses that justice also includes our responsibilities toward God himself" (Ratzinger 2005). For example, Catholic charities seeking to find loving homes for abandoned or abused or orphaned children will understand that social justice, rightly understood, requires placing such children inside monogamous marriages between a man and a woman. Catholic social agencies will understand that their commitment to feeding the poor or assisting AIDS patients must be integrated into the whole of the Church's teaching—and must entail the freedom, for example, to witness to that teaching in the "benefits" the agencies provide to workers (such as distinct support for married couples, exclusion of contraceptive devices from insurance packages, and so on). Catholic hospitals will understand that their care cannot include abortions and the "morning-after" pill. And so on.

What *Deus Caritas Est* makes clear is that these distinct practices demanded of Catholic social institutions are not at all, rightly understood, a matter of a failure to recognize the dignity of all human beings or indeed to be sensitive to the suffering (for example) of homosexuals or of women seeking abortions. On the contrary, it is a matter—and it can be justified finally only as a matter—of protecting what Christians believe is the deepest *érōs* of *every human being*, including and especially those who suffer the most, who are the weakest and most vulnerable and most rejected by society: of protecting the *érōs* whose deepest search is for a happiness liberated into the generosity of *agápē*, an *agápē* that in Jesus takes the form of sacrificing himself—suffering with all of us and for all of us—unto death. It is a matter of seeing that *érōs* and all of its passion can be realized in the end only by being somehow integrated in and through what is *naturally*—hence "objectively"—given by God as the way to share in the truth of his love and life.

At any rate, professional-social skills and conventional-managerial social service methods combined with generous intentions do not suffice to account for the love that "is the light ... that can always illumine a world grown dim" (*DCE* 39). Man is created in the image of God who is Logos and Love, and Christian charity workers are called to form every phase and aspect of their activities in the image of this God. "To experience love and in this way to cause the light of God to enter into the world—this is the invitation [that Benedict] extend[s] with the present encyclical" (*DCE* 39).

Bibliography

Balthasar, Hans Urs von. 1993a. "The Council of the Holy Spirit". In *Creator Spiritus*. Explorations in Theology, vol. 3. Translated by Brian McNeil, C.R.V. San Francisco: Ignatius Press.

———. 1993b. *Razing the Bastions*. Translated by Brian McNeil, C.R.V. San Francisco: Ignatius Press.

———. 1994. *A Theology of History*. San Francisco: Ignatius Press.

———. 2003. *The Laity and the Life of the Counsels: The Church's Mission in the World*. Translated by Brian McNeil with D. C. Schindler. San Francisco: Ignatius Press.

Benedict XVI. 2006. "Charity Exceeds Philanthropy by 'Showing Christ'". Address of His Holiness Benedict XVI to the Participants at the Meeting Promoted by the Pontifical Council "Cor Unum", January 23. *L'Osservatore Romano*, no. 5 (February 1, 2006): 4.

Benedict XVI and Marcello Pera. 2006. *Without Roots: Europe, Relativism, Christianity, Islam*. Translated by Michael R. Moore. New York: Basic Books.

Day, Dorothy. 1999. *On Pilgrimage*. Grand Rapids, Mich.: William B. Eerdmans.

Delbrêl, Madeleine. 2000. *We the Ordinary People of the Streets*. Translated by David Louis Schindler, Jr., and Charles F. Mann. Grand Rapids, Mich.: William B. Eerdmans.

Péguy, Charles. 1958. *Temporal and Eternal*. Translated by Alexander Dru. New York: Harper and Brothers.

Ratzinger, Joseph. 1969. "Commentary on *Gaudium et Spes*, Chapter I". In *Commentary on the Documents of Vatican II*, edited by Herbert Vorgrimler, 5:115–63. New York: Herder and Herder.

_____. 1988. *Introduction to Christianity*. Translated by J. R. Foster. New York: Crossroad.

_____. 1992. *Co-Workers of the Truth: Meditations for Every Day of the Year*. Edited by Sr. Irene Grassl. Translated by Sr. Mary Frances McCarthy, S.N.D., and Rev. Lothar Krauth. San Francisco: Ignatius Press.

_____. 2002. *God and the World: A Conversation with Peter Seewald*. Translated by Henry Taylor. San Francisco: Ignatius Press.

_____. 2005. "Homily on the Fortieth Anniversary of *Gaudium et Spes*". March 18.

Schindler, David L. 2005. "Truth, Freedom, and Relativism in Western Democracies: Pope Benedict XVI's Contributions to *Without Roots*". *Communio* 32, 4:669–81.

Schmemann, Alexander. 2000a. *For the Life of the World*. Crestwood, N.Y.: St. Vladimir's Seminary Press.

_____. 2000b. *The Journals of Father Alexander Schmemann 1973–1983*. Crestwood, N.Y.: St. Vladimir's Seminary Press.

Schürmann, Heinz, Joseph Ratzinger, and Hans Urs von Balthasar. 1986. *Principles of Christian Morality*. Translated by Graham Harrison. San Francisco: Ignatius Press.

Zwick, Mark, and Louise Zwick. 2005. *The Catholic Worker Movement: Intellectual and Spiritual Origins*. New York: Paulist Press.

"The Love that Moves the Sun and the Other Stars": Light and Love

*Stanislaw Grygiel**

We risk missing a great deal in Pope Benedict XVI's encyclical *Deus Caritas Est* if we do not read it alongside his address to the participants of the meeting promoted by the Pontifical Council *Cor Unum* on the theme "But the Greatest of These is Love" (Benedict XVI 2006). In my opinion, this address forms an integral part of the encyclical and helps us to understand it better.

This discourse begins with the words with which Dante, having reached Mary with the help of the woman Beatrice and the support of the prayers of St. Bernard, concludes his *Divine Comedy* (*Paradise* 33.145): "the Love that moves the sun and the other stars". The Pope observes that this vision of the love that moves the universe, although bearing an Aristotelian stamp, is substantially different from Aristotle's. I would even make so bold as to say that Dante's vision of the event that takes place between God and the entire universe is so far from Aristotle's vision as not to have much to do with the latter. In Aristotle's philosophy, human *érōs*, lacking *agápē*, loses itself in pure reaction; it is determined by the attracting power of a god closed into thinking only of his own reality. When Dante says,

> O Light Eternal fixed in Self alone,
> known only to Yourself, and knowing Self,
> You love and glow, knowing and being known!
>
> (33.124–26)

*Karol Wojtyla Professor of Philosophical Anthropology, Pontifical John Paul II Institute for Studies on Marriage and Family, Rome.

46

we do indeed think of Thought thinking itself (*nóesis noéseos nóesis*; cf. Aristotle, *Metaphysics* 1074b), attracting everything and everyone to itself as a magnet attracts metal shavings. These shavings desire the magnet, but the magnet does not turn its "gaze" toward the shavings. Aristotle's god, loving and knowing no one but himself, will never be Emmanuel, "God with us". In the Aristotelian world, the metal shavings move toward a god that resembles the god of Deism.

Dante is totally different. The words "the Love that moves the sun and the other stars" have their source in a mind struck by "a great flash of understanding . . . / and suddenly its wish was granted" (33.140–41). That is to say, they have their source in a mind overcome by the light in whose radiance we see that which the human intellect and heart desire to see. In the presence of the "Virgin Mother, daughter of your son", through the mystery of the Incarnation, Dante sees "within its depthless clarity of substance / . . . the Great Light shine into three circles / in three clear colors bound in one same space" (33.115–17). The light of these "three clear colors bound in one same space", shining on man, renders both man and the whole universe visible and comprehensible. Aristotle did not know this because he could not know it, inasmuch as this light shines forth in God's self-revelation that takes place when he gives himself to man in the mystery of the Incarnation and Redemption. The light of love that is God, in his being Dialogue and Person, encompasses man by creating and saving him. Precisely for this reason, the word "love" conceived in an Aristotelian fashion distances itself not only from the word as Dante understands it, but from human truth itself.

Whoever speaks of love without thinking of the triune Love of the Divine Persons will never know what love is. For such a person, *érōs*, since it has nothing in itself in "the image and likeness" of the *agápē* that is God—and therefore is not *capax Dei*—will always be alienating itself in useful or pleasurable things. If, "within its depthless clarity of substance", there were not "three circles / in three clear colors bound in one same space", love would be tantamount to a dissolution and unmaking of man. Human *érōs* can be saved only if it ascends in the hope that *agápē*, who is God himself, descends from his heavenly Jerusalem. Contemplating Mary, Dante sees the Love of the Trinity so near to us that, he writes, the second circling "seemed in itself and in its own Self-color / to be depicted with man's very image" (33.127, 130–31). For someone whose reason depends on *érōs* alone, love can be everything because it is in itself nothing. It is not "in the image and likeness" of *agápē*, or, as Dante would perhaps say, it is not "depicted with his very image". Not reflecting this "image", it is reduced to a web of different interests and desires tossed to and fro.

At the beginning of the first canto of the *Paradise*, Dante says that the intellect "fathoms to the depths" the "glory of the One Who moves all things / penetrates all the universe, reflecting / in one part more and in another less", and that "memory is powerless to follow" (*Paradise*, 1.8, 1–3, 9). Because of the failure of memory, man must constantly begin all over again to contemplate the love that shows itself in the glory of God's ceaseless activity. Only the person for whom each day is the first day of creation knows that human words, if they are not reborn each day in the Silence of the Ineffable, will never be able to tell, or better, to sing the glory of the Love that is God.

The address in which, with the help of Dante's poetic song, the Pope speaks of the mystery of the Trinity forms an introduction to the encyclical and at the same time provides the context for an adequate understanding of the latter. Without this brief text, the encyclical would lack the perspective that makes the human desire to be loved and to love comprehensible. It is true that in the second part of the encyclical, the Pope turns to St. Augustine, the doctor of charity, and cites the words of the prologue to *De Trinitate* that inspired Dante: "If you see charity, you see the Trinity" (*De Trinitate* VIII, 8, 12) It is, however, from the poetic heights upon which the Pope elaborates his discussion that we glimpse the divine-human mystery of love. Outside the contemplation of the mystery of triune Love, men will never be satisfied if they remain bound to what is seen and experienced in this world. The Fire of Love that is God draws the universe out of darkness. At first glance, the sparks from that Fire seem to flit confusedly about the universe. Each one of them, however, carries within itself a memory of the Fire; more, it is made in its "image and likeness" and rises above itself: it ascends. Does it find the Fire again? Does it fall into it?

I remember the late evenings, or even the first hours of the night, when, as young people years ago, we sat around the bonfire at camp. We gazed on it with piety, because it warmed us and made us feel that we were not lost in the darkness. Sparks flew high above us and within us. They kindled our wonder, creating such a fairy-tale home that we did not want to go to sleep. Every now and then, one of us would say a few words, but the brevity of what was said only served to bring out the silence. It was precisely in this silence that we heard the fire speaking its friendly word, a word refracted into each one's interior as light is refracted in a crystal. There was a pathos in the light of the fire, a pathos in our receiving its light, a pathos in the silence that made discussion superfluous. Illumined by the fire, we felt ourselves to be loved by it. Being loved, we became lovable to one another; our friendship was strengthened to the extent that it could overcome all the difficulties that might cloud our relationships. We illumined one another in the light of the bonfire whose reflection continued to play over us, and this drew us closer to each other.

The experience of that pathos has kept me company till now and helps me to understand the goodness of the light as well as its negation, the night. This pathos is present in the questions that do not cease to emerge in the lights and shadows of life. That is, it is present in the daily calling into question of the darkness by the light and of the light by the darkness. It makes me experience more deeply both the goodness of the light and the dangers hidden in the night.

* * *

Benedict XVI tells us in his address that Dante's vision of the human face taken on by God "reveals, on the one hand, the continuity between Christian faith in God and the search developed by reason and by the world of religions; on the other, however, a novelty appears that surpasses all human research, the novelty that only God himself can reveal to us: the novelty of a love that moved God to take on a human face, even to take on flesh and blood, the entire human being" (Benedict XVI 2006).

John Paul II said that the path of the Church is humanity; Benedict XVI says that the path of humanity is love. This path has been obscured today. In his address, he writes, "Today, the word 'love' is so spoiled, worn out and abused that one almost fears to pronounce it. And yet, it is a fundamental word, an expression of the primordial reality. We cannot simply abandon it, but we must take it up again, purify it and bring it to its original splendor so that it can illumine our life and guide it on the right path" (ibid.).

In part 1 of the encyclical, Benedict recalls the two loves: the love proper to *érōs* and that proper to *agápē*. Erotic love, which is constituted by desire, is not reduced to the passion with which a man thinks of a woman or a woman thinks of a man. *Érōs* has a broader scope. True, it has been reduced to the man-woman relation, but in the beginning it was not so.

Erotic love is the desire for the salvific presence of the other. *Érōs* burns in the poor man who, assaulted and wounded by evil, feels the misery of not having anyone to turn to, anyone from whom he can seek healing. He lies on the roadside and asks the passers-by for help. His love ascends and at the same time prophetically awaits the love that will descend to him. Between the love proper to *érōs* and the love proper to *agápē*, Christ's parable of the Good Samaritan takes place every day: *érōs* ascends from Jericho to Jerusalem, while *agápē* descends from Jerusalem to Jericho. The one who descends gives himself; he wants to love. The one who ascends asks to be given what he lacks; he wants to be loved. The one descending illuminates, the one ascending is illuminated. The Samaritan, descending, radiates light all around him, light that heals his neighbors enfolded in darkness. The Good Samaritan dwells in light; in it, his *agápē* is revealed and accomplished. Every love is light. Even erotic love is such, but as a reflection. Each love sheds a different light on us and, consequently, on the world. The light of *agápē* reveals those whom we ought to love, whereas the light of *érōs* shows us who we are. It shows this in the measure in which we allow ourselves to be illuminated by the light of *agápē*. In fact, it is thanks to the light of *agápē* that we understand our own *érōs* and can glimpse the orientation it must be given in order not to be destroyed. The future makes the present comprehensible. *Agápē* descends from eternity, and *érōs* desires to move out of time: eternity is its future. For this reason, only those who, with faith, hope, and love, in some way already dwell in eternity understand time and know how to carry themselves in it. This is the truth of freedom, that is, of the event that is the human person.

The fundamental question about man has to do with the meeting of *érōs* and *agápē*, and an essential moment of this question is a question about God. The question about *erōs*, that is, about man, would be exhausted and bristling with mortal perils if, at the same time, it were not also a question about *agápē*, which is God. If it were not also this latter, the question would destroy man. The God-question, however, is really a question about God only if it is posed within the question about man. Outside of this context, the God-question would become an abstraction, this time deadly for God himself. The light that indicates the true path toward God has its source in the question arising from primordial experience. In this experience, man becomes the *magna quaestio* (the "great question": "Where do I come from, and where am I going?") and is tormented by this. The God-question without the *magna quaestio* is an attempt to detach curiosity from reason. Curiosity is not the desire for love. Rather, by killing love, it also kills man. When read from this perspective, a poem by Rilke gives terrible voice to this:

> What will you do, God, when I'm dead?
> I am your pot (when I crash into potsherds?)
> I am your drink (when I go bad?)
> I am your cloak and your career;
> without me you end up losing making sense. . . .
>
> I fret about you, God. (Rilke 2001: 47)*

God is infinite *agápē*. All he wants is to give himself, that is, to be present for man. The only thing he ever asks of us is to accept his agapic desire. We should not wonder, then, that the light in which he dwells, the light of *agápē*, is inaccessible (cf. 1 Tim 6:16) for someone who is not a great *erōs*. No one has seen God, but his invisible Light is refracted by our being, illuminating it and allowing us to glimpse this Light precisely as it touches our own being. This experience allows us to discern the Invisible and, with poetry, in our turn to touch the Ineffable.

---

* The last line of the German original, "*Was wirst du tun, Gott? Ich bin bange*", conveys more pointedly the torment to which the present article refers: literally, "What will you do, God? I am afraid."—TRANS.

He who loves wants to see at least the shadow of the beloved,
This is how we love our mother—our father—our brothers—
A lover—even God. . . .

He who loves—wants to see eye to eye,
to catch the sweet tresses' scent;
To him who loves—the small becomes immense
And the faintest beam of light causes hope to grow. (Norwid 1971:
  III, 441, 443)

In mystical contemplation, St. Benedict of Nursia saw the whole world in a small beam of light. Indeed, if light draws the world out of darkness, the true light creates the world; it separates creation from the darkness as creation shines with the true Light. St. John states this unequivocally. Everything was created through the Word, in whom "was life, and the life was the light of men. The light shines in the darkness" (Jn 1:4–5). "God is light" (1 Jn 1:5). From this light, the filial light, Jesus, was born: "I am the light of the world; he who follows me will not walk in darkness, but will have the light of life" (Jn 8:12). "While you have the light, believe in the light, that you may become sons of light" (Jn 12:36).

The path traced out by the light ends in the world of matter; the latter represents the final point attained by the "Love that moves the sun and the other stars". "After" this, there is only the lack of Love, that is, nothingness, *nihilum.*

No light emanates from Thought thinking only itself. Self-thinking thought attracts but does not descend to men and, consequently, is not present to them. In reality, they are not even present to it, because they do not ascend but are merely attracted by it. Between such a god and men, who have been turned into metal shavings, there can be no love, no friendship; they are separated by an unbridgeable abyss (cf. Aristotle, *Nicomachean Ethics*, 1159a). "Chained" to this absolute magnet, man is not free. Lacking the freedom of love, the freedom of entrustment to the other, and, awaiting from that other fruits that do not deceive, man can depend only on the powers of his own reason. In consequence, rationalism, atheism, and indifference possess him, enter into his interior, and destroy his capacity for knowing himself, others, and the world of things. Thus destroyed, man contents himself with the appearances of knowledge, love, faith, and hope.

In other words, where the freedom of love, faith, and hope are lacking, human freedom is transformed into unthinking license. Only the gift, grace, is able to defend freedom from this mortal danger. Only the gift bears in itself the commandments, which orient freedom toward its Source and its End. Human freedom comes to be in the unity of these two things. "The commandment of the Lord is pure, enlightening the eyes" (Ps 19:8). "Your word is a lamp to my feet and a light to my path" (Ps 119:105). The Word of God is the Source and the End of human freedom.

The things of this world say nothing to man's freedom. They do not call to it. The word adequate to freedom is spoken only by grace, which rekindles acts of faith, hope, and love in man. People said all sorts of things about Jesus. Some said that he was an exceptional man; others, that he was a prophet; still others, that he was John the Baptist. And "Who do you say that I am?" Simon Peter answered, "You are the Christ, the Son of the living God." Jesus said, "Blessed are you, Simon, Bar-Jonah! For flesh and blood has not revealed this to you, but my Father who is in heaven" (Mt 16:15–17). Freedom descends, or, rather, falls on us like a bolt of lightning, as it fell on Simon the son of Jonah. This freedom comes from beyond the world. It comes in the light that surrounds and converts us, as happened to St. Paul: "As he journeyed he approached Damascus, and suddenly a light from heaven flashed about him. And he fell to the ground and heard a voice saying to him, 'Saul, Saul, why do you persecute me?'" (Acts 9:3–4).

Knowledge comes when light surrounds man and sets him free, rekindling love, faith, and hope within him. "Per ardorem caritatis datur cognitio veritatis" (St. Thomas Aquinas, *In Ev. Jo.* 5, 6). "Non intratur in veritatem nisi per caritatem" (St. Augustine, *Contra Faustum* 41, 32, 18; *PL* 45, 507). "Ubi amor ibi oculus" (St. Thomas Aquinas, *In Sent.* 3d, 35, 1, 2, 1). "One sees clearly only with the heart" (Saint-Exupéry 2000, XXI), because "the heart has its reasons, which reason does not know" (B. Pascal, *Pensées* 477). The heart is the very event of love, faith, and hope. Those who remain outside these epiphanies of freedom will never be able to free themselves from the relativism of *doxa* (opinion) and of the experiments that verify it.

The struggle of good against evil takes place in the freedom of faith, hope, and love. *Érōs*, enraptured by the light of beauty radiated by *agápē*, fights the glitter with which evil tries to attract man. Without the gift of *agápē*, *érōs* would end up in an unthinking license that would be the destruction of the human person. For the person who has been thus destroyed, both good and evil are merely empty categories.

A person who is present to others radiates light for them. There is a lack of persons present to one another; there is a lack of light. Darkness fills their solitude. That person alone is present for the other who loves this other; light radiates from love. That person alone who reveals himself, that is, who gives himself, is present for the other. For this reason, man is illuminated and made visible, both to self and to others, in the measure in which he receives the other. The light of *agápē* dazzles *érōs*. It disturbs the wicked eye. "Oculis aegris odiosa lux, quae puris amabilis" (St. Augustine 1961: VII, 16: "Light is hateful to sore eyes, although we welcome it when our sight is hale and clear"). The light of *agápē* judges *érōs* because it dissipates the appearances among which it hides and to which it lets itself grow accustomed. The light seeks it and cries out to it, "Where are you?" (cf. Gen 3:9). We should not marvel, then, that those who are not yet good are afraid of the light, afraid of the gift, afraid of the other. "He who loves his brother abides in the light, and in it there is no cause for stumbling. But he who hates his brother is in the darkness and walks in the darkness, and does not know where he is going, because the darkness has blinded his eyes" (1 Jn 2:10). "Therefore ... walk as children of light (for the fruit of light is found in all that is good and right and true).... Take no part in the unfruitful works of darkness, but instead expose them" (Eph 5:7–9, 11).

But the light has no need to fear because the eyes of man belong to it. It need have no fear of *érōs*, because *érōs* receives its identity from *agápē*. The identity of every event originates in its belonging to the other, ultimately, to that Transcendence which, descending to man, illumines him and draws him out of the darkness of nothingness. That Transcendence is love.

Bibliography

Augustine, St. 1961. *Confessions*. Translated by R. S. Pine-Coffin. London and New York: Penguin Books.

Benedict XVI. 2006. "Charity Exceeds Philanthropy by 'Showing Christ' ". Address of His Holiness Benedict XVI to the Participants at the Meeting Promoted by the Pontifical Council "Cor Unum". January 23. *L'Osservatore Romano*, no. 5 (February 1, 2006): 4.

Dante Alighieri. 1984. *The Divine Comedy*. Vol. 3: *Paradise*. Translated by Mark Musa. New York: Penguin Books.

Norwid, Cyprian. 1971. "*Promethidion—Bogumił*": "*Pisma wszystkie*". Warsaw. [Here translated from the Italian.]

Rilke, Rainer Maria. 2001. *The Book of Hours: Prayers to a Lowly God*. Translated by Annemarie S. Kidder. Evanston, Ill.: Northwestern University Press.

Saint-Exupéry, A. de. 2000. *The Little Prince*. Translated by R. Howard. San Diego and New York: Harcourt.

Has Christianity Poisoned *Eros*?

Jarosław Merecki*

Introduction

It is not surprising that at the beginning of his pontificate Benedict XVI has chosen to dedicate his first encyclical to the topic of love. "God is love": These words from the First Letter of John convey the very essence of the Christian faith, according to which God is not withdrawn into himself, does not only receive love. God, whose intimate essence is made up of the love communicated among the Divine Persons, wants to share his love, starting with the act of creation, through the history of his chosen people, culminating in the event of Jesus Christ. What might instead be surprising—or at least it may be surprising to those who do not know much about how the Church's Magisterium has evolved over the past few decades—is the fact that the love between man and woman is taken as the paradigm of love. Indeed, in mentioning the different meanings that are attached to the word "love" in modern-day culture, Benedict XVI writes: "Amid this multiplicity of meanings, however, one in particular stands out: love between man and woman, where body and soul are inseparably joined and human beings glimpse an apparently irresistible promise of happiness. This would seem to be the very epitome of love; all other kinds of love immediately seem to fade in comparison" (*DCE* 2).

The Pope's statement is very interesting from a philosophical point of view. Indeed, it seems to suggest that man's most natural experience, the experience that involves the entire human being—body, emotions,

---

* Assistant Professor of Philosophy, Pontifical John Paul II Institute for Studies on Marriage and Family, Rome.

and spirit—is seen as the prototype of love, which helps us to understand the essence of love and therefore also its other forms, including God's love for man. The love between man and woman, with the promise of happiness that it brings, allows us to glimpse the possibility of accessing a reality that is far greater than our everyday experience (cf. *DCE* 5). Plato would say that a voice speaks to us through *érōs* that is not the voice of our calculating reason; it is a voice that drives us to do something that perhaps we would never have risked doing. In other words—no longer speaking in Platonic terms—it impels us to go beyond ourselves and devote ourselves to another person. This implies giving up part of our autonomy for the sake of the greater value that we have discovered; it implies depending on the other although such a dependence is not experienced as the loss of our freedom but rather as its accomplishment.

In this sense, loving the other means wanting what is good for him and, ultimately, his salvation. Gabriel Marcel wrote: "Loving the other means: You must not die." From this perspective, it is easy to see the correlation between the experience of human love and that of divine love, of which the Holy Scriptures speak, especially the Song of Songs, but also the prophets Hosea and Ezekiel, who, as Benedict XVI reminds us, described God's love for his people "using boldly erotic images" (*DCE* 9). God's love, which is manifested in different ways throughout the history of Israel, is just like human love and must appear as "madness" to calculating reason. But God's love of man and the world—"God so loved the world that he gave his only-begotten Son ..." (Jn 3:16)—culminates in the Cross, which Paul does not dare to refer to as "madness". It is in this "divine madness" that God fully reveals his very essence.

From Nietzsche to the Sexual Revolution

In modern times, however, and especially in the past century, the opinion has spread according to which the Church, in teaching the moral norms that must be observed in the sphere of sexuality, has not valued, but has rather unjustly limited and suppressed, human *érōs*. In this regard, Benedict XVI refers to Friedrich Nietzsche, who, in his usual biting language, states: "Christianity had poisoned eros, which for its part, while not completely succumbing, gradually degenerated into vice" (*DCE* 3; in the German: "Das Christentum ... habe dem Eros Gift zu trinken gegeben; er sei zwar nicht daran gestorben, aber zum Laster entartet"). In his attack on Christianity, which he believed was responsible for this degeneration and for the onset of the process whereby the values of the weak prevailed over those of the strong, Nietzsche exalted the impulse of Dionysus. The Dionysian attitude extols the morals of exuberant life, not subjected to restrictions, even natural and instinctive ones. He opposed this attitude to that of Apollonian morality, which was too orderly and reasonable. Restrained by exceedingly rigid morals, *érōs* could not unleash all its energies, which ultimately reflect the basic foundation of all reality, that is, the "will to power".

On the other hand, it is likewise true that Nietzsche himself was not in favor of allowing instincts to run free. Since instinct is—or rather, should be—at the service of the will to power, according to Nietzsche, it was necessary to exercise some caution in the sexual sphere. For Nietzsche, sexual instincts were to be curbed, not for the sake of a higher purpose, that is, not for love understood as a recognition of the other, but rather for the sake of asserting oneself, one's will to power.

The idea of sexuality freed from moral control was proposed by the so-called sexual revolution. It is true that already in nineteenth-century libertine thought we find a similar view of sexuality, although libertines did not propose it for all of society but only for a restricted circle of the "enlightened" (Buttiglione 1991: 239–44). The sexual revolution instead tries to form part of the great modern movement of liberation that took different forms in the social sphere and now also involves customs. At the same time, a significant part of the movement also refers to anti-authoritarian thought, which was especially strong after World War II. Liberation from authoritarianism also involves abolishing prior sexual morals that prevented people from fully enjoying their sexuality and was imposed by the authority of tradition and the Church. Freed from moral constraints in the sexual sphere, man would not only be happier but also less aggressive, since—always according to this current of thought—sexual repression generates aggressiveness.

Such assumptions have been proved wrong not only by history, in which aggressiveness has anything but disappeared, but also by one of the leading exponents of anti-authoritarian thought, Max Horkheimer, who sided with Paul VI and the encyclical *Humanae Vitae* rather than with the premises of the sexual revolution (cf. Horkheimer 1970: 74ff.). On the other hand, even the father of psychoanalysis, Sigmund Freud, who considered sexual energy, the *libido*, as one of the primary forces of the human being, upheld that if this energy is left unrestrained it becomes destructive rather than liberating. He thus placed the plea-sure principle next to the principle of reality, which must govern the satisfaction of instincts (cf. Freud 1990). In non-Freudian terms, the concept can be expressed as follows: Our mature personality is formed through the process of denying the immediate satisfaction of our instinc-tive drives for the sake of the truth that we have come to know and identify with our reason. Only in this way can we act consistently and give unity to our conscious personality. Those who fail to do so remain in the grip of the drives that rise from the unconscious.

In antiquity, Plato had shown this fact with perspicacity. The man who does not subordinate the impulses of his drives to the higher cri-terion of truth and good becomes a "democratic" man. Who is the dem-ocratic man? He is a man whose actions are not guided by any governing principle—which in the case of man is precisely reason and freedom, which reconcile the needs of instincts with the needs of truth—and who acts under the impulse of whatever drives prevail at a given moment. In *The Republic*, Plato wrote:

> After this he lives on, spending his money and labor and time on unnecessary pleasures quite as much as on necessary ones; but if he be fortunate and is not too much disordered in his wits, when years have elapsed and the heyday of passion is over—supposing that he then readmits into the city some part of the exiled virtues and does not wholly give himself up to their successors—in that case he bal-ances his pleasures and lives in a sort of equilibrium. (561 a–b)

And farther on: "As the result of all, see how sensitive the citizens become; they chafe impatiently at the least touch of authority, and at length, as you know, they cease to care even for the laws, written or unwritten; they will have no one over them" (563 d–e).

Plato's logic could also be extended to how *érōs* is lived. If *érōs* is not subordinated to a higher criterion, it can easily become demo-cratic, that is, it merely seeks satisfaction indulging its momentary drives and recognizing no other values to which it should be submitted. In this way, *érōs* can also easily use other people for its own gratification. It does not want to submit itself to higher values, and everything revolves around it. Rather than helping to build the unity of the individual and unity among people, *érōs* becomes a disruptive force. That is why Benedict XVI concludes his reflection on intoxicated and undisciplined *érōs* as follows, "Evidently, eros needs to be disciplined and purified if it is to provide, not just fleeting pleasure, but a certain foretaste of the pinnacle of our existence, of that beatitude for which our whole being yearns" (*DCE* 4).

Naturally, we must not think ill of *érōs*. Benedict XVI is against identifying *érōs* with selfish and possessive pride or opposing it to *agápē*, understood as unselfish and specifically Christian love. Rather, he upholds the *gratia supponit naturam* principle according to which human nature has been so offended by original sin that human *érōs* needs the individual to make the effort to lead it back to its truth. All prohibitions existing in this sphere ultimately refer to the positive value: it is a matter of strengthening the positive role that *érōs* plays in human life.

The Internal Dynamics of *Érōs*

What is the truth about *érōs*? What meaning does it have in human life? In order to answer these questions, we should start from the beginning, that is, from the story of creation, especially reading it in light of the commentary that John Paul II provides in his catechesis *The Theology of the Body: Human Love in the Divine Plan*. According to his interpretation, in the Bible story there are two essential points that help us to understand the true meaning of *érōs*: the incomparable value of the human person and the need for the other that flows from its very nature. Thus, *érōs* itself, understood as the desire for communion with the other, is seen as part of God's original plan and is therefore deeply valued from the very beginning.

Let us begin with the first point. Man, created in God's image and likeness, does not find anyone in the world who is like him. This original experience is, on the one hand, negative, because this original loneliness makes him feel incomplete, but, on the other hand, it holds an important truth about man: Man cannot identify with the

world that surrounds him because he is ontologically different from
the material world and axiologically superior to it. Man does not exist
as some worldly thing but as person, a being at once material and
spiritual. Because of this, he has a value that cannot be compared to
other worldly values. Speaking in Kantian terms, we can say that man
does not have a "value" but rather "dignity". Whoever has dignity
can never be used as an object but must be recognized as a person. In
personalistic ethics, this truth about the human person was expressed
in the norm that constitutes the very foundation of the moral order:
Persona est affirmanda per seipsam. This is another way of expressing the
concept of love: love understood not as *éros* but as *agápē*. The person,
by virtue of human ontological and axiological nature, is the first and
primary recipient of this love.

Let us now move on to the second point. As we said, Adam's
original loneliness makes him feel that something is missing, he feels
incomplete. Indeed, God himself says, "It is not good that the man
should be alone." Only when woman is created does man find someone with whom he can enter into a mutual relationship leading to
their communion. Benedict XVI says, "Only together do the two represent complete humanity and become 'one flesh' " (*DCE* 11). Only
in this need of the other, which is part of human nature, do we find
the most profound meaning of *éros*. On the existential level, *éros* expresses
the very truth we find in the book of Genesis: "It is not good that the
man should be alone." Man is not self-contained; he finds himself
only by entering into communion with the other. But this "other"
cannot be seen only as the object of desire, as something that satisfies
our needs. Treating the other in this way would mean crushing his
dignity. The encounter with the other starts with desire but goes beyond
it; human *éros* is not self-referential but turns to a value that demands
to be recognized in itself.

How is this unique value of the person to be recognized? Every person demands to be recognized, but in the love between man and woman,
recognizing the other reaches another, and in some ways deeper, level.
Every person is unique, but in the love of a man for a woman, and of a
woman for a man, the uniqueness of the individual is discovered in a concrete and existential way: this man, this woman is unique, unique to me
among all people. Hence, in the heart of man and woman the desire arises

to give oneself to the other; in other words, *érōs* also becomes *agápē*. That is the truth about *érōs*: because of its internal dynamics, it leads to *agápē*. If this does not happen, *érōs* has not fulfilled its purpose. In a way it has betrayed its vocation, which consists in discovering the most profound truth about man: man finds himself only by sincerely giving himself to the other (cf. *GS* 24). Benedict XVI writes, "Even if *eros* is at first mainly covetous and ascending, a fascination for the great promise of happiness, in drawing near to the other, it is less and less concerned with itself, increasingly seeks the happiness of the other, is concerned more and more with the beloved, bestows itself and wants to 'be there for' the other" (*DCE* 7).

The gift of oneself to the other, *agápē*, is therefore a natural consequence of *érōs*. At the same time, covetous love is not suppressed but transformed. Also, the response of the other to the desire for mutual self-giving is experienced as a gift; it cannot be demanded or extorted, but only given freely. Thus, according to this vision that flows from human experience and from the revelation that sheds further light upon this experience, *érōs* is lived as an integral part of personal love, the love that is both desire and recognition of the person. Yes, love as *érōs* is desire, but finding ourselves before our beloved makes us see that that other cannot be treated as merely an object for our own gratification. Instead, the beauty of that other is so striking that it even makes us capable of defending and protecting our beloved, capable of self-sacrifice.

This way of experiencing and understanding love as *érōs* goes beyond and transforms the Greek understanding of it The Greeks also believed that *érōs* can induce man even to "die for the other". In the *Symposium*, Plato speaks of the heroes who, in sacrificing their lives for others, do so "in an extraordinary condition of *érōs*, to achieve fame and gain immortal and everlasting glory" (208 c). According to this view, *érōs* can lead us to heroic gestures, but it does so, not for the sake of the other, but for our own personal glory and honor. Commenting on this passage of the *Symposium*, Guido Calogero says that when one

> investigates the most typical form of *érōs*, the love for other persons, the latter count so little in the concept that the regard for them, considered singularly, is placed only at the bottom of the

scale of the best forms of *érōs* and is destined to be immediately surpassed by an increasingly generalized love and distanced from the concrete personalities, in an ascent toward absolute reality and impersonality of the Idea. A love considered as substantial devotion and self-sacrifice in favor of the other is not even deemed conceivable. (Reale 1997: 196)

If we consider Nietzsche's statement from this standpoint, we can say that the German philosopher was right in stating that Christianity has deeply transformed *érōs*. This transformation, however, does not imply a poisoning of but rather a sublimation of *érōs*. It can be rightly thought that Nietzsche, who had a profound knowledge and appreciation of ancient culture, wanted to return precisely to the notion of *érōs* according to which love is a way for the individual to assert himself, or, as Nietzsche would put it, to strengthen and develop the "will to power". It is clear that in such a process others are not recognized in themselves; on the contrary, they merely provide an opportunity or a means to assert oneself, just as according to Plato they merely represented a stepping stone in the individual's ascent toward the absolute world of ideas.

The great contribution of Christianity consists precisely in discovering that both the Absolute-God and man are persons. As a person, man cannot be exploited for the sake of the highest ends because he represents the ultimate end in the visible world—the image of God himself. *Érōs* thus becomes a personal reality par excellence. Naturally, the temptation to use others always exists, and we must always fight it. The prohibitions the Church speaks of are meant precisely to protect the dignity of the person and prevent it from being crushed by *érōs*. Actually, the temptation to use others is especially strong in the sexual sphere. Love is about giving, but one can pretend to give in order to obtain pleasure. *Érōs* itself can be used to pursue ends that are contrary to its true nature. It can happen that love, which for its very nature can be only given gratuitously, is subordinated to the laws of the market, in other words, can be bought and sold. Those who buy sexual love may assert power over others but at the same time they crush their own dignity.

In short, *érōs* used to assert one's will to power is truly a vice. In this sense, Christianity does not poison *érōs* but heals it.

The Fullness of the Gift of Self

In *The Ballad of Reading Gaol*, Oscar Wilde wrote: "All men kill the thing they love." Human love is always ambiguous because man is unable to keep fully the promise made through his very being and his gift of love. We also find this notion in Karol Wojtyła's play *The Jeweler's Shop*. The author, in reflecting upon the weakness of human love, wrote, "It is strange, yet necessary, to move away from each other because man will not endure in man forever and man will not suffice."

Is it possible to give oneself completely? Is there such a thing as love that does not kill? Here again, Christianity brings the good news: Yes, in this world there lived a man who did not want to kill but rather let himself be killed for others. In him, God's desire— God's *érōs*—was expressed as the pinnacle of oblative love—God's *agápē*. "His death on the Cross is the culmination of that turning of God against himself in which he gives himself in order to raise man up and save him. This is love in its most radical form" (*DCE* 12).

When the soldiers brought Jesus to Pilate, the latter said, "*Idu ho anthropos! Ecce homo*", "Behold the man." In commenting on these words spoken by Pilate, Cardinal Ratzinger observed that on the lips of the cynical Roman governor they meant: "We are proud of being men, we aspire to greater things, but behold, this is what man is: he is nothing, a worm, weak and alone, and he deserves to be despised" (Ratzinger 2005: 58–59). John the Evangelist, however, saw precisely in these words and in this image the deepest truth about God and man. Yes, in Christ we can see the sin of a person who is capable of reducing another to this state, who in order to assert himself will go as far as to kill another, but at the same time we can see the response of God, who, through Christ, gives himself fully to others. Thus, in the offering of Christ, the calling of man, who is created in God's image and likeness, is fully revealed. Whenever we express our love, even with all our human weakness, as a sincere gift of self, we participate in a crucial way in this higher revelation of the meaning of the world, of man, and of our history; we become witnesses of the truth that God is love.

Bibliography

Buttiglione, R. 1991. *L'uomo e la famiglia.* Rome: Dino Editore.

Freud, S. 1990. *Beyond the Pleasure Principle.* New York: W. W. Norton.

Horkheimer, M. 1970. *Die Sehnsucht nach dem ganz Anderen.* Hamburg: Furche Verlag.

Nietzsche, F. 1989. *Beyond Good and Evil: Prelude to a Philosophy of the Future.* Translated by Walter Kaufmann. New York: Vintage.

Ratzinger, J. 2005. *Im Anfang schuf Gott: Vier Predigten über Schöpfung und Fall: Konsequenzen des Schöpfungsglaubens.* Einsiedeln: Johannes Verlag. [*In the Beginning . . . A Catholic Understanding of the Story of the Creation and the Fall.* Grand Rapids: Eerdmans, 1995.]

Reale, G. 1997. *Eros: Dèmone mediatore.* Milan: Rizzoli.

Love between Man and Woman: The Epitome of Love

*William E. May**

1. Introduction: The Encyclical *Deus Caritas Est* on the Love (*Amor*) between Man and Woman as Uniting *Érōs* and *Agápē*

1.1. In his first encyclical, *Deus Caritas Est*, Pope Benedict XVI wished "to speak of the love [*amor*] which God lavishes upon us and which we in turn must share with others" (*DCE* 1). Noting the "vast semantic range of the word 'love' [*amor*]", he then said:

> Amid this multiplicity of [its] meanings, ... one in particular stands out: love [*amor*] between man and woman, where body and soul are inseparably joined and human beings glimpse an apparently irresistible promise of happiness. This would seem to be the very epitome of love [*amoris per excellentiam imago perfecta*]: all other kinds of love [*cetera universa amoris genera*] immediately seem to fade in comparison. So we need to ask: are all these forms of love [*omnesne amoris hae formae*] basically one, so that love [*amor*], in its many and varied manifestations, is ultimately a single reality, or are we merely using the same word to designate totally different realities? (*DCE* 2)

1.2. I inserted the Latin word *amor* in brackets in this passage because the Latin text of the encyclical uses several different words for "love": the title uses *caritas*, the word used in the Latin text of Scripture to

*Michael J. McGivney Professor of Moral Theology, Pontifical John Paul II Institute for Studies on Marriage and Family at The Catholic University of America, Washington, D.C.

66

translate the Greek *agápē*. In citing Scripture, the Latin text of the encyclical uses the verb *diligo* to translate the Greek *agapáō*, for example, "Sic enim *dilexit* Deus mundum, ut Filium suum unigenitum daret ..." (Jn 3:16; *DCE* 1) (God so *loved* the world that he gave his only Son ...). But, and it is most important to note this, the Latin text of the encyclical more frequently uses the laical *amo* to speak of God's love for man: for example, "In his Nostris primis Encyclicis Litteris de *amore* cupimus loqui quo Deus nos replet quique a nobis cum aliis communicari debet" (*DCE* 1); "Dei *amor* nobis quaestio est de vita principalis" (*DCE* 2); and "Deus hic hominem *amat*" (*DCE* 9). In fact, Pope Benedict says: "Since God has first loved [*dilexit*] us (cf. 1 Jn 4:10), love [*amor*] is now no longer a mere 'command'; it is the response to the gift of love with which God draws near to us [*verum est responsio erga* amoris *donum, quo Deus nobis occurrit*]" (*DCE* 1).

1.3. In Latin, consequently, the word *amor* is the more universal word for "love" and is so used in the official Latin text of Benedict's encyclical. In fact, in the first part of the document Pope Benedict argues that *amor* integrates into one the different kinds of "love" identified by the Greek words *érōs* and *agápē*. Here I will not attempt to summarize his entire argument but will rather focus on those elements of it concerned with showing how authentic love (*amor*) between man and woman unites *érōs* and *agápē*.

1.4. After noting that "the love [*amor*] between man and woman which is neither planned nor willed, but somehow imposes itself upon human beings, was called *eros* by the ancient Greeks" (*DCE* 3), the Pope is subsequently at pains to show that biblical faith in no way rejects *érōs* as such. While declaring "war on a warped and destructive form" of *érōs* (cf. *DCE* 4), biblical faith leads us to understand that there is an underlying unity between *érōs*, or "ascending" love, and *agápē*, or "descending" love.

1.5. Thus in his reflections on the Song of Songs, whose poems were "originally love-songs [*cantus amoris*], perhaps intended for a Jewish wedding feast and meant to exalt conjugal love [*coniugalis amor*]", Benedict says:

Love [*amor*] now becomes concern and care for the other. No longer is it self-seeking, a sinking in the intoxication of happiness; instead it seeks the good of the beloved: it becomes renunciation, and it is ready, and even willing, for sacrifice.

It is part of love's [*amoris*] growth towards higher levels and inward purification that it now seeks to become definitive, and it does so in a twofold sense: both in the sense of exclusivity (this particular person alone) and in the sense of being "for ever".... Love is indeed "ecstasy", not in the sense of a moment of intoxication, but rather as a journey, an ongoing exodus out of the closed inward-looking self towards its liberation through self-giving, and thus towards authentic self-discovery and indeed the discovery of God. "Whoever seeks to gain his life will lose it, but whoever loses his life will preserve it" (Lk 17:33), as Jesus says throughout the Gospels (cf. Mt 10:39; 16:25; Mk 8:35; Lk 9:24; Jn 12:25). In these words, Jesus portrays his own path, which leads through the Cross to the Resurrection: the path of the grain of wheat that falls to the ground and dies and in this way bears much fruit. Starting from the depths of his own sacrifice and of the love [*amoris*] that reaches fulfillment therein, he also portrays in these words the essence of love [*amoris essentiam*] and indeed of human life itself. (*DCE* 6)

1.6. He emphasizes that "the more the two [*érōs* and *agápē*], in their different aspects, find a proper unity in the one reality [*veritate*] of love [*amoris*], the more the true nature of love [*vera amoris natura*] in general is realized. Even if *eros* is at first mainly covetous and ascending ... in drawing near to the other, it is less and less concerned with itself, increasingly seeks the happiness of the other, is concerned more and more with the beloved, bestows itself and wants to 'be there for' the other" (*DCE* 7).

1.7. In commenting on the Genesis accounts of creation, the Pope declares:

From the standpoint of creation, *eros* directs man towards marriage, to a bond which is unique and definitive; thus, and only thus, does it fulfill its deepest purpose. Corresponding to the image of a monotheistic God is monogamous marriage. Marriage based on exclusive and definitive love [*in amore unico et definito fundatur*] becomes the icon of the relationship between God and his people and vice versa. God's way of loving [*ratio qua Deus amat* (for example, as the passionate lover and spouse of Israel) (Hosea, Ezekiel; cf. *DCE* 9) whose love is at once both *eros* and *agape*] becomes the measure of human love [*humani amoris*]". (*DCE* 11)

1.8. From all this we can see that when Pope Benedict declares that the "love [*amor*] between man and woman" is the "very epitome of love", the love he is talking about is the love between husband and wife, that is, marital or conjugal love, *amor coniugalis*. This love, moreover, has an essentially *bodily* component: Thus in the text already cited in which he proclaims the "love [*amor*] between man and woman" to be "the very epitome of love", Benedict had emphasized that in this love "body and soul are inseparably joined" (*DCE* 2). Elsewhere he also stressed that "man is a being made up of body and soul ... [and] is truly himself when his body and soul are intimately united; the challenge of *eros* can be said to be truly overcome when this unification is achieved ... [and that] Christian faith ... has always considered man a unity in duality, a reality in which spirit and matter compenetrate, and in which each is brought to a new nobility" (*DCE* 5).

1.9. In what follows I will therefore focus on *conjugal* or *marital love*. I will argue that this kind of love is the "life-giving principle" of marriage, enabling spouses "to do" what married persons are supposed to do and, in this way, attain the "ends" intrinsically perfecting both marriage and marital love, namely, the "good of the spouses" (*bonum coniugum*) and the "procreation and education of children".

2. Vatican II: Conjugal Love as the Life-Giving Principle of Marriage

2.1. A major idea about marriage central to Vatican Council II's *Pastoral Constitution on the Church in the Modern World* (*Gaudium et Spes*) is that conjugal love is the "life-giving principle" of marriage. An important essay by Francisco Gil Hellín, "El lugar propio del amor conyugal en la estructura del matrimonio según la *Gaudium et spes*" (1980), summarized by Ramón García de Haro in *Marriage and the Family in the Documents of the Magisterium* (García de Haro 1993: 234–56), shows that for the Council Fathers, marriage is the *institution* of conjugal love; and this love, which like marriage itself is ordained of its very nature to the *bonum prolis*, is the *life-giving principle* of the entire institution of marriage.

2.2. *Gaudium et Spes* consistently teaches that *marriage* is a personal communion and uses the terms *marriage, the conjugal community*, and *the conjugal covenant* interchangeably to designate this communion (see *GS* 48, 1, 2, 4; 49, 2; 50, 1, 3; 52, 1, 2, 4). Both this community—the institution of marriage itself, the conjugal covenant—and conjugal love are ordained by their very nature to the procreation and education of children (see *GS* 48, 2).

2.3. A passage revealing the difference and, at the same time, the complementarity between the *institution* of marriage and *conjugal love* is found in *Gaudium et Spes* 47, 2: "But not everywhere does the dignity of this *institution* [*huius institutionis dignitas*] shine forth with the same clarity, for it is obscured by polygamy, the plague of divorce, so-called free love, and other deformations. Moreover, *marital love* [*amor nuptialis*] is too often profaned by selfishness, hedonism, and illicit acts against the generation of life."* As García de Haro notes: "the text distinguishes two kinds of errors [concerning marriage]: the first kind—polygamy, divorce, and free love—obscure the dignity of the institution of marriage itself; among the others that are then enumerated—selfishness, hedonism, and illicit practices against conception—none directly attacks the essential properties of marriage and hence can co-exist with the institution; but they are opposed to conjugal love, which is protected by the institution, and they thus destroy it, ending up, as it were, by corrupting the institution of marriage" (García de Haro 1993: 239).

2.4. In short, marriage is the *institution of conjugal love*, and *conjugal love* is the life-giving or animating *principle* of this institution. Both institution and conjugal love have the same ends and properties, that is, the properties of unity and indissolubility.

2.5. Moreover, "what distinguishes and, at the same time, inseparably unites love and the institution, as elements of the marital community, is that *love constitutes the personal reality that the institution confirms,*

---

*The quotations from *Gaudium et Spes* and *Humanae Vitae* have been translated by the author.

protects, and sanctions before God and man" (ibid., 240). As the Fathers
of Vatican II themselves say: "from the conjugal covenant ..., that
is, from the human act by which the spouses mutually give and
receive each other, there arises in society an institution [marriage],
confirmed by divine ordination; this holy bond [*hoc sacrum vinculum*],
for the good of the spouses [*intuitu boni ... coniugum*] themselves, for
the good of their children, and for the good of society, does not
depend on human choice. God himself is the author of marriage,
endowed with various goods and ends" (*GS* 48, 1). Note that in
this passage reference is made to the "good of the spouses" (*bonum
coniugum*). However, this expression is not used here to designate an
end of marriage, as it will be used later in the 1983 Code of Canon
Law and the 1992 *Catechism of the Catholic Church*, as will be seen
below.

2.6. The institution of marriage arises from an act of love ("the
human act whereby spouses mutually bestow and accept each other"),
and the institution protects love, for true conjugal love is not limited
or impeded by the institution; rather both these elements, institution
and conjugal love, mutually require and complete each other as integrative elements of the one same reality, marriage or the conjugal community, a point emphasized later by Pope John Paul II in *Familiaris
Consortio*: "The institution of marriage is not an undue interference
by society or authority, nor the extrinsic imposition of a form. Rather
it is an interior requirement of the covenant of conjugal love which is
publicly affirmed as unique and exclusive" (*FC* 11).

2.7. Conjugal love, as noted already, *is intrinsically ordained, by its
very nature, to the end of procreating and educating children* (cf. GS 48, 1;
50, 1; and 50, 2). As Gil Hellín observes:

> What distinguishes this text [*GS* 50, 1], in relationship to the
> previous Magisterium on the ends of marriage, is that it distin-
> guishes between two formally diverse elements contained in the
> conjugal community [the institution of marriage and conjugal
> love]. It thus makes explicit "the significance of conjugal love
> even for the procreating and educating of children" [a citation
> from a *relatio* to the *Schema receptum*]. While up to now the Mag-
> isterium of the Church affirmed that marriage "tends toward [the
> procreation and education of children]", Vatican Council II tells

us that both the institutional aspect and conjugal love "tend toward [the procreation and education of children]". (Gil Hellín 1980: 16)

2.8. Conjugal love plays a different role in *establishing the marriage* (*matrimonium in fieri*) and in *the marital community once established* (*matrimonium in facto esse*). As García de Haro notes, the act of matrimonial consent is itself an act of conjugal love, indeed, its first act, and conjugal love is one of the essential goods on which consent bears (García de Haro 1993: 247; cf. *GS* 48, 1 and 2). Thus, "in the conjugal community love is the life-giving principle, owed by virtue of the very consent that has generated it, but whose actual absence does not destroy it" (García de Haro 1993: 248).

2.9. The text of *Gaudium et Spes* makes it clear that love is essential to marriage once it has been consented to *as a requirement* of marriage, even if, because of human will, this love is not actually present. But this obviously "does not mean to make marriage dependent upon the contingent presence of this love in fact" (ibid., 249–50).

3. Conjugal Love Enables Spouses to "Do" What Spouses Are Supposed to Do

I. To Give Conjugal Love

3.1. What are spouses supposed to do? First of all, they are supposed to *love* each other with conjugal love. Men and women engaged to each other *aspire* to conjugal love, but they are not capable of *giving* this kind of love to each other. As we have seen above, the first act of conjugal love is the act of matrimonial consent that establishes the marriage and in doing so enables husbands and wives to give each other *conjugal love*. Pope John Paul II thus declared that the account of creation in Genesis 2 makes it clear that the reality of marriage comes into being when a man and a woman "give" themselves one to the other through the act of irrevocable personal consent. He wrote:

The formulation of Genesis 2:24 indicates that human beings, created as man and woman, were created for unity. It also indicates that precisely this unity, through which they become one flesh, has right from the beginning a character of union derived from a choice. We read: "A man leaves his father and mother and cleaves to his wife." If the man belongs "by nature" to his father and mother by virtue of procreation, on the other hand he cleaves by choice to his wife (and she to her husband). (John Paul II 1997: 50)

3.2. The act of matrimonial consent is an act of self-giving love. It is a freely chosen act, by means of which a man, forswearing all others, freely chooses this particular woman as the non-substitutable and irreplaceable person with whom he wills to share his life *as a married man* until death and by means of which a woman on her part freely chooses this particular man as the non-substitutable and irreplaceable person with whom she wills to share her life *as a married woman* until death. In and through this act a man and a woman give to themselves new capacities and new rights, and they freely take upon themselves new responsibilities. They are now able to do things that non-married men and women simply cannot do precisely because the latter, by refusing to marry, have failed to capacitate themselves to do them. In short, men and women who give themselves irrevocably to one another in marriage have the right and capacity to do what husbands and wives are supposed to do. And the first thing that married persons are supposed to do is to give one another a unique kind of love, conjugal or spousal or marital love.

3.3. Conjugal love (*amor coniugalis*), *Gaudium et Spes* teaches, is no mere sentiment or passion but an "eminently human" affection proceeding from free will, embracing "the good of the whole person and therefore capable of enriching with a peculiar dignity the manifestations of both mind and body and of ennobling them as elements and special signs of conjugal friendship" (*GS* 49, 1). Conjugal love is a special kind of *love of friendship*. Moreover, "Our Lord has deigned to heal, perfect, and elevate this love (*hunc amorem*) with a special gift of grace and of charity", so that this love, "bringing together the human and the divine, leads the spouses to the free and mutual gift of themselves, experienced in tender affection and action, and permeates the whole of their lives; moreover, this love is perfected and grows by its generous exercise" (ibid.).

II. To Engage in the Conjugal Act, One Proper and Exclusive to Spouses

3.4. Moreover "this love [dilectio] is singularly expressed and perfected by the act proper to marriage [proprio matrimonio opere]. For the acts by which spouses intimately and chastely become one [inter se uniuntur] are good [honesti] and worthy. Exercised in a truly human way [modo vero humano], these acts signify and foster the mutual gift whereby they enrich one another with a joyful and grateful spirit" (GS 49, 2). This shows us that the conjugal act is not simply a genital act between men and women who happen to be married. Husbands and wives have the capacity to engage in genital acts because they have genitals, and nonmarried men and women have the same capacity. But husbands and wives have the capacity to engage in the conjugal act only because they are married, that is, husbands and wives, spouses. The conjugal act, therefore, is more than a simple genital act between people who just happen to be married. As conjugal, it is an act that inwardly participates in their marital union, in their one-flesh unity, a unity open to the communication of love and to the gift of children.

3.5. In and through the conjugal act husband and wife literally become "one flesh", "one body". In and through this act they come to "know" each other in a unique and unforgettable way, and they come to know each other precisely as male and female, in their masculinity and femininity. Pope John Paul II offered a deepening of the truth that in and through the conjugal act husband and wife attain a unique "knowledge" of one another. In this act, first of all, "together they become almost the one subject of that act and that experience, while remaining, in this unity, two really different subjects." Second, in and through this act:

> They reveal themselves to each other, with that specific depth of their own human self. Precisely this self is revealed also by means of their sex, their masculinity and femininity. Then in a unique way the woman "is given" to the man to be known, and he to her. . . . The reality of the conjugal union, in which the man and the woman become one flesh, contains in itself a new and, in a way, definitive discovery of the meaning of the human body in its masculinity and femininity. (John Paul II 1997: 79)

In the conjugal act they are speaking the "language of the body" and realizing its "nuptial meaning".

3.6. The conjugal act reveals the *complementarity* of male and female, of husband and wife. This act is possible only by reason of their sexual differences. The wife does not have the male sexual organ; therefore, in this act of conjugal union, she is not able to enter into the body, the person, of her husband, whereas he can and does personally enter into the body, the person, of his wife. He gives his very self to her and, in doing so, receives her. On the other hand, his wife is uniquely capable of receiving her husband personally into her own body, her own person, and, in so doing, gives her very self to him. The wife's giving of herself to her husband in this receiving sort of way is just as essential to the unique meaning of this act as is her husband's receiving of his wife in this giving sort of way. The husband cannot, in this act, give himself to his wife in this receiving sort of way unless she gives herself to him by receiving him, and she cannot receive him in this giving sort of way unless he gives himself to her in this receiving sort of way (Joyce 1980; May 1992).

III. To "Give Life Lovingly, Nurture It Humanely, and Educate
It in the Love and Service of God and Neighbor" and Thereby
Attain One of the Ends of Marriage and of Marital Love,
That Is, the Procreation and Education of Children

3.7. Because they have genitals, non-married men and women can generate life through genital acts, but they do not have the right to do so because it is not good for human life to be generated through acts of fornication and adultery. Doing so, as St. Thomas Aquinas, Karol Wojtyła, W. Bradford Wilcox, and others have clearly shown, violates the *good* of the child begotten insofar as fornicators and adulterers cannot give to the child the home to which he has a right and in which he is meant to take root and grow (Aquinas, *Summa Contra Gentiles* 3.122; Wojtyła 1981; Wilcox 2005). But conjugal love, because it enables spouses to engage in the conjugal act, also enables them to "welcome life lovingly, nourish it humanely, and educate it religiously" (cf. Augustine, *De Genesi ad Litteram* 1.9), that is, "in the love and service of God and neighbor". Conjugal love does this because of the intimate nature of the conjugal act that signifies and expresses it. As Pope Paul VI put the matter so well in *Humanae Vitae*: The intimate nature of this act, "which unites husband and wife with the closest of bonds, also *makes them fit* [*eos idoneos facit*] to bring forth new human life according to laws inscribed in their very being as men and women" (*HV* 12).

4. Conjugal Love and the Realization of the "Good of the Spouses" [*Bonum Coniugum*]

4.1. Conjugal love also "enables" spouses to realize this end of marriage and of marital love. Hence this topic could have been taken up in section 3 above. But because this issue is of such significance, I devote a special section to it. I believe that the relationship between conjugal love and the "good of the spouses" shows most fully why conjugal love, the "love [*amor*] between man and woman" celebrated in *Deus Caritas Est*, is indeed the "epitome of love".

4.2. The very first canon on marriage in the 1983 Code of Canon Law declares: "the matrimonial covenant, by which a man and a woman establish between themselves a partnership for the whole of life, is by its nature ordered toward the good of the spouses [*bonum coniugum*] and the procreation and education of offspring" (can. 1055, §1). The *Catechism of the Catholic Church* reaffirms this in its opening number devoted to the sacrament of matrimony (*CCC* 1601). Thus the Church today identifies as the principal ends of marriage both the procreation and education of children and what she calls the "good of the spouses", the *bonum coniugum*, and in fact the Church names this end first.

4.3. The expression "good of the spouses" to refer to an *end of marriage* is very recent and was first used in this sense in the revised Code of Canon Law in 1983. Theologians have not given much attention to it. In fact, the expression "good of the spouses" is not even mentioned in the works on marriage by several noted authors faithful to the Magisterium published after the 1983 revision of the Code of Canon Law: Peter Elliott (1989), Agostino Sarmiento (1998), Francisco Gil Hellín (1995); Germain Grisez (1993: 553–751); Ramón García de Haro (1993). Some theologians, for example, Antonio Miralles, identify the "good of the spouses" with the good of "mutual assistance" and discuss it only very briefly (Miralles 1993: 102). Canon lawyers, however, have debated its meaning to considerable extent, and the studies of Cormac Burke (1989, 1993a and b) and Dominic Kimengich (1997) have proved helpful to me.

4.4. I will try to show that the "good of the spouses" ultimately consists in the holiness that husbands and wives are meant to attain precisely in and through their married life and that the teaching of Pope Pius XI in his 1930 encyclical *Casti Connubii* is central in understanding this.

4.5. To show the intimate, indeed, essential bond between the "good of the spouses" and the vocation of husband and wife to holiness precisely insofar as they are husband and wife, it is helpful to consult the "sources" for canon 1055 identified by the Pontifical Commission for the Interpretation of the Code in its annotated version of the new Code (1989). One of these sources is the teaching of Pius XI in *Casti Connubii*, which, in my opinion, is the most important source. In this passage Pius XI declared that married love "demands not only mutual help but must go further; must have as its *primary purpose* [emphasis added] that man and wife help each other day by day *in forming and perfecting themselves in the interior life* [emphasis in original], so that through their partnership in life they may advance ever more and more in virtue, and above all that they may grow in true love toward God and their neighbor" (*CC* 23).

4.6. I believe that this statement of Pius XI, together with one immediately following it, is the major source of the teaching that the "good of the spouses" is an essential end of marriage. Surprisingly, the Pontifical Commission did not call attention to the paragraph in *Casti Connubii* immediately following this citation. This is surprising because this text is of the utmost importance in understanding the *bonum coniugum* as an end of marriage and how this end is intrinsically related to the spouses' vocation to holiness precisely as spouses. In it Pope Pius XI declared:

This mutual molding of husband and wife, this determined effort to perfect each other, can in a very real sense, as the Roman

Catechism teaches [pt. 2, chap. 8, 13], be said to be the chief
reason and purpose of matrimony, provided matrimony be looked
at not in the restricted sense as instituted for the proper conception and education of the child, but more widely as the blending
of life as a whole and the mutual interchange and sharing thereof.
(CC 24)

4.7. Pius XI in my judgment is here speaking of what the 1983
Code would call the "good of the spouses", and he clearly identifies
it as an *end* of marriage, in fact, in a real sense, its *primary end* or
"chief reason and purpose". He unequivocally claims that this end
consists in the endeavor of the spouses, rooted in their unique and
exclusive love for one another, to help each other perfect themselves
and grow in holiness. In short, a married person's path to holiness has
a name: his or her spouse, and the way to holiness, the ultimate "good
of the spouses", is conjugal love.

5. Conclusion

5.1. Conjugal love (*amor coniugalis*) is the love uniting *érōs* and
agápē, or, as *Gaudium et Spes* says, "bringing together the divine with
the human" (*GS* 49, 1), that is identified in Benedict XVI's *Deus
Caritas Est* as "the epitome of love". It is the life-giving principle of
marriage that enables spouses to do what married persons are supposed to do, that is, to give one another a unique kind of love, conjugal love, to express it in the act proper and exclusive to spouses, the
conjugal act, and to realize the ends toward which this love and the
institution of marriage that protects it are ordered, that is, the procreation and education of children and the "good of the spouses", which
ultimately consists in their mutual sanctification. These ends are *not*
extrinsic ends to which marriage and conjugal love are merely instrumental; rather they are ends inwardly perfecting both marriage and
conjugal, the ultimate "gifts" of marriage.

Bibliography

Burke, C. 1989. "The *Bonum Coniugum* and the *Bonum Prolis*: Ends or Properties of Marriage?" *The Jurist* 49:704–13.

———. 1993a. "Marriage: A Personalist or an Institutional Understanding?" *Communio* 19, 2:278–304.

———. 1993b. "Personalism and the *Bona* of Marriage". *Studia Canonica* 27:401–12.

Elliott, P. 1989. *What God Has Joined: The Sacramentality of Marriage.* New York: Alba House.

García de Haro, R. 1993. *Marriage and Family in the Documents of the Magisterium: A Course in the Theology of Marriage.* Translated by William E. May. San Francisco: Ignatius Press.

Gil Hellín, F. 1980. "El lugar propio del amor conyugal en la estructura del matrimonio segun la *Gaudium et Spes*". *Annales Valentinos* 6, 11:1–35.

———. 1995. *El Matrimonio y la Vida Conyugal.* Valencia: Edicep C.B.

Grisez, G. 1993. *Living a Christian Life.* Quincy, Ill.: Franciscan Press.

John Paul II. 1997. *The Theology of the Body: Human Love in the Divine Plan.* Boston: Pauline Books and Media.

Joyce, R. 1980. *Human Sexual Ecology: A Philosophy of Man and Woman.* Lanham, Md.: University Publications of America.

Kimengich, D. 1997. *The Bonum Coniugum: A Canonical Appraisal.* Rome: Pontificium Athenaeum Sanctae Crucis.

May, W. 1992. "Marriage and the Complementarity of Male and Female". *Anthropotes* 8, 2:41–60.

Miralles, A. 1993. *El Matrimonio.* Pamplona: EUNSA.

Sarmiento, A. 1998. *El Matrimonio.* Pamplona: EUNSA.

Wilcox, W. B. 2005. "The Facts of Life and Marriage: Social Science and the Vindication of Christian Moral Teaching". *Touchstone* 18, 1.

Wojtyła, K. 1981. *Love and Responsibility.* New York: Farrar, Straus, and Giroux.

Eros: Ambiguity and the Drama of Love

*Giovanni Salmeri**

A False Contraposition

When one begins to ascertain the meaning of *érōs* within a Christian context, it seems particularly opportune to distinguish the level of words from that of concepts and of reality. Words alone do not resolve anything, as their meanings can fluctuate and subordinate concepts may then traverse the phenomena of decomposition and recomposition, still leaving open the task of describing and understanding reality. Concerning the duplicity of *érōs* and *agápē*, a philologist, for example, could suggest simply that the difference between the two is one of a linguistic nature: the first being more elevated and classical with the second being colloquial (at least concerning the meaning that is of interest to us). Such a difference in nature then would have been reflected in the distance between the classical Greek and the Hellenistic *koiné* (used by early Christianity) and would have led to a certain specialization of senses, but more radically to the victory of the common term (the only one suitable in the neo-Hellenistic language to express one's own love being that of "*s'agapó!*").

A thesis such as this one has the support of an exceptional witness like Origen—who most certainly could not be accused of having inadequate linguistic preparation—who calmly observes how the two words want to express the same thing except for the fact that, so he says, on the one hand, the term *érōs* has a sensual connotation, while, on the

*Assistant Professor of Philosophy, Pontifical John Paul II Institute for Studies on Marriage and Family, Rome. Associate Professor of History of Theological Thought, Università Tor Vergata, Rome.

other, it is more vague. Linguistic studies, moreover, have abundantly confirmed this very simple thesis, concluding that Christianity did not operate according to any autonomous lexical innovation whatsoever but rather simply followed an independent evolutionary trend. The most evident confirmation (so evident that, paradoxically, it is often overlooked) of this notion is the systematic and ample usage of the term *agápē* in versions of the Septuagint—thus in a pre-Christian era— with a range of meanings that, much like the term "love" in English, extend without embarrassment from the radical choice of the one God, on one extreme, to sensual attraction, on the other, accepting seven years' labor just to reap the reward of two sweet eyes (cf. Gen 29:15–30).

Without a doubt, these observations enjoy the fundamental merit of not assuming any dichotomy with prejudice or of imposing any ready-made thesis requiring demonstration on the history of ideas. However, they are insufficient by far to resolve the problem. When during the last century—with Anders Nygren on one side and Karl Barth on the other—these authors used the pair *érōs* and *agápē* to set the Christian vision of love against that of the pagan world as if they were two hostile and irreconcilable entities, most certainly they wanted, not to conduct a simple operation of lexical distinction, but, above all, to draw attention to the experience of love itself. In both visions, of course, there is in reality nothing "ambiguous" either in the Christian *agápē*, with its abyssal message of a gratuitous donation of God, or in the pagan *érōs*, with its aspiration to a brilliant egoism. Rather, according to the two, the ambiguity originates in ever-returning attempts to fuse and to blur the two into one thing; an ambiguity, therefore, which, if not within the human soul, is at least rooted in human history.

The theses they sustain, undoubtedly exaggerated and frankly untenable from a historical and conceptual point of view, take nothing away from the seriousness of the problem they intend to highlight. One could say further that to unravel and to distinguish the various meanings of love is not something very different from what Plato did when he noted how wolves also "love" lambs or from what Aristotle did when he observed how delinquents are "good friends" of each other. In brief, independently of linguistic questions, and even independently of either true or supposed Christian novelties, it seems that love itself, and the way of understanding it, offers itself to human experience in a splendid but fragile way. Precisely the fact that love crosses every path of the human being means, however, that it inherits its tensions as well as its uncertainties and discontinuities. This notion applies to *whatever* understanding of love there might be. Carnal love is ambiguous, but is the spiritual one (as Christos Yannaras wisely asked himself years ago) less so? Love as a search for satisfaction has the taste of selfishness about it, but where could we find a pure giving completely stripped of the egoistic search for joy that one has "more in giving than in receiving?" And so on.

From this point of view, an unambiguous concept of love seems to be a simple *petitio principii*. Of course, one could reply that with respect to its predominantly theological meaning, that of divine love, love suffers no ambiguity. Here we would not be dealing with a matter of simple *petitio principii* because the experience of faith consists precisely in perceiving this love and in living according to it. However, one could then reply that a love so radically intended coincides with the very nature of God and is, therefore, unknowable in its essence. No love that offers itself to human knowledge is free from ambiguity, and thus no other way remains than to begin from the basis of human experience, experience that, in the history of the West, has reflected love above all by way of the key term *érōs*.

The Impersonal Face of *Érōs*

Platonic thought, from this point of view, was, not only the starting point of the reflection, but also the constant reservoir for all those who wanted to see something more than mere sentiment in love. Plato's strategy does not consist in challenging the fact that love is above all a sentiment, with all of its fragility and instability. On the contrary, according to him this precise point of departure reveals the peculiar nature of *érōs* (something that often is ignored). Continually subject to death and rebirth, love would in this way manifest its hybrid nature, half mortal and half immortal. Therefore, being neither fully human nor fully divine, but something in the middle, it has the role of connecting the human and divine worlds; giving to the former an impulse that alone has the capacity to reach the perception of something absolute and eternal.

The moment of falling in love is the first one in which a human being can, not only can think abstractly, but truly perceive something that is worth living and dying for, something worth the effort to do foolish things and to abandon all calculations of what is valuable in the finite world. The attraction that is caused by seeing a beautiful body is thus the first step of a journey that, in one way, touches upon the universal idea of beauty (not only the beauty of *this* body that enamors me, but that which reveals itself in every beautiful thing) and, in another way, deepens beauty itself by passing progressively from a sensible appeal to one that is spiritual, to that which reveals itself in the greatest moral ideas.

Here, the torments of love are not useless sufferings from which a sober spirit could simply back away; rather, they are the sign of effort and affliction in a journey that leads a person from the first amorous look—awakening us to our eternal destination—toward the vision of truth. Certainly, *érōs* in this framework is moved by lack, by the perception of one's own incompleteness, in a word, by desire. However, is it not exactly this particular discovery out of many that makes us aware, without illusions or masquerades, of our own nature? Religious instinct, human sentiment, and aspiration for knowledge, in the best-case scenario, thus come together in a unique way, full of both enthusiasm and effort.

But is everything as clear and exciting in *érōs* as Plato speaks of it? Certainly not. Going over all three of his dialogues dedicated to this theme (*Lysis*, *Phaedrus*, and the *Symposium*), one recurring element arouses perplexity. Love, as it is described, originates in encountering the other person and is continually nourished by this encounter, but in the final analysis it is also not directed toward the other. The beloved is rather the opportunity of discovering a transcendent universal value, one that is as impersonal as much as the "Good" that constitutes the ultimate goal of human knowledge and action. In the final analysis, therefore, the beloved person is replaceable, and the emotion one has regarding that beloved (Plato himself states so explicitly) is destined to appear as very small when the lover's path crosses a universal beauty that reflects upon *everything* beautiful.

Of course, one could defend Plato and reply that it serves as part of the most common human experience to appreciate a person and also to nourish love for that person thanks to the qualities discovered in him; also, in order to be recognized there must be something of the universal present (grace, intelligence, courage). To love the universal in a person, for Plato, thus means precisely to discover what constitutes the most profound identity of a person and, in the end, of myself. The idea of the Good, to Plato, is ultimately exactly what bestows being upon every reality. The problem, however, is that it is precisely this last identity that is not considered in personal terms. The most certain sign of this impersonal drift manifests itself in Plato's strong distrust of the relation of conjugal love. Surely, the underestimation of woman's intellectual value (who evidently would be incapable of sufficiently establishing spiritual and profound relationships) plays a part in this and, thus, also that form of spiritualized homosexuality which is typical of Platonic anthropology. However, a more profound part is played by the distrust of a relation (such as the conjugal one) that is so essentially individualized and personal that by its nature it tends to generate new persons.

More than drifting toward abstract values, what still makes Platonic love incurably impersonal is the fact that it programmatically refuses to find its paradigm in the real fertility of human beings, in the extraordinary capacity that love has to be the origin of new life. Whoever turns to conjugal love, thus Plato suggests, frustrates the real desire of immortality in that of a surrogate immortality passed down from generation to generation. Hence, the impersonality of love in Plato is not an immediate problem of a theological nature. In fact, it will not resolve itself simply by another more complete philosophical image of the human person or by substituting the anonymous Good with the face of a personal God to which man aspires. The problem consists precisely, so to speak, in the face of a love that cannot limit itself to assuming the feminine face of the priestess Diotima, who teaches the reality of love by myths, but who *also* must have the feminine face of a beloved woman and a mother.

A Reality to Decipher

In ancient times, in fact, at least two voices have tried to merge the Platonic proposal into the language of conjugal love. One of them is the pagan voice of Plutarch in the *Erotikós*. The other is the Christian voice of Origen in his commentary on the Song of Songs. While the first development, as interesting as it is, is in a certain sense organic to the Platonic tradition, the second provides a somewhat new depth to Western culture. Origen indeed follows in the footsteps of Jewish exegesis, which already had been adept at allegorically interpreting this sacred poem of love as an encoded description of the history of God with his people. However, he obviously unites to this perspective not only his Christian faith but also his classical erudition, which enables him to read the Song of Songs as precisely the Christian successor to Plato's *Symposium*. In fact, the former would also be a philosophical text and, moreover, represents, among the three books of Solomon, that which is properly metaphysical. After the ethical purification of customs in Proverbs and after the "physical" lesson of Ecclesiastes on the transitory nature of every earthly thing, the Song of Songs presents authentic contemplation, that of the Christian faith that proclaims God as one who is both love and the contemplation of love.

Surely Origen, like Jewish tradition, is attentive in distinguishing a literal meaning of the text, which here concerns the love between man and woman, from the spiritual meanings to which the reader is called in reality: the love of God for the soul and the love of Christ for the Church, both cases having a "fecundity" that is obviously not identical to natural and biological fertility. Only the allegorical sense is Scripture's "eternal" meaning. The literal surface, even though to be studied carefully, risks being misleading or at least useless as is so true of the Song of Songs, which to Origen, in a certain sense, serves as the center of the Christian Bible and is a reading meant only for adults. All of this, surprisingly, in no way means that Origen intended to contrast earthly to heavenly love. The love of which the Song of Songs speaks is that which indeed leads to God, but it is exactly the same love that "from puberty onward" begins to bind every human being with its strength. Love may either be holy or degenerate to vulgarity, but this degeneration concerns the love of honors, wealth, or carnal love bought for money, while love for a spouse is precisely holy love, just like love for God. It is in this context, as previously mentioned, that Origen does not hesitate to recognize how the biblical language of *agápē* and the Platonic language of *érōs* talk about the same thing, observing furthermore that in some rare passages, the use of a term with more sensual connotations could not be misinterpreted. The Greek Bible also speaks of *érōs*, for example, the "*érōs* of wisdom".

While the history of exegesis, and Christian theology in general, has bestowed huge success upon this work of Origen (the work in which, after he had exceeded all others, Origen surpassed himself, as the fastidious Jerome enthusiastically confirms), the phantasmagoria of allegorical interpretations along with their inevitable liberties, only weakly guaranteed by the "spiritual" intelligence of the interpreter, brings to light the difficult problem of that relation between the spiritual and the mundane, between the eternal and the temporal. It is true that Origen's line of demarcation actually does not stand between *érōs* and *agápē* (whatever they may mean), or between human love and divine love. The latter, however, is still always the line that divides the two senses of reading the Song of Songs. Moreover, at the same time it divides and entangles them, for the announced love is concurrently eternal love of God and temporal human love, with all of its uncertainties and flutterings as the dramatic material of the biblical book witnesses.

Also, when one accepts as philologically correct a reading of the Song of Songs that is consonant with the Platonic theory of *érōs* (an attempt that, even if with great discussion, has been revisited in recent years), the problem remains completely open as to what entails a human love that, remaining itself, *signifies* divine love. It offers itself, thus, to human experience, not as simple language to interpret, but as a *reality* to decipher, as a realization that at the same time serves as a promise. Plato could skip over this problem with his depersonalized conception of *érōs*, but it now comes to be suggested again in all its power by the dignity of conjugal love within which the goodness of divine creation is manifested. However they are understood, do not Paul's words concerning the interior "division" of married persons propose, in a certain fashion, precisely the empirical difficulty of this integral interpretation of human love?

The Ambiguity of Folly

Several centuries later, this problem would be proposed dramatically as a theme in one of the most surprising medieval mystical treatises,

The Four Steps of Ardent Love, by Richard of Saint Victor. By that time, Origen's discourse had been completely assumed and, what is more, had also been couched in the form of a sacramental theory that would see the Christian value of matrimony precisely in its capacity to *signify* the infinite depth of divine love. Dionysius the Aeropagite's mediation in the treatise *On the Divine Names* then taught *érōs* (in Latin, *amor*) as a divine name that, even if it never appears literally in Scripture, shines and is experienced in the mystical life as the embrace of God himself, impelling humans ecstatically to leave themselves behind, conducting them toward unspeakable unity with God.

Richard of Saint Victor in fact, qualifying *caritas* as "ardent", rediscovers the spirit of Plato's erotic phenomenology and describes, with a surprising abundance of details, the effect of falling in love on the human life. Love takes on the whole person and, in upsetting one's life, becomes an obsessive thought that impedes other concerns and completely absorbs all one's strength, thus hampering work and in the end destroying and exhausting existence, leading to folly. This is the effect of *ardent love* that is presented with a mixture of fright and satisfaction. However, is he talking here about human or divine love? Richard's surprising thesis is that the description applies to both forms; the first part of the treatise, dedicated to human *érōs*, is followed by another one, perfectly mirrored, concerning divine *érōs*. While in the first case the successive steps demarcate a progressive degeneration, in the second case the concern is about falling into the mystery of divine love, that is, onto the most sublime path that man may travel.

Nevertheless, Richard is very careful not to contrast passion and rationality. Even if (and this is admitted) the love for God always presumes a preliminary rational knowledge, both ways of love are equally characterized by the progressive victory of passion. He would also allude, however, to the commandment to love God "with all your heart, and with all your soul, and with all your strength", in which three successive specifications indicate the irrepressible way of divine love that arrives at conquering the whole of human existence and even conducts man toward complete folly. This folly allows man (as with Abraham) to have discussions on an equal footing with God or to arrive at the point where he desires (as in the case of Paul) to be damned for the good of his own brethren. They are expressions impious in themselves, almost blasphemous, that somehow do not need to be pardoned, for they are a sign of the complete burning of the *ardent love* of God.

Does this mystical perspective succeed in resolving the problem of the relationship between human and divine love? Certainly not. Even if the contrast between the foolish love of creatures and the wise love of eternity, with its noble Augustinian ancestry, were to signal with certainty the general structure of the work, the appropriate and willful identity of language in the two cases leaves the question concerning their relation open, like a wound. This question is strengthened by the fact that Richard, noting explicitly that the strongest human love is that found between a husband and a wife, observes that in this case the first step of ardent love, already described with unequivocally erotic terms, is fully good and is, in other words, the expression of discovery of the other and of unreserved self-giving. Only successive steps are improper, as they would lead the spouses, dragged by the eagerness of their love, to neglect their duties, to isolate themselves from the world, and ultimately to revoke their own lives.

In brief, the force of spousal love should not hinder one's work, the relations within the broader human community, or the preservation of one's very existence. Only in the case of divine love is the complete turmoil of one's life justified by the infinite and absolute value that is at play. In the end, everything happens as if human experience had presented, by way of its corporality, a model of the first encounter with God (both the first and second forms of *érōs*) but then had suggested progression to a folly of which only God is worthy. However, the subtle distinctions made by Richard, even if they are faithful to a phenomenology that is within the reach of every reader, leave the question open as to how it is possible that this destructive folly—which can be described empirically only by way of the experience of human love—then could assume a value that is literally reversed in divine love. More radically, one must ask if the good sense that is evoked to limit the range of human *érōs* is really consistent with the discourse that is being carried out, or if the goodness shared within the first steps of both spousal and divine *ardent love* might not rather be the sign of *another* meaning that still needs to be brought to light.

Érōs and Its Narration

But what meaning would that be exactly? The examples that we have provided, modestly describing a fragment of the history of understanding *érōs*, cannot be banally interpreted as incomplete discourses that are merely waiting for an ever-better theory in order to be complete. The Platonic tension between a personal falling in love and the attractive force of universal values, Origen's problem of a human love intertwined with divine love that continually needs to "signify", and the progressive and problematic distance in Richard between human and divine folly in the end all indicate the complexity of the experience of human love itself—more intimate to man than any other feeling and, maybe precisely because of that, more incomprehensible than any other.

Appealing to naturalness and the impulse through which sentiment may be lived out resolves nothing here. As Plato taught, these are the tensions (or at least some of them) that are refracted by crises and fluctuations that are not *alien* incidents in themselves (as only ignorance or a banal romanticism can suggest). Rather, they serve as constitutive elements of the experience of love itself: the fear of disappointment of a person who is never up to the promises made, the stages of opacity of a love by which one also desires to *signify*, with its wholeness, the totality of one's own faith and the disquietude of a happy folly that must come to terms with reality alongside its depth and heaviness. Considering all of these factors, it becomes understandable that one repeatedly tries, for example by confining human *érōs* to a secular framework or by a fantastical contraposition between *érōs* and *agápē*, to skip over these problems all together and to assign them to the level of an intellectual confusion that need only be declared and eliminated. As has been said before, the same problems are found again on a different level, even in the concept of love that we would like to have finally purified.

It is, therefore, certainly true that this discourse necessarily passes on from a theory of *érōs* to anthropology and theology. With the Christian *érōs*, the entire image of God (if *érōs* in fact is a divine name, as Thomas confirms in his reading of Dionysius) as well as the entire image of man are at stake. *Érōs* in its human perfection cannot but coincide with the theological image of man as he was willed to be "at the beginning", or rather with waiting for the final destination where, messianically, each thing finds its own face. Eventually, the claim of Christian "novelty", at least according to Jesus' words, stands right here. Nevertheless, is there room to speak of *érōs*? Certainly. However, it is noteworthy that every voice we put into play uses a *dramatic* language for love: either in the more stylized way of an evolutionary description of the often a-linear experience of love or even in a fully dialogical form, as Christian tradition inherited from the Song of Songs.

If love is a *drama*, this love comes to pass, not only in the sense of the burden of suffering and pain that always is involved, but above all in its etymological sense, in which it is the development of an event, and in its theatrical sense, according to which there are always supposed to be actors who meet each other, talk and act together, and put their own lives at stake. This is no different from what happens within the Christian event itself, which, as far as it can and should be understood and is thus translated into concepts, is always irreducibly a history of love narrated and heard in biblical testimony.

Bibliography

Barth, Karl. 1936–1977. *Church Dogmatics*, Edinburgh: T. & T. Clark.

Joly, Robert. 1968. *Le Vocabulaire chrétien de l'amour est-il original? Philein et agapan dans le grec antique*. Brussels: Presses Universitaires de Bruxelles.

Nygren, Anders. 1953. *Agape and Eros*. Philadelphia: Westminster Press.

Origen. 1957. *The Song of Songs, Commentary and Homilies*. Ancient Christian Writers. New York: Paulist Press.

Plato. 1997. *Complete Works*. Edited by J. M. Cooper and D. S. Hutchinson. Indianapolis: Hackett.

Plutarch. 1969. *Moralia X: Love Stories*. Loeb Classical Library. Harvard: Harvard University Press.

Richard of Saint Victor. 1999. *I quattro gradi della violenta carità*. Luni: Trento.

Rist, John M. 1965. *Eros and Psyche: Studies in Plato, Plotinus and Origen*. Toronto: University of Toronto Press.

Yannarás, Christos. 2005. *Variations on the Song of Songs*. Brookline, Mass.: Holy Cross Orthodox Press.

The Unity of the Human Person under the Light of Love

José Granados [*]

How does the Christian Gospel respond to that great question which, in the words of St. Augustine, man is for man (*Confessions* IV, 4, 9)? Much of modern thought has looked at Christianity as a repression of human happiness. According to this position, the Church responds to man's deepest aspirations with a dreary, resounding No.

In its turn, our culture offers different versions of a Yes to man. Without exception, however, each of these Yeses turns out to be partial, equivocal, and trapped within the bounds of temporality. Behind these Yeses to the body, to sexuality, to love and its desires, are hidden the most destructive Noes to other dimensions of the human person.

It is in light of this that Pope Benedict, in his first encyclical, wishes to present Christianity unhesitatingly as a great Yes, a Yes that is capable of integrating all of human reality. The way the Pope has chosen to do this can be called the way of love. What were his reasons for this choice? Let us begin by reviewing briefly some of the visions of man that pronounce only a partial Yes about him (1); this will give us the key for understanding the importance of the path chosen by the Pope (2); the way of love will then enable us to consider Christian anthropology from a privileged point of view (3–6).

---

[*] Assistant Professor of Patrology and Systematic Theology, Pontifical John Paul II Institute for Studies on Marriage and Family at The Catholic University of America, Washington, D.C.

91

1. The Incomplete Yes of Some Conceptions of Man

Many seeming Yeses to man are deceptive because they present a human
reality that is fractured, with cracks that in some cases do more than
disfigure the building: they threaten its ruin.

a. Let us first turn our attention to a rupture that is present at the
heart of man's being. The dualism ratified by Descartes has never abandoned the Western soul, which carefully delimits the objective from
the subjective. To the objective side are relegated those things that are
licit for discussion in the public forum. These are restricted, in the
final analysis, to the domain of the natural sciences; that is to say,
more or less, to that which can be measured in the laboratory. The
remaining aspects of human life, such as religion and morality, seek
refuge in the privacy of each individual, where the subject lives them
out according to his will. In this second realm is included that which
is properly human: spirituality and freedom.

Now, every Yes to man that so radically distinguishes the private
sphere from the public, the personal from the natural, is condemned
in the end to remaining a Yes characterized by lasting conflict—and
especially if those questions relegated to the private sphere are the
specifically human ones, which are then prevented from ever playing
any significant role in the construction of society (Ratzinger 2004b:
139).

b. This dualism within man corresponds to another division: that
which separates man from God. Our society divides the human from
the divine with an excessive sharpness. The love of God proper to
religion is considered alien to other types of love. Some expressions of
religious fanaticism, having assumed destructive forms, appear to have
confirmed this point of view. It is therefore said that religion should
not express itself in public, because through its own dynamic, religion
ends by destroying the "city of man". The separation between life and
faith is seen as a good by those who think that this is the only means
of establishing a pluralistic society. One can pronounce a Yes to life in
this world and a Yes to faith in God as long as both Yeses remain
unconnected to each other.

What is the response of Christianity to these partial Yeses to
man?

2. The Point of Departure: The Experience of Love

The great Yes to man given in the Christian Gospel is not a Yes "from outside", pronounced, as it were, by an impartial observer. It has been the particular desire of Benedict XVI in his first encyclical to begin directly with human experience, giving a Yes "from inside" to the question that man is for man. In this way he is continuing the path marked out by John Paul II in his catechesis on human love (John Paul II 1997: 34).

What is this experience with which he begins? Underlying the encyclical is the conviction that only *the experience of love* can recover the unity of the subject that has been lost. After speaking of how Gassendi greeted Descartes with the salutation, "O Soul!", and of the response, "O Flesh!", that followed, the Pope affirms the unity of the person, who is one in body and soul. In order to justify this unity, he appeals to the experience of love: "It is neither the spirit alone nor the body alone that loves: it is man, the person, a unified creature" (*DCE* 5). The crucial proof of the unity of man seems to be the classic "*da amantem*" argument of Augustine (*In Iohannis Evangelium* 26, 4): Give me someone who loves, and he will understand, by the light of his own love, that man is one, in body and soul.

What is proposed, therefore, is an understanding of man that considers him as a loving subject, as a person who loves. What might result from an anthropology that took this as the cornerstone of its response? In light of the encyclical, we may adopt the point of view of love as that which provides the key for understanding all of the traditional concerns of philosophical and theological anthropology, from freedom and self-consciousness to the imaging of God.

This choice of love as an interpretive key has two immediate consequences that respond to the encyclical's concern for seeking the unity of man.

a. It shows us the fundamental *unity of human experience*, which has so often been broken in the history of thought. The foundation of experience is not the aridity of the Cartesian "I think, therefore I am." Over the centuries the isolated action of the thinking subject has been taken as the fundamental human experience, from which all other human experiences could be derived. The existence of the exterior world and the company of my neighbor form part of this experience only as elements brought in as an afterthought.

But suppose the primary experience is, not isolated thought, but love? Here we might follow the brilliant intuition that Calderón de la Barca places in the mouth of Segismundo, the protagonist of *La vida es sueño* (Life is a dream). After many years in prison, he is granted the possibility of returning to the palace and assuming the responsibilities of a king. However, in view of the fact that he behaves as a tyrant, his father re-imprisons him, making him believe that everything has been a dream. The baroque theme of life as a dream, an empty illusion or a deceptive counter-reality is presented to Segismundo in a radical way. He can no longer be sure of anything; could not he himself, along with the prison where he suffers, also be a dream?

It is here that Segismundo recalls the love that united him, in the palace, to Rosaura. He exclaims: "I loved one woman alone; I believe that that really happened / because everything else has vanished / but that love alone stays with me" (Calderón 2002: 56). Upon realizing that he is a subject who loves, Segismundo discovers the anchor that grounds him in reality and is capable of bringing back to him the meaning of all of his experiences. Love confers a particular unity upon all the dimensions of human life (Marías 1987: 166).

Indeed, setting out from love helps us avoid the various partial Yeses to man from the start. In the first place, we avoid a Yes to the body that consists in giving free rein to all of its impulses. The partiality of this Yes is revealed in the consequences to which it leads. The Pope uses an example from another era to demonstrate this: sacred prostitution (*DCE* 4). In such cases, the desire for the mystical hid a depreciation of the person in the final analysis. The victims were the women who were made into objects of abuse. What occurred in the temples of pagans continues today, without the reference to the sacred, in the frantic Yes given to sexuality, a Yes that often ends up abusing the other person. Now it is precisely the experience of love, when embraced in its integrity, that denounces unambiguously every reduction of the person to an object of pleasure. This is because the goal to which *érōs* is directed from the beginning surpasses *érōs* itself and culminates in a welcome of and respect for the beloved.

What is to be done? We could, as Kant did, view passionate love as a kind of malady. The German philosopher understood *erōs* as a threat to the autonomy of the subject and the dignity of the person. As a result, *erōs* was banished from Kant's moral theory. Yet this Yes to the dignity of the person likewise turns out to be a partial Yes. In effect, the dynamism proper to *erōs*, far from obscuring the dignity of the person, is the only way that allows us to affirm this dignity from the very beginning of our experience. Whoever depreciates *erōs*, which is rooted in the body, will be able to justify the importance of his neighbor only secondarily, as a phenomenon that is superadded onto the already established loneliness of self-consciousness, the isolation of the Cartesian *cogito*. To the one who loves, on the contrary, the dignity of the beloved makes itself evident from the very first moment because it is necessary for defining his own identity as one who loves, as a loving subject. To disregard *erōs* is, thus, to close the door from the start to any convincing foundation for human dignity.

We can therefore see how, starting from the experience of love, we safeguard the unity of the subject, who is one in body and soul. *Erōs* embraces in a single dynamism the personal and the natural, the corporal and the spiritual.

b. On the other hand, beginning with the experience of love can show the profound unity between divine love and human love, religion and culture. What is decisive is not simply the affirmation that God is love, for love can take a thousand different forms, some of which are not at all reassuring. Above all it is a matter of disclosing what is proper to Christian love, which, far from destroying other forms of love, ennobles them by bringing their own dynamism to its fullness. Moreover, in highlighting the centrality of love, Christianity offers us from the beginning a profound harmony between human experience and divine revelation, between that which man discovers on his own and that which God grants him gratuitously.

To the "thinking subject" of Descartes, as well as to Kant's "autonomous man", any kind of revelation must necessarily come as something alien since revelation always arrives from outside the subject. Something different occurs for the subject who loves: he lives already rooted in an event that was not in his hands to produce, nor is it in his power alone to keep it alive. Love is, from the very elements that constitute it, essentially a certain experience of revelation. Love *happens*; it sneaks up on us without our choosing it (*DCE* 3), continuously drawing its life from a primordial gratitude. Christianity can thus present itself as that which perfects human experience while working in accord with its innermost law (because this law is already a law of revelation). In fact, as we will see, this human experience opens for us the way to God, the basis of the very possibility of loving.

We have indicated, then, a double rupture: (a) in the interiority of the subject; (b) between the subject and God. Benedict's interest in healing this rupture is confirmed by an analysis of the term *érōs* in his encyclical. If Plato understood *érōs* as the noblest aspiration of the human soul, its impulse toward the divine, for the modern mind-set its meaning is fused with that of "sex". For his part, Benedict has chosen to respect the entire range of meanings of the word. *Érōs* refers, in the first instance, to the love between a man and a woman and is linked in a special way to human bodiliness. Yet at the same time, it veils within itself a mysterious promise, a call to union with the other and, ultimately, with the divine. In fact, the integrity of *érōs* depends precisely on both of its aspects being affirmed at the same time in the human being, in whom are joined the spiritual and the corporeal, the image of man and the image of God (*DCE* 5; this coincides with the treatment of *érōs* by John Paul II, 1997: 168–71).

Throughout the encyclical, then, the aspect of unity pervades everything. In fact, it seems that, in order to specify the novelty of Christianity, Benedict makes reference to its unifying power, to the fact that it leaves out nothing of the human experience. This novelty consists in the fact that "*eros* is healed and its grandeur restored", that "Christian faith ... has always considered man a unity in duality" (*DCE* 5). The Christian Yes is a comprehensive Yes: a Yes that does not wish to exclude any part of what is human.

In continuity with his predecessor, Benedict XVI affirms that this unity, confirmed by an analysis of *érōs*, leads us to a new interpretation of the material and the spiritual, one from which both dimensions emerge ennobled. Let us consider, individually, this dual ennobling.

3. The Body, Seen in a New Light

An appreciation for the material is now in vogue in many anthropologies that isolate what is properly human and reduce man to a biological product (*DCE* 5). Consider, for example, how today the theory of evolution is much more than a scientific explanation—here what we encounter is an ideology that pretends to be able to explain every facet of reality (Ratzinger 1973: 147–60).

And yet, is it possible to give a complete explanation of reality beginning with what is material? If we do wish to proceed in this manner, we must listen attentively to all that material reality has to say to us. A true appreciation of materiality means paying careful attention to all of its manifestations. Let us consider, then, the experience of love. *Érōs*, being primarily a corporeal phenomenon, rooted in the body, points beyond itself: it reveals to us the dignity that is proper to the beloved, who cannot be reduced to an object of pleasure. In *érōs*, the material phenomena themselves indicate the dignity of the person. Hence we are faced with a paradox: the only way to affirm the body and pronounce a complete Yes to it consists in affirming much more than the body. To deny *érōs* the vocation to which it aspires is to suppress *érōs* as such.

We can say, then, that to consider material reality deterministically as pure extension does not result in a true Yes to material phenomena— and it is precisely fidelity to the observed data itself that leads us to interpret materiality in a new way. If the body forms part of the experience of love, if the unity that love reveals to us is real, then materiality cannot be reduced to an ordered collision of molecules, a mere *res extensa* that is deprived of meaning and voice.

This vantage point offers us a different way of understanding the phenomena with which physics and biology are concerned. Abandoning a suffocating mechanism allows for visions of the world that are much more open. It is true that we must keep in mind the autonomy of each area of being; but this does not demand its fortification against any external intrusion. Inert material, for example, retains its laws upon being assumed into living being, but it will never be able on its own to account for the phenomenon of life. What is proposed is a vision of the material world, not as detached from man or from his liberty, consciousness, and love, but instead a vision that admits what is properly human as the fullness of its innermost laws (Granados 2005).

It is precisely love, which testifies to this unity, that presents itself to us as the unifying point of view that encompasses everything. As Cardinal Ratzinger said some years ago: "The natural event [of reproduction], guided by natural laws, is borne and made possible by the personal event of love, in which human beings give to one another nothing less than themselves" (Ratzinger 1989a: 209 [*translation slightly modified*]).

In sum: the body ceases to be what Plato calls the *regio dissimilitudinis*, the region of what is different and, in the last analysis, does not pertain to the properly human. In contrast to the Platonic definition, we read in the encyclical a bold expression of Benedict XVI, which designates the body *provincia libertatis*, the arena of freedom (*DCE* 5). This is an indication of how Christianity desires to accord a new dignity to matter. One early Church Father went so far as to say that precisely this is the Good News of the Gospel: the body is called to enter the kingdom of heaven (St. Justin Martyr, *De Resurrectione* X). Let us consider now how this new conception of the body permits a new description of the spiritual.

4. Reinterpreting the Spiritual in Light of the Body

Beginning with the experience of *érōs*, which offers us a synthesis between the corporeal and the spiritual, we will arrive at a new vision, not only of material reality, but also of the spiritual. What is biological in man, as we have just said, far from being meaningless raw material, already bears a primordial meaning. We can, therefore, speak of a "language of the body": the body, once it is admitted into the company of the soul, communicates something to it. To take the body into account means, therefore, to define anew what is "spiritual". Let us think, for example, of freedom, to which we have referred above. The fact that freedom is embodied, that it has its sphere of action in the body, must change the very notion of the "free man".

Let us now enumerate the key principles of a new definition of "spirit":

a. What the body first reveals, once it is admitted into the sphere of the self, is our poverty, our vulnerability. The body introduces an original dependence, revealed especially in the sphere of affectivity. In this sphere it is clear that there is a dimension to the person in which he is passive before that which happens to him; it is the fact that man is capable of suffering (Ricoeur 1992: 318). In this respect the phenomenon of suffering is illuminating: various attempts by Greek philosophy to escape from the body simply endeavored to deny such a fragility.

Once again it is the light of *érōs* that brings clarity to our analysis; here, bodiliness reveals its meaning in an even more radical way. *Érōs* comes over us like an imposing force, one that presents itself without having been invited (*DCE* 3). Not everything is under the control of sheer willpower or an alert intellect. The "other", thanks to *érōs*, can enter into my existence and settle there. Being open to the possibility of this happening indicates a radical vulnerability.

b. Such a vulnerability draws us toward an enrichment of our personal life by way of the other's entrance into that life. Here we must recall that any consideration of the body as a fundamental anthropological element entails a necessary reference to the fact that human beings exist only as gendered. The grammar of *érōs* expresses itself precisely in this unity between the man and the woman, in the fact that neither is complete without the other (*DCE* 11). In this way the body, especially because of its sexual character, reveals that the person is fundamentally, not an imprisoned intellect, but rather openness and dependence, who is called in turn to transcend himself through faithful love. The body becomes a bridge for communication and unity (Ratzinger 2003: 79); it becomes *provincia communionis*.

When we allow the voice of the body to be heard, it becomes clear that the concept of the "spiritual", which for centuries was united to self-consciousness and the immaterial mind, must of necessity change: to speak of the "spiritual" is to speak of openness to the other person; it is to refer to the sphere of communion (Ratzinger 1998).

c. However, this must be developed even further, listening attentively to the language of the body. The passivity to which *érōs* testifies goes deeper than simply a relationality, however concrete, to other persons. The experience of love as a gift, as a grace that arises within the encounter with another person and affects, in the first place, our bodiliness, allows us to connect the body with an original gift, with a first love. If we move from the phenomenon to the foundation (*FR* 83), we will be able to read in the body not only a given (*datum*) that man finds when he comes into existence, but also and more fundamentally a true original *gift* (*donum*). The original receptivity of the body leads us to God, the original giver. In this sense the philosophical experience of love remains open to the love of God as a creating love. One can only give love, indicates Benedict XVI, if one has first received love (*DCE* 7). This "first love" is evident in corporeal existence in a radical way, as the creating love of God that brings his creatures into existence and declares them good (Pérez-Soba 2001).

This primordial foundation of *érōs* makes it possible for us to understand why the first movement of *érōs* is not that of giving. Before we are able to give, there is always something we have received. God, the original giver, ensures already from the beginning the possibility for *érōs* to be transformed into *agápē* without losing itself in the process. Whoever understands the abundance of the first gift of creation will not fear the oblation of himself, for he knows that this oblation will not fall into the void of indifference. *Agápē* is the handing on of the gift received (*DCE* 7).

Hence, even when *érōs* is allowed to point beyond itself to the reality of the person, it is not content merely with this; *érōs* points, by virtue of its own dynamism, to a foundation (the original love of God) and a horizon (communion with the Father), which is fully in accord with the Pope's interest in underscoring the profound unity between divine and human love.

There is, then, a dynamism that, beginning with our human experience, reveals to us the presence of God. This is not the case, however, of an analysis of self-consciousness that, being oriented to the infinite, finds in the Supreme Being the origin of its own power of knowing. The emphasis, on the contrary, is on the affectivity of the body as the first place where we perceive our neighbor and the presence of God (Pannenberg 2004).

This would be an appropriate place for a detailed consideration of the relationship between the image of God and the image of man. The dynamism of love, which begins precisely with the original gift, is based on the presence of a creating God who loves the world with a true passion and calls it to communion with himself, all the while respecting its creaturely identity. Behind this conception of the divine is the trinitarian face of the Christian God, the ultimate ground of the Christian vision of *erōs* as capable of containing *agápē* within itself, without thereby losing its innermost essence.

Let us conclude. The body helps us better to understand various dimensions of the person: (a) his dependence and openness, (b) his call to communion, (c) his ultimate reference to an original gift and giver. Let us note the significance of these three points for the concept of freedom, which is of such importance in our culture: (a) If the proper realm for the realization of freedom is the body, then freedom cannot mean pure autonomy, the flight from all limitation. On the contrary, freedom must be rooted in its environment, depending upon it and receiving from it its foundation. (b) Likewise, just as the body, in which the phenomenon of *erōs* is rooted, points beyond itself to a dynamism of communion, so freedom must be understood in the horizon of love. Freedom is indeed creative; but it is creative precisely with the creativity of *erōs*, which transcends itself in *agápē* in order to transform itself in faithfulness to the beloved. (c) Finally, if we keep in mind this reference to the first love, we see that freedom is always born as a response to an original gift of God; from this point, the free man is able to surpass himself, to reach a newness of being through the communion of persons.

5. An Image: The Temple of the Body

Allow me to expound on these ideas a bit by returning to the notion of the body as the *provincia libertatis* (arena of freedom). Then-Cardinal Ratzinger, speaking of the Church, commented that the concept of freedom in antiquity was always associated with the home. A free man, in contrast to a slave, was one who had his own home. The home was the sphere that made the family possible, the point from which the person became open to the life of society. Ratzinger extended this similitude to the Church, the only home in which the Christian is truly free (Ratzinger 1998).

I believe that this idea can be applied in a similar way to the human body, which comes to be the original home of the free man. Today's understanding, however, is diametrically opposed to the conception of the body as the *provincia libertatis*. Man today regards his own body as an unwelcome interference of nature in his personal life. It suffices to mention the desire to abandon the man–woman distinction, a desire that at times regards sex as an accident of the person, comparable to race or social class. The body, therefore, is seen as an obstacle to the realization of the person, something opposed to freedom. Its voice is silenced when it becomes unpleasant; and, when it invites us to start the costly ascent of love, we reduce it to the monotony of pleasure.

The proposal of Benedict is that we make the body, once again, the house of man, his true home, outside of which he ceases to be himself. The image of the body as a house was used by St. Paul, in whose footsteps many of the Church Fathers followed. The difference between conceiving of the body as a house or, in a Platonic fashion, as a prison, is obvious, even though in both cases we speak of a building. In the image of the house, we must not see something external to the person. On the contrary: the image is valid insofar as it refers to a dwelling, to that which necessarily pertains to the human being, without which man is exiled from himself, forced to turn his back upon himself. In the body, the person encounters that house where communion is lived in a concrete form. The way of the purification of *érōs* consists precisely of being able to make this house of the body into a *human* place, into one that is habitable.

In St. Paul the reference to the body as a house goes deeper, for it refers to the Temple of God. Today it seems strange to us to think of bodiliness as a place of God's presence. Of some help to us might be the biblical concept of the heart, the seat of the bodily affections and, at the same time, the core of the person. Man enters into relation with God when his heart belongs to the Lord. It is interesting to note, as well, the connection between the heart and *érōs*, that human love which, according to the encyclical, points to the divine. The Pope's letter invites us to take into greater consideration this fundamental anthropological element (cf. Spaemann 1996: 29–30; Hildebrand 1977).

6. From Extasis to Exodus

Our analysis of *érōs* has brought us to affirm the unity of man in all of his dimensions. Now we must direct our attention to a decisive element of this unity: the fact that it is a dynamic unity, one that takes the historical dimension of man seriously. This is a constant thread throughout the encyclical: the Pope repeats that *érōs* is always "open-ended"; he speaks of a journey, of an ascension in which love attains its own truth.

At the beginning of its journey, *érōs* hears the call to go out of itself. But a mere "being outside of oneself" can end up as nothing more than inebriation, a loss of oneself. What Benedict XVI is proposing is that this *ecstasy* be transformed into an *exodus*, that is to say, not in a simple "being outside" (ex-stasis), but in a "being outside" that is a "setting out on the way" (ex-odos). This raises the question of the search for meaning that governs the whole journey of *érōs*. The answer is given in the dynamism of the gift: with the original gift as starting point, the person who seeks meaning is able to make the gift of self in order, by so doing, to discover himself fully in communion with the beloved.

The idea of the exodus of *érōs* suggests an interpretation of human life as a journey that must be traveled over time. Our culture has fractured time; it lives in between the universal time of the cosmos and those relative times that each individual creates for himself. Man has always desired to make his time into something eternal; today this is pursued in the form of ecstasy, of a perpetuation of the present instant, isolated from the whole of one's existential project.

This is simply part of the current global crisis in the configuration of time, in which the absence of direction toward the future is coupled with an indifference under which the past is viewed as dead weight. In order to overcome this situation, the German philosopher Hannah Arendt has underscored the necessity of recovering two fundamental human actions: forgiveness, which breaks the rigidity of the past; and the promise, which assuages our fears before the future (Arendt 1958). Forgiveness and promise pertain precisely to the dynamism of love just as it is outlined by the Pope: love is born of divine forgiveness and seeks to devote itself forever in fidelity (*DCE* 10–11).

In this way the consideration of the exodus of love makes it possible to conceive of human time in a new way: time is a gift given for the building up of communion. Hence we have a glimpse of a Christian interpretation of time, which is capable of offering an alternative to the vision of evolution. It is the conception of time as *exitus-reditus*: man goes out from God, who creates the world in love, and returns to him by a free response to this love. "Time is a movement of freedom; ... the cosmos is created with freedom in mind ... , a freedom that gives itself back and finds itself completely in so doing ... , an illuminated freedom that finds its definitive state in the fusion of truth and love" (Ratzinger 2004a: 22). Love appears, therefore, as a point of reference for understanding all of the temporal phenomena in which man, his society, and his history are enveloped.

This idea of the exodus of *érōs* clearly shows the connection between human experience and divine revelation. The fundamental law of revelation is precisely the "Exi", the "Go out" that God gives as a command to Abraham (Gen 12:1) and that continues in the Exodus of Israel, until it is completed in the mystery of the Passion. "Thus the Cross becomes transformed, not in the crucifixion of man, in the sense intended by Nietzsche, but rather in his genuine healing" (Ratzinger 1973: 181). The *iter* of love is shown especially in the *iter* of Christ, which culminates in the Passion.

We can see, then, that the exodus of Christ—which refers especially to the mysteries of his life in the flesh—is a real exodus that Christian *érōs* must undertake. Hence the way of love enables us better to understand how anthropology and Christology are connected. The journey of the incarnate Christ in time, his learning what it is to give fully of oneself, can be seen as an affirmation of the journeys of man and, at the same time, as that which both judges man and always surpasses him. Since *érōs* is always "on the way", there is nothing strange in another Wayfarer joining his steps with ours and, by admonishing our foolishness of heart, causing our paths to extend beyond the twilight (cf. Lk 24:15–32).

In this way we can return to the point where the vision of man offered us in the encyclical originated. In the commentary that he wrote on the pastoral constitution *Gaudium et Spes*, Ratzinger noted that the document, in paragraph 22, attained its *reductio in theologiam* (Ratzinger 1967, *ad locum*): "The mystery of being human is only made fully clear in the mystery of Christ, the Word Incarnate." Immediately after this, *Gaudium et Spes* makes reference to the "revelation of the Father and of his love". In this love, revealed in Christ, consists therefore God's definitive Yes to all of the promises there are in our hearts (cf. 2 Cor 1:19).

We have tried to explain why, in order to give the Yes of Christianity to the desires of man's heart, Benedict has chosen the way of love. Let us note here that this Yes, because it is the Yes of love, cannot remain simply a word: it must go out, seeking the neighbor who suffers. This makes it possible to understand the unity of the two parts of the encyclical: the Christian affirmation of man, as the affirmation of love, cannot be only a theoretical one. To conclude: one could not choose a better way to present the Yes given in the Gospel to man; for it is proper of love, in a unique way, to confirm the existence of the beloved (Ratzinger 2005: 89–90); love testifies to his goodness and upholds it, correcting his defects and overcoming his limits. Only love affirms in a radical way.

Bibliography

Arendt, H. 1958. *The Human Condition*. Chicago: University of Chicago Press.

Calderón de la Barca, Pedro. 2002. *Life Is a Dream*. Translated by Stanley Applebaum. Edited by Drew Silver. Dover Thrift Editions, edited by Paul Negri. Mineola, N.Y.: Dover Publications.

Granados, J. 2005. "Love and the Organism: A Theological Contribution to the Study of Life". *Communio* 32:435–69.

Hildebrand, D. von. 1997. *The Heart: An Analysis of Human and Divine Affectivity*. Chicago: Franciscan Herald Press.

John Paul II. 1997. *The Theology of the Body: Human Love in the Divine Plan*. Boston: Pauline Books & Media.

Marías, J. 1987. *Antropología Metafísica*. Madrid: Alianza Editorial.

Pannenberg, W. 2004. "Geist und Bewußtsein". *Theologie und Philosophie* 79:481–90.

Pérez-Soba, J. J. 2001. "Operari sequitur esse?" In L. Melina, J. Noriega, and J. J. Pérez-Soba, *La plenitud del obrar cristiano: Dinámica de la acción y perspectiva teológica de la moral*, 65–83. Madrid: Palabra.

Ratzinger, J. 1967. "Commentary on the Dogmatic Constitution on Divine Revelation". In *Commentary on the Documents of Vatican II*, edited by H. Vorgrimler. New York: Herder and Herder.

_____. 1969. "Zur Theologie der Ehe". In *Theologie der Ehe*, edited by G. Krems and R. Mumm, 81–115. Regensburg and Göttingen.

_____. 1973. *Dogma und Verkündigung*. Munich: Wewel.

_____. 1985. *Dogma and Preaching*. Chicago: Franciscan Herald Press.

_____. 1989a. "Man between Reproduction and Creation". *Communio* 16, no. 2:197–211.

_____. 1989b. "'You Are Full of Grace': Elements of Biblical Devotion to Mary". *Communio* 16, no. 1:54–68.

_____. 1998. "The Holy Spirit as *Communio*: Concerning the Relationship of Pneumatology and Spirituality in Augustine". *Communio* 25, no. 2:324–39.

_____. 2003. *God Is Near Us*. San Francisco: Ignatius Press.

_____. 2004a. "The End of Time". In *The End of Time? The Provocation of Talking about God*, edited by C. Urban and T. R. Peters. New York: Paulist Press.

_____. 2004b. *Truth and Tolerance: Christian Belief and World Religions*. San Francisco: Ignatius Press.

_____. 2005. *The Yes of Jesus Christ: Spiritual Exercises in Faith, Hope and Love*. New York: Crossroad.

Ricoeur, P. 1992. *Oneself as Another*. Chicago: University of Chicago Press.

Spaemann, R. 1996. *Personen: Versuche über den Unterschied zwischen "Etwas" und "Jemand"*. Stuttgart: Klett-Cotta.

Agape, the Revelation of Love and Its Appeal to the Heart: A Comment on *Deus Caritas Est* in Light of John Paul II's Category of "Elementary Experience"

*Margaret Harper McCarthy**

Introduction

At a certain point in time, well along in human history, something new appeared on the horizon: the *event* of Jesus Christ by which the Eternal Son became a man. In that event the Mystery of God was fully revealed and, insofar as the Son was permanently conjoined to the humanity of Jesus, the meaning of man and all of reality was also revealed (*GS* 22). More specifically, what was revealed is that God is Father from all eternity and that he, by no necessity, extends to mankind the love he has for the Son in the Holy Spirit, making us to be always in and through the freedom that that very love implies—*filii in Filio*. Also revealed in that event is the divine fidelity of the God of the Covenant, shouldered by the incarnate Son, who hands himself over "even to death on the cross" and rises from that death as Spouse of a Bride. With the revelation of God in Jesus Christ, as Pope Benedict XVI says in *Deus Caritas Est*, we are before a novelty that concerns both the image of God and the image of man. That is, we stand before the novelty of *agápē*, which names "something new and distinct about the Christian understanding of love" (*DCE* 3).

*Assistant Professor of Theology, Pontifical John Paul II Institute for Studies on Marriage and Family at The Catholic University of America, Washington, D.C.

The Greek term *agápē*, a word almost entirely unknown in secular Greek (De Andia 1997: 29), makes its first biblical appearance in the Septuagint, in the Song of Songs, where it refers to the love of the bridegroom for his bride. The poem was held to be inspired scripture insofar as it described, metaphorically, the Hebrew people's experience of God's electing love (ibid., 29–30). The term is used again, with greater force, in the New Testament to identify the love of the Father for his Son, in the Holy Spirit, gratuitously bestowed on mankind (ibid., 32–33). In its many instances, *agápē* can be characterized as a self-sacrificing love that, moving beyond the selfishness that marks other forms of love, "involves a real discovery of the other" and "seeks the good of the beloved" (*DCE* 6).

But what is this love to the person who encounters it? If it is so strikingly new, must it not also be alien, foreign to the naturally human manifold experience of love? Although many were attracted to this unprecedented revelation of love that is Christ and were ready to follow him without calculating the cost, others, such as the young rich man, took note especially of the sacrifices their following would entail and, fearing the burden to be too great, turned away (Mt 19: 16–21). Is not this new love, as Nietzsche and others have suggested, alien to *érōs*, to that deeply human desire and striving for what is fulfilling and ultimately, therefore, for what is truly beautiful (Nygren 1982: 30)? It is true that the Septuagint and the New Testament reserve the term *érōs* for loves that are in some way impure, but it seems that what is there in view is not really *érōs* per se but perverted forms of the erotic (De Andia 1997: 31). *Agápē* would not then so much oppose *érōs* as rectify and purify it and ultimately fulfill it by placing it before an utterly gratuitous and unforeseen object (*DCE* 5). Indeed, the greatest instance of Christian (*agapic*) love was indicated as the path to authentic self-discovery and recovery (*érōs?*) when Jesus said to his disciples: "Whoever loses his life will preserve it" (Lk 17:33).

Should we recall the thoroughly paradoxical character of human nature (De Lubac), we can hear how the Christian experience of the surprising and altogether gratuitous *novitas* of *agápē* strikes a chord deep within us. This is the theme of "original" or "elementary experience" (Giussani 1997: 7–9), and, according to John Paul II, it is crucial for seeing that the revelation of Christian love is, even if demanding, the fulfillment of an original promise (John Paul II 1997: 51–54).

It is to this theme that John Paul II turns, following Jesus' own appeal to "the beginning" (Mt 19:4), in addressing the specific case of human spousal love. And it is to this same theme that we turn, in this brief comment on *Deus Caritas Est*, in order to see how the ever new revelation of love and its demands corresponds to the ancient and abiding demand of the human heart, to its original desire—even if that heart could never have adequately anticipated such love, in all its gratuitousness, and even if it had been dealt a mortal blow of doubt, somewhere near the beginning of its history, making it and its desire fragile and vulnerable (Giussani 1997: 11). More specifically, I wish to consider how spousal love is exalted once love descends in the form of a Spouse; by appealing to the notion of original experience, I also hope to show how the love revealed by this divine Spouse corresponds to the heart of man, notwithstanding the wounds it has suffered.

The Problem of Marriage

It need hardly be said that marriage is an old story. Men and women were joining together in marriage long before the advent of Christian love. The treasury of the world's great literary works testifies that marriage has always somehow been at the heart of the human drama. Yet, despite the significance the married state must always have had in human life, when the philosophers of pagan antiquity considered the question of love and friendship in a thematic way, the love specific to man and woman was not foremost on their minds (cf. Plato, *Lysis*, *Phaedrus*, *Symposium*; Aristotle, *Nicomachean Ethics* 8–9). Spousal love was for them one of the many cases of love, but by no means its paradigm (McCarthy 2005: 260–82).

One does not have to strain too much to see, for it is a fairly common experience, that the difference between the man and the woman, which is precisely what specifies their love as a form of love, stands at the origin of their love as a powerful source of attraction between the two. But while the allure of that difference between them may remain, it also often gives way over time to other, less alluring, differences. Moreover, the terrain of sexual difference is one of the more privileged theaters for the objectification of the other: whether by force or by seduction we attempt to reduce the otherness of the sexual other to an instrument wholly of our own purposes. For these and other reasons, the experience of marriage is often, in varying degrees and in varying ways, a mortifying experience. And after all, did not Eve's appearance deprive Adam of a rib? It should therefore come as no surprise that according to a very ancient view, the mortifications involved in the marital state are themselves an inevitable consequence of the task specific to marriage, the generation of new human life, which is itself intimately connected to the phenomenon of physical death (Balthasar 1990: 374; cf. Augustine *Enarratio in Psalmum* 127:15). Surely all this accounts, in no small measure, for the almost universal practice of making allowances for divorce. In view of such "realism", one can understand the objection made to Jesus' new prohibition: Impossible! "If such is the case of a man with his wife, it is not expedient to marry!" (Mt 19:10).

While the many real benefits and blessings that issue from the love between a man and woman cannot be denied, it is difficult to see how spousal love, precisely as such (in that difference which specifies it), can be said to be so congruent with the human heart that a man and a woman should commit themselves to an indissoluble union, no matter the consequences that might ensue. On the more theoretical level, it is difficult to see how spousal love *as such* can be the expression of the highest form of love, the "love of friendship" (*amor amicitiae*), where each loves the other for his own sake and not, rather, as an "object for oneself", as in the case of "love of concupiscence" (*amor concupiscentiae*) (*STh* I–II 26, 4), unless, of course, something unexpected were to happen to show that, in facing the other, one is not, in the end, alienated or deprived of one's heart's deepest desire, even within the most difficult circumstances.

The *Status Quaestionis*

When St. Thomas forged his famous distinction between the two basic loves, he was echoing an ancient view that a love that calculatingly moves out toward the beloved only to take back what had previously been lacking is lower than a love that looks wholeheartedly to the good of the beloved and for *that* reason is happy, together with the beloved. In the *Phaedrus*, Socrates argues for *érōs*, that awe and reverence for the beloved akin to that for a god (251a–b), holding it to be superior to Phaedrus' carefully regulated, risk-free, and, for that matter, love-free exchange of (sexual) favors in view of his own interests (230e–34d). Most notable is Aristotle's extended discussion of love and friendship in his *Ethics*, wherein the philosopher distinguishes between friends who love each other *accidentally*, on account of the utility or pleasure that ensues from the friendship, and friends who love each other *absolutely*, "for themselves", and who for that reason are also pleasant and useful to each other (*Ethics* 1156b12–16). St. Thomas links his celebrated distinction between *amor concupiscentiae* and *amor amicitiae* back to Aristotle's distinction between friendships of use or pleasure, on the one hand, and the friendship of virtue, on the other (*STh* I–II, 26, 4 ad 3).

Now for Aristotle and Thomas it is not the case that the distinction in question has to do with the difference between the self-seeking lover with something to gain and the other-centered lover, who is no better off for this love and this loving than before. It would be a strange thing if one of the greatest *joys* in life, friendship, were, in its highest expression, of no benefit to the two friends; it would be stranger still to think of such an altruistic conception coming from the "eudaimonistic" Aristotle or from Thomas, who begins his treatise on moral theology with an extended discussion of the desire for happiness (*STh* I–II, qq. 1–5). There is certainly a reward in the higher forms of love; it is just that it comes only by way of an affirmation of the good of the beloved, an embrace of the entirety of the beloved's person. Thus, the reward is not merely some aspect of the other (some accidental quality) from which the lover benefits, because it perfects his individual well-being. The reward is the beloved, the joy of *being with* that person whom the lover takes as good *in se* and whose good the lover pursues so that, by it, the beloved may be more perfect and flourish (Gallagher 1996: 26). In his treatise *On the Love of God*, St. Bernard of Clairvaux expresses this distinction exquisitely: "All true love is without calculation and nevertheless is instantly given its reward; in fact it can receive its reward only when it is without calculation" (*De diligendo Deo* 32).

Reasons for love in either of its two modalities are not lacking: one does not love something or someone voluntaristically. According to St. Thomas, one loves on account of some sort of unity that is perceived to exist between the lover and the thing or person loved. Before love is a passionate movement toward something desirable, or a *dilectio*, the rational act of choosing one over another and willing that person's good, it is an "affective union" (*complacentia, coaptatio*) with a good (*STh* I–II, 25, 2c and ad 2; 26, 2), which the good itself has forged with the lover as a kind of promise of communion (Melina 2001: 24–25; Pérez-Soba 2001). According to this same account, if there are two loves, or rather, if love is twofold—involving as it does the "wanting *some* good" (*amor concupiscentiae*), "for *someone*" (*amor amicitiae*), whether for oneself or another (*STh* I, 20, 1 ad 3; I–II, 26, 4)—that is because of the twofold nature of the union that stands at the beginning of love (as its formal cause). The affective union can be either one whereby the lover takes the beloved (thing or person) "as something belonging to himself", his well-being, or one whereby the lover takes the beloved (person) "as himself", "his other self", and therefore "wills good to him, just as he wills good to himself" (*STh* I–II, 28, 1c and ad 2).

It is, moreover, precisely the apprehension of a likeness (*similitudo*) between the lover and the beloved that gives rise to the twofold union of affection in the lover. This likeness, as might be expected, is twofold. In the case of the union at the heart of the love of concupiscence, the "similarity" is between one who possesses actually what the other has potentially (*STh* I–II, 27, 3c). Thus, for example, a needy man, lacking material means, has a kind of similitude with a rich man and takes him, in his affections, to be one with him, *as pertaining to his well-being*. But this is also the case between two "equals" in the Aristotelian friendship of pleasure or use, between, for example, two equally witty men who are recurrently in potency for what each already possesses in himself *but desires from the other* (Mansini 1995: 185–87). In any case where love arises from this kind of likeness and *where this likeness is the reason for the friendship*, there is a love of concupiscence. Here the friend is not loved, in the ultimate analysis, *for himself*, but only to the extent that he can provide or offer something the lover lacks or wants.

The likeness that gives rise to the love of friendship, on the other hand, is that between two who possess the same quality actually. Our common humanity is, of course, the most basic of such likenesses and is the reason for which one can love any human being with the highest of loves. But of course there are other more particular qualities by which friends can be said to be similar in this second way. When such likenesses are seen—it goes without saying that the similar qualities should also be lovable—one perceives the friend as another self, "as identified with oneself" (*quasi reputans amicum idem sibi*), or "as though become one with the beloved" (*quasi idem factus amato*) (*STh* I–II, 27, 3c), extending love for self to love for the friend, loving the friend for his own sake.

From this second sense of likeness one can see how much love of another in the higher sense is an extension and overflow of the love one has for oneself (Gallagher 1996: 32). It is because the beloved is similar (in the second sense) and therefore looked upon as "another self" that the lover can love that other "for his own sake". This follows from Thomas' argument that since love is an affective union, and since a person's substantial self-unity (and likeness) is stronger than the union (of likeness) with another, the former unity is the "form and root" of the latter (*STh* I–II, 27, 3; *STh* II–II, 25, 4). Scripture is called upon as an authority on this point: "You shall love your neighbor as yourself" (Lev 19:18), as is Aristotle: "The origin of friendly relations with others lies in our relations to ourselves" (*Nicomachean Ethics* 1166a1–2; cf. *STh* II–II, 24, 4c). So, paradoxically, likeness (in the second sense) gives rise to the utterly other-directed love of friendship, but always insofar as the other is identified with the self, not the narrow individual of the love of concupiscence to be sure, but the expanded self whose good is now a common good (*STh* II–II, 26, 4 ad 3).

Returning to spousal love, the love specific to a man and a woman, where does it fit in this account of love and friendship? It almost goes without saying that between man and woman, the highest kind of friendship can exist on the grounds of their common humanity or on the grounds of some other more particular similarity by which each, taking the other as an other self, loves the other by wanting his good. The question is whether the highest kind of friendship can exist between

them on the grounds of the difference that is so instrumental in drawing the two together and that so specifies their love (in both conjugal
and domestic life). Aristotle considered that friendship to be chiefly a
combination of use and pleasure, where each, having different func-
tions, fulfills the other's distinctive needs and wants (*Ethics* 1162a15–
28). And Thomas more or less accepts this association in his commentary
on the *Ethics* (*In VIII Eth. lect.* 12, 1721) as well as when he takes up
one of the "effects" of love, namely, zeal, and offers as an example of
zeal, in the case of a love of concupiscence, the jealousy specific to a
husband for his wife (*STh* I–II, 28, 4c).

One could at this point note the elements in Thomas' theology of
marriage that extol spousal love (*STh* III, 42), especially there where
he argues for indissolubility and monogamy (*SCG* 123, 4–6); but the
question remains whether that friendship, when confronted with his
celebrated distinction, is still not ultimately ranked on the lower end.
For it seems that according to the terms of that distinction, the difference (of sex) that specifies spousal love suggests a love whereby
each loves the other, not for himself, but "accidentally", that is, in a
kind of exchange where each appropriates some particular aspect of
the beloved that is lacking in and beneficial to the lover. If, however,
there are elements indicating that spousal love is not, in the end, reducible to the love of concupiscence, then must this not affect the way
we understand the place of sexual difference in the friendship between
the man and the woman?

The Turning Point

When *agápē* erupts into history, all the newness of a gratuitous and
supernatural event appears. One stands before the revelation of the
mysterion, in no way owed to us and in no way deducible from our
nature, in which the manifestation of the eternal communion that
God is becomes a union (Ratzinger 1968: 175). The Eternal Son
becomes man, and in time, through his Cross whereupon he makes
the gift of his body, he brings forth the Church, his Body, his Bride,
and is with her the "one flesh", she thereby participating in a new
nature (Eph 5:31–32). In this revelation of God, where man, too, drawing near to Christ, finds himself (*RH* 10), "God's way of loving becomes

the measure of human love" (*DCE* 11), and spousal love comes forward front and center (Balthasar 1992: 283–360; Scola 1998: 630–62). Ultimately, as Balthasar labored tirelessly to show, the possibility of this particular manifestation of love for the world and union with it is found in the God of Jesus Christ, for whom the Other is thoroughly positive and, thus, for whom a world can be created (*ex nihilo*) and subsequently receive its Creator without the overcoming of the difference (between Creator and creature) (Balthasar 1998: 61–109). Indeed, the *dissimilitudo* between Creator and creature is the precondition for, and is therefore directly related to, the gratuitous bestowal of human *similitudo* with God, fully given in unity with Jesus Christ (Balthasar 1983: 68).

A Return to "The Beginning"

But for all of its novelty, *agápē* is not so new that nothing has been prepared for it, so that it encounters no correspondence in the one to whom it is revealed, once it comes along. On the contrary! This revelation is possible precisely because we have already encountered its traces in experience (Scola 2003: 50), and this is because the full human image was already "hidden for ages" in the Father who created all things and in the predestination of the Son (Eph 3:8–9; Balthasar 1992: 250–59; Scola 1997: 206).

When Jesus gave his new and radical teaching on divorce—no circumstance can make that other, that man or that woman, ultimately alien, for one *is*, with him or her, "one flesh"—he indicated just such a correspondence, turning his interlocutors to "the beginning", some deep experience lurking in the depths of man, and staking its claim therein even now. It is not insignificant that it was in front of Jesus that the "beginning" could now, more than ever, be recalled in all of its persuasiveness. For as the disciples' response to the new teaching on the indissolubility of marriage attests, that beginning was by no means unscathed and unobscured. Indeed, if the new teaching came as a shock ("impossible!"), it is not because it accompanies an alien imposition, "detached from the vital relations fundamental to human existence" (*DCE* 7) but because somewhere at the dawn of time that "beginning" had suffered a blow when the image of the other, both divine and human, was disfigured, becoming the object of distrust (Batut 1997: 8–10; Ratzinger 1985: 25). This is when, as a result, human freedom became disordered precisely at the level of human vital relations (Batut 1997: 10–13). So it is that, abiding in the new love that is Jesus, one does so not without the cross, but now—now that death is no longer the final word—that cross can be embraced as the path on the way to the fulfillment of one's very self.

Elementary Experience

In his famous *Wednesday Catechesis*, John Paul II identified that "beginning" to which Jesus referred not only with a "theological prehistory", that state of original innocence which man enjoyed before original sin, but also and more significantly with an "elementary" or "essential" experience that he possessed and continues to possess, as Jesus' dialogue suggests (John Paul II 1997: 51–54).

For John Paul II the experience in question is not the reductive accumulation of facts, bodily sensations, and psychological emotions that results from the mere trying of things (Giussani 1997: 6). It connotes rather "a unifying and complex act constituted by the sensible, psychic, and intellectual dynamic . . . which institutes a direct contact with the object, in force of which the object itself is given in its original form" (Caffarra 2001: 8); for if it is human, experience cannot be separated from the intellectual act (judgment) by which one attempts to understand that reality with which one is engaged (Scola 2003: 49).

But more specifically, the experience that John Paul II identifies with "the beginning" is "elementary experience", that *human* act in which is given direct contact with man, the *integrum humanum* (Caffarra 2001: 9). This experience, this contact with the whole of "the human thing", is the very impetus that launches human beings into the world to engage with it and that therefore dwells within every experience of reality as its root even if it is "so intermingled with the ordinary things of life that we do not generally notice [its] extraordinary character" and we pay it little attention (John Paul II 1997: 51–54). Even if human experience is that of "historical man", with his historical sinfulness, which places him at such a remove from elementary experience, even *that* experience must ultimately refer back to and be judged by something more elementary, something more original (John Paul II 1997: 32–34).

Original Solitude

There are, following the reflection of John Paul II, three elements of elementary experience: original solitude, original unity, and original nakedness or innocence (John Paul II 1997: 51–54). The first of these, "original solitude", names that experience Adam has of himself after accomplishing the task God gives him of naming the animals. Through that activity, Adam begins to know (experience) himself, first by what he is not, as one who is distinguished from the *animalia*. They do not name themselves, and there is not one of them that can be for him a partner. But this *via negativa* leads toward a positive self-definition as well: Adam finds himself alone before God and discovers that he, "through his own humanity, through what he is, is constituted at the same time in a unique, exclusive and unrepeatable relationship with God himself" (ibid., 37–39). "Original solitude" is the experience of human uniqueness as person with all of the fullness that the doctrine of creation brings to it, so perfectly expressed in the text of *Gaudium et Spes* 24, constantly cited by John Paul II: "*Man . . . is the only creature on earth which God willed for itself.*"

This first meaning of Adam's original solitude—his uniqueness in the world by which he stands "alone" before God—is the ontological basis for its second meaning: Adam's lack of a human companion. It is on account of the "good" of Adam's aloneness before God that it can be said that "it is not good for man to be alone"; for, indeed, if man is "the only creature on earth which God willed for itself", "*man . . . cannot fully find himself except through a sincere gift of himself*" (GS 24).

Original Unity

The second meaning of original solitude thus leads us to the second element of elementary experience, that of original unity. By this expression John Paul II does not, as it might seem, indicate the *union* that the first man and woman form once each has discovered the other. Rather, he uses it to point to the deep reason why they should do so and why doing so is not a mere matter of choice or "diversion"; for it is because of original unity, presented in the "myth of beginnings" as the woman coming forth from the donation of Adam's rib, that we see that the "help" of the woman for the man (and that of man for the woman) is nothing less than helping the other *to be*, to find himself completely (cf. John Paul II, *Mulieris Dignitatem* 7).

This constitutive character of the person's relation to the other (sex) can be readily seen in the figure of the "sleeping Adam". For unlike "Androgyny" in Plato's *Symposium*, Adam *from the beginning* longs for a helper—"it is *not good*"—and *always already* carries within himself the tendency toward her (the "rib"). Moreover—and this banishes any idea of exteriorness between the two—the fact of the woman's coming from man's rib does not present us with two individuals, each of whom has come independently "from different" places and who, with their complementary compatibility, meet in the middle. Woman, *'issah*, literally "comes from man", but then so does the man, since it is not until she appears that the man (*'is*) appears in his definitive form. Each is constituted by the other and cannot therefore be without reference to the other, the reason for which their eventual meeting face to face is a fulfillment ("this at last!").

Now, on the basis of this original unity, the woman for the man (and the man for the woman) is a kind of "second self" (John Paul II 1997: 42–45), for she is of the *same* humanity. Not on the basis, in the first instance, of an "abstract" belonging to human nature (Balthasar 1983: 227), but rather on account of a gift of self. The woman is *similar* to man because she is "bone *of bones* and flesh *of flesh*". It is precisely on account of this (kenotic) origin of the similarity between man and woman that it always resides in and coincides with a difference, each being given and taking possession of that similar humanity in uniquely different ways. We have here a difference that is no mere accidental aspect of the person (to be appropriated in an exchange as an "object for me") but the bodily manifestation of a common humanity that is "dual", that is, which is always possessed as either male or female (John Paul II 1997: 45–48). Thus, when Adam takes Eve as his "second self", and not merely as an object for himself, he does so, not only on account of her similarity to him (that is, through his having identified her with himself and thereby achieved a more expansive

substantial unity in himself), but also on account of her being different, another person, before which difference he must "lose himself"
in order to have himself back, to find himself completely ("dual unity").
So much from the rib of which he had been "deprived"!

When Jesus returned to "the beginning", as an argument for the
indissolubility of marriage, it was precisely this element of the beginning, original unity, so seemingly remote, to which he pointed. "For
this reason," he said, quoting Genesis 2, "the two shall become one
flesh." It is because the "one flesh" of marriage is the fulfillment of
original unity that a husband can never be for his wife, and a wife
never be for her husband, ultimately alien.

Original Innocence

"Original innocence", or "original nakedness", is the third element
of elementary experience. Unlike the first two elements, however, Adam
and Eve, as John Paul II notes, become aware of this innocence, or
nakedness, only from within the "boundary experience" of shame
"when their eyes were opened" (John Paul II 1997: 51–54). Here the
movement signifies, not the passage from not knowing to knowing,
but rather a radical change in the gaze of each upon the other. Now
each, with his newfound shame, is urged to hide for fear of the "other
self" who no longer sees the depths and rightful value of one's own
self and therefore tends to reduce it to an object to be appropriated
and taken back (John Paul II 1997: 66–69). Shame, though it comes
with sin, is now at their service by bringing about a distance that will
serve, paradoxically, "to draw them closer together personally, creating
a suitable basis and level to do so" (John Paul II 1997: 54–57).

It is now with shame that the first man and woman can "remi-
niscently" experience a more original nakedness, that of a body that
could manifest all of the depth of the human person, when each could
see the other with the vision of God (John Paul II 1997: 57–60),
according to the truth of his being. John Paul II identifies that truth
with the mystery of creation, when mankind was loved into being *for
its own sake*, from which fact follows the very particular human path
to self-finding: a sincere "gift of self", that is, a "deep availability for
the affirmation of the person", by which the gift of the other is

welcomed in all of his truth, as one who is also willed "for his or her own sake" (John Paul II 1997: 63–66). When each ceases to be for the other this "disinterested" gift, as each was in the beginning, then they see that "they are naked" and the fear of extortion is justifiably aroused (John Paul II 1997: 69–72).

Conclusion

When Jesus turned his disciples back to the beginning, he did so, not in order to "naturalize" the newness that he brought, by bringing himself, but rather to show that the measure of love that he is, is not, for all its being "from beyond", alien to the human heart. *Agápē* does not crush the love that man has known up until that point. On the contrary, it fulfills an ancient promise, a "mystery" hidden within *érōs* itself, by the God "who created all things" (Eph 3:8–9). That *érōs* was poised from the beginning (in man's "original solitude" before God) to be satisfied only in the gratuitous and surprising "love of friendship" with Another (*STh* I–II, 5, 5 ad 1). As an echo of that ultimate desire, it was also directed toward a friendship with one's neighbor, the first of whom is "another self" ("original unity") of a *nuptial* sort ("dual unity"). If it became difficult—for some "impossible"—to bind the fulfillment of one's very self to that love (so tied, by its difference, to a "love of concupiscence"), it became so on account of a deep wound that affected man's very vision of the other as well as his desire (*érōs*). However, in light of the Incarnation of *agápē*, with its deep and enduring fidelity, that vision of the Other has now been restored and exalted, so that in Christ spousal love can be lived as a love of friendship in the deepest sense—because it involves the real discovery of the other as such—even if the often demanding sacrifice of "losing one's self" is the way to the happiness it promises. "This at last!"

Bibliography

Balthasar, Hans Urs von. 1983. *The Christian State of Life*. San Francisco: Ignatius Press.

————. 1990. *Theo-Drama*. Vol. 2: *Dramatis Personae: Man in God*. Translated by G. Harrison. San Francisco: Ignatius Press.

————. 1992. *Theo-Drama*. Vol. 3: *Dramatis Personae: The Person in Christ*. Translated by G. Harrison. San Francisco: Ignatius Press.

————. 1998. *Theo-Drama*. Vol. 5: *The Last Act*. Translated by G. Harrison. San Francisco: Ignatius Press.

Batut, Jean-Pierre. 1997. "The Chastity of Jesus and the 'Refusal to Grasp'". *Communio* 24:5–13.

Caffarra, Carlo. 2001. "Introduzione Generale". In *L'Uomo e Donna lo Creò: Catechesi sull'amore umano*, 5–24. 5th ed. Rome: Città Nuova.

De Andia, Ysabel. 1997. "*Eros* and *Agape*: The Divine Passion of Love". *Communio* 24:29–50.

De Lubac, Henri. 1967. *The Mystery of the Supernatural*. Translated by G. Chapman. New York: Herder.

Gallagher, David. 1996. "Desire for Beatitude and Love of Friendship in Thomas Aquinas". *Medieval Studies* 58:1–47.

Giussani, Luigi. 1997. *The Religious Sense*. Translated by J. Zucchi. Montreal: McGill-Queen's University Press.

John Paul II. 1997. *The Theology of the Body: Human Love in the Divine Plan*. Boston: Pauline Books and Media.

Maggiolini, Alessandro. 1996. "Magisterial Teaching on Experience in the Twentieth Century: From the Modernist Crisis to the Second Vatican Council". *Communio* 23:225–43.

Mansini, G. 1995. "Duplex Amor and the Structure of Love in Aquinas". In *Thomistica: Recherches de théologie ancienne et médiévale*. Supplementa 1:137–96. Edited by E. Manning. Leuven: Peeters.

McCarthy, Margaret Harper. 2005. "'Husbands, Love Your Wives as Your Own Bodies': Is Nuptial Love a Case of Love or Its Paradigm?" *Communio* 32:260–94.

Melina, Livio. 2001. *Cristo e il dinamismo dell'agire: Linee di rinnovamento della teologia morale fondamentale*. Rome: PUL–Mursia.

Nygren, Anders. 1982. *Eros and Agape*. Translated by P. Watson. London: SPCK.

Pérez-Soba, J. J. 2001. *Amor es nombre de persona: Estudio de la interpersonalidad en el amor en Santo Tomás de Aquino*. Rome: PUL–Mursia.

Pieper, Joseph. 1997. *Faith, Hope, Love*. Translated by R. and C. Winston. San Francisco: Ignatius Press.

Ratzinger, Joseph. 1968. "Commentary on the Dogmatic Constitution on Divine Revelation". Translated by W. Glen-Doepel. In

Commentary on the Documents of Vatican II, edited by H. Vorgrimler, 3:167–272. Freiburg: Herder.

———. 1985. *Dogma and Preaching*. Chicago: Franciscan Herald Press.

Scola, Angelo. 1997. *Questioni di antropologia teologica*. Rome: PUL.

———. 1998. "The Nuptial Mystery at the Heart of the Church". *Communio* 25:630–62.

———. 2000. *Uomo-Donna: Il "Caso Serio" dell' Amore*. Genoa: Marietti.

———. 2003. *L'Esperienza elementare: La vena profonda del magistero di Giovanni Paolo II*. Genoa: Marietti.

The Revelation of Love in the Song of Songs

Joseph C. Atkinson*

Introduction

In his encyclical *Deus Caritas Est,* Benedict XVI sets himself the daunting but much needed task of recovering the true meaning and significance of the word "love". It has become gravely disfigured in the modern world, but, as it lies at the heart of the Gospel, the word cannot simply be abandoned. Rather, it must receive its true value once again and be re-inserted into our theological and social consciousness.

The Holy Father begins this project by linking the truth of love to the person of God in the startlingly simple phrase taken from 1 John 4:16: "God is love." It is the bare simplicity of this statement that is so striking and captivating. It embodies the heart of the Gospel as it was known at creation (Gen 3:15), at the calling of Abraham into the first salvific covenant (Gen 12, 15, 17), as it was experienced within the prophetic vision of God's undying and unchanging love for his people (Hos 2:19–23), until finally it was fully revealed and embodied in the Incarnation itself. To consummate his love for his people, he who is God became flesh. Precisely through taking a body, God showed forth his nature as love on the Cross.

The simplicity of the encyclical is refreshing on several levels. First, in a world weary of religious violence and maniacal intolerance offered up in the name of God, the Holy Father has given us a single Word

---

* Assistant Professor of Sacred Scripture, Pontifical John Paul Institute for Studies on Marriage and Family at The Catholic University of America, Washington, D.C. Most Scripture passages in this chapter have been translated by the author.

to speak into this situation: "God is love." Secondly, in a world that is weary of empty and oppressive theological posturing, *Deus Caritas Est* brings us back to the foundational truth that clarifies the being of the Christian: "God is love." This return to the simple foundation of our faith resonates with the style of the Gospel itself. The evangelists communicate the reality of God with simplicity of language and economy of expression and, because of this, engage listeners at the most profound levels of their being.

The Purpose of the Song of Songs in *Deus Caritas Est*

One of the main theses of the encyclical is that a correct anthropology is essential if a valid understanding of love is to be achieved. The human person is not merely a material substance (body) or only spirit. Rather, he is a dual unity of body-and-soul which forms a single composite reality. "Man is a being made up of body and soul. Man is truly himself when his body and soul are intimately united" (*DCE* 5). This becomes a key hermeneutical principle by which to decipher human beings and their longings because only when both dimensions of the human personality are acknowledged and given their proper valuation can the distortions of human longing (both spiritual and corporeal) be overcome. Benedict XVI specifically alludes to this when he states that "the challenge of *eros* can be said to be truly overcome when this unification is achieved" (ibid.).

Biblically, this is rooted in the Semitic understanding of creation and constitutive human nature. The Hebrew phrase used in Genesis 2:7 to describe the first *'adam* is *nephesh hayyah*. Yahweh had formed the body out of the dust (*'aphar*) of the ground and then breathed into this corpse-like reality the breath of life (*nishmat hayyim*). With the combination of these two elements (the body and the spirit) the man becomes a *nephesh hayyah*. The whole living, animated human reality, body and soul, is a single unified reality (Pedersen 1973: 97–112). Both dimensions of the human person must be given their proper place and *understood to interpenetrate each other* if the value of the human person is to be safeguarded. Otherwise, both body and soul will suffer damage.

It is the fatal bifurcation between these two essential elements that has characterized the modern world. Human sexual love in its bodily dimension (*érōs*) has been separated from the spiritual faculties and has thus become a mere commodity.

> Yet the contemporary way of exalting the body is deceptive. *Eros*, reduced to pure "sex", has become a commodity, a mere "thing" to be bought and sold, or rather, man himself becomes a commodity.... He now considers his body and his sexuality as the purely material part of himself, to be used and exploited at will. Nor does he see it as an arena for the exercise of his freedom.... Here we are actually dealing with a debasement of the human body: no longer is it integrated into our overall existential freedom. (*DCE* 5)

While the contemporary assessment of Christianity is that it is opposed to the body, *Deus Caritas Est* shows that while such tendencies have existed, nonetheless the fundamental valuation of the body has always been positive and ultimately related to salvation itself. It is here that the Song of Songs (later abbreviated: Song) becomes a critical witness, and its inclusion in the canon makes it impossible to assert that the tradition has eschewed physical human love as being incompatible with divine love.

The Structure of the Song

Delitzsch was surely right when he commented that the Song of Songs was the most obscure of the books of the Bible, defying any single hermeneutical key to unlock its meaning in a totally integrative fashion. Always, there are parts left over, images left unexplained, with phrases and whole sections that do not fit neatly into the interpreter's scheme. While being composed of only eight small chapters, the Song has thirty-seven *hapax legomena* whose meaning is fairly conjectural (Murphy 1990: 75). Added to this is the complication that there is no other book or writings in the canon to which it can authentically be compared. The Song contains the only texts that deal in a positive and sustained manner with the physical realities of human love and use the human body and affective nature as vehicles of expression.

Because of this uniqueness, the interpreter is at times hard pressed to understand the value or meaning of certain images or actions. But despite all this, the very fact that a whole book of the Scriptures is given over to the theme of human sexual desire and longing is a profound statement in and of itself. Its acceptance into the canon allows us (indeed requires us) to analyze the Song to understand the structure (and revelation) of human love within the structure of salvation history.

Genre

As noted in *Deus Caritas Est*, many modern-day commentators have concluded that the Song is a collection of love poems that may or may not have been recited at a wedding feast (see Murphy 1990: 57–60 for an overview). However, more must be grasped if the unique nature of this text is to be understood. Not all love poetry is the same. By comparing these poems with those of ancient Egypt, a difference of orientation or direction emerges that is fundamental to the biblical view of love. As Michael Fox noted, Egyptian love poetry was inwardly directed, whereas the Song was more objective and outwardly directed. "The Egyptian poets [are] fascinated by what goes on inside a lover's heart.... The poet of the Song, on the other hand, has the lovers concentrate on each other rather than on their emotions" (ibid., 47). While there are emotional intensity and strong expressions of affectivity in the Song, yet lovers concentrate primarily on the other and not on themselves, even when the other is absent. Thus, their *érōs* is always outwardly directed.

While the medium of love poetry provides the mechanical structure of the Song, this classification does not do justice to the dynamic that lies at the heart of the poem. From the first words of the text, we enter immediately into the emotional (or, better still, sexual) landscape of two protagonists. This is not a third-person account of affective experiences or a first-person journal of interior longings and perturbations. Rather the Song is a dialogue between two lovers who are exploring the depths of human love. Here we encounter their deepest desires and longings as they seek for each other. As one would expect, the imagery is highly personalized, free flowing, and, at times, almost riotous—like love itself. Yet there is an odd gap between the surety of the love imagery (neck like the tower of David, legs like columns of alabaster, and so on) and the fragility of the love affair itself (the times of absences, seeking, confusion, and even violence in the persons of the watchmen).

The Song in Salvation History

One can best approach the Song by seeing it as the middle panel of a triptych about love. The first panel shows Eden, where human love was first created. Here man and woman exist without shame as the body, the spirit, and all affections and longings are properly integrated. The body and soul fully interpenetrate each other, and there is no sin or tension. The primordial wedding of Genesis 2 culminates with the ecstatic cry of the man: "This one is bone of my bones and flesh of my flesh", presenting us with human love in its uncorrupt form. As the interaction between the original couple shows, the focus is on the totality of the other received as gift and is characterized by joy.

The third panel is the Wedding Banquet of the Lamb which ushers in the eschaton. This is at the other side of history where the mystery of evil has been vanquished. The consummation of God's love for his people takes on the form of the nuptial banquet of the One who was slain. Human marriage is the image used to present the sacrificial love of God for his creation.

In these two panels we have "love as created" and "love as restored". But what lies between these two experiences? Where is the presentation of human love as experienced in our fallen state? Here is where the Song comes in. It also speaks of love, but it is human love against the backdrop of the Fall. Emotions and judgments are not all totally integrated; there is confusion, absence, and a question of danger. The Song knows all this but also knows that human sexual love is still a gift from God from the time of our innocence, which was not totally destroyed at the Fall. But the Song is also aware that the Fall has left its mark.

The Revelation of Love

Canonicity

What does the Song teach or reveal about human sexual love? As stated above, by the very inclusion of the Song in the canon, physical, sexual love was accorded a positive value that was linked to salvation history. Much of the history of this text has amounted to attempts to establish this spiritual link and to develop an analogical interpretation of the text (see Murphy 1990: 12–41 for an overview). Mainly, the effect of this effort was a downplaying of the literal meaning of the text. This attitude is possibly behind Aqiba's commentary, which stated that anyone who sang the Song in a frivolous manner would lose his place in the world to come (ibid., 13). But the fact remains that what was accepted into the canon was the poetical longings of two human lovers, seeking each other out. There is only one place, itself debatable, where the name of God is perhaps even mentioned (8:6). While it is perfectly legitimate to seek to divine a further and more spiritual meaning of the text, it would still be grounded in the created and bodily experience of human love. On the other hand, modern exegesis has gone the other direction by eschewing all reading of the Song on a symbolic level. It can only be about human love. But this reading surely isolates the text from its context within salvation history.

A comparison can be made between Genesis 2 and the Song. Both deal with the articulation of the relationship between man and woman, but, in both texts, the subject of God does not dominate thematically. In Genesis 2, even though God is Creator, he retires from the center of the (dramatic) stage when he acts as the groomsman and presents the first woman (Eve) to the man (Adam). At this point, the primordial couple take center stage and become the primary characters. In the Song, God is hardly (if at all) mentioned, and the focus is properly on the lovers' relationship. In both cases, the human dimension controls the presentation. But while God is not the textual focus, the biblical witness still affirms that the foundation for this human encounter still lies within the nature of God, who is revealed as the Creator of all.

Waṣf

One of the great contributions of the Song is its frank use and appreciation of the human body. There are no other comparable texts in Scripture. In the nineteenty century, it was discovered that this use of the body was similar to an Arabic taxonomy (called the *waṣf*) and used in modern Arabic poetry. In the *waṣf* (an Arabic word meaning *description*), the person was described from top to bottom with comments on each of the constitutive parts (Falk 1982: 80–87). There are four sections of the Song that are like this, all but one dedicated to extolling the beauty of the woman. The imagery is bold, earthy, sensuous, and at times unsettling:

The Woman: *Your eyes are doves behind your veil. . . .*
Your teeth are like a flock shorn that has come up from washing. . . .
Your temple is like an opened pomegranate behind your veil.
Your neck like the tower of David. (4:1–4)

The Man: *His head is pure gold. . . .*
His lips are lilies, dripping fragrant myrrh
His legs are columns of alabaster. (5:11–15)

That the Song has a mystical meaning is a part of the Church's reception of it at this point. Exegetes, however, make a fundamental mistake when, instead of entering into the cognitive and sexual landscape of the speaker, they rush to determine the analogical partner for each body part and image too quickly. When dealing with the *waṣf*, it is probably better to determine the meaning of the experience as a whole (intoxication with love, exclusive focus on the other, appreciation of corporeal reality, and so on) and apply that to the spiritual realm. In this way, each order is allowed its own integrity. Only after this can the way in which both realities co-penetrate each other begin to come to light. The mystical meaning is not something extrinsic to the experienced phenomenon of the body but is revealed through it.

Journey

This is perhaps one of the major differences between the Edenic experience of human love and the Song's presentation. In the garden, the love of each person was transparent ("and they were not ashamed [*ve lo' yitboshashu*]"; Gen 2:25). The integrity of the couple was so perfect that the communication of their love was unencumbered. Here, there is no formal "search" or "journey" theme associated with love. The Father, aware of the man's need for communion, properly meets this need through his creation of the "other". But with the Fall, man begins to experience separation from the woman and from his own true self. Life becomes a journey, a search for the original peace and integrity that has been lost. No longer are the man and woman unashamed, but rather the very structure of their relationality is fractured.

The Song, on the other hand, is thematically structured around the archetypal theme of searching and the concomitant emotions that surround it. The text oscillates between the ache for communion (1:2–4), the tension of seeking (3:4), the joy of finding (2:8–9), the rapture of contemplating the beloved (4:1–6), the ardor of anticipation (5:8), the fear of losing (5:6), and the peace of attainment (8:10). In contrast to Eden, these are now the constitutive dimensions of human love and part of the human dynamic by which resolution and peace are finally achieved. Thus, they mark the way for the human heart.

Sexuality and Shame

One point of comparison holds good for both the Song and Eden. In both situations, there is no shame involved with the contemplation of and desire for the beloved. The young woman initiates the Song by her unselfconscious announcement that her longing is for the physical kisses of her beloved ("Let him kiss me with the kisses of his mouth", 1:2a). Her ache is for communion with her beloved ("For your love is better than wine", 1:2b). But in this fallen world, love has become a fragile reality. There are times when it is elusive and must be sought after, sometimes in vain. In the Song, the beloved stands at the woman's door, but she hesitates to open to him, and so he disappears (5:2–6). The woman frantically begins to search for him in the dead of night only to suffer abuse at the hands of the city's watchmen (5:7–8). Love for the other makes one vulnerable, even to the violence of others. In many ways, this is the test of love. As *Deus Caritas Est* states, *érōs* is purified by the love of the other: "No longer is it self-seeking ... ; instead it seeks the good of the beloved: it becomes renunciation, and it is ready, and even willing, for sacrifice" (*DCE* 6).

Nephesh

Because of love, the seeking of the beloved engages the whole person. This is particularly seen in the text's use of *naphshi*. Five of the seven occurrences talk about loving the beloved with my *nephesh*, my whole being (1:7; 3:1–5). The Hebrew phrase *naphshi* refers to "the totality of who I am", that is, to the integrated and animated reality of the person, body and soul. Love here is not a moment of intoxication but a movement within and of the whole person. This is the juncture spoken of in *Deus Caritas Est* where *agápē* begins to inform and purify *érōs*. Through this process, the person becomes increasingly free from self-centeredness and begins to desire to give of oneself to and for the beloved, even if it means pain.

> Yet *eros* and *agape*—ascending love and descending love—can never be completely separated. The more the two, in their different aspects, find a proper unity in the one reality of love, the more the true nature of love in general is realized. Even if *eros* is at first mainly covetous and ascending, ... in drawing near to the other, it is less and less concerned with itself, ... is concerned more and more with the beloved, bestows itself and wants to "be there for" the other. The element of *agape* thus enters into this love, for otherwise *eros* is impoverished and even loses its own nature. (*DCE* 7)

Because the searching has been with the woman's whole being, the discovery of the loved one is of equal magnitude. "When I found the one that my soul [*nephesh*] loved, I grasped him and did not slacken my hold on him" (3:4). "All of you is beautiful, my companion and there is no blemish in you" (4:7). The very descriptions on the part of both the man and woman show the sheer intoxication with the contemplation of the effects of the other. "Behold, you are beautiful, my companion; behold, you are beautiful. Your eyes are doves from behind your veil ... your neck is like the tower of David" (4:1–4). Also, this sexual appreciation of the beloved is mutual and sustained, and there is no shame for either.

Shalom

But this journey toward love is also marked by disappearances and absences of the beloved. These hiatus periods are marked by the lovesickness of anticipation. "His banner over me is love ... sustain me with apples; for I am lovesick" (2:4–5). Unlike Eden, there will always be a certain note of fragility that accompanies our relationships (if for no other reason than that we are subject to death). Thus, the journey toward love is not straightforward or easy, yet, at the conclusion of the Song, comes the longed-for resolution. "At that time, I became in his eyes as the one who finds peace" (8:10). In Eden, all is ordered to God, and this naturally yields peace (*shalom*). Outside of Eden, it is in the fulfillment of our masculine and feminine natures through our yielding to one another (and precisely because the Song has a canonical context, it must therefore be in the covenantal relationship of marriage) that we find our *shalom*.

Deus Caritas Est carefully and properly articulates this relationship between *érōs* and permanency. "From the standpoint of creation, *eros* directs man towards marriage, to a bond which is unique and definitive; thus, and only thus, does it fulfill its deepest purpose. Corresponding to the image of a monotheistic God is monogamous marriage" (*DCE* 11).

Intimate and Exclusive

The use of language, particularly the terms of endearment and the forms used for the verb "to love", also reveals the nature of human love. *Deus Caritas Est* shows the important distinction between the two primary words in the poem used for love and the tendencies of each. *Dodim* is only used in the section of the Song where the man appears before his beloved but she does not open to him (5:1). Trouble ensues as he hides himself from her and she begins to seek him. The opening that immediately precedes this appears almost to be trifling with love. "I have drunk my wine with my milk. Eat, friends, and drink. Be intoxicated, O beloved ones" (5:1). *Dodim* is a plural form that, in this context, reduces love to mere sensate intoxication aroused by stimulants. There can be no genuine intimacy here because there is no protection offered. A multiplicity of encounters prevents true openness from occurring. Here, there is no focus on the beloved but rather a wild satiating of the senses.

The other word used for human love in the Song is *'ahabah*. This concept of love, as the encyclical points out, was translated by the word *agápē* when the Hebrew texts were translated into Greek. The noun occurs ten times in the Song, while there are seven instances of various verbal forms built upon this root. In contradistinction to *dodim*, this verb has the sense of exclusivity and election about it ("I have chosen you and not another").

The language of the Song also underscores the mutuality that exists in a genuine relationship of love. Nowhere is there evidence of a movement toward interchangeability between the protagonists within the text. Yet, there is a profound sense of each person being a subject in the cosmic drama of love. The man's favorite term for the woman is *ra'eyati*, which means companion. He uses this nine times (1:9, 15; 2:2, 10, 13; 4:1, 7; 5:2; and 6:4). Once, the woman uses the same noun (only in the masculine form) for her beloved (5:16) (Murphy 1990: 172). This demonstrates that the sense of companionship was operative for both partners. On the other hand, the most common name the woman has for the man is *dodi* ("my beloved"), which is used a total of twenty-one times.

The accumulative effect of these terms of endearment (with certain instances of actual reciprocity of terms) demonstrates that the vision of human love was constructed on the basis of two subjects, without hint of domination or manipulation on either part. It becomes clear that they were not chattel for each other but truly the "other" in whom they could rest their heart (see Prov 31:11). (It is interesting to note that Leviticus 19:18 brings these concepts together: "You shall love [*'ahab*] your neighbor [*re'a*] as yourself.")

Communion

One other use of language that is of note is found in the phrases that have an almost Johannine or Pauline sensibility to them. These are the phrases and words used to express the semantic category of communion. In three instances, the Song attempts to portray the interpenetration of the two lovers' realities: "I am my beloved's and my beloved is mine" (cf. 2:16; 6:3; 7:10). There is a faint resonance with the much later phrase used by John: "The Father is in me and I am in the Father" (Jn 10:38). The basis of comparison is simply that both are expressions of profound communion, a communion that brings about unity but does not destroy the integrity of the participating subjects.

Also, there is the ever-recurring imagery of eating and (affective) fulfillment. In the Song, the woman is compared to a luscious garden. "Your lips drip honey, [my] bride; honey and milk are under your tongue" (4:11). The woman extols the man by saying, "His fruit was sweetness to my palate" (2:3). There is an intuition here that communion with another is analogous to being nourished with food. This of course finds its fulfillment in the messianic banquet, which provides the food of redemption and communion in terms of the flesh of Christ: "Take, eat." This effects not only eternal nourishment but also communion with God himself (Jn 6:54–56). What is noteworthy here is that John emphasizes the physical realism of the sacrament by which this communion is achieved, and in a parallel fashion the Song emphasizes the physical dimensions of human love. The point is that the dominant theme in each text is the physical realism that underlies communion, but this very corporeity points to a greater spiritual reality.

Caution

Finally, the Song also contains a note of caution. In Eden and in the eschaton, this is not needed, but, in our postlapsarian context, this warning element is essential when dealing with the erotic impulse in the human situation. The drama and the glory of human sexuality unfold according to their own logic within the text, but the narrative is also punctuated with a stylized warning: "Do not stir up love until it is pleased" (2:7; 3:5; 8:4). While the phrase remains somewhat enigmatic, it nonetheless conveys the sense that love as a passion has inherent dangers that can easily destroy as well as fulfill. It is not that our passionate desires are somehow disordered in themselves, but that love requires the proper context (such as maturity, commitment, marriage, and so on) that allows, in terms of the encyclical, *érōs* to become informed by *agápē*. There is a timing to all things that must be respected, and we ignore such warnings at our own peril.

In summary fashion, the Song concludes with a dramatic revelation of the nature of love. Here, the images are stark and somewhat disconcerting. Love is said to be "strong as death" (8:6). The listener has just been warned not to arouse this love before its time. The comparison seems to be that this "love" will not let go once it has claimed someone. In the right context this would bring great fulfillment. But, if awakened inappropriately, it would also be difficult to extract oneself from the mesh of problems it would create. The text goes on and says that "ardor/jealousy is severe as Sheol." Here, the warning is to avoid entanglement with jealousy, which often accompanies love. Once again, the wise person steers clear of such emotional problems.

On a more positive note, this warning ends with two final images. Many waters (representing troubles, opposition, and so on) cannot quench love; it remains steadfast regardless of what happens. This again, feels like an adumbration of Romans 8: "Neither death, nor life, . . . nor any other created thing will be able to separate us from the love of God." Finally, the Song speaks of how anyone who attempts to buy love would be utterly despised, since love is not a commodity to be bought or sold like merchandise. Its value is beyond material calculation.

Conclusion

In the Song we do not have the atmosphere of either Eden or the Eschatological Banquet. Nor is there some idealized vision of human love, unattainable except in fantasy. Instead, the Song presents us with the reality of human love as it is now experienced—a created joy with multiple pleasures but fraught also with tensions, dangers, and disappointments. The wonder of love in the Song is that it is precisely through our bodily realities and the problems that are encountered because of our fallen nature that love reaches its fulfillment. This is truly a redemptive understanding of love.

There is a wondrous mutuality between the partners, who always remain subjects and whose identities, while united, never fuse into some form of monadic reality. Rather, the principle operative within human love is *communion*, which, if properly attained, yields forth *shalom*, whose roots lie in Eden itself.

Bibliography

Falk, Marica. 1982. *Love Lyrics from the Bible*. Sheffield: Almond Press.

Fox, Michael. 1985. *The Song of Songs and the Ancient Egyptian Love Songs*. Madison, Wis.: University of Wisconsin Press.

Hess, Richard S. 2005. *Song of Songs*. Grand Rapids, Mich.: Baker Academic.

Murphy, Roland E. 1990. *The Song of Songs*. Hermeneia Series. Minneapolis, Minn.: Fortress Press.

Neusner, Jacob. 1993. *Israel's Love Affair with God: Song of Songs*. Valley Forge: Trinity Press International.

Origen. 1956. *The Song of Songs: Commentary and Homilies*. Translated by R. P. Lawson. New York: Newman Press.

Pedersen, Johannes. 1973. *Israel: Its Life and Culture I–II*. London: Oxford University Press.

Ratzinger, J. 1989. *Biblical Interpretation in Crisis: The Ratzinger Conference on Bible and Church*. Grand Rapids, Mich.: Eerdmans.

Robert, A., and R. Tournay. 1963. *Le Cantique des Cantiques*. Paris: Librairie LeCoffre.

Schwab, George. 2002. *The Song of Song's Cautionary Message concerning Human Love*. New York: Peter Lang.

The Novelty of Christian *Agape*: The New Testament Testimony

*Luis Sánchez-Navarro**

In *Deus Caritas Est*, charity appears as a central element of both revelation and the Christian life in all its forms. This doctrine is fully in conformity with the witness of the New Testament, which presents *agápē*, or the love of charity, as an essential component of revelation. A reading of the relevant texts is enough to ascertain this. The noun *agápē* appears 116 times; the verb *agapáō*, "to love", 143 times; the adjective *agapētós*, "beloved", sixty-one times. In all we find it appears on 320 occasions. It is present in all of the New Testament texts, in contexts that are singularly important. Thus it is, not a secondary concept, but rather a primordial one. In the following pages we present a synthesis that confirms this reality as well as outlines its richness. We must note from the beginning, however, that in the New Testament the word *érōs*, which Benedict XVI presents as an aspect of biblical *agápē* (9–10), does not appear. Must we conclude from this fact that a passionate dimension is absent from the *agápē* preached by Jesus and witnessed to by the Scriptures of the New Covenant? Our study will allow us to answer this question.

In the Vulgate, there is no uniform translation for *agápē* in the New Testament. It is translated sometimes as *caritas* (in the majority of the cases), other times as *dilectio* (twenty-five times in all: always in John, as well as in other texts, particularly the Pauline corpus). On the other hand, *caritas* also occasionally translates the Greek noun *philadelphía*

---

*Visiting Professor of New Testament, Pontifical John Paul II Institute for Studies on Marriage and Family at The Catholic University of America, Washington, D.C. Assistant Professor of New Testament, Facultad de Teología San Dámaso, Madrid.

(Rom 12:10; 1 Thess 4:9; Heb 13:1; 1 Pet 1:22), which is translated as *amor fraternitatis* in 1 Peter 1:22 and 2 Peter 1:7 (these are the only times that the word *amor* appears in the New Testament Latin). *Agapētós* is translated as *dilectus* twenty-one times (four of these as a superlative) and forty-two times as *carissimus*. The only time the word *philía* appears it is translated as *amicitia* (Jas 4:4). The verb *agapáō* is always translated as *diligere*; it can only be found once as *amare* (2 Pet 2:15), a verb that also uniformly translates *philéō*. We can see, therefore, that with the exception of the verb, the translations do vary substantially. In this study we will translate *agapáō* as "to love" and *agápē* as "love" and "charity" without distinction.

In the Old Testament, love (Hebrew *'ahăbāh*) is a central element of the Yahwist faith. It is enough to recall two key texts: the *Shemá* (Deut 6:4–5), where the love of God is seen as the basic duty of the Israelite, and the commandment of love of one's neighbor (Lev 19:18), which is singularly relevant because it synthesizes the "second tablet" of the Decalogue and serves as the rule for all interactions among the children of Israel. The New Testament does not suppose a rupture with the Old Testament; in fact, we can verify that Jesus' teaching on the centrality of *agápē* echoes God's requirements in the Old Testament Scriptures. On the other hand, there is not simply continuity between the two Testaments: a recent document from the Pontifical Biblical Commission describes the relationship between the Old Testament and New Testament in terms of continuity, discontinuity, and progression (Pontifical Biblical Commission 2001: 64–65). Thus the New Testament is both rooted in the Hebrew Scriptures as well as irreducibly novel in comparison. It represents the fullness of the Old Testament teaching, and this fullness is in direct dependence upon the person of Jesus Christ. This is the first element we will address below.

1. A New Context: Jesus Christ

"The real novelty of the New Testament lies not so much in new ideas as in the figure of Christ himself, who gives flesh and blood to those concepts—an unprecedented realism" (*DCE* 12). As we have indicated, it is certain that the New Testament teaching about charity would not make sense without an implicit reference to the Old Testament: "Without the Old Testament, the New Testament would be an incomprehensible book, a plant deprived of its roots and destined to dry up and wither" (Pontifical Biblical Commission 2001: 84a). In the writings of the New Covenant, however, we discover more than just a new interpretation of the Hebrew Scriptures in the style of the Rabbinic teachers—we discover a dazzling new synthesis, a synthesis that has everything to do with the person of Jesus. He is the new context of his teaching. All of the inspired texts must be read using Christ's life as a hermeneutic principle; this is true particularly of the canonical Gospels. These books reveal Jesus' teaching as illustrated through his actions (Stock 2004); this fact gains special relevance in regard to his teaching on *agápē*, which is the synthesis of his mission.

Below we will present the testimony of the various New Testament books about Christian charity. Rather than being guided by chronological criteria, we will follow the groupings of texts that make up the canon. The distinct theologies of charity that we will find are harmonic, rather than dissonant, in their polyphony; they complement one another and in doing so allow us to capture the richness of Jesus' teaching.

2. The Testimony of the Synoptic Gospels and the Acts of the Apostles

Although they are distinct, there are enough common elements in the Gospels according to Matthew, Mark, and Luke that they may be studied together. The principal theories today regarding the composition of the Synoptics (the Q hypothesis, or the documentary theories) are based on the abundant common material and the common basic schema found in the three Gospels. These literary elements distinguish them from the Gospel of John. We will focus on the main passages that treat our topic; some are common to all three Gospels, while others lack Synoptic parallels. Due to the singular nature of the double Lucan work, we will discuss Acts following the section on the third Gospel.

a. The Gospel of Matthew

At the baptism of Jesus, the voice of the Father introduces him as "my beloved [*agapētós*] Son, with whom I am well pleased" (Mt 3:17). This celestial declaration—repeated in the Transfiguration (17:5)—characterizes the public life of Jesus. The Father is pleased with him: love and good pleasure (*eudokía*) mutually illuminate one another and thus become an explanation of *agápē* (Spicq 1994: 102). These concepts solemnly proclaim the Father's love for Jesus at the outset of his earthly activity. Jesus' teaching must be considered from this perspective: it is a concretization of the Father's will carried out by the one whom the Father loves in a unique way.

The Father's love, rather than imperfect human love, is the overarching criterion that must determine the action of the disciple; Jesus explains this in the last antithesis of the Sermon on the Mount (5:43–48). In giving his gifts, the Father does not stop to consider if men are worthy of them or not; he constantly offers his love to the good and the bad, the just and the unjust, in the same way he gives to all people that which is necessary for life (the light of the sun and the rains, 5:45). The "greater justice" required of the disciples by Jesus must become their rule of life; only in this way can they become perfect (5:48). At the root of their Christian charity is their relationship with the heavenly Father (Sánchez-Navarro 2005: 124–25).

This charity is both the nucleus and the synthesis of evangelical justice; Jesus declares this in his response to the question about the "great commandment" (Mt 22:34–40). The "law and the prophets" (Mt 22:40), which Jesus has come to fulfill (cf. 5:17), depend on the inseparable keystones of the love of God (Deut 6:5) and of neighbor (Lev 19:18). How does one put such love into practice? The disciple's own desires are to guide his interactions with others as well as to reveal the intensity of his love: "So whatever you wish that men would do to you, do so to them; for this is the law and the prophets" (7:12). In the eschatological discourse in Matthew 24–25, Jesus describes the trials that await the Church, saying that the charity of many will "grow cold" (24:12). The use of the "thermal metaphor", a universal way to express the passions, implies the "burning" nature of charity (cf. Song 8:6–7; Rev 3:15) and gives an idea of its affective intensity.

The Gospel of Matthew does not describe Jesus' actions in terms of charity; the verb "to love" never has Jesus as its subject. Yet in 20:28 Jesus says: "The Son of Man came not to be served but to serve, and to give his life as a ransom for many." After what we have said above, we can understand that this giving over of one's own life is the most perfect form of love. Jesus' entire existence is proof of this.

> Matthew, to be sure, never says, in so many words, "Jesus loved".
> Yet take away this tacit idea and the gospel becomes incoherent.
> As the lover of men and women, Jesus heals the afflicted (4:23–25; 8:2–17; etc.), and proffers encouragement (6:25–34; 7:7–11).
> He forgives sin (9:1–8) and exhibits mercy (9:10—13:27–31; 12:1–8; 20:29–34). He shows compassion (9:36; 12:20; 14:14; 15:32) and gives rest to the weary (11:28). And having done all this he does even more: he hands over his life for the sake of others (20:28; 26:28). Jesus is, in fine, the example in love. It follows that the evangelist would ... have concurred ... with the author of 1 John, who wrote: "We love, because he first loved us." (Davies and Allison 1988: 691)

Finally, we must note that the love Jesus speaks of has a double dimension. The love of the Father is a complete giving of self; Jesus will say this later: "All things have been delivered to me by my Father" (11:27). It is also described as desire or will (thélēma): the third petition of the Our Father verifies this ("your will [tò thélēmá sou] be done": 6:10). What is the will of the Father? "That [not] one of these little ones should perish" (18:14). The Father's limitless love (5:45) also has the intensity of a profound desire. Something similar must be said of the disciple's agápē: in imitation of the Father this love must become a generous self-gift without conditions (5:45), filled with affective intensity, as the sentence "the love of many will grow cold", found in 24:12, shows.

b. The Gospel of Mark

The brevity of the second Gospel leads to a more infrequent occurrence of words in the lexical family of agápē, however this does not imply that there is any less richness to be found in Mark. What we have said about Matthew 3:17 and 17:5 is true for Mark 1:11 and 9:7 (*agapētós*); the adjective reappears in 12:6 (par. Lk 20:13), referring also—allegorically—to Jesus, who is, in the same way, "God's beloved". Mark also emphasizes the centrality of the love for God and neighbor in the controversy between Jesus and one of the scribes (Mk 12:28–34; cf. Mt 22:34–40); charity is essential in the life of the disciple.

Nevertheless, there is a use of *agapáō* without parallels in Matthew or Luke that attracts our attention. When the rich man affirms that he has observed all of the commandments of the Decalogue since his youth (10:19–20), the evangelist says: "Jesus looking upon him *loved him*, and said to him, 'You lack one thing; go, sell what you have, ... and come, follow me'" (10:21; emphasis added). Jesus invites this man to discipleship, just as he has done in the past with Peter, Andrew, James, and John (1:16–20). This is an invitation made in love. From the evangelist's telling description in this passage, we discover the profound motivation of Christ's relationship with his disciples: the call to follow him flows from love. Only the Gospel of John, which speaks of the disciple whom Jesus loved, testifies to Jesus behaving in a similar way (Stock 2003: 201). His love is shown in the desire to establish a personal tie of communion; this intentional dimension of Jesus' *agápē* will remain present even in the sacrificial dimension of the giving over of his own life, which is anticipated in 10:45 (par. Mt 20:28): "The Son of Man also came ... to give his life as a ransom for many." In the evangelical narrative, the Passion of Jesus appears as the perfect fulfillment of the double commandment to love God and neighbor (cf. Keerankeri 2003: 189–238).

c. The Gospel of Luke

The lexical family of *agápē* appears more frequently in the third Gospel than in the two previous Gospels. In Luke 6:27–36, the central section of the "Sermon on the Plain" (Lk 6:17–49), charity is presented as *active, compassionate benevolence* toward one's neighbor, especially toward one's enemy. Here again the disciple's desire is the criterion that determines his treatment of others: "And as you wish that men would do to you, do so to them" (6:31). In the scene with the sinful woman who repented (7:36–50), it is clear that intense love is the type that pleases Jesus. The woman's gestures express her love (she washes Jesus' feet with her tears, wipes them with her hair, kisses them and anoints them with perfume: 7:38) as well as her affective intensity (cf. Spicq 1958–1959: 1:124). Jesus will declare "her sins, which are many, are forgiven, for *she loved much*" (7:47; emphasis added).

In the Lucan development of the question about the greatest commandment, Jesus illustrates the love of neighbor with the parable of the Good Samaritan (10:25–37; Ratzinger 2005: 119–24). This love is described as active, committed, and intelligent compassion (*splankhnízō*: v. 33) and mercy (*éleos*: v. 37) for the suffering. In this way any stranger becomes a neighbor (vv. 36–37); charity creates authentic community among all people, independent of their condition (Spicq 1958–1959: 1:140). With this parable Jesus fulfills and at the same time universalizes the precept found in Leviticus 19:18: "My neighbor is the first man I meet who is in need, for, as such, he is simply a brother of the Master who is always present to me in the lowliest of men" (Ratzinger 1993: 29).

Finally, we note a last text in which *agápē* does not appear but is expressed: "I came to cast fire upon the earth; and would that it were already kindled!" (Lk 12:49). Few New Testament texts describe in the way that this one does Jesus' desire to give his life through the Paschal Mystery (his "baptism": 12:50). For Jesus, death is an object of intense desire, an event with a passionate dimension that is inseparable from the sacrificial one. With a special insistence on Christ's mercy (23:34; 23:43), Luke describes this death as the preeminent sign of his love. Christ's self-giving begins to reveal itself in the eagerly desired (22:15) institution of the Eucharist: "This is my body which is given for you" (22:19).

d. The Paradox of Acts

In the Acts of the Apostles, the second part of the Lucan "diptych", the adjective *agapētós* appears only once (Acts 15:25). Surprisingly, in this canonical record of the life of the early Church, neither the verb *agapáō* nor the noun *agápē* ever appears. This fact is even more striking if we compare Acts to the Gospel of Luke and the Pauline letters, the New Testament texts that are closest to Acts. It brings to light the point that reality can transcend terminology. It is enough to recall the great "summaries" in Acts 2:42–47 and 4:32–37, with their insistence on prayer and the sharing of goods, to verify that the love for God and neighbor was normative among the first Christians (Coda 1994: 129). Communion (*koinōnía*: Acts 2:42) "consists in the fact that believers hold all things in common and that among them, there is no longer any distinction between rich and poor" (*DCE* 20). The life of the first Church in Jerusalem, sustained by the Eucharist ("the breaking of the bread", 2:42, 46), is presided over above all by fraternal charity; this is the same charity that will inspire Paul to his tireless apostolic labor and which we find admirably reflected in his farewell address to the presbyters of Ephesus (Acts 20:18–35) and in his fiery exhortation to King Agrippa to embrace the Christian faith (26:29).

3. The Testimony of John

Charity is a fundamental concept in the Johannine writings, as can be seen even in its origins; the fourth Gospel speaks of its author as "the disciple whom Jesus loved" (Jn 21:20). It is impossible to give a detailed vision of this topic in John; here we offer only some of its principal elements.

a. The Gospel of John

The Gospel mentions *agápē* for the first time in John 3:16: "For God so loved the world that he gave his only-begotten Son, that whoever believes in him should not perish but have eternal life." The giving over of the only-begotten Son for the life of the world is interpreted as the Father's act of gratuitous and generous love. The world that does not love him (3:19) is the object of God's loving care. The Father's *agápē* appears as the preeminent example of seeking the good of the other, his salvation. This salvation requires a complete giving of self, and its effect is "eternal life", which is to say, participation in the very life of God; definitively this is the reciprocity of love. The main response that this requires of us is faith. "It is fitting, then, that this verse is considered to be the summary of the Gospel of John, and the verb *agapân* is considered to be the key word of revelation, of the mystery of God, of Christology, and of soteriology" (Spicq 1959b, 132).

Although charity makes an appearance early in the Gospel of John, it is particularly present in the last part of the Gospel, known as "the book of glory" or "of the hour" (chaps. 13–21). The Passion of Jesus, a key part of these chapters, is a work of love. John 13:1 represents a synthesis of the entire Gospel; all of the existence of Jesus is seen as *agápē*: "He loved his own who were in the world, he loved them to the end." Up until this point he had loved his own, as part of the work of love that was his public life (Spicq 1958–1959, 3:145). From this moment on he will love them "to the end", evidenced by his sacrifice, which is the supreme act of love. This expression, "to the end" (*eis télos*), anticipates the death of Jesus on the Cross (19:28–30); the verb *teléō* (to fulfill) appears twice, and the verb *teleióō* (to consecrate) appears once; both are derived from *télos* (Spicq 1958–1959, 3:144). The sacrifice that Jesus accomplishes as the culmination of his work and the fulfillment of the Scriptures (19:28) is synthesized in 13:1 with the verb *agapáō*. Love characterizes the life and work of Jesus.

In this context, Jesus declares his main teaching: "that you love one another; even as I have loved you, that you also love one another" (Jn 13:34). This is a "new commandment" that could not have been articulated previous to Jesus' shared life with the disciples; the "new covenant" will be cemented upon it (cf. Jer 31:31). Love "to the end" (cf. 13:1) directs the interactions between Christ's disciples and identifies them as his followers (13:35). Just as the Pharisees are characterized by their attention to ritual prescriptions (cf. Mk 7:3–4) and their exactitude in interpretation of the law (cf. Acts 22:3; 26:5), and the Sadducees by their rejection of the resurrection (Mk 12:18; Acts 23:8), the Christians must be distinguished by the Christ-like love they have for others. In this way the history of Jesus' own love is prolonged; it is for this reason he founded his Church (Spicq 1958–1959, 3:176). In John 15:12–17, Jesus calls this instruction "my commandment". Before he had defined it by its novelty; now he defines it according to its intrinsic tie with him. Love consists in giving one's life for one's friends (15:13). The Master invites his disciples to propagate in this way the new love that he is at the point of consummating by laying down his life (cf. Jn 10:17).

b. The Letters of St. John

John's three letters, with their repeated mention of *agápē* (sixty-two times), evidence to what extent the beloved disciple has made the Master's teaching his own. The first letter is the most important as well as the most extensive, and it defines God in two moments: 1 John 1:5 ("God is light") and 4:8 ("God is love"); this last affirmation is central to the letter and is repeated in 4:16. These two themes, light and love, structure the text as well as explain each other. God is love, *agápē*, complete self-gift, and he is also light, *phōs*, the beauty that draws others to itself. Walking in the light (1:7) is remaining in love (4:16), which means remaining in Jesus himself (2:6, 28). Whoever renounces love lives in darkness; while "he who loves his brother abides in the light" (2:10). God's charity can be seen in his Son's sacrifice for the life of the world (4:9), which is eminently gratuitous (4:10). This love demands that we as Christians love one another (4:11, 21) and excludes all fear in our relationship with God (4:18). Christian charity, is, finally, a love that responds to the gift of God: "By this we know love, that he laid down his life for us; and we ought to lay down our lives for the brethren" (3:16). Even beyond this, the Christian who loves is enacting God's own love and, in this way, becomes "perfected" (4:12).

4. The Testimony of Paul

In the Pauline writings, *agápē* also enjoys a notable importance; it appears 141 times and is the object of an important theological development. *Agápē* is an essential element of the "gospel" of Paul (Spicq 1958–1959, 2:9); due to this, the Pauline tradition is an important milestone in the New Testament understanding of charity. We will focus on some principal texts that allow us to understand the dynamics of *agápē*: God, in loving man, creates in him—through his Spirit—the capacity to respond to this love.

In the Letter to the Galatians, Paul synthesizes the Paschal Mystery of Christ, saying: "I live by faith in the Son of God, who loved me and gave himself for me" (Gal 2:20). What is peculiar about this dense affirmation is, precisely, its audacious reference to Paul: "for me". The life, death, and Resurrection of Jesus (all a work of love, as we see in the Gospels) is understood by Paul as the fruit of Christ's love for him. Thus we can see the fecundity of Christ's love, which Paul feels as a personal call to communion. That this is not an exclusive privilege of Paul will be seen in his exhortation to the Christians of Ephesus: "And walk in love, as Christ loved us [many manuscripts read: "loved you"] and gave himself up for us, a fragrant offering and sacrifice to God" (Eph 5:2). This offering, ultimately, is proof of the Father's love (Rom 5:8). The sacrifice of Christ on the Cross, a work of love, is in its very reality a call to communion with him. The Christian is called to reproduce this offering which, in the love of the spouses, brings about a particular synthesis between *agápē* and *érōs* (cf. Eph 5:25–33).

Upon welcoming the love of Christ, believers open themselves to an immense horizon: divine filiation. The Holy Spirit has poured out the *agápē* of God into their hearts; this same Spirit is what permits them to call God "Abba! Father!" (Rom 8:15; Gal 4:6). For the Apostle, the love of God is the most valuable reality: "Who shall separate us from the love of Christ? ... Neither death, nor life, ... nor anything else in all creation, will be able to separate us from the love of God in Christ Jesus our Lord" (Rom 8:35–39).

Those who have experienced the love of God in Christ cannot but make *agápē* the key of their very existence. Paul incessantly exhorts the faithful to mutual love; this is not an external imposition, but rather—as the Thessalonians show in their lives—an intimate teaching of God: "But concerning love of the brethren you have no need to have any one to write to you, for you yourselves have been taught by God to love one another" (1 Thess 4:9). Among all of the spiritual gifts that might appeal to the Christian, none is comparable to charity. In chapter 13 of the First Letter to the Corinthians, "without a doubt the most important page of the entire NT—being the most formal and explicit—referring to charity" (Spicq 1958–1959, 2:54), Paul extols *agápē* in what the tradition has called, due to its beauty and profundity, the "hymn to charity". The most excellent gifts, without charity, are sterile (1 Cor 13:1–3); charity originates and enlivens all of the human virtues (13:4–7). Even the other theological virtues (faith and hope) are inferior to charity, as *agápē* is eternal (13:13). Love is the center and summit of the Christian life.

Paul demonstrates this with his life, through his own particular concretization of brotherly *agápē*: pastoral charity. All of his ministry is motivated by this: "For the love of Christ urges us on" (2 Cor 5:14). Numerous expressions of tenderness toward the faithful in his communities appear in his letters (2 Cor 2:4; Phil 4:1; 1 Thess 2:8), particularly for those he calls "my beloved" (1 Cor 10:14; Phil 2:12); in Romans 16:5–12 *agapētós*, "beloved", appears four times in the singular, referring to other brothers in the community in Rome. Paul's desire, ultimately, is that "my love be with you all in Christ Jesus" (1 Cor 16:24) (Spicq 1958–1959, 2:122).

What are the characteristics of this *agápē*? We find them in the Letter to the Romans: "Let love be genuine [*hē agápē anypókritos*]; hate what is evil, hold fast to what is good" (Rom 12:9). Sincere charity not only avoids evil and does good, it *hates* evil and *holds fast* to what is good. The "abhorrence" expresses a radical rejection that touches the passionate realm of the Christian. Before evil, one must feel horror and express it. On the other hand, one must hold fast to the good. Using a verb (*kolláō*) that in the Old Testament expresses allegiance to the Covenant and to God himself, Paul refers to a complete adherence of will and affectivity. Before evil Paul asks for complete abhorrence and before good a complete allegiance; this is what "genuine charity" consists of. Christian perfection is rooted, not only in doing the good, but in loving it and holding fast to it with all of one's heart. As a permanent behavior, which belongs to the very core of the moral life, such love is possible only by virtue of the Spirit who has poured out the *agápē* of God in our hearts (Rom 5:5) and has introduced us into divine filiation as well as a new world of affective interactions (8:15).

5. Other New Testament Testimonies

The other books of the New Testament speak of various forms of the novelty of *agápē*; the love of God is the root of the Christian life (Jude 1.21) and translates into fraternal charity (1 Pet 1:22; 2 Pet 1:7), which "covers a multitude of sins" (1 Pet 4:8). We will pause briefly on two writings: the Letter of James and Revelation.

The Letter of James contains a well-known teaching on faith and works (Jas 2:14–26). In light of James 2:8, where the command of love of neighbor (Lev 19:18) is called "the royal law", we understand that the issue behind this is fraternal charity. Without works, that is to say, without charity, faith is dead (2:17, 26). Prejudice (2:1–9) and lack of mercy before the needy (2:14–17) both express a lack of love that mortally wounds faith. The letter explains that the breaking of even one precept of the law makes one guilty of breaking all of it (2:10): transgression of a commandment implies a lack of charity, which is what enlivens Christian faith.

The letters to the seven churches of Asia (Rev 2–3) corroborate the centrality of *agápē* in the vocation of the Christian as well as its passionate nature. After enumerating the merits of the church of Ephesus, patient in her sufferings for Jesus (Rev 2:2–3), Jesus himself gives an unexpected warning: "But I have this against you, that you have abandoned the love [*agápē*] you had at first" (2:4). The gravity of the accusation is evident in the exhortation that follows: "Remember then from what you have fallen, repent and do the works you did at first. If not, I will come to you and remove your lampstand from its place, unless you repent" (2:5). The Christians of Ephesus had failed in their love for God and neighbor; they needed a true conversion if they did not want to see themselves deprived of their communion with God. Here we see the absolute primacy of love for Christ and neighbor in the life of the Church; it is her true center, without which everything else is worthless. In the seventh and last letter, to the angel of the church in Laodicea, Jesus makes an accusation that is even graver: "You are neither cold nor hot. Would that you were cold or hot! So, because you are lukewarm, and neither cold nor hot, I will spew you out of my mouth" (3:15–16). The "thermal metaphor"—of which we have spoken earlier—makes reference to *agápē*. The dominant trend in this particular church is being lukewarm and lacking in love; it lacks what is essential: a passionate tie to Jesus (Stock 1995: 62–63). Jesus does not tolerate ambiguity in faith, because it directly affects communion with him and, therefore, the ecclesial communion. Neither does he tolerate ambiguities in love: a lukewarm love is a love that does not exist, because love is intense by nature. The vitality of a church depends on its adherence in faith and love to Jesus Christ. It is to this that the Resurrected One invites the seven churches, through perseverance in the good and through repentance.

6. Conclusion: A Convergent Witness

In our necessarily summary and thus incomplete overview, we have been able to verify the profound harmony of the New Testament teaching about charity. In the diverse texts that make up the canon of the New Testament, the love of God revealed in Christ is presented as the fundamental element of the Christian life, while the love of God and of neighbor, distinct but inseparable, comprise the vocation of man, who is called to participate in the life of God through Jesus Christ. This *agápē* is the giving over of one's self, but without a reduction to the sacrificial dimension: It has an undeniable passionate element, which is expressed principally through the "will" or "desire" (*thélēma, thélō*). In Christ, the Father has loved us passionately; this is how he wishes to be loved by us. Mutual love—the Christian commandment par excellence, which culminates in giving one's own life "for one's friends"— also cannot be lacking in the affective dimension. On the contrary, it is fed and strengthened by it. Christians respond to the call of Christ when they gives themselves over with and for love to God and their brethren. Their communion with Christ makes them capable of this. Christ, upon loving us and sacrificing himself for us, gave in his flesh and blood an unsuspected fullness to charity (cf. *DCE* 12); he lives today in the Christian (cf. Gal 2:20).

Bibliography

Coda, P. 1994. *L'agape come grazia e libertà: Alla radice della teologia e prassi dei cristiani*. Rome.

Davies, W. D., and D. C. Allison. 1988. *The Gospel according to Saint Matthew* I. International Critical Commentary. Edinburgh.

Keerankeri, G. 2003. *The Love Commandment in Mark: An Exegetico-Theological Study of Mk 12:28–34*. Analecta Biblica 150. Rome.

Pontifical Biblical Commission. 2001. *The Jewish People and Their Sacred Scriptures in the Christian Bible*. Vatican City. [=PBC]

Ratzinger, J. 1993. *The Meaning of Christian Brotherhood*. San Francisco: Ignatius Press.

———. 2005. *The Yes of Jesus Christ: Exercises in Faith, Hope and Love*. New York.

Sánchez-Navarro, L. 2001. "Verità nell'amore: la carità sincera (Rm 12,9)". In *Verità e libertà nella teologia morale*, edited by L. Melina and J. Larrú, 179–85. Rome.

_____. 2004. "El enfriarse del amor (Mt 24,12)". In *On His Way: Studies in Honour of Professor Klemens Stock, S.J.*, edited by A. Malina, 121–34. Katowice.

_____. 2005. *La Enseñanza de la Montaña: Comentario contextual a Mateo 5–7*. Estella.

Spicq, C. 1958–1959. *AGAPÈ dans le Nouveau Testament: Analyse des textes*. 3 vols. Paris. [*Agape in the New Testament*. 3 vols. St. Louis and London: Herder, 1963, 1965.]

_____. 1994. "*Eudokéō, eudokía*". In *Theological Lexicon of the New Testament*, vol. 2. Peabody, Mass.

Stock, K. 1995. *L'ultima parola è di Dio: L'Apocalisse come Buona Notizia*. BibPr 21. Rome.

_____. 2003. *Marco: Commento contestuale al secondo Vangelo*. Rome.

_____. 2004. *Las bienaventuranzas de Mateo 5,3–10 a la luz del comportamiento de Jesús*. Madrid.

Commandment and Love:
From Friedrich Nietzsche to Benedict XVI

Olivier Bonnewijn*

Introduction

"Since God has first loved us (cf. 1 Jn 4:10), love is now no longer a mere 'command'; it is the response to the gift of love with which God draws near to us" (*DCE* 1). The encyclical letter of Benedict XVI approaches commandment by means of the way of love. "No longer is it a question, then, of a 'commandment' imposed from without and calling for the impossible, but rather of a freely-bestowed experience of love from within" (*DCE* 18, concluding the first section).

Right away, such an inscription may seem strange to a mentality strongly influenced by the thought—without doubt one should say by the mysticism—of Friedrich Nietzsche. Are not love and commandment in an opposing relationship? Is not love's spontaneous emergence from a joyous and overflowing life not contrary to the petty scope of law? Or worse, is it not "poisoned" (cf. *DCE* 5) by mortified precepts, shaped and promulgated in large part by a Christianity that is an enemy to the world and servant of a glacial world long past? "Doesn't the Church, with all her commandments and prohibitions, turn to bitterness the most precious thing in life? Doesn't she blow the whistle just when the joy which is the Creator's gift offers us a happiness which is itself a certain foretaste of the Divine?" (*DCE* 3). Even from his first citation, the Pope poses

---

*Visiting Professor of Fundamental Moral Theology, Pontifical John Paul II Institute for Studies on Marriage and Family, African session, Benin. Assistant Professor of Moral Theology, Institut d'Etudes Théologiques, Brussels.

the question of commandment in a peaceful, loyal, and original confrontation with German philosophy.

In this article, we propose to enter into this dialogue, keeping our attention fixed on some aspects of the connection between love and commandment. To this effect, we will begin by accompanying Friedrich Nietzsche in his famous text on the three metamorphoses of the spirit. "I will tell you ... how the spirit becomes a camel, the camel a lion, and the lion a child in the end" (*TSZ* I, 2). Who, then, is this child, this orphan living in "the pure love of Destiny", rebellious against every commandment different from that of his own desire? On the basis of this exchange, we will then see how the first section of the encyclical *Deus Caritas Est* links commandment, love-*érōs*, and love-*agápē*. Finally, we will continue our study by bringing to light, in the third place, the intimate relationship that exists, at a theological level, between love, history, and commandment.

A. *Érōs* and Commandment according to Friedrich Nietzsche

1. *The Camel, or the Negation of* Érōs

The camel is an animal of the desert, a place of desolation, of sickness, of death, and of nothingness. It manifests its strength, not by affirming itself, but by bearing patiently the heavy load imposed by others, in this case the commandments that drive us to the hatred of life. The camel is similar to the donkey, the Christian animal par excellence. It also is known to put forth grotesque cries of approval or happiness ("Hee-haw, Hee-haw", close to the sounds that make up the German *Ja*), a parody of the sacred Yes of the child. These animals take monstrous delight in their burden. They feel "robust"—powerful—in constantly transporting the weight of an antihuman morality of which Christianity is the finest expression and the most dangerous.

According to Nietzsche, Christian morality could be summarized by the following verse: "Whoever seeks to gain his life will lose it, but whoever loses his life will preserve it" (Lk 17:33, quoted by Benedict XVI in paragraph 6 with its variants: Mt 10:39, 16:25; Mk 8:35; Lk 9:24; Jn 12:25). This maxim and others like it serve as the foundation, invented by Socrates and especially by Paul of Tarsus, for the prohibitions and values of beings that are weak, incapable of living as lords, perverted by resentment, and denatured by their thirst for revenge. These values intersect in their manner of hating love, cursing the passions, slandering this world, turning away from the sublime in order to seek refuge—by pure resentment—in an illusory and deathly world.

With its ascetic ideal of chastity, poverty, and obedience, Christianity in effect commands a fleeing from the earth in order to reach an afterlife that is purely negative and without consistency. The temptation is to "destroy *eros*" (*DCE* 4), referring again to a key term of our encyclical. It poisons Dionysus, the god of wine, inebriation, immoderation, fecundity, play, music, and the night. It "had poisoned" (*DCE* 3) this unpredictable and joyous king, under whose reign the values of the good life triumph spontaneously, in a perpetual "divine madness" (*DCE* 4), without being impeded by any commandment, duty, asceticism, or "spirituality" whatever. In condemning this Kingdom of the world, Christianity perverts life and delivers the individual over to an "extreme solitude".

2. The Lion, or the Negation of the Negation of Érōs

"And there, in this extreme solitude, the second metamorphosis is produced; the spirit becomes a lion" (*TSZ* I, 2). The desert of nothingness provokes a jolt, a revolt. The camel transforms into a lion. Certainly, the lion still lives in the desert, in nihilism. But it is not a submissive animal, domesticated, that likes to kneel down. It does not put up with any burden. Noble and savage, it roars with pride and ferocity. It is closer to the earth with its broad paws than the camel. It wants to live freely, according to the law of its own will. An animal of prey, it looks for a master or a god only in order to defy or vanquish him.

The lion also drives out the great dragon that symbolizes all of the values promoted by decadent men, those of the metaphysicians who slander the world, those of Socrates and Paul of Tarsus, those of *agápē*, to use the terminology of Benedict XVI. The lion calls the dragon by its true name: the categorical imperative, the Kantian "Thou shalt." It refuses to prostrate itself in front of him and adore him (cf. Jn 20:28).

"What is the great dragon which the spirit no longer wants to call lord and God? The great dragon is called 'Thou shalt.' But the spirit of the lion says, 'I will!' 'Thou shalt' lies in its path, sparkling with gold, a scale-covered beast, and on every scale glitters golden 'Thou shalt'" (*TSZ* 1, 2). The dragon lacks neither prestige nor power. Robust with age-old traditions, it is the bearer of Athenian metaphysics, of the Jewish *Torah*, of all Christian morality, of which Kantian philosophy is the most refined expression in the eyes of Nietzsche. It shines with the splendor of its innumerable "Thou shalt". It does not stand for the "I will", that is to say, an absolute liberty that would precede all standards of the past.

The prophet Zarathustra announces the putting to death of this terrible dragon by the power of the lion's will, which thus prepares for the rule of "love". This reign cannot happen solely by the revolt of the lion. Its "not sacred" is not yet a "creative yes". The lion delivers, unburdens, liberates from all attachment, beginning with metaphysics, religion, and morality. It dwells in a pure negation. It negates the negation of *érōs*. But at this phase, nothing is yet in play! All can be turned upside down in the search for new forms of burdens to carry. The rebellious, for example, may in resentment desire sexual pleasure, money, and the arrogance of power. They may act strictly in reaction to chastity, poverty, and humble obedience. These "material" values would thus appear as opposed to the "spiritual" values, and their very differentiation would never be overcome. The "kingdom of God" would survive in an inverted manner, under another form. The idol would change its mask but would not truly disappear. The lion again would become a camel.

3. The Child or the Holy Affirmation of Érōs

The negation of the negation, therefore, does not suffice. The lion must become a child. A child is a new being. He does not carry the burdens of the past. All begins—or begins again—with him and remains unfinished. A being without history, the child is forgotten. He does not retain anything. He springs up always new. He opens his wide eyes at each moment upon the life that he savors with every taste. He utters a big Yes to this Life. His will does not know blame, regret, or negativity. He is only a "holy affirmation" at each new instant. "The Yes is multiple, the Yes is a becoming: The spirit becomes a child, and the child is multiple. This becoming is an always-new beginning for those who forget the Yes they speak. And the multiple is always one, for those who play all their games in a Yes" (Piret 1994: 324).

This child wants his own desire. It coincides perfectly with him. Even better, it is a pure will to power. It "only wants its own affirmation, in all solitude. . . . It is not at all the mediocrity of domination over others or the possession of things. The will wants nothing other than what it itself wants" (ibid., 304). Such is the essence without essence of the will to power. "The will (or desire: *der Wille*) is to itself its principle and its end. Desire wants its desire. More precisely (because desire is not, according to Nietzsche, a good onto which to hold): Desire wants in order to desire. It is the will to power (*zu Macht*): it must have what it wants" (ibid., 350).

Over and above the unhealthy Yes of the robust camel, over and beyond the proud No of the formidable lion, the Yes of the child thus springs up always new, without beginning or end other than that of wanting above all its own desire. The ethical values that he continually creates in this supreme activity are only worth as much as they are put forth to be at each instant by his will that wills itself. They have no other value except that of the end in themselves. In an analogous fashion, even though at a level less cosmic and more "leonine", Jean-Paul Sartre wrote in *Existentialism Is a Humanism*: "For I declare that freedom, in respect of concrete circumstances, can have no other end and aim but itself; and when once a man has seen that values depend upon himself, in that state of forsakenness he can will only one thing, and that is freedom as the foundation of all values" (Sartre 1977).

Nietzschean morality then situates itself "beyond good and evil", in the same act by which the "ethical subject" values and devalues, or "transvalues" according to his desire. The only commandment with which it is identified is that of the "desiring will" ("volonté voulante"; Blondel 1973: 132) willing itself. Values have interest only insofar as they are the effect of this absolutely creative act. The moral life consists in a perpetual "transmutation" of the joyous dance of values. It is pure evaluation. It evaluates in order to evaluate. The creative and playful world of the child offers the purest symbol of it.

"Ethic" here meets "mysticism" and ruins it. The "holy affirmation" of the child coincides perfectly with reality. It totally identifies with his Will to Power, with the Eternal Return or again with Destiny. *Amor Fati. Ego Fatum.* "Love of *Fatum*. I (am) *Fatum*" (cf. De Lubac 1983: 510). From eternity to eternity, the *Ego* determines existence. The child no longer needs to bow before Destiny: he wants to be Destiny. When he "discovers that he coincides with such a principle, he truly discovers that there was no other rule superior to that to which he needed to be attached: The law of the world is, at each instant, the result of his freedom. He has conquered any spirit of heaviness. He is eternal in himself and not by participation" (ibid., 513). He no longer inhabits the worrisome margins of the circle but rather its center, the center that also is everywhere. He has himself become the center and the source of all life. He is pure creativity, a game of dice, fantasy, crazy and unbridled dances. Lucid, he participates in the tragedy of existence in its absurd ugliness as much as in its sublime beauty, in its chaos in perpetual movement. And what is more, he is this tragedy and this chaos. He is desire "in the movement of power": *Wille zu Macht.*

4. *The Dialectic of* Érōs *and Commandment*

In the two first metamorphoses, *érōs* and commandment thus are in a dialectical relationship of opposition, in an inversely proportional way. That which one possesses is possessed at the detriment of the other, and vice versa. The Dionysian *érōs* and the Kantian commandment appear as two forces, as two powers that knock into each other. The "I will" and the "Thou shalt" are and invincibly remain strangers to each other, even if they have in common the fact that they are both will to power.

Our philosopher in this way places himself within the voluntarist tradition that carries him in some way to his end, to his final entrenchments. The child, or the Superhuman, must himself produce at each instant "new charts of what is good", in a movement of perpetual self-legalization, "beyond good and evil". Law without law exists only by the power of his will. That which is ordained by God is good—*Bonum quia iussum*—wrote William of Ockham. Equally for Nietzsche, morality and legality coincide. But according to the latter, it is a question of the will of the Superhuman. There is no longer an encounter of two distinct beings as with Ockham, with the superior imposing his arbitrary law upon the inferior. No, "God is dead" (*TSZ*, prologue, 2). He has disappeared from the horizon from which he rose, made by the metaphysicians and above all by the priests filled with resentment. Man is thus alone, haunted by two enemy wills to power. The child, in the innocence of his perpetual birth, spontaneously surpasses this intimate antagonism in order to affirm himself simply and absolutely. *Bonum quia iussum*: what is good is that which his innocent desire commands at each instant.

This "child" is delivered over to the good pleasure of his arbitrary power. Along with God, the other—of whom the commandment is the trace and the witness—is erased from the field of vision. He is no longer there to save the human being from the vertiginous solitude within which he enslaves himself by his absolute voluntarism. Without origin, without father, the child gives birth to himself to no end. He only proceeds from himself for himself. Real alterity is desperately absent. Zarathustra, calling out in vain to his flock by some pathetic "my brothers", only utters unending monologues. Like his Superhuman, the prophet is at the same time too full and too empty of himself to hear anything else but himself. He does not communicate, but rather affirms. However, his Yes addresses only himself, not anyone else. Generous, he gives in overabundance but refuses to receive. He "loves", but he does not let himself be loved. The child is neither son nor brother nor friend nor citizen. He trembles with love only in front of the abyss of his own greatness. Outside of time and history, he no longer inhabits the world of humans, their relations, or their societies.

This prophecy of the triumph of *érōs* over commandment has been reaped by a contemporary culture that has been covertly nourished with it. Identifying morality and commandment in the voluntaristic sense of the term, our era tends to contrast the latter with individual liberty, defined as being the power of self-affirmation. "I call liberty", wrote William of Ockham in the fourteenth century, "the power by which I am able to carry out diverse acts indifferently and in a contingent manner, in the same way that I may cause the same effect and not cause it, no diversity whatsoever existing outside of power itself"

(*Quodlibet* I, 16). Like the "Thou shalt" and the "I will" of the first two Nietzschean metamorphoses, morality and liberty are perceived as incompatible. They confront each other in vigorous battles from which the outcome is envisaged in terms of all or nothing: The ground lost by laws is gained by liberty, and vice versa. How does one welcome such a challenge that at the same moment is spiritual, intellectual, and ethical? The first encyclical of Benedict XVI offers a precise contribution to this subject while articulating the history of *érōs*, commandment, and *agápē*.

B. *Érōs*, *Agápē*, and Commandment

Have the commandments issued by Christianity truly poisoned *érōs* in order to destroy it, the Holy Father asks? "Jesus united into a single precept this commandment of love for God and the commandment of love for neighbor found in the *Book of Leviticus*: 'You shall love your neighbor as yourself' (19:18; cf. Mk 12:29–31)" (*DCE* 1). Is this unique precept, of which the "Hebrew Jesus" is at the same time both the exegete and the exegesis, opposed to the fulfillment of *érōs*? Does "the man who wants to die", as Nietzsche calls him, live at midnight far from Dionysus?

No! The Old Testament—and the New by extension—"in no way rejected eros as such; rather, it declared war on a warped and destructive form of it, because this counterfeit divinization of eros ... strips it of its dignity and dehumanizes it" (*DCE* 4). Benedict XVI evaluates *érōs* from the point of view of human dignity, or, in speaking with the voice of John Paul II, from the "personalistic norm" (John Paul II 1993). When the *érōs* is idolized—that is to say, taken as absolute—it drives inexorably toward the "degradation of man" (*DCE* 4). The sacred prostitutes are in themselves a sign, they who "were not treated as human beings and persons" but rather were "exploited" (*DCE* 4). *Érōs* cannot be abandoned to itself, under pain of disfiguring man in his deepest identity, which is concurrently spiritual and corporal. It must be purified, disciplined, healed, educated, developed, realized. Thus, it is not a question at all of negating *érōs*, but well to the contrary, of leading it to "maturation" in order to "restore its true grandeur" (*DCE* 5). But how?

In order to respond to such a question, one usually appeals to natural law such as it is expressed in condensed form in the Decalogue. Does it not help man to open out according to all that he is and to all that he is called to become? Benedict XVI, however, does not refer immediately to these "unwritten" laws. He remains strictly in the logic and internal dynamic of love. "Even if *eros* is at first mainly covetous and ascending, a fascination for the great promise of happiness, in drawing near to the other, it is less and less concerned with itself, increasingly seeks the happiness of the other, is concerned more and more with the beloved, bestows itself and wants to 'be there for' the other. The element of *agape* thus enters into this love" (*DCE* 7).

This *agápē* is crystallized, expressed, and implemented in the fulfillment of the "single commandment" (*DCE* 18) of love of God and of neighbor. This commandment thus informs *érōs* in its "ongoing exodus out of the closed inward-looking self towards its liberation through self-giving" (*DCE* 6). "Whoever seeks to gain his life will lose it, but whoever loses his life will preserve it" (Lk 17:33). Human *érōs*, by virtue of what it is and of what it is not yet, necessarily must traverse this "path" of *agápē* toward the other under pain of "impoverishment" or "losing its own nature" (cf. *DCE* 7). "Love now becomes concern and care for the other. No longer is it self-seeking, a sinking in the intoxication of happiness; instead it seeks the good of the beloved: it becomes renunciation, and it is ready, and even willing, for sacrifice" (*DCE* 6).

In combating this "moment of *agápē*" with violence and irony, Nietzsche voluntarily removed himself from others in order to try desperately to join his "brothers" in the Eternal Return of his own divinized *érōs* or, to be more precise, of the Universal *Érōs* with which he wanted to coincide, with which he claims to identify. *Amor Fati. Ego Fatum.* Our philosopher perhaps would retort that this identification, always at the same time already realized and to be realized, transcends the distinction between *érōs* and *agápē*. It is nevertheless true that this very movement of "passing" designates a disproportional form of *érōs* in the final analysis. He identifies with an absolute "love" of his own will to power, which consequently does not guide *érōs* to its end. Nietzschean mysticism, as distinct from Christian mysticism, distorts *érōs*, preventing it from being realized and diverting it from the human fullness it promises. The study of love in its integral reality as scrutinized by Benedict XVI implicitly turns the Nietzschean critique of Christianity against itself.

Reciprocally, without *érōs*, *agápē* is also distorted. Cutting man off from his vital wellsprings, which are at the same time both biological and spiritual, it dehumanizes him. It makes him lose his consistency. "Love" thus becomes a sort of ideal and abstract reality. Pure "exodus", it leads the person to a subtle disappearance. Man "cannot always give, he must also receive. Anyone who wishes to give love must also receive love as a gift" (*DCE* 7). The law that shines in the gaze of the other, to use the vocabulary of Emmanuel Levinas, is not only a "taking hostage". It is equally a call to an exchange, to a communion. *Agápē* implies *érōs*, and vice versa. "The more the two, in their different aspects, find a proper unity in the one reality of love, the more the true nature of love in general is realized" (*DCE* 7).

This mutual implication at the heart of the one reality of love is revealed most preeminently in the "personal path" of Christ, which "leads through the Cross to the Resurrection: the path of the grain of wheat that falls to the ground and dies and in this way bears much fruit" (*DCE* 6). Not only does he lose his life, but he finds it. More precisely, it is in losing his life by his sacrifice that he gains it, that he comes back to life, that he comes to fulfillment in love. The Christianity denounced by Nietzsche does not give sufficient attention to the mystery of the Resurrection. It concentrates above all on that of the Passion. In addition, to our philosopher the Crucified is a curse against life. In him, the concept of God contradicts, degenerates, and corrupts the whole existence of man and the cosmos. He makes nothingness sacred. He proposes it as "Ideal", as "Being". The Crucified leads men by all of his commandments to live such an *agápē*, that is, to die with him in order to gain his lifeless afterlife built upon a gigantic mystification. "If Christ has not been raised," St. Paul observed, "your faith is futile.... If for this life only we have hoped in Christ, we are of all men most to be pitied" (1 Cor 15:17–19). In the love of Christ, there is no *agápē* without *érōs*, and vice versa.

As Christ reveals him, man is not pure *agápē*. And neither is God! Hosea, Ezekiel, and the Song of Songs testify powerfully to this reality. Unlike the Unmoved Mover of Aristotle, the God of the Scriptures "is at the same time a lover with all the passion of a true love. *Eros* is thus supremely ennobled, yet at the same time it is so purified as to become one with *agape*" (*DCE* 10). The pardon continually offered is the most profound testimony and sign of it. These considerations reveal the economy of salvation that culminates in the Passion and Resurrection of Christ. They introduce us to a contemplation of the very being of God as love, the title of our encyclical. In God, *érōs* and *agápē* coincide perfectly within the infinite fullness of trinitarian communion. Is such a God what Nietzsche wanted to become himself, he who would sign his notes at the end of his conscious life by a pathetic "Dionysus or the Crucified"?

In conclusion, this vital junction between *érōs* and *agápē*—with the commandment of the love of the other that is united to it—helps Benedict XVI to overcome the contemporary cultural extrinsicism between love and law. It offers a tranquil and integrated response to the dialectic of opposition between *érōs* and commandment, while giving new dimension to these two realities within the same reality of human love, the latter itself referring to the personal dignity of man as man. It thus balances in a dynamic and circular way two sides of the fertile tension between the Aristotelian perspective of the final end and the Platonic perspective of the Good.

Such an approach also permits us to base the intrinsic truth of the commandment of love in the very being of God-love. The ethic that follows from it, far from appearing strange or arbitrary in relation to human destiny, emerges out of the heart of man created in his image and likeness. It gushes forth as a light and an interior force at the service of the education and the unfolding of love in history.

C. History and Commandment

By absolutizing *érōs*, Nietzsche propelled himself outside of time and history. The universe that he wanted to create at each moment is without origin or end, without generation. "The before and after are confused in the immediate assumption of the will to life and to power" (Hausman 1984: 99). Everything is always already both unaccomplished and accomplished, in the spontaneity of a becoming in perpetual forgetfulness of itself. Did Nietzsche not conceive his Zarathustra "6,000 feet away from man and time?"

On the contrary, *erōs*, when it is brought to maturity by *agápē*, brings forth a history. In fact, these two essential dimensions of love are linked, not only from the ontological, structural, or dialectical point of view, but from the point of view of history as well. A path is traced by a series of encounters with the other. Events take place one after the other, one inside the other, and thus constitute a communal memory, a narrative bearing the future. This consideration is equally true in what concerns the love of man for God. But what is the love of God for man? Does it also live in history? Is it at the origin of a history?

Yes, as Holy Scripture reveals. God loves man and desires to be loved in return. In addition, he educates his people to love, particularly in giving them the Decalogue. "The history of the love-relationship between God and Israel consists, at the deepest level, in the fact that he gives her the *Torah*" (*DCE* 9). In Hebrew, *Torah* has a broader significance that is less strictly juridical than νομος in Greek. It designates the path God teaches man to walk toward him in uprightness and justice, in tenderness and fidelity.

The gift of this law is made within a theophany, a manifest encounter between God and his people for whom Moses is the mediator. "Moses brought the people out of the camp to meet God; and they took their stand at the foot of the mountain" (Ex 19:17). During the course of these events, God offers them the "Ten Commandments", or the "Ten Words of Life" (*dabar*; cf. Ex 20:1–21 and Deut 5:6–11). "If you obey the commandments ... by loving the LORD your God, by walking in his ways, and by keeping his commandments and his statutes and his ordinances, then you shall live and multiply" (Deut 30:16).

These words are thus not arbitrary. They enable a fully human life. They express the identity and the profound vocation of man. They open "Israel's eyes to man's true nature and [show] her the path leading to true humanism" (*DCE* 9). In their fragmentary and imperfect form, they belong to the patrimony of the civilizations of Israel's neighbors. "The Ten Commandments ... teach us the true humanity of man. They ... contain a privileged expression of the natural law.... The Ten Commandments are engraved by God in the human heart" (*CCC* 2070, 2072). According to the concepts of our encyclical, these commandments bring to light the itinerary of *erōs* in its process of humanization, of the dynamic intersection between *érōs* and *agápē*. They guide the "work" of authentic love in all human being.

The principal originality of the Decalogue does not primarily lie in the exceptionally clear and concise expression of this natural law but in the historic experience that makes Israel loved and saved by God. The theophany, which passes through the episode of idolatry and concludes with a communion meal, is its hallmark. The historical prologue of the Decalogue is its memorial: "I am the LORD your God, who brought you out of the land of Egypt, out of the house of bondage" (Ex 20:1). "The first of the 'ten words' recalls that God loved his people first" (*CCC* 2061).

The other words engraved on the two tablets then express, each according to its specificity, the love that man is called to give in return to God and to neighbor. "Since God has first loved us (cf. 1 Jn 4:10), love is now no longer a mere 'command'; it is the response to the gift of love with which God draws near to us" (*DCE* 1).

> The moral life [wrote John Paul II] presents itself as the response due to the many gratuitous initiatives taken by God out of love for man. It is a response of love, according to the statement made in Deuteronomy about the fundamental commandment: "Hear, O Israel: The Lord our God is one Lord; and you shall love the Lord your God with all your heart, and with all your soul, and with all your might. And these words which I command you this day shall be upon your heart; and you shall teach them diligently to your children" (Deut 6:4–7 [taken up in this sense by *DCE* 1]). (*VS* 10; cf. also *CCC* 2062)

Biblical morality thus is not "autonomous" or exclusively conceptual, but rather dialogic and historical. It is a theological ethic, inscribed in the heart of a covenant history. We are very far here from the atemporal confrontation between the Kantian dragon of "Thou shalt" and the roaring lion of "I will". The relationship between commandment and will is subsumed into a loving encounter. It reemerges as profoundly transfigured. "The Commandments take on their full meaning within the covenant" (*CCC* 2061).

This theology of covenant in time underlies the entire subject of our encyclical, without being developed immediately for itself. "In the love-story recounted by the Bible, he [God] comes towards us, he seeks to win our hearts, all the way to the Last Supper, to the piercing of his heart on the Cross, to his appearances after the Resurrection and to the great deeds by which, through the activity of the Apostles, he guided the nascent Church along her path" (*DCE* 17). Covenant, redeeming Incarnation, and the mystery of the Church are many aspects of the singular reality of the love of God who "came to his own home" (Jn 1:11), in their history, a history that also becomes—analogously— God's own "history". "Being Christian is not the result of an ethical choice or a lofty idea, but the encounter with an event, a person, which gives life a new horizon and a decisive direction" (*DCE* 1). This encounter—of which the event of the rich young man amply meditated upon by John Paul II is in some way an archetype (cf. *VS* 6 through 27)—awakens, renders possible, carries, and finalizes the double commandment of love.

This event is not confined to the memory of a past that is definitively finished. "And behold, I am with you always, to the close of the age" (Mt 28:20), Christ promises to his disciples. "In order to make this 'encounter' with Christ possible," wrote John Paul II, "God willed his Church. Indeed, the Church 'wishes to serve this single end: that each person may be able to find Christ, in order that Christ may walk with each person the path of life' (*Redemptor hominis* 13)" (*VS* 7). The Church renders Christ present. In a certain fashion, she extends his Incarnation. "Nor has the Lord been absent from subsequent Church history: he encounters us ever anew, in the men and women who reflect his presence, in his Word, in the sacraments, and especially in the Eucharist. In the Church's Liturgy, in her prayer, in the living community of believers, we experience the love of God, we perceive his presence, and we thus learn to recognize that presence in our daily lives" (*DCE* 17).

This is why the rejection of the institutional and "historical" Church, proper to certain ideologies, contrasts radically with the dynamic of covenant and accordingly with the very nature of commandment, in the Christian sense of the term. Without the Church—in which Benedict XVI roots the text—it would become much more difficult today to experience that God first has loved us, that he continues to love us first, and that our action is called to respond to it.

To conclude this third section, let us consider for an instant the Eucharist celebrated by the Church each day and throughout the world. This memorial, in the strongest sense of the term, "draws us into Jesus' act of self-oblation. More than just statically receiving the incarnate Logos, we enter into the very dynamic of his self-giving" (*DCE* 13). The "mysticism" of this sacrament (*DCE* 14), referred to historically as God's *agápē*, is consequently very different from that of the Nietzschean *érōs*. It carries the baptized into the *érōs-agápē* of Christ himself in his different mysteries, that is, in the perfect accomplishment of the double commandment of love. This event, this communion *hic et nunc*, becomes the source, permanent force, and crowning of Christian moral action. "Here the usual contraposition between worship and ethics simply falls apart. 'Worship' itself, Eucharistic communion, includes the reality both of being loved and of loving others in turn" (*DCE* 14).

The eucharistic meal, therefore, necessarily and concretely nourishes an action of charity, that is, an action constituted in its intimate core by the love of Christ. Such a consideration agrees with the great Augustinian and Thomistic tradition that sees the virtue of charity as "the mother and the root of all the virtues, inasmuch as it is the form of them all" (*STh* I–II, 62, 4). The second major section of the encyclical—that which treats of "The Practice of Love by the Church as a 'Community of Love'"—is consequently in no way heterogeneous to the first, but rather is its "natural" extension at a social level.

Conclusion

Friedrich Nietzsche invites people as "his brothers" not to renounce the vertiginous call of their most profound appetites. He exalts *érōs*, not in the vulgar or biological fashion for which he is sometimes reproached, but in an intense, completely mystical impulse. His Zarathustra wants to sweep us beyond the distinction between spiritual and carnal, rational and irrational, space and time, father and son, simple and complex, true and false, good and evil, necessity and chance, beyond all distinction as such. To this effect, he struggles powerfully against the Kantian categorical imperative and the Christianity that fills it.

Stimulated by this challenge, Benedict XVI very clearly sets off commandment in relation to its Kantian conception. Commandment, in the way the Pope sketches his portrait, is not at all reducible to an imperative of pure reason, postulating practically the existence of God, the immortality of the soul, and fair retribution. It is no longer cut from its vital roots. It is not uprooted from its native soil—that is, from human *érōs*—as is the case with the great philosopher from Königsberg. No, it accompanies the progressive maturation of *érōs* in *agápē*. It is not the work of practical reason in the Kantian sense of the term. It springs forth within a history of love as its intrinsic demand and abides there practically ordered.

Consequently, commandment no longer appears to be a menacing enemy, issued out of some dragon or Leviathan. No, it is revealed as the benevolent expression of a love that precedes me and wants my beatitude, educating me and guiding me patiently into the infinite realization of love. Commandment is in no way the strange manifestation of a negative or reactive will to power, animated by resentment. On the contrary, it is "more intimate to me than I am to myself", entirely devoted to the communion of thought, will, and sentiments with God and with my neighbor. It is not an obstacle against absolute and "divine" love, but rather is its means of accomplishment.

Such a love transforms us, not into a meta-human Eternal Destiny, but into "a 'we' which transcends our divisions and makes us one, until in the end God is 'all in all' (1 Cor 15:28)" (*DCE* 18).

Bibliography

Blondel, Maurice. 1973. *L'Action (1893): Essai d'une critique de la vie et d'une science de la pratique.* Paris. [*Action (1893): Essay on a Critique of Life and a Science of Practice.* South Bend, Ind.: University of Notre Dame Press, 2004.]

Hausman, Noëlle. 1984. *Frédéric Nietzsche et Thérèse de Lisieux: Deux poétiques de la Modernité.* Paris: Beauchesne.

John Paul II. 1993. *Love and Responsibility.* San Francisco: Ignatius Press.

De Lubac, Henri. 1983. *Le Drame de l'humanisme athée.* Paris: Cerf. [*The Drama of Atheist Humanism.* San Francisco: Ignatius Press, 1995.]

Nietzsche, Friedrich. 1969. *Thus Spoke Zarathustra*. Translated by R. J. Hollingdale. New York: Penguin. (= TSZ)

Piret, Pierre. 1994. *Les Athéismes et la théologie trinitaire: A. Comte, L. Feuerbach, K. Marx, F. Nietzsche*. Brussels: Institut d'Études Théologiques.

Sartre, Jean-Paul. 1977. *Existentialism and Humanism*. Translated by Philip Mairet. New York: Haskell House.

Love and Forgiveness

Jean Laffitte*

In a way, the delay of a few weeks in the publication of the encyclical *Deus Caritas Est* was an advantage: 2006 marks the fiftieth anniversary of the publication of another encyclical, *Haurietis Aquas in Gaudio*, which Pope Pius XII offered to the Church and to the world on May 15, 1956. A truly christological encyclical, the latter text laid out the fundamental principles, inspired by Scripture and tradition, for a genuine devotion to the Sacred Heart and explained the symbolism of this devotion. Contemplating the Heart of Christ from a trinitarian perspective, Pius XII saw in it the symbol and recapitulation of all the fundamental mysteries of Christianity, from the eternal Trinity to the Church. More precisely, he saw the place of the gift of divine love (*caritas*) and the gift of the Spirit:

> [The] Paraclete, who is the mutual personal love between the Father and the Son, is sent by both.... [T]his charity is the gift of Jesus Christ and of His Spirit, for He is indeed the spirit of the Father and the Son from whom the origin of the Church and its marvelous extension is revealed.... This divine charity is the most precious gift of the Heart of Christ and of His Spirit. It is this which imparted to the Apostles and martyrs that fortitude, by the strength of which they fought their battles like heroes till death in order to preach the truth

* Professor of Theological Anthropology, General Ethics, and Spirituality, Pontifical John Paul II Institute for Studies on Marriage and Family, Rome.

of the Gospel and bear witness to it by the shedding of their blood. (*HA* 81–83)

At a distance of fifty years, *Deus Caritas Est* further explores the dimensions of love (*érōs* and *agápē*), showing its presence in God, not in a trinitarian key—this is not the encyclical's aim—but in terms of the gift made to man, a gift that kindles a loving response. An approach strictly along the lines of dogmatic theology would doubtless have developed further the relationships between the Father and the Son as well as the pneumatological dimension of Love in God; these aspects are indeed present in *Deus Caritas Est*, but by way of suggestion, while the focus is on the gift God makes to man. In offering himself, God offers his Love. The encyclical's intent is profoundly one of evangelization: it seems to be possessed by the urgent need for proclaiming God's love for man, for each particular man, which makes him capable of loving in turn, not only God, in a response to the gift received, but also his neighbor. At bottom, the text thus reformulates the content and the exercise of faith: to believe in God is to believe in his active love (the content of faith). In this perspective, the Church cannot be reduced to a conglomeration of believers who adhere to the same articles of faith; rather, she is an active "community of love".

The directly evangelizing nature of the encyclical does not economize, with a rigorous, double methodological principle:

—understanding the Love of God presupposes a contemplation of the opened side of Christ (*DCE* 7 and 12);

—the eucharistic nature of divine Love offers the "Christological and sacramental basis" from which "we correctly understand Jesus' teaching on love" (*DCE* 14).

Numerous passages explicitly referring to the pierced Heart of Christ in a way make *Deus Caritas Est* a prolongation of *Haurietis Aquas*. More fundamentally, the encyclical joins forgiveness to divine Love; the former is one of the essential themes of this text. We do not understand the nature of the Love God bears for man if we forget that this Love is a Love that forgives. We will look at (1) the encyclical's references to the Heart of Christ as the place of divine love and forgiveness; (2) how the logic of forgiveness meets the logic of love; (3) eucharistic logic as the unity of gift and response.

I. The Heart of Christ in the Encyclical *Deus Caritas Est*

a. *The Gaze and Witness of the Disciple*

The first passage that mentions the Heart of Christ (*DCE* 7) joins in a classical vein the two texts of the fourth Gospel: John 19:34 and John 7:37–38. The event of Jesus' death and the blood and water pouring forth from his side are the source allowing the disciple to become, in his turn, a "spring of living water", according to the Lord's prophetic words. The encyclical's perspective is specifically Johannine.

The verses recounting Jesus' death are among those that have received the most commentary by the tradition, especially during the Middle Ages. Ignace de la Potterie shrewdly remarked that this abundance contrasts with a certain type of contemporary exegesis (La Potterie 1990). According to the Gospel text, "One of the soldiers pierced his side with a spear, and at once there came out blood and water. He who saw it has borne witness—his testimony is true, and he knows that he tells the truth—that you also may believe. For these things took place that the Scripture might be fulfilled, 'Not a bone of him shall be broken.' And again another Scripture says, 'They shall look on him whom they have pierced'" (Jn 19:34–37). The encyclical does not enter into the debate regarding the traditional interpretation of the "pierced heart"; in St. John's text, the wound is referred to as the "pierced side". In no. 7, Benedict XVI makes the traditional expression his own, whereas in no. 12, taking up John 19:37, he speaks of "contemplating the pierced side of Christ". Here we find a confirmation of Pius XII's broad interpretation, in which he indicates that "What is ... written [in John 19:34] of the side of Christ, opened by the wound from the soldier, should also be said of the Heart which was certainly reached by the stab of the lance, since the soldier pierced it precisely to make certain that Jesus Christ was really dead" (*HA* 78). A second point of interpretation characterizes the encyclical: it speaks of the "opened" side, while the verb *nussô* (*enuxen* in the aorist) used by the evangelist means "struck" or "pierced". Here, too, the choice of the tradition, inspired by the translation of the Vulgate, is particularly felicitous: "he opened" translates "*ênoixen*". In "opening" the side of Christ, the lance traces a path to his heart. According to Benedict

XVI, to contemplate this opened side is to understand that God is love: "It is there that this truth can be contemplated" (*DCE* 12). The opened side has opened to us the door of life (the *vitae ostium* so dear to St. Augustine).

This contemplation is not passive; it transforms. By this act, the disciple, that is to say, the one who believes in Christ, quenches his thirst, according to Jesus' own words. He drinks from the springs of the Holy Spirit: "'if any one thirst, let him come to me and drink. He who believes in me, as the Scripture has said, "Out of his heart shall flow rivers of living water." ' Now this he said about the Spirit, which those who believed in him were to receive; for as yet the Spirit had not been given, because Jesus was not yet glorified" (Jn 7:37–39). The juxtaposition of the two texts falls within the context of the dialectic illustrated in the encyclical between ascending and descending love (the love that seeks God and the love that transmits). The encyclical affirms the primacy of the gift received, the anteriority of divine love. We observe that *the love of God does not cease to have primacy*. It is thus a constant invitation to a response as well as the content of that which the encyclical several times calls an "experience": "Man, through a life of fidelity to the one God, comes to *experience* himself as loved by God" (*DCE* 9; emphasis added). With regard to the God-man relationship expressed by the Song of Songs, we read that the latter "became, both in Christian and Jewish literature, a source of mystical knowledge and *experience*" (*DCE* 10; emphasis added). In no. 17, the Pope speaks of the Church's liturgy, her prayer, and the living community of believers, in which "we experience the love of God"; later on, the communion of will between man and God refers to the "realization [experience] that God is in fact more deeply present to me than I am to myself" (*DCE* 17).

b. The Singular Experience of the Love of God

The experience described in the various passages cited above specifies a primordial event, an "intimate" encounter (*DCE* 18) with a loving and personal God. This encounter is fundamental, for it places man in a relationship with God that casts out fear, leaving nothing but a loving awe. The latter is made up of sentiments of both reverence (the

God who is so near does not cease being God) and a concern to correspond to the love that has been offered (a response that, beyond the level of sentiments, truly establishes the disciple in love).

The experience of the love of God appears unexpectedly in human existence and re-centers the latter in what is essential, broadening it to the dimensions of the world, and hence to all neighbors, and ultimately leading us back to the pierced Heart. Through grace, the disciple who loves appropriates and integrates in himself the action of his Lord. In this sense, the Cross is both the place where the oblative love of God gives itself to be contemplated and the place where the disciple rejoins his Master.

The experience we have been considering places man in a loving relationship to God. In the encyclical, the love of God is specified by its function of reconciliation. The dimension of forgiveness is introduced in no. 10: "We have seen that God's *eros* for man is also totally *agape*. This is not only because it is bestowed in a completely gratuitous manner, without any previous merit, but also because it is love which forgives." Later in the same paragraph, we are told that this love "goes far beyond the aspect of gratuity" (*DCE* 10). Gratuity, as we will see farther on, characterizes every act of love and every act of forgiveness. The gratuity of love, as well as that of forgiveness, expresses the fact that neither of these can be instrumentalized for the sake of anything else. By observing that gratuity alone does not suffice to characterize forgiveness, the encyclical introduces a notion that is not explicitly expressed but that we might call the "excellence of forgiveness". This points to the unique, limitless character of forgiveness.

Christian experience, in its profound sense, is accompanied by signs of the transcendence of human existence (the forgiving love of which the encyclical speaks refers first of all to the transcendent love of God). This transcendence is translated into human life through the integration into it of a new way of life (conversion). The response of the convert is part of the experience of the love of God, because it verifies the authenticity of the latter. We simply observe that such an experience is totally singular and is distinguished by unique circumstances and personal history. Nevertheless, it possesses an intelligibility so that it can be passed on in testimony, in two senses of the word: the recounting of facts (the event) and the testimony of a life (the coherence of the response). Moreover, this experience becomes part of the objective riches of the entire Body of Christ. The fundamental experiences of those who have surrendered themselves to the divine love that revealed itself to them are able not only to enrich the community of believers with new members; they can even give rise to a teaching modeled on the founding event of a primordial encounter, authenticated as an objective richness for all believers.*

c. The Heart of Man in Tune with the Heart of Christ

The offering that Jesus makes of himself on the Cross acts on human hearts by making them capable of offering themselves in turn. It would be helpful here to take up again the Pope's comments on how imperative it is not to reduce the life of Christ to a moral example and, for this reason, to begin from the christological and sacramental foundations (eucharistic logic, to which we shall return): "The transition which [Jesus] makes from the Law and the Prophets to the twofold commandment of love of God and of neighbor, and his grounding the whole life of faith on this central precept, is not simply a matter of morality—something that could exist apart from and alongside faith in Christ and its sacramental re-actualization. Faith, worship and *ethos* are interwoven as a single reality which takes shape in our encounter with God's *agape*" (*DCE* 14). We have to avoid two pitfalls: on the one hand, moral reductionism, in which the Christian life is presented as a mere imitation of Christ's action, and, on the other hand, understanding this conforming of ourselves to Christ as a sort of indistinct union with the divine, a grace without the real engagement of personal responsibility. There should be neither Pelagianism nor spiritualism: our being conformed to Christ is born of a Gift of the Holy Spirit, who comes to dwell in the person's interior. In other words,

---

* As, for example, the experience of Saul of Tarsus on the road to Damascus was a source of fruitfulness for the whole Church, because it gave the teaching of Paul the Apostle its specific traits. In the same way, Augustine's discovery of the love of God and its demand for a change of life gave to the future Doctor of the Church his extreme sensibility for the primacy of grace and the dramatic character of salvation (the Augustinian *conversio*). The same observation could be made of all the saints: the form their sanctity took became a universal source of teaching for the Church.

the Spirit dwells in that intimate place where the person receives and honors him: the heart. Thus renewed, human action flows from a contemplation of the Heart of Christ, where the supreme act of love was accomplished and from which springs the Gift of the Spirit of God. In this way, the Heart of Christ makes man capable of acting in a way that is supernaturally fruitful. The presence of the Holy Spirit in his heart becomes the condition for action that can resemble the action of Christ and thus be pleasing to the Father. In this Johannine light, two of Jesus' actions in particular become paradigmatic: his washing of the disciples' feet, which is the act of the servant par excellence, and the offering of his own life, which is the supreme act of love.

We find two final references to the Heart of Christ at the end of the second part of the encyclical. The first exalts the example, in Mary, of the most intimate union with God. In her, the conditions for this transformation of the human heart were fulfilled, allowing her to become, as her Son promised in the verse we cited above, a source from which flows "rivers of living water." The second reference expresses, in the final prayer addressed to Mary, the intention that we, too, may become "fountains of living water in the midst of a thirsting world" (*DCE* 42).

II. The Logic of Love and the Logic of Forgiveness

Regarding the dynamism of human love, the encyclical insists first of all on its unifying activity: love unites the two terms of the relation, each of them being in its turn the starting and the ending point of a twofold movement. It does this through a whole process of maturation, which the philosopher Karl Wojtyła readily terms "integration". With this word, he signifies, in an ethical perspective, the human capacity to submit the physical and affective dynamisms to the government of the spiritual faculties. In the text of the encyclical, Benedict XVI uses the term "purification", which places in greater relief the permanence of *érōs* totally taken up (purified) by *agápē*. Indeed, the text's primary intention is to present a realistic vision of love, avoiding the familiar oppositions between the two dimensions. With such an explanation of human love as our starting point, it will become possible to speak of the Love of God.

Early on, the encyclical also highlights another constitutive element of love, though without developing it: the presence of the two movements of giving and receiving. The act of receiving, welcoming the other's love, structures the person. We can even say that it is originally structuring in the psychological and affective genesis of man (cf. Laffitte 2003; 2005). It is an experience offered to each one, who discovers himself to be preceded by the unconditional love of his parents (at least in a normal experience of a family). Beginning with human love allows the encyclical to introduce the theme of divine Love by first considering it from the side of its recipient, who then becomes capable of transmitting it in turn. Where does the disciple find this Love? At its source, the pierced Heart of Jesus, which is the place where this Love of God is offered inexhaustibly to man: "Anyone who wishes to give love must also receive love as a gift. Certainly, as the Lord tells us, one can become a source from which rivers of living water flow (cf. Jn 7:37–38). Yet to become such a source, one must constantly drink anew from the original source, which is Jesus Christ, from whose pierced heart flows the love of God (cf. Jn 19:34)" (*DCE* 7). We are reminded here of the chief affirmation of *Dives in Misericordia*: "Making the Father present as love and mercy is, in Christ's own consciousness, the fundamental touchstone of His mission as the Messiah" (*DM* 3, 4). Elsewhere in the same text: "It is precisely this drawing close to Christ in the mystery of His Heart which enables us to dwell on this point—a point in a sense central and also most accessible on the human level—of the revelation of the merciful love of the Father, a revelation which constituted the central content of the messianic mission of the Son of Man" (*DM* 13, 2).

The experience of the Love of God begins with a gift welcomed and received.

The encyclical illustrates the contours of a Christian existence informed by divine charity. The Love God offers to every man is always an act of forgiveness, since it is sinners who, in every case except Mary, are thus united with him. Everything that can be said of divine Love *ad extra* can be said absolutely of divine Forgiveness: God's forgiveness always has and never ceases to have primacy ("I was a sinner from my mother's womb"). It expresses a divine fidelity that never fails and that remains infinitely open to us [*disponible*]. The encyclical expresses this first of all in the manifestation of divine Holiness in the face of an unfaithful and adulterous people. The cardinal sin, if we can call it this, is always couched in terms of a betrayal of love. Every fault committed against God is a betrayal of love because it is committed against the One who loves unconditionally (gratuitously) and never ceases to do so. The forgiveness offered is the glory of God, and this forgiveness defines his conduct toward the people of Israel: "I will not execute my fierce anger, I will not again destroy Ephraim; for I am God and not man, the Holy One in your midst, and I will not come to destroy" (Hos 11:9). In these words, the encyclical sees a "dim prefiguration" of the mystery of the Cross. The realization of divine Forgiveness at Calvary is here expressed by the original image of God who "follows" man (*DCE* 10). The demands of the mystery of the Incarnation include taking on human mortality. In this sense, Jesus' crucifixion is the way in which God made man "follows" man even into death. The image is suggestive; it conveys clearly that in this act, the Word takes on everything belonging to human nature, and especially death, the consequence of his transgression.

For man, the passage from the gratuity of love to the surpassing gratuity of pardon has its source in contemplation. The attitude of the true pastor, according to Gregory the Great, whom Benedict XVI quotes, consists in carrying the infirmities and the needs of others, but in a profoundly interior manner (*per pietatis viscera*). Doing this requires that transformation of the heart we discussed above. What is involved here is active compassion (*transferat*), which does not confine itself to a superficial, emotional compassion. The *viscera pietatis* evoke the "bowels of mercy" (*splagchna*) of the father of the prodigal son; St. Luke tells us that his "bowels trembled with compassion" in the moment between when he caught sight of his son and when he ran to meet him (Lk 15:20). According to Gregory, the pastor, by virtue of his contemplation, reproduces the father's sentiments. Compassion is a moment of forgiveness, just as it is a moment of love. It is the desire and the will for the good of the other that makes the one see the sufferings of the other as a burden to be removed and carried oneself: at first sight, they are in themselves an obstacle to the good of the beloved.* In the figure of the merciful father of the parable, who incarnates the figure of the Father of all mercy, love and forgiveness are one. His forgiveness expresses to the highest degree the quality of his love.

The experience had by every human being of the Love of God is inseparable from the experience of his forgiveness, because of what God is and because of the holiness of his Name. Man finds himself not only to be loved, but that this love is such that it transforms him and makes him righteous. God does not excuse. There is no complicity in him with the failings and betrayals of his children; but he justifies them, penetrating to the depths of their subjectivity with his Spirit. He makes them better, that is to say, he makes them fully themselves, capable of loving and forgiving. Their hearts are changed.

The human experience of forgiveness is also structured by a double movement, forgiving and being forgiven. The experience of forgiveness desired, requested, and received requires a process of maturation: it introduces the offender into a work of truth accomplished in him, and this requires time. The demand that he acknowledge his fault and its consequences for the victim (the avowal and confession of his transgressions) both reveals him to himself as unjust and places him before the necessity of having his debt removed. This last element implies that, through the act he committed, he wounded the nature of a relationship. An offense is always unjust on a human level, because it shatters a natural order of the relationship between persons. Peace can come to a society only if this initial order of justice is restored. No doubt, human justice requires punishment. On a personal level, however, the guilty party realizes that, beyond his victim, he has violated an absolute dimension. The experience of remorse and guilt that sometimes persist after the punishment has already taken place shows that a full reconciliation of the guilty person with himself is made possible only by the *other's* forgiveness. Precisely this latter is able to justify the offender in the depths of his interiority, where no human justice can penetrate. The experience of a forgiveness that is awaited after a grave

---

*It is only in a second instance that the sufferings of the beloved can be seen as a necessary step toward their true good. The initial movement of love moves us to consider them first with compassion.

injustice cries out for divine action, the Gift of an ever-available Love. The Mercy that forgives man takes on all the demands of justice in the efficaciousness that distinguishes it as divine, making the unjust just: "Men exercise mercy as men, but God will have mercy on them as God. There is a great difference between human compassion and the compassion of God; and they are as distant from one another as malice is from goodness" (St. John Chrysostom, *In Matthaeum Homil.* XV: PG 57, 227).

The second movement of human reconciliation is the granting of forgiveness. The decision to forgive also requires a progressive maturation, since it is not until it takes the form of a decision that forgiveness can be efficacious. The steps that precede it make the human itinerary of forgiveness complex: the desire for vengeance, which is a distortion of the natural demand for justice (the *vindicta* of the Romans); rancor, which identifies the guilty party in the transgression committed and inevitably gives rise to a hatred of the aggressor; and lastly, the false reasons for forgiving that make forgiveness impure: a desire to establish a personal superiority, a seeking after the glory of clemency, political calculation. When the aspiration to forgive overcomes these possible obstacles, forgiveness becomes an act of love and is not disinterested in its recipient. To the contrary, it is offered *to him*; it is the guilty person whom forgiveness intends to reestablish in his dignity and freedom. Forgiveness is fundamentally altruistic, and, in this sense, it is as gratuitous as every act of disinterested love. Nevertheless, it goes beyond gratuity in the measure in which, humanly, the one who forgives renounces the exercise of a personal right to justice being done for him. Thus, forgiveness is essentially sacrificial. Sacrifice goes beyond the gratuitous gift, for it reestablishes a balance in the order of relationships without necessarily taking the detour of distributive justice, which at any rate is often impotent. The one who forgives in some way takes on the debt of the one who offended him. We have seen that love is a gift bearing a unitive finality. Forgiveness is a perfect gift (*per-donum*, pardon) bearing a redemptive finality. It aims at giving back to the guilty person his dignity and the justice that was his before the offense.

The two logics, of love and of forgiveness, meet here, since every act of genuine forgiveness is an act of love that acknowledges and gives honor to the dignity of the other.

Two common objections arise here. The first holds that forgiveness ought not to be considered a duty, because in some way it does not respect the demands of justice that are basic to human society. There is, according to this position, a sort of irrationality in forgiveness that disturbs the rules of social life, makes laws obsolete, and represents a danger for the well-balanced juridical regulation of the citizens. Forgiveness does not respect the nature of the moral obligation inscribed in justice, since there are what we call "unforgivable" acts. On the level of jurisprudence, these acts are called "imprescriptible". (The terms "unforgivable" and "imprescriptible" have been the object of ample development in the philosophical and political literature of the last half-century. In the French-speaking context, they were popularized by various authors, among whom are: Jankélévitch 1966; 1967; 1971; 1986; Wiesel 1979; Wiesenthal 1969; Derrida 1999; for a Christian contribution to this debate, cf. Laffitte 1995.)

The second objection is that forgiveness is acceptable only when it remains an exception. "I will risk the following proposition: each time forgiveness serves an end, however noble and spiritual (atonement or redemption, reconciliation, salvation), each time it attempts to reestablish a normality (social, national, political, psychological) through a grieving process, through some sort of therapy or ecology of memory, then forgiveness is not pure—nor its concept. Forgiveness is not, it should not be either normal or normative or normalizing. It should remain exceptional and extraordinary" (Derrida 1999: 2). Basically, it would be the prerogative of an aristocratic ethics.

The first difficulty mentioned is a genuine one: the term "unforgivable" refers first to the fact that an act is at times juridically or morally irreparable, even on a symbolic level. The term contains another nuance, however: that of "inexpiable", which implies a definitive judgment regarding the impossibility of an eventual transformation of the guilty person. Expiation inarguably aims at reparation, but also at changing the guilty person through the suffering of the chastisement that has been endured. Such a judgment, it is clear, is religious in nature, even if it is a sort of secularization of hell. In the concrete, the question of the unforgivable cannot long remain in the realm of philosophy. It very quickly becomes theological, when it takes the form of a theoretically formulated refusal that forgiveness, be it divine, might be granted. The question can be summed up as follows: "Does God have the right to forgive a crime that is humanly unforgivable?" Does his power extend so far as to "cover the unexpiated side of the transgression", to borrow W. Jankélévitch's beautiful definition of forgiveness? There are no easy answers to this dramatic question. Only a loving adherence to the words the prophet Isaiah places on God's lips, "I am God and not man", allows us, in the encyclical's words, to see in them "a dim prefigurement of the mystery of the Cross: so great is God's love for man that by becoming man he follows him even into death and so reconciles justice and love" (DCE 10).

The second difficulty misjudges the very essence of the act of forgiveness, which always presupposes, above and beyond the person pronouncing it, a person to whom it is directed: Why should it remain exceptional and be offered only exceptionally? If this were the case, forgiveness would lose all exemplary value; it would no longer be able to represent a richness and a virtuous ethical norm for human society. A culture of forgiveness would become impossible. The very foundations of civil peace would irremediably be called into question.

III. Eucharistic Logic: The Unity of Gift and Response

The encyclical establishes a direct link between the mystery of the "opened side" of Christ and the institution of the Eucharist (DCE 12 and 13). In terms of doctrine, this is nothing new: the Church has always held that at each celebration of the Eucharist, the work of our redemption is accomplished. The Council of Trent states,

> [Christ], our Lord and God, was once and for all to offer himself to God the Father by his death on the altar of the Cross, to accomplish there an everlasting redemption. But because his priesthood was not to end with his death, at the Last Supper "on the night when he was betrayed," [he wanted] to leave his beloved spouse the Church a visible sacrifice (as the nature of man demands) by which the bloody sacrifice which he was to accomplish once for all on the Cross would be re-presented, its memory perpetuated until the end of the world, and its salutary power be applied to the forgiveness of the sins we daily commit. (Council of Trent (1562): DS 1740)

More recently, John Paul II's encyclical *Ecclesia de Eucharistia* expressed Christ's intention of leaving to those who belonged to him this salvific heritage: "This sacrifice is so decisive for the salvation of the human race that Jesus Christ offered it and returned to the Father only *after he had left us a means of sharing in it* as if we had been present there" (*Ecclesia de Eucharistia* 11; cf. also 12 and 13). The novelty is not doctrinal; rather, in the perspective of evangelization mentioned above, it resides in a twofold insistence on the nature of the participation by Christ's disciples in this mystery.

The first element joins the subjective dimension of eucharistic communion to its objective dimension: remarking boldly that the dream of the ancient world (to nourish oneself with the food of eternal wisdom, the *logos*) has become a reality for us, Benedict XVI insists on the loving character of such an assimilation, which simultaneously understands itself to be a gift of love: "This same *Logos* now truly becomes food for us—*as love*" and as a response that is necessarily loving: "The Eucharist draws us into Jesus' act of self-oblation.... *We enter into the very dynamic of his self-giving*" (*DCE* 13; italics mine).

Only the contemplation of Christ's sacrifice on Calvary lets us allow ourselves to be drawn into his self-giving. Throughout the ages, the Church in her wisdom has ceaselessly encouraged the faithful to meditate on the sufferings of the Passion: on the Cross is accomplished both the horrible unleashing of evil and of human sin and the self-giving of God that is worthy of adoration. He did not despise any means of saving men by giving himself to them, through the very act by which they rejected him and put him to death. What was done against him was, humanly speaking, irreparable. The massacre of the supremely Innocent One was a crime that no human legislation could prescribe. The act of self-giving annihilated the abominable act; forgiveness without limits was offered to man.

The encyclical's second point of insistence has to do with the social dimension of the Eucharist. The Eucharist builds up the Church in the sense that it gives her her form and consistency. It is possible to participate in the Eucharist without uniting oneself to Christ in love. The faith inspiring such an act is a dead faith; indeed, it is not even an act of faith. Such a participation does not allow one to remain in the Church "body and soul", according to the expression of *Ecclesia de*

Eucharistia. Christ comes in his Body and Blood to unite himself to the one receiving him. But as he unites himself to each person who receives him, he brings about this humanly impossible unity between the members of his Body. The love transmitted to each member is not a human love; it is really divine charity, the *caritas* of God, which is communicated to each of the members and makes them to be a true Body and in the Family of God. "God incarnate draws us all to himself" (*DCE* 14). Hence, eucharistic communion necessarily unites us to all his other members. Eucharistic finality, from the point of view of the baptized person, is effective communion in the Savior's redemptive sacrifice. For the same reason, it is at the same time communion with all the redeemed. In this communion, the twofold commandment of the love of God and the love of neighbor is fulfilled, because that love is received from God and because, in the eucharistic communion, it possesses the most complete form it can have here on earth.

When we receive communion, we receive the Body of Christ who, in giving himself to us, in some way prolongs his Incarnation. It is also true, however, that, in a movement exactly opposite from the kinds of metabolism we observe in nature, we in some fashion become Christ, participating in his eternal life. In the Eucharist, Christ receives us. We become that which we receive: the work accomplished is truly divine.

The Eucharist is presented, as we noted above, as the "Christological and sacramental basis" for a correct understanding of "Jesus' teaching on love" (*DCE* 14). We find in it the twofold movement of love between God and man. In the sacrifice made really present in the Eucharist, the source of all forgiveness is offered to us; in it, each one of us is given the means to respond to the Lord's invitation: "If any one thirst, let him come to me and drink. He who believes in me, as the Scripture has said, 'Out of his heart shall flow rivers of living water'" (Jn 7:37–38).

Bibliography

Derrida, J. 1999. "Le Siècle et le pardon". *Le Monde des débats*. December 1999.

———. 2001. *Foi et savoir: Le Siècle et le pardon*. Paris: Seuil.

Jankélévitch, W. 1966. *La Mauvaise Conscience*. Paris: Aubier Montaigne.

———. 1967. *Le Pardon*. Paris: Aubier Montaigne.

———. 1971. *Pardonner?* (1971) In *L'Imprescriptible. Pardonner? Dans l'honneur et la dignité*. Paris: Seuil, 1996.

———. 1986. *L'Imprescriptible*. Paris: Editions de Seuil.

Laffitte, J. 1995. *Le Pardon transfigure*. Paray-le-Monial: L'Emmanuel/ Desclée.

———. 2003. "Qu'est-ce qu'une anthropologie filiale?" In *Anthropologie filiale*, in the collected proceedings of a colloquium organized by the Congregation for the Doctrine of the Faith in September 2003, now being prepared for publication.

———. 2005. "Esperienza dell'amore e Rivelazione". *Anthropotes* 21/1 (2005): 23–34.

La Potterie, I. de. 1990. "Le Côté transpercé de Jésus". An address delivered at a conference at Paray-le-Monial, France, in October 1990.

Wiesenthal, S. 1969. *Les Fleurs du Soleil*. Paris: Albin Michel.

Wiesel, E. 1979. *Le Procès de Shamgorod tel qu'il se déroula le 25 février 1649*. Paris: Seuil.

The God Who Loves Personally

*Antonio López, F.S.C.B.**

Introduction

Like the Roman centurion at the foot of the Cross (Mt 27:54), those who allow themselves, with a childlike heart, to be known by the gaze of the "one whom they have pierced" (Jn 19:37) cannot help but wonder at how King David's ancient question wells up anew from their own lips: "What is . . . the son of man that you care for him?" (Ps 8:4). The presence of the crucified Lord also prompts them to ask, with an unspeakable and loving respect, for the same answer sought by the disciples of John the Baptist: "Who are you?" (Jn 1:22). Without claiming that the fragile net of human concepts is able to capture and contain the mystery hidden behind these two questions, this brief essay would like to show that Pope Benedict XVI's first encyclical, *Deus Caritas Est* (*DCE*), perceives the path to an answer in the term "person".

Love reveals that the mystery of God and of man is a personal mystery. In his encyclical, the Pope addresses and advances a very rich and controversial term with simplicity and lucidity, seeking to overcome a restricted understanding of the category of "person" as well as a certain embarrassment that seems sometimes to accompany theological reflection's recourse to this concept. Before exploring the depth and richness of this point in the encyclical, I would ask the reader to bear in mind that this essay, divided in three parts, makes no claim to be an exhaustive treatment of the argument or of the Pope's own

* Assistant Professor of Theology, Pontifical John Paul II Institute for Studies on Marriage and Family at The Catholic University of America, Washington, D.C.

account. The first part of the paper addresses what it means for the one God to love man "with a personal love" (*DCE* 9). The second part illustrates that God loves in this way because he, the God of love (1 Jn 4:16), is a "communion" of persons (Ratzinger 1987: 23). Lastly, the paper concludes with some brief remarks indicating that, as the figure of Mary witnesses, God loves man personally because he wishes man to become, as he himself is in his own being, a person within a communion of love, the Church (*DCE* 41–42).

God's Love for Man

In a world in which Nietzsche's voice proclaimed God to be dead, Feuerbach attempted to sketch a God who is in-different to human existence and thus identical to human essence, and many, perhaps still under Spinoza's influence, associate God with "vengeance or even a duty of hatred" (*DCE* 1), it is crucial to see that the task that *Deus Caritas Est* sets for itself is not so much to overcome atheism and religious fanaticism either by proposing a more accurate concept of God or by making all beliefs equal (and thus void of any content). Rather, the encyclical sets out, first, to be a help toward acknowledging that God is an ever-greater "mystery" that makes himself visible in Christ (1 Jn 1:1–4) without, however, being at the disposal of man's capricious reason—*si comprehendis non est Deus* (*DCE* 38; see 17); and second, to be an invitation "to experience love" (*DCE* 39). Hence, *Deus Caritas Est* invites us, not so much to "know" that God is love, but to "understand" that God is a mystery of love. The encyclical wants to assist in our efforts to "remain", to "stand", in wonder and contemplation of this mystery, of this "ground", love, that precedes us and gives itself to us as "truth" and "meaning". This mystery allows itself to be seen only by those who entrust themselves to it—where we are ourselves understood and can finally understand. "Love is the light—and in the end, the only light—that can always illuminate a world grown dim" (*DCE* 39; see Ratzinger 1990: 46–47).

To understand that the love God has for us is personal, it is first necessary to see that "there is no other [God] besides him" (Deut 4:35). Benedict XVI clarifies that God's absolute oneness indicates more than simply "absolute identity". God is not an Aristotelian unmoved mover, always loved and never loving (*Metaphysics* 1071b3–1076a4). He is not the self-contained Plotinian One, an utterly ineffable being of which only a few are granted a "mystical" vision (*Enneads* 6, 8–9). God's oneness is radically transcendent, and yet, precisely because of it, he can make himself present in history without either identifying his own being with the historical process (à la Hegel) or making himself subservient to history. God is one, and, despite all Enlightened reason's best efforts to seal him away within a self-enclosed isolationism, he freely establishes a relationship with man without losing his transcendence. *Non coerceri maximo, contineri tamen a minimo, divinum est.*

Grasping God's method in revealing himself sheds light on the uniqueness of his nature and of his love for mankind. God chooses a particular event in history and reaches out to all the rest only through this concrete point (*DCE* 9; Ratzinger 1987: 153–90). Out of many other peoples, God chose the people of Israel and, through them, showed himself to be, not only one and ever-greater, but also one who loves and cares for his chosen ones. God decided not to be "for" himself alone. He decided to be "for" and "with" his people and to be so "passionately", that is, desiring that his love be reciprocated (*DCE* 10). God's love for his people is personal because it is an "exclusive" and "eternal" love for someone (*DCE* 6). This divine pedagogy could be deemed "unjust" in its seemingly arbitrary preference of some over and against others had God not shown that the "choice" of a particular people is for the sake of all. The universal significance of this choice, however, should not be reductively interpreted in terms of progressive egalitarianism, as though God's care for all, to whom he reaches out through the particular, would relativize and ultimately nullify the choice of that very particular. Instead, God himself teaches that this choice is to be seen as an expression of love and not of power. Only love, in fact, can demonstrate the harmonious but dramatic balance between the universality and particularity. Through their relationship with the God who is love, the people of Israel were brought to see, on the one hand, that their being chosen among all the other peoples also bore a positive meaning for all of human history, and, on the other, that God's choice presupposes the entire cosmos' original vocation to existence (Ratzinger 2005b, 90–92). The one, ever-greater, and personal love is not only the one who takes care of his people throughout history; much more, he is the Creator and the destiny of all being and history.

We can understand how Israel's awareness of God's being "for" them, along with their conception of their own identity, moved forward from the covenant to the further realization that God is Creator if we briefly look at the dynamic of human love. True love is nothing other than the radical and unconditional Yes pronounced to the presence and existence of the beloved. This exclusivity, however, does not consist in the affirmation of the beloved over and against others. The "exclusive" preference for the beloved is true only inasmuch as it seeks and loves others and the world through the beloved. At the same time, the Yes to the beloved would fall short if it could not rest in being's primordial goodness; that is, one can say to the beloved, "It is good that you exist", only because that person's being is good. We can say Yes to another because, ultimately, being in itself is good. Thus the lover's Yes to the beloved presupposes a prior, grounding Yes, which is both the wellspring of the human Yes and the guarantor of the fulfillment of the promise of eternity that forms part of human love (*DCE* 6). Human love without a Creator lacks its ultimate ground. In a similar way, then, Israel realized that God's covenant with them, his being-for them, implied that he, who alone is, loved the world into existence.

The connection between covenant and creation allows one to see that God's love is "personal" not only because he chooses and remains faithful to someone, but because God creates, that is, calls, man to be in relationship with him. If this is so, then "person" is not a synonym for "individual". It is instead a theological category and entails the ontological constitution of the subject: the person is called into existence (created), to an existence whose logic develops as a dramatic relationship with God. That God's love is universal and particular, exclusive and eternal, that it creates and seeks a finite person, indicates, then, that his love is that of a personal being who, as the Psalms teach us, desires to be addressed by the personal pronoun "you". A God who loves in this way cannot but be a person himself. This is not, of course, because he is *causa sui* or because he is in relation to the cosmos. As we shall see later, he is a person because relationship is internal to him.

In keeping with this understanding of God's pedagogy, *Deus Caritas Est* adopts a nuptial imagery that allows a bold but apt description of God's love for mankind as erotic (*DCE* 9) and agapic (*DCE* 10). It is erotic in that he creates and continuously "seeks" us. Availing ourselves of the full, positive meaning of *érōs* allows us to say that God not only seeks mankind, but he seeks unity with mankind—a unity that fully respects and preserves the difference between us. This first dimension of divine love can be seen as one of the elements behind the rationale for both the Incarnation of the Logos and the eschatological participation of man in God, the communion of saints. This dimension is one that could easily lead to a misunderstanding—an assumption about God's dependence upon creation. What prevents this misunderstanding is the equal affirmation that God's love is at the same time totally agapic. God's love is *agápē* because God loves man "in a completely gratuitous manner", for his own sake and, more radically, because he "forgives" us (*DCE* 10). The Logos "emptied himself, taking the form of a servant", and became man (Phil 2:7), seeking to redeem "a suffering and lost humanity" (*DCE* 12).

The Pope provocatively states that God's willingness to give everything to man (Rom 8:32) who had rejected his friendship is so "passionate" that his search for us mysteriously "turns God against himself" (*DCE* 10). Christ dies on the Cross, where he cries out to the Father and sends the Spirit to restore the friendship between man and God (Jn 15:15). Hegel once said that a love that fails to measure up to death lacks ultimate seriousness (Hegel 1998: 219–22). Nevertheless, unlike Hegel, for whom the absolute spirit dies on the Cross in order to become itself, for Benedict XVI, God's "turning against himself" does not refer to a diremption or fragmentation in God's essence, according to which God would contradict his own original plan or, more radically, his very self. It is the question that the incarnate Logos asked the Father on the Cross, "Why have you forsaken me?" (Mk 15:34), that seems to create an insurmountable distance ("against himself") between the two. This would truly be the case if it were not for the fact that this distance from the Father, a distance so great that no sinner will ever know it, is held within that greater unity—"Father, into your hands I commit my spirit" (Lk 23:46)—which the Spirit confirms (Jn 19:30). The "turning against himself" refers to the historical event of the Cross, which Christ embraced without being determined either by man's sin or by any sort of internal negative process of absolute spirit's self-determination (Hegel). The Cross is, in fact, "the culmination of that turning of God against himself in which he gives himself in order to raise man up and save him" (*DCE* 12); it is "the gesture of love that gives all—... the true and final feast of reconciliation" (Ratzinger 1990a: 218).

In order to advance an answer to the delicate question of the relation between God's passionate love for man and his death on the Cross, it is necessary to consider the bond between personal love and truth as it is revealed in the Cross. God is gift (*Dominum et Vivificantem* 10). He gives himself to us because he created us free and redeems us gratuitously. If the forgiveness offered by divine *agápē* were just a dismissal of man's evil, if, in other terms, it were logically opposed to divine wrath, then, instead of showing the "path ... to true humanism" (*DCE* 9), the Cross would do away with man's freedom and reduce history to tragic irrelevance. The Cross seems utter "folly" only when one loses sight of the relationship between love and truth. Forgiveness uncovers man's deep-seated lie and renews man. It is the restoration of the truth of man as a gift given to itself and called to live a loving, personal relationship with God. God's agapic love for us thus "requires [both] the Cross of the Son and ... our conversion" (Ratzinger 2005b: 95).

God's personal love and the offer of himself reconstitute the human person, that is, they change and transfigure man. The relationship between God and man is a "personal" one, not because it is "private", but because love requires a free interlocutor. God created us free so that we might possess the good that we are created to choose. Christ's eucharistic sacrifice on the Cross then purifies human erotic love by removing its egotistic self-centeredness and by transfiguring our presumptuous endeavors to save ourselves into the agapic being-for the human and divine other (*DCE* 7). It is only by turning to God himself, however, that we can fully perceive why being "person" means being-for and being-with another and why other-centeredness and service are the measure of true personal love.

A Communion of Persons

"When Jesus speaks in his parables", he does not simply give examples. The parables "constitute an explanation of his very being and activity" (*DCE* 12). Looking at Christ's words and deeds, the Pope tells us, we are granted access to God's being. In expressing what we are allowed to see of God, however, we have to resist the temptation of searching for an adequate "concept" of God that could, in principle, synthesize all the different aspects of the Godhead that human reason, on its own, can only juxtapose; it is incapable of integrating them into a greater, all-encompassing unity. Christ is the only way to God's eternal life. The contemplation of the "Pierced One" (*DCE* 12; 19; 39; and Ratzinger 1986) allows Pope Benedict XVI to formulate one of his most fundamental theological and anthropological insights: God's personhood is sheer relation, gift. In fact, in contrast to any other understanding of God, in Christian revelation we have been allowed to see that "the highest unity there is—the unity of God—is not a unity of something inseparable and indistinguishable; rather, it is a unity in the mode of communion—the unity that love creates and love is" (Ratzinger 2005a: 81). The one God, then, exemplifies "ecstasy, a complete going-out-from himself". In Christ, it has been revealed that "the ground of being is *communio*" (Ratzinger 1987: 22–23).

We do not need to rehearse here the recent debate regarding the use of this concept. It suffices for our purposes to note, first, that *communio* here does not simply mean, as it did for the Cappadocian Fathers, one essence that is shared by the three Persons and, second, that the use of the term *communio* does not need to be seen in opposition to the so-called intrapersonal models of the Trinity. *Communio*, as Balthasar suggests, indicates that God is one eternal essence that is both "co-extensive with the event of the eternal processions" and "concomitantly determined by the unrepeatably unique participation of Father, Son, and Spirit in this event" (Balthasar 2004: 137; ibid. 1988; López 2005).

In fact, looking at the person of Christ with the help of St. John's Gospel, three decisive aspects emerge to indicate that his being is total relation, eucharistic gift, and that God is a communion of Persons in the way just mentioned. They are: (1) Christ is the "Son" of the Father,

(2) the one who is "sent" to redeem mankind by giving his life to the end on the Cross for man, (3) and the Logos. By calling God "Father" with the familiar term "Abba" (Mk 14:36), Christ proves that he is not in the same creaturely dependence on God as man is. Thus, there is in God a primordial origin, which, however, is not first complete in itself and then gives itself. His Person "*is* the act of begetting, of giving oneself, of streaming forth. It is identical with the act of giving. Only as this act is it person, and therefore it is not the giver but the act of giving" (Ratzinger 1990a: 132). The way of being of this origin, *fons et origo totius divinitatis*, is in his being-for another. The fullness of love, then, is always coupled with an absolute poverty, not in the sense of lacking something, but in the sense of that "law of fullness" according to which a thing is itself only inasmuch as it gives all of itself to the other (Ratzinger 1990a: 193–98; Ulrich 1999: 122–43).

If the Father's being is that of being-for the other, the Son's is nothing but the eternal coming-from and being-for the Father. The Son does not consider what the Father gives him to be his own property; there is no room for anything private. Since there is nothing in the Son that is not relative to the Father, he is one with the Father. "Son" in fact indicates the totality of the union between the Father and the Son. Sheer relation is sheer unity, that is, an always-new communion in which the difference is always preserved. The mystery of the Trinity shows that, paradoxically, the greater the unity, the greater the difference, and vice versa. This mystery is what Jesus Christ indicates when he says both, "the Son can do nothing of his own accord" (Jn 5:19), and, "I and the Father are one" (Jn 10:30).

We said earlier that love is saying Yes to another and that the affirmation of the other's goodness rested in the original goodness of creation and being, in God's Yes to man and to creation. Now we are able to see that this divine Yes to human existence, which undergirds the exchange of Yeses between men, is rooted in an eternal, ever-new Yes in God. God's desiring not to exist for himself alone, prior to any reference to a creative act, points to the immemorial decision of the generation of the Son and the procession of the Holy Spirit. This affirmation in God means, on the one hand, that the Father and the Son are the two poles of a relation that has an eternal existence and, on the other hand, that the generation of the Son is also the positing of the Son (Aquinas *De Potentia Dei*, q. 10, a. 3).

The eternal exchange of Yeses in God is freely inserted into history. The Father, moved by love (Jn 3:16), sends the Son (Jn 6:44), who, in turn, empties himself to take the form of the servant (Phil 2:7) to redeem man (*DCE* 17). In the form of a servant, Christ presents himself as the "sent one" (Jn 17:23), that is to say, as the one who is eternally loved and generated by the Father. It is important not to reduce Christ's self-awareness of being the sent-one to an action or a mission that he performs. Christ is not one more prophet to whom God entrusted a specific mission. The awareness of his mission concerns his very being. In Christ it is not possible to distinguish his office from his person. There is no disinterested "man Jesus" standing behind the work of Jesus. Contrary to the situation of human beings, who cannot give themselves completely in what they say or do because they are not the origin of their own being, Christ's work is his "self" and his "self" is his work.

What this means, then, is that his work is not just a "doing" that ultimately remains extrinsic to his person but is the very gift of his entire self to humanity (Jn 12:20–28). The eucharistic sacrifice is, above all, the gift of his very self to us. His being, then, is sheer *actualitas* of "from" and "for" (Ratzinger 1990: 170). It is this coincidence between the mission of the Son and his eternal procession (*STh* I, 43) that undergirds Christ's action, not only in the sense that it is its theological ground, but because, in a deeper way, it illustrates that when Christ forgives sins, he is reintroducing man into the never-ending dialogue of love between the Father and the Son. Forgiveness needs to be viewed from the mystery of Christ's Transfiguration: it is the transformation and fulfillment of all that is in man. Christ's self-presentation as the "sent one" is yet another confirmation that Christ's eternal being, his person, is "from" and "for". Christ reveals that the personal character of God comes from the fact that his being is "absolute openness without reservation, ... relatedness and hence ... unity" (Ratzinger 1990a: 136).

The third moment that serves as a window into an understanding of how divine personhood is total relativity and union is the Johannine use of the Greek term *logos*. In St. John's Gospel, however, Christ is understood, not so much in terms of "intelligence" (*ratio*), but in terms of "word" (*verbum*). It is true that Christ is the hermeneutical principle of reality; but only because in him, the Logos, the Father speaks himself and all of the cosmos (*DCE* 10). The meaning of reality that he discloses here stems from the fact that he himself is the Word. Undoubtedly, Christ's message was uttered in words. But the characterization of Christ as the Word, and not only as the one who comes bearing a message, intends to show the mystery of his divine personality through the coincidence of person, work, and word. John's Gospel "is, as it were, the thorough reading of the words of Jesus from the angle of the person and of the person from the words" (Ratzinger 1990a: 152–53). What matters is to see that the Word is the personal reality of Jesus Christ inasmuch as he is eternally uttered by the Father. A "word" is "essentially from someone else and toward someone else; word is existence that is completely path and openness" (Ratzinger 1990b: 446). If this is the case, then the wisdom that nourishes man is the participation of the entire human being in the eucharistic "dynamic of self-giving" of the Logos (*DCE* 13). Christ's gift of himself is thus the hermeneutical key to both the cosmos and God.

The dynamic of gift, of being-from, -with, and -for the Father that we have discussed would remain incomplete or threaten to collapse into a monadic identity if the Father and the Son were not "for" the other in yet a third Person, the Holy Spirit. The affirmation of the existence of the third is not required by logical necessity, as in Hegel, but rather by faithfulness to Christ's self-revelation and gift of himself. The Spirit within God brings the dyad of Father and Son into unity without dissolving the reciprocation of love into a monadic exchange. The Holy Spirit, then, "is the unity which God gives himself" (Ratzinger 1998: 327), a unity that preserves the (theological) difference and secures the infinity of love. As Augustine already intuited, it is in the Person of the Holy Spirit that union and relation in God—the being-for, -from, and -with of the Divine Persons—is best understood in terms of *communio*: three Persons who are one divine essence, and one essence that only exists in three Persons who are themselves only insofar as each gives himself to the other. In the Holy Spirit, the Father and the Son give themselves back to one another. He is the Person in whom God abides in himself and through whom

God gives himself to himself; he is the Person in whom God becomes gift. Because of this, he is also the eternal fruitfulness of the Father and the Son, which can be bestowed gratuitously to man. The gift of the Spirit is the gift of divine communion. Thus it becomes clear that the circumincession of the Divine Persons is their reciprocal "being" the space where the others are; it is the triune unity in which each one is totally for and with the others.

Before I indicate the implications for man that arise from understanding "person" within the communion of love that God is, I would like to highlight the significance of this approach. This is, without a doubt, one of the greatest fruits that Vatican II has given to theological reflection and also a path that requires further and careful development. To say that person is not a self-enclosed substance, but the phenomenon of complete relativity, means upholding a radically dynamic understanding of being as *communio*. The Divine Persons are eternally for and with each other. Relation is not what "comes after" substance; it is the way in which the most excellent being, that is, person, is. God's being is relation, and relation of donation. To affirm that the identity of God's essence must be held together with the way this essence is itself takes the classical understanding of "person" as subsisting relation a step farther and affects the definition of person *tout court*. This insight of person understood in terms of relation governs all of the Pope's thought. If "person as relation" were applicable only to God, it would be a "theological exception" and Christ would simply be "a unique ontological exception" (Ratzinger 1990b: 445). If this were the case, the richness of the understanding of person deriving from God as a communion of love would be lost. Without reducing "person" to a univocal concept, it remains now to see how this theological concept of person illumines the mystery of the human person.

Anima Ecclesiastica

The doctrine of the Trinity outlined in the previous section is not an abstract elucidation of the concept of Love. This doctrine is the tradition's expression of the awareness of the truth regarding the mystery of God, to which the Spirit of truth continuously guides the Church.

This revealed truth, according to which God is a communion of Love, sheds a precious light on the nature of man and of reality. Christ not only reveals God to man, he reveals man to himself. I said earlier that God's sacrificial death purifies human erotic love and, without eliminating the dimension of desire for unity, leads it to become agapic love, that is, love seeking the other for the other's own sake. *Agápē* is the truth of *érōs*. The reflection on the personal nature of divine love enables us now to see that this being other-centered is not simply a pious exercise put forth by those who cannot manage to be self-sufficient. It regards the person's very being. The circumincession of the Divine Persons points to this mystery in which one person is the space where another exists, in total unity and total (theological) difference.

If this mystery, as claimed, also indicates the direction of all personal being, then the archetype of the human person is not the hero but the saint; that is, the one whose life no longer revolves around self but around Christ. The saint is the one who knows and experiences that true love of self comes with total belonging to that Other who has given himself for him. If Christ opens the path to a new humanism, the saint is the human person par excellence. *Deus Caritas Est* is a powerful witness to the need to move beyond both a Pelagian or moralistic anthropology and an anti-cultural and spiritualistic understanding of sanctity, in order to rediscover that Christianity is the fulfillment of one's own humanity.

The Virgin Mary is in this regard the paradigm of true humanity. In her, one learns that existing as a person consists in both thankfulness (*Magnificat*) and service. The *Magnificat*, the Pope tells us, represents Mary's fundamental decision: "not setting herself at the center, but leaving space for God, who is encountered both in prayer and in the service of neighbor" (*DCE* 41). Thankfulness for the gifts received (herself and God's love) elicits in her an obedient gratitude that places her person at the service of the other, even "after death" (*DCE* 42). "Service", an unpleasant word to contemporary ears, indicates before all else the total availability to friendship with Christ (Jn 15:15). Being at the disposal of others and of Christ, however, does not consist in giving everything but, rather, in allowing Christ to take everything. In this way one grows, like Mary, speaking, thinking, and willing in and with the Word, into the full stature of one's humanity (*DCE* 41).

This radical being other-centered is not an individualistic endeavor. The being-for proper to person is, in an analogous way to the Trinity, being part of a communion. The saint, both the great saints recognized by the Church (*DCE* 40) and all those who live from the gift of Christ's Body and Blood, is himself only in his being with others. The Eucharist, perennial memorial of Christ's self-oblation, continuously draws man out of himself toward Christ and, "thus, towards unity with all Christians" (*DCE* 14; De Lubac 1999). This unity to which the Christian belongs is the Church, a communion of love that can be perceived in the birth both of a new mentality and of a new way of being with the other, of being at the service of the other—a culture of love, as our dear late Pope liked to describe it (*EV* 101). The human person, in receiving self and the other, is made responsible for the other's destiny. We carry the wounds and the joys of the other within ourselves and bring them in Christ through the Spirit to the Father (De Lubac 1988). It is through the communion of the Church that God wishes to save all, to make us become "persons" (Ratzinger 1991). In living out what we are and what we are called to be, the communion of saints, which is still *in via*, becomes the marvelous witness of the beauty to which the human person is called, *anima ecclesiastica*.

Bibliography

Balthasar, H. U. von. 1988. *Theo-Drama: Theological Dramatic Theory.* Vol. 5: *The Last Act.* San Francisco: Ignatius Press.

———. 2004. *Theo-Logic: Theological Logical Theory.* Vol. 2: *Truth of God.* San Francisco: Ignatius Press.

De Lubac, H. 1988. *Catholicism: Christ and the Common Destiny of Man.* San Francisco: Ignatius Press.

———. 1999. *The Splendor of the Church.* San Francisco: Ignatius Press.

Hegel, G. W. F. 1998. *Lectures on the Philosophy of Religion.* Vol. 3: *The Consummate Religion.* Berkeley, Calif.: University of California Press.

López, A. 2005. "Eternal Happening: God as an Event of Love". *Communio* 32 no. 2: 214–45.

Pieper, J. 1997. *Faith, Hope, Love*. San Francisco: Ignatius Press.

Ratzinger, J. 1983. *Daughter Zion*. San Francisco: Ignatius Press.

————. 1986. *Behold the Pierced One: An Approach to Spiritual Christology*. San Francisco: Ignatius Press.

————. 1987. *Principles of Catholic Theology: Building Stones for a Fundamental Theology*. San Francisco: Ignatius Press.

————. 1990a. *Introduction to Christianity*. San Francisco: Ignatius Press.

————. 1990b. "Concerning the Notion of Person in Theology". *Communio* 17, no. 3: 439–54 RT.

————. 1991. *Called to Communion: Understanding the Church Today*. San Francisco: Ignatius Press.

————. 1998. "The Holy Spirit as *Communio*: Concerning the Relationship of Pneumatology and Spirituality in Augustine". *Communio* 25, no. 2: 324–39.

————. 2003. *God Is Near Us: The Eucharist, the Heart of Life*. San Francisco: Ignatius Press.

————. 2004. *Truth and Tolerance: Christian Belief and World Religions*. San Francisco: Ignatius Press.

————. 2005a. *Pilgrim Fellowship of Faith: The Church as Communion*. San Francisco: Ignatius Press.

————. 2005b. *The Yes of Jesus Christ: Spiritual Exercises in Faith, Hope, and Love*. New York: Crossroad.

Ulrich, F. 1999. *Leben in der Einheit von Leben und Tod*. Freiburg: Johannes Verlag.

The Original Source of Love: The Pierced Heart

*Juan de Dios Larrú** *

Introduction: The Path toward Original Love

"If you see charity, you see the Trinity" (Augustine, *De Trinitate* 8.8; *CCL* 50, 287). St. Augustine's sentence, which is intimately bound to man, the trinitarian mystery, and the gift of charity, is found at the heart of the encyclical *Deus Caritas Est*, established like a bond of union between the two hemistiches of the diptych that they make up. Understanding the correspondence and unity of the two parts of the document is essential for discovering the encyclical's ultimate meaning. The verse from the First Letter of St. John with which the encyclical opens already points to the changing and dynamic relationship between God and man by the bond of charity through the eternal Word. This endurance, this durability in time, is known precisely of charity as a nexus of union that implies the mutual endurance of those who wish to be united. According to the Bishop of Hippo, *agápē*, which joins persons to one another and to God, is found in close relationship with the Holy Spirit (Granados 2002). Augustine locates the key of this affirmation in Scripture, more specifically in the Gospel and the First Letter of St. John. The Holy Spirit's work is precisely to bring about, to make this endurance of charity possible.

That is why Augustine is going to match the verse that begins the encyclical, "God is love, and he who abides in love abides in God,

* Assistant Professor of Fundamental Moral Theology, Pontifical John Paul II Institute for Studies on Marriage and Family, Spanish session, Valencia. Assistant Professor of Ethics, Facultad de Teología San Dámaso, Madrid.

and God abides in him" (1 Jn 4:16) to the above-mentioned sentence when he affirms: "But one may object: 'I see love and I conceive it in my mind as best I can, and I believe the Scripture when it says: "God is love, and he who abides in love abides in God", but when I see it I do not see the Trinity in it.' But as a matter of fact you do see the Trinity if you see love" (Augustine, *De Trinitate* 8.8; *CCL* 50, 287).

With this the Bishop of Hippo points to the fact that God, in his unfathomable mystery, is not a direct object of our knowledge. However, this does not mean that he is totally inaccessible. The Augustinian intuition is that the love recorded in the human soul is the path that leads us to God. Knowledge of love, however, is not sufficient unless, when reflecting on love, we also discover the Trinity. To know God, it is more important to know how to love than just to know love. The person who loves another knows that other in an original way. If we know him in the measure that we love him, then love becomes a singular source of knowing. This circularity between love and knowing is expressed by St. Gregory the Great in the elegantly concise formula: "When we love the higher than heavenly things of which we have heard, we already know the things loved, because that love itself is knowledge" (*ipse amor notitia est*) (Gregory the Great, *Homiliae in Evangelia*, homily 27; *CCL* 141, 232; Catry 1975).

For the encyclical, charity, found at the heart, at the center of the Christian faith, constitutes the keystone to understanding simultaneously who God is (the image of God) as well as who we are (the image of man) and our path toward God (*DCE* 4).

To situate properly the intrinsic relationship between the love of God and love of neighbor, it is necessary to attend to what John Paul II termed "the mystery of man's original innocence" (John Paul II 1997: 66). The importance of going back to original innocence is rooted in discovering that divine charity does not come from any other previous reality. The absolute precedence of divine love makes all that exists come to be. Gratuity and the unconditional nature of God's creating love allow us to go deeper into the meaning of St. John's affirmation, according to which God has loved us first (1 Jn 4:10) and continues loving us first. This original love, God's *érōs*, is not solely a primordial cosmic force; rather, it is the creative love that is directed, before all else, to human beings as man and woman. They are created to love and be loved; herein lies the fundamental and innate vocation of every human being (*FC* 11).

St. Augustine wonderfully described the path of seeking out original love as a pilgrimage on the interior path and at the same time on the path toward the heights of transcendence (*intimior intimo meo et superior summo meo*) (Augustine, *Confessions* 3, 6, 11; *CCL* 27, 32). The mystery of original innocence remains hidden from man, veiled to his eyes, and therefore does not allow him to search for it. In St. Augustine, desire is presented in the symbol of the experience of thirst (Debbasch 2001: 4–75). The centrality of desire in contemporary Western societies is obvious. When the relation of the one desiring and the object desired appears in an external form, however, the satisfaction of the desire takes the form of a consumption that feeds on its constant repetition. The phenomenon of consumerism, the repeated and insatiable consumption of material goods, significantly affects human sexuality. The pansexual culture that reduces sexuality to genitality, eroticizing and converting it into a product for consumption, is a cultural challenge for evangelization. In order to overcome this reduction, it is necessary to respond to the paradox of desire, of *érōs*, which is impossible to satisfy fully or extinguish. Plato already knew this ambiguity of *érōs* which he conceived as the son of a god (*poros*) and a mortal (*penía*) (Plato, *Symposium* 199c–212b).

For Augustine, the desire for happiness becomes a desire for salvation because of its ties to loving desire in those who discover that God not only calls them but loves them profoundly. That is why the reality of desire places them in intimate connection with prayer: to pray is to perfect desire. In the collection of poems *Roman Triptych*, John Paul II, following in Augustine's footsteps, formulates longing desire in this beautiful way: "Let me wet my lips in spring water" (John Paul II 2003). The Augustinian image of desire as the thirst of the soul (Augustine, *Enarratio in Psalmum* 42, 5; *CCL* 39, 796) evokes Psalm 42, which has an obvious baptismal character. The desire for salvation urges us to look for this living water that is capable of quenching the thirst of love. God gives us what we yearn for in baptism as the first gift, as the most beautiful and magnificent of his gifts. This is the great intuition that the saint from Hippo will live during his conversion experience and that, later, Thomas Aquinas will masterfully formulate this way in his more unifying vision of love: "amor praecedit desiderium" (Thomas Aquinas, *STh* I–II, 25, 2, resp.; Melina 1999). This precedence of love directs desire toward its fullness, redeeming its insatiability and transforming it into hope.

In effect, if desire is directed toward a transcendent, transforming future, because it ultimately rests in the desire for a happy eternal life, so for Augustine recollection, the recognition of desire's dispersion, also guides it to a transcendent and primordial past. This movement that memory makes toward the mystery of original innocence is not governed by a yearning love but rather by the "love of Your love", which is not and could not be the object of desire (Augustine, *Confessions* 11, 1; *CCL* 27, 18).

Consequently, life is not a theater in which each chooses, before entering, which role he wants to play. Finding ourselves in a constitutive loving relationship with our Creator makes us grateful for all we have received, beginning with the gift of life. This gratitude becomes the very first form of human love (Schwarz 1968; Von Hildebrand 1980). We gratefully recognize the original source of our happiness— that we are loved by God. The recognition of the gifts we have received, which implies gratitude, is profoundly tied to the virtue of humility. In effect, grateful persons are aware of the fact that they are beggars before God. The close relationship between humility and charity, which has a clearly christological foundation, is a key aspect of Augustinian morality. Christ is the master of humility; this is why only the humble can traverse the path of charity (Augustine, *Enarratio in Psalmum* 141, 7; *CCL* 40, 2050; *In Iohannis Evangelium Tractatus*, pro.: *PL* 35, 1977). The encyclical relates humility ("which accepts God's mystery and trusts him even at times of darkness" *DCE* 39) and patience ("which continues to do good even in the face of apparent failure" *DCE* 39) to the theological virtue of hope, which in turn is united with faith and charity. In this way, the virtues appear in their intimate, mutual connection with the theological virtues as well as with the moral virtues. A virtuous person's integrity has its source in Christ's heart. He is the source of all virtues. Kenosis, the emptying and privations of the Lord, has become for us the source of our virtuous habits (*héxeis*) (Maximus the Confessor, *Quaestiones et Dubia*, q. 1, 12; *CCG* 10, 143–44). In the exchange and reciprocity of friendship, Christ invites us to make progress in the virtues that culminate in charity, since when we do not live in genuine love we take refuge in lesser loves.

In this context we can better understand the encyclical's affirmation that love is not only a "commandment" but the answer to the gift of love with which God draws near to us (*DCE* 1). Love can be commanded, ordered, because first it is offered, given (*DCE* 14). In this regard, "Saint Augustine asks: 'Does love bring about the keeping of the commandments, or does the keeping of the commandments bring about love?' And he answers: 'But who can doubt that love comes first? For the one who does not love has no reason for keeping the commandments'" (*VS* 22; Augustine, *In Iohannis Evangelium Tractatus* 82, 3; *CCL* 36, 533).

The newness of creation that comes from the Christian faith is found in a fundamental gift (Schmitz 1982). God not only is the creative principle of all things—the *logos*, primordial reason—but at the same time is also a lover having all the passion of true love (*DCE* 10). Rationality, divine logic, is nothing other than mutual love. Light and love are one in God's creative love. To love and be loved, to give and to accept a gift, are the moments proper to this logic of reciprocity that is always called to grow because it is asymmetrical. In this sense the encyclical affirms that "anyone who wishes to give love must also receive love as a gift" (*DCE* 7). In this way, mutual love is superior to purely oblative love.

It is also important to note that this logic contemplates difference, not as a synonym of discrimination, but rather as that which makes the unity proper to love possible. From this perspective the encyclical affirms that loving unification is never identified with an anonymous fusion with a principle (*DCE* 10) and that whoever goes toward God does not draw away from men but rather truly draws near to them (*DCE* 42).

The Supreme Manifestation of Trinitarian Love

God has first loved us, and this love becomes present, becomes visible to us in many ways (*DCE* 17). The completion or culmination of the creative task takes time. The revelation of original love is, therefore, an entire progressive and growing history of love by which God desires

to attract man to himself. The apex of this history is found in the
mystery of Christ. The newness of Christianity is focused on the human
face of Christ, on the human heart of Jesus of Nazareth. In this way,
creation and redemption have a delicate and sophisticated integration
in the encyclical.

In Christ and through Christ, God is truly made concrete: Christ
is Emmanuel, God with us. We can say that the function of the
Incarnation is that, in seeing Christ visibly, we can come to love
what is invisible (Gregorian Sacramentary, *In Die Natalis Domini*, prae-
fatio, 110: *PL* 78, 31). As the way, Christ has not only offered us
love but has lived and followed the way first, knocking at the door
of our hearts in many ways to elicit our answer of love and our
discipleship. He makes us feel the Father's love to the point that
whoever sees him sees the Father (Jn 14:9), the mysterious source of
trinitarian love. Our love as an answer to this first love supposes, as
the encyclical affirms, that one does not begin to be Christian because
of ethical will or a great belief, but rather because of the encounter
with a Person (*DCE* 1). God opens an interpersonal relationship in
which our love is always a response to divine charity, that is, a love
of correspondence to the original love that comes from God. The
Father delights in Christ's human action because in it is found the
full response to a loving initiative.

Jesus' humanity is, undoubtedly, the fruit of the Spirit's action.
The Spirit's action in and through Christ affects the Son as incarnate.
God's Spirit works through Jesus in that he is able to be sanctified and
to walk a path in history, in his human nature, that exists only in that
it has been assumed by the Son.

Now, if, on one hand, the Spirit moves Jesus, on the other, Jesus
works in the Spirit in that he is a power that can, for example, expel
demons. In this way, Jesus as the Son made man is not only the place
of the Spirit's presence in the world but is also the principle of his
emanation through his glorification. From the Incarnation to the Resurrection the filial path of Jesus' life as man is completely marked by
the Spirit. Christ lives under his constant influence, or, as St. Basil
affirms, where Christ acts he does so by the Holy Spirit's presence
(Basil the Great, *De Spiritu Sancto* 49: *PG* 32, 157a). This docility to
the Spirit is proof of Christ's divine descent, "for I have come down

from heaven, not to do my own will, but the will of him who sent me" (Jn 6:38; also cf. Jn 5:30).

The Spirit's action in the humanity of Christ consists in a dynamic indwelling of a new operating principle so that the Lord's human will might naturally fulfill the Father's original plan of salvation. The Spirit, instilling his gifts in Jesus' humanity, interiorly impels him to carry out the mission and the work that the Father has entrusted to him. It is clear that Christ received this mission and work as man because only as man could he save and sanctify men in a way "conforming to our nature". In this way, the Holy Spirit's gift that we receive depends on the anointing that the Word made flesh receives in his humanity. The necessity of the mediation of Christ's humanity to fulfill our communion with God thus becomes evident.

In his unpredictable and unprecedented action, God himself in the person of Jesus Christ draws near to man in order to show him the most dramatic and radical form of the mystery of his love. These are not just words but rather the human action of Christ, who gives himself up, both in handing himself over to his disciples and in perpetuating this handing over in the sacrament of the Eucharist. In the Eucharist, the divine gift and human action meet in their most perfect reciprocity. In effect, Christ knows himself to be loved with an ineffable love, living an unceasing and total exchange with the Father. His answer to the Father's love is his bodily surrender for men. In the action of the eucharistic sacrifice he shows us that the gift of love is most fully received when it is fully communicated.

In order to penetrate the meaning of the Augustinian phrase "if you see charity, you see the Trinity" and also, therefore, the encyclical's point of departure, it is necessary to place our gaze upon the pierced side of Christ (Jn 19:37; DCE 12). The Augustinian aphorism can now be reformulated in the following way: "If you see Christ's heart, you see the Trinity." The most profound and most radical truth of God's love can be contemplated in the Cross: "For God so loved the world that he gave his only-begotten Son, that whoever believes in him should not perish but have eternal life" (Jn 3:16). Fixing our gaze upon the Crucified One makes it possible to recognize the Father's plan, the reason why he sent his only begotten Son to the world through the work of the Holy Spirit to redeem man (DCE 19). Now, this

gaze embraces a newness irreducible to the observation of pagan astrolo-
gers or the contemplation of Greek philosophers; Christians do not
look to the past with the melancholy of absence or to the future as an
unreachable ideal; they rather look forward with true hope. This gaze
moves them to act because they feel addressed by Christ's call, Follow
me!, which in the great invitation of Jesus' Heart is expressed as "Come
to me!" (Mt 11:28). "Come and see" is the formula that the disciples
use to communicate their encounter with Christ to others (Jn 1:46).
The answer to this call is fulfilled in our way of following him,
and following Christ means living where Jesus dwells (Ratzinger 2005:
13–31). Only the one who follows Jesus begins to see. In this sense, as
St. Gregory of Nyssa affirms: "To follow God wherever he might lead
is to behold God" (Gregory of Nyssa, *Vitae Moysis* 252: PG 44, 408d).

Fixing our gaze upon the Pierced One allows us to recognize the
plan of the Father who, moved by love (Jn 3:16), sent his only Son
into the world to redeem us. Zechariah's prophecy, to which John
19:37 alludes, begins literally in the first person: "They shall look on
me whom they have pierced" (Zech 12:10, LXX). This accentuates
the personal relationship of all believers with Christ, which has to
bring them to sorrow and the desire of reparation through love.

Dying on the Cross, Jesus "gave up his Spirit" (Jn 19:30) as a
prelude to the Holy Spirit's gift that would be granted after his Resurrection (Jn 20:22). Thus would be fulfilled the promise of the
"rivers of living water" that, emanating from the Spirit, would flow
from within the believers (cf. Jn 7:38–39). In this way, through the
Paschal Mystery, Christ becomes the fountain of living water that
makes the world fruitful. The logic of the overabundance in communication of the gift delivered and received is thus seen: Christ
who has received the Spirit without mediation becomes its source
for all mankind in such a way that we receive the Spirit by means of
Christ. Christ's open Heart is the symbol of what he has become in
the full revelation of trinitarian love and in the original source of all
human love.

In this way, as the encyclical affirms, the Spirit is that inner force
that harmonizes, that attunes the hearts of all believers with the Heart
of Christ and moves them to love their brothers as he has loved them.
This love of Christ reached its fullness when he knelt to wash the feet

of his disciples (cf. Jn 13:1–13) and, above all, when he gave his life for us (cf. Jn 13:1; 15:13; *DCE* 19). The Eucharist generates the communion of the Church, sent to communicate Christ's gift of himself to all men of all times.

It is in Christ's Paschal Mystery that God's *érōs* for man is revealed, in an unprecedented way, to be at the same time *agápē*. God's gratuitous love for man is now shown in a new way as love that forgives, merciful love. Here the encyclical turns to Hosea: "How can I give you up, O Ephraim! How can I hand you over, O Israel! ... My heart recoils within me, my compassion grows warm and tender. I will not execute my fierce anger, I will not again destroy Ephraim; for I am God and not man, the Holy One in your midst" (Hos 11:8–9), which prophetically indicates the mystery of Golgotha (*DCE* 10). Here God's heart is moved by the impulse to mercy, changing the procession of punishment that seems logical at the beginning.

In the Spiritual Exercises preached to the Roman Curia at the beginning of Lent 1983, then-Cardinal Ratzinger commented on this passage from the prophet Hosea: "The mystery of the open heart of the Son, the mystery of the God who in his Son takes upon himself the curse of the law so as to free and to justify his creature, is already outlined in this text. It is no exaggeration to say that these words from the heart of God are a first and important foundation to the devotion to the Sacred Heart" (Ratzinger 1987b: 46).

The symbol of the heart as the center of the intellectual life was a reason for dialogue between the biblical tradition and the pagan philosophies, mainly with the anthropological conception of Platonic origin that located the source of the soul in the head (Pozo 1994). Joseph Cardinal Ratzinger showed the role of the bridge that Stoic ideas offer in this dialogue between the center of the universe, which they called the "heart of the cosmos", and the *pneuma* that resides in the human heart and is the body's sun (Ratzinger 1987a). Both Origen and Augustine (Maxsein 1966), who were influenced by Platonic ideas in many aspects, have traces of Stoic anthropology. According to ideal Stoic morality, however, the person does not have to take his emotions into account in any way. This forgetfulness of emotion reappears in modern morality and, in reaction, unleashes the Romantic Movement. Some contemporary authors have struggled to develop a new synthesis to

recuperate the emotional dimension, avoiding superficial emotional-
ism (Von Hildebrand 1977). In effect, the symbol of the heart points
to the importance of affectivity and its dispositional character in the
dynamism of action. The unifying (symbolic) dimension of affect also
allows a deepening in the relationship between the divine gift of grace
and human action, so that the divine gift animates human action from
within its dynamism. Grace, described in terms of a personal presence, generates an affective union between the lover and the beloved.
Human action is the specific modality for receiving the divine gift
and making it grow. From this perspective, it becomes possible to situate the encyclical's affirmation that places the moment of *agápē* within
the initial *érōs* (*DCE* 9).

Christ's Heart, which reveals the depth of God's love to us, is a
wounded Heart. The detail of the side pierced by the lance is enormously meaningful to St. John the Evangelist. Christ's pierced "side"
(*pleurá*, rib) evokes the passage of Genesis 2:21–23 that narrates how
Eve is formed of Adam. Similarly, the opened side of the New Adam
gives birth to a new creation. The love that Christ reveals to us is not
impassive; it is a love that knows suffering. Christ's Heart, wounded
by the lance, is opened to become the inexhaustible source of love's
vitality. The symbol of the heart is the symbol of the center; from the
side of the New Adam comes forth new life capable of integrating *érōs*
and *agápē*. In the nuptial mystery of Christ, God's way of loving becomes
the measure for human love. In this way, conjugal love as well as virginal love encounter their light and definitive reciprocity in Christ's
gift of self.

Conclusion: A Heart that Sees

In the famous story *The Little Prince*, the fox tells his friend before
departing: "Now here is my secret, a very simple secret: It is only with
the heart that one can see rightly; what is essential is invisible to the
eye" (Saint-Exupéry 2000). The hidden secret, the source of divine
love, is found in the human Heart of Christ. In order to recognize it,
it is necessary to ask, as St. Paul does, "that the God of our Lord Jesus
Christ, the Father of glory, may give you a spirit of wisdom and of
revelation in the knowledge of him, having the eyes of your hearts

enlightened, that you may know what is the hope to which he has called you, what are the riches of his glorious inheritance in the saints" (Eph 1:17–18). The enlightened eyes of our hearts thus become capable of living charity, so that, as the Apostle affirms a little farther on: "Christ may dwell in your hearts through faith; that you, being rooted and grounded in love, may have power to comprehend with all the saints what is the breadth and length and height and depth, and to know the love of Christ which surpasses knowledge, that you may be filled with all the fullness of God" (Eph 3:17–19).

The vision to which St. Augustine invites us in the sentence that begins the second part of the encyclical is completely unique. The Doctor of Grace goes on to explain it in the following passage: "Blessed are the pure in heart, for they will see God (Mt 5:8).... Those who have love see everything at once with the intellect. Live within love and love will live within you; abide in it and it will abide in you" (Augustine, *In Epistolam Iohannis* 7, 10: PL 35, 2034). Faced with the hardness of heart that resistance to the Spirit represents, the "eyedrops" of faith have to purify the heart so that we might come to see God as he is (1 Jn 3:2). The heart's gaze is the gaze of love (*ubi amor, ibi oculus*, say the medieval theologians). This is not, therefore, a partial, superficial vision that banalizes or objectifies what surrounds it, but a synthetic and inclusive gaze capable of penetrating the mystery of unity in difference.

The encyclical points out to us, in this sense, that the Christian plan (which is no other than Jesus' plan) is a "heart which sees" (*DCE* 31), a heart capable of recognizing where love is needed and of acting accordingly, that is, moved permanently by its light. The saints are the paradigm of this heart that sees, since in them the flame of love shines eminently. The Virgin Mary, who gave the world the true Light and who reflects it like the morning star, stands out among them, offering herself to God's call and thus becoming a source of divine goodness. As the encyclical notes at its conclusion, she pours out from the depths of her heart inexhaustible love and in this way shows us what love is and whence it draws its origin and its constantly renewed power (*DCE* 42).

The purpose of Benedict XVI's letter is clearly stated by the author himself: "to speak of the love which God lavishes upon us and which we in turn must share with others" (*DCE* 1). This double and inseparable movement, descending and ascending, comes to be a constant throughout the document. The image of Jacob's ladder and the symbolism that the Church Fathers saw in it is a graphic image of this double movement (*DCE* 7).

Christian life and action are called to be permanently moved and unified by this double activity that has its inspiration in Christ's Heart. The attraction of his person invites us to intimacy with him; the outpouring nature of his saving love sends us forth to announce it and to communicate it to our brothers. The inseparability and mutual reciprocity of these two moments can be reflected in the image of the heart's systolic and diastolic movement. To be loved and to love, vocation and mission, worship and ethics, *érōs* and *agápē* encounter their deepest unity in Jesus Christ, the first and original source of God's love (*DCE* 7).

In this way, Christian charity has its inexhaustible spring in the wood of the Cross from which comes forth never-ending new life. St. Thomas Aquinas, commenting on the verse of Ephesians 3:19 mentioned earlier, affirms:

> At this point it should be realized that it was within Christ's power to choose what type of death he wanted. And since he underwent death out of charity, he chose the death of the cross in which the aforesaid four dimensions are present. The cross-beam has *breadth* and to it his hands were nailed because through charity our good works ought to stretch out even to adversaries: "The Lord brought me forth into a broad place" (Ps 17:20). The trunk of the cross has *length* against which the whole body leans since charity ought to be enduring, thus sustaining and saving man: "He that shall persevere unto the end, he shall be saved" (Mt 10:22). The projection of wood [above the cross-beam], against which the head is thrown back, has *height* since our hope must rise toward the eternal and the divine: "The head of every man is Christ" (1 Cor 11:3). The cross is braced by its *depth* which lies concealed beneath the ground; it is not seen because the depth of the divine love which sustains us is not visible insofar as the plans of predestination, as was said above, are beyond our intelligence. (Thomas Aquinas, *Super Epistolam ad Ephesios* 3, 5; see Thomas Aquinas 1966)

Bibliography

Catry, P. 1975. "Désir et amour de Dieu chez Grégoire le Grand". *Récherches Augustiniennes* 10: 269–303.

Debbasch, H. 2001. *L'Homme de désir: Icône de Dieu.* Paris: Beauchesne.

Granados, J. 2002. "Vides Trinitatem si caritatem vides: Vía del amor y Espíritu Santo en el *De Trinitate* de San Agustín". *Revista Agustiniana* 43: 23–61.

John Paul II. 2003. *The Poetry of John Paul II.* Washington, D.C.: USCCB Publishing.

———. 1997. *The Theology of the Body: Human Love in the Divine Plan.* Boston, Mass.: Pauline Books & Media.

Maxsein, A. 1966. *Philosophia cordis: Das Wesen der Personalität bei Augustinus.* Salzburg: Otto Müller Verlag.

Melina, L. 1999. "Amore, desiderio, e azione". In *Domanda sul bene e domanda su Dio,* edited by Livio Melina and José Noriega, 91–108. Rome: PUL-Mursia.

Plato. 1980. *Symposium.* Translated by Michael Joyce. Princeton, N.J.: Princeton University Press.

Pozo, C. 1994. "Simbología del corazón en la Biblia y en la Tradición cristiana". In *Reino de Cristo,* 1:11–13, 2:11–13, 3:11–13.

Ratzinger, J. 1987a. *Behold the Pierced One.* San Francisco: Ignatius Press.

———. 1987b. *Journey towards Easter: Retreat Given in the Vatican in the Presence of Pope John Paul II.* New York: Crossroad Publishing.

———. 2005. *On the Way to Jesus Christ.* San Francisco: Ignatius Press.

Saint-Exupéry, A. de. 2000. *The Little Prince.* Richard Howard, trans. New York: Harcourt.

Schmitz, K. L. 1982. *The Gift: Creation.* Milwaukee, Wis.: Marquette University Press.

Schwarz, B. 1968. "Über die Dankbarkeit". In *Wirklichkeit der Mitte: Beiträge zu einer Strukturanthropologie, Festgabe für August Vetter,* edited by Johannes Tenzler, 697–704. Freiburg: Karl Alber.

Thomas Aquinas. 1966. *Commentary on Saint Paul's Epistle to the Ephesians.* Albany, N.Y.: Magi Books.

Von Hildebrand, D. 1977. *The Heart: An Analysis of Human and Divine Affectivity.* Chicago: Franciscan Herald Press.

———. 1980. *Über die Dankbarkeit.* St. Ottilien: Eos Verlag.

Eros and Agape:
The Unique Dynamics of Love

*Antonio Prieto**

Introduction

"Érōs, a god for the Ancients, is a problem for the Moderns. The god was winged, charming, and of secondary importance; the problem is serious, complex, and cumbersome" (Rougemont 1996: 11). This affirmation by Denis de Rougemont sums up in a concise and provocative way the panorama of meaning in which the Pope, Benedict XVI, wished to set the vigorous revaluation of human love that he has penned in his encyclical letter *Deus Caritas Est*.

Love, which used to be a secondary god in the context of ancient Greece, was purified and made worthy enough to occupy a privileged place in Christian revelation. Nowadays, however, it has become a complex, widespread, and ambiguous reality that has lost its capacity to illuminate and guide the lives of men. What path should we take to retrieve this love in its original splendor?

The Need for an Interpretation

The first step proposed by the Pope in his encyclical is to clear up the question of terminology. "Today, the term 'love' has become one of the most frequently used and misused of words, a word to which we attach quite different meanings" (*DCE* 2). Within this vast semantic

* Assistant Professor of Dogmatic Theology, Pontifical John Paul II Institute for Studies on Marriage and Family, Spanish session, Madrid. Assistant Professor of Dogmatic Theology, Seminario diocesano San Pelagio, Córdoba, Spain.

field and multiplicity of meanings, it is nevertheless possible to find a fundamental archetype: the love between man and woman, which stands out because of its completeness and because it contains within it the promise of an irresistible happiness (cf. Noriega 2005: 15–89).

This archetype of love, which received the name of *érōs* in the days of classical Greece, is both the starting point and guiding thread of all the reflections in the first part of the encyclical. Nevertheless, the Pope does not restrict the meaning of *érōs* to the confines of Greek culture, nor does he take it to mean only the love between a man and a woman. In a more general manner he presents it as an impulse "which is neither planned nor willed, but somehow imposes itself upon human beings" (*DCE* 3). It is an "intoxication, the overpowering of reason by a 'divine madness'" (*DCE* 4a).

In this manner Benedict XVI indicates a necessary and universal characteristic of *érōs*: that it envelops and transcends man, engaging him totally as he truly is, and even his very destiny, and he applies it to the concrete fact of sexual difference (cf. Zuanazzi 1991: 55). In the true process of falling in love, there is in effect a particular integration of the whole person that does not exclude bodiliness (cf. Giuliodori 2001: 45–55). This characteristic of *érōs* can be found in all cultures and in literature all over the world, containing countless testimonies of impossible love between a man and a woman whose cultural and social differences render such a relationship practically incomprehensible.

However, this general description of an erotic phenomenon places us before its essential ambiguity. If, on the one hand, *érōs* manages to tear us away from the limitations of our existence and allows us to experience supreme happiness (cf. *DCE* 4), on the other, the fact of being beyond reason makes this a phenomenon difficult to interpret, at the mercy of any deviation, which could even turn out to be harmful to human dignity. Love, as simply a phenomenon, is not a justification for action and can lead to the greatest excesses.

It is for this reason that, with such a level of transcendence perceived in the human experience of *érōs*, it ended by being turned into a divinity as the only possible adequate interpretation of it in people's lives. Nevertheless, because of its radical ambiguity, *érōs* the god was looked upon with suspicion when explaining the destiny of mankind and relegated to the sidelines in Homeric mythology (cf. West 1987: 148).

A relationship exists between love and the divine that requires discernment, therefore. As Benedict XVI notes: "Love promises infinity, eternity—a reality far greater and totally other than our everyday existence. Yet we have also seen that the way to attain this goal is not simply by submitting to instinct. Purification and growth in maturity are called for; and these also pass through the path of renunciation" (*DCE* 5).

Logos to the Aid of *Érōs*

From Hesiod and the Orphean cosmogonies onward, the way in which *érōs* was considered in classical culture changed significantly (see Rougemont 1972: 62). The cosmogonic *érōs* was to emerge, no longer a small, winged, playful god, as he used to be portrayed in the most archaic forms of poetry and art, but rather one of those that rank first (*arché*) and govern the destiny of the world (see Zuanazzi 1991: 142). In this way, the divine weight of *érōs* ceases to be solely that of worship and psychology and comes to be associated with the contemplation and admiration of reality (see West 1987: 148; Méndez 1990: 219–28).

It was *logos*, rational effort motivated by admiration of reality, that finally conferred consistency and relevance on *érōs* in the time of ancient Greece and that turned love into an essential element for understanding Western culture. The history of that culture consequently shows that the human experience of love needs reason if it is to find a solid basis in all of human existence and be able to serve as its guide.

As is pointed out in the encyclical *Deus Caritas Est*, anyone who simply allows himself to be dominated by instinct is on the wrong path for love. "Eros, reduced to pure 'sex', has become a commodity, a mere 'thing' to be bought and sold, or rather, man himself becomes a commodity" (*DCE* 5). That is why love needs to be "healed", so that it can attain its true grandeur, and this is the task of *logos* (cf. Solov'ëv 1983: 93).

Thanks to *logos*, in effect, body and sexuality may be integrated into the totality of our existential freedom, so that love may be transformed into the living expression of our whole being and not remain a purely biological phenomenon. Both in the history of mankind as in the conduct of our personal lives, therefore, we see that love needs to be redeemed by *logos*. Love has been a source for reflection in history, and solely because of that has it been given its privileged position as the principle that clarifies human existence (cf. Simonin 1936: 65–72; Noriega 2004: 699–713).

This need for rationality, which is necessary for the survival of love, was the reason why it moved out of the ancient religious sphere that had previously been the context for understanding the erotic phenomenon. That is why the privileged place that love found in Christian revelation emphasizes Christianity's originality among the early, mythical religions. Indeed, Christianity, in order to demonstrate the novelty of its faith, began by entering into a dialogue, not with the religions of the times, but with philosophical reason, endeavoring in this manner to demonstrate its claim to the religion of *Logos*, capable of integrating into itself all that was human (cf. Ratzinger 1996: 110).

The phenomenon of love is at the center of Christianity and therefore receives decisive support from human *logos*, since it is through rational thought that love is directly linked to a metaphysical reality in which good plays the main part. This link with what is good calls for a reasonable discernment of the truth of this love, so that if love departs from the truth of what is good, it begins to disappear and could even turn against man.

The fact that nowadays the rationality of love is questioned and even despised can be connected to the process of marginalization that the Christian faith has suffered since the end of the eighteenth century. Rationality, which has closed itself to faith because it considers it the source of a knowledge that is imperfect and inadequate for science, has also removed love from philosophical reflection (cf. Nussbaum 1990: 336) and interpreted it in a romantic way (cf. Pope 1980: 1–26). Love has thus been reduced to an irrational impulse or sentiment, which might perhaps contain some substance, but whose value is basically emotional.

We are, therefore, able to understand why Benedict XVI should establish the interplay between faith and reason in his encyclical as the frame of reference for understanding the relationship between *érōs* and *agápē*. The Holy Father tackles this relationship, starting with the

distinction mentioned in the Song of Songs between *dodim*, the love
that is still insecure, and *ahabá*, the new love, which presumes the
discovery and seeking of the good of the beloved, with a readiness for
renunciation and self-sacrifice (cf. *DCE* 6).

The philosophical re-appropriation of love proposed by the Pope
in his encyclical, therefore, implies opening up a path of unusual dimension for the encounter between reason and faith. Man needs to "believe"
in love for this love to be able to achieve that role in his life which
the experience of love would appear to reserve for him (cf. Solov'ëv
1983: 132). In other words, the *logos* of *érōs* needs faith as a necessary
element, since the inner workings of every *érōs* contain a promise
of plenitude that is much sought after and can only be received as a
gift. At that point, *logos* opens itself up to faith and the revelation of
new love with the awareness that it is not the final measure of all
reality.

The Phenomenon of Desirability and Wonder in the Presence of the Gift

The above reflection confronts us with the problem of the circularity
that exists between the human experience of love (*érōs*) and the revelation of a new love (*agápē*) passed down by Holy Scripture and the
tradition of the Church. As Benedict XVI frequently points out, these
two concepts of love are contrasted "as 'ascending' love and 'descending' love" (*DCE* 7), and he confirms that it is the descending and
oblative love that is typically Christian, while ascending, covetous, and
possessive love would be typical of non-Christian culture, particularly
Greek culture.

Behind this last reference it is possible to glimpse the binomial
interpretation of *érōs-agápē* of the Swedish pastor Anders Nygren that
led to a heated dispute about love, a dispute that lasted throughout the
twentieth century. Nygren's study shows a tendency to consider the
phenomenon of love in depth from a purely descriptive point of view,
analyzing the different types of love, but without taking the time to
study what love itself actually is (cf. Pérez-Soba 2001: 25). This approach,
which understands different types of love to be irreconcilable terms,
claims to present the division of these various kinds of love as being

the most original synthesis of Christian tradition, although, in Nygren's case, the outright rejection of any possible integration between the different types of love is also the result of an attempt to defend Lutheran doctrine (cf. Dietz 1976: 29).

By describing the movement of *érōs* as being ascending, typical of an egoistic nature focusing on its own interests and trying to achieve satisfaction, Nygren is chiefly attempting to emphasize the movement of *agápē* as being descending so as to defend the supernatural quality of divine revelation (see Nygren 1962: 2:10). From this point of view, *érōs* and *agápē* would be two types of love with nothing in common and which, in mankind and in history, would be found mixed up and even in opposition to each other (see ibid., 1:49).

At the same time, Nygren attacks the Catholic word *caritas*, interpreting it as a symbiosis of the two above-mentioned types of love (see ibid., 1:50) and consequently as a corruption of a genuinely Christian love. It is on this point that he focuses his accusation against St. Thomas Aquinas for being, in his opinion, the theologian who studied charity in the most systematic manner in order to come upon a novel synthesis in the notion of friendship (see ibid., 2:216).

In his encyclical, Benedict XVI highlights the negative consequences and the fallacy of such an affirmation as Nygren's: "Were this antithesis to be taken to extremes, the essence of Christianity would be detached from the vital relations fundamental to human existence and would become a world apart, admirable perhaps, but decisively cut off from the complex fabric of human life" (*DCE* 7).

How can we relate erotic love to agapic love in a suitable way? The encyclical itself indicates the way: "The element of *agape* thus enters into this love, for otherwise *eros* is impoverished and even loses its own nature" (*DCE* 7). This statement completely refutes Nygren's concept of love, because, from this standpoint, it is no longer possible to imprison *érōs* in appetitive desire, of which it could be the noblest expression.

Érōs cannot of course, as the Swedish pastor would have it, be its own measure because all idea of perfection far outstrips mere desire, which is a phenomenon incapable of recognizing its own origin and purpose (cf. Melina 1999: 91–108). To go even farther, it would appear that the purpose of desire would necessarily have to be its own annihilation, since the moment desire has been satisfied it ceases to exist as such. The desire for good, therefore, contains a truth that refers to a principle far beyond self-interest. A truth that can in no way be tainted with selfishness (cf. D'Arcy 1958: 58).

Nygren's concept of desire, finally, is connected with the philo-sophical explanation of *érōs* offered by Plato in the *Symposium*, through the words spoken by Diotima, priestess of Mantinea (201a–204d; cf. Robin 1922). Diotima explains the birth of love as starting from *Poros* (resource) and *Penia* (poverty) and combining the qualities of both in itself. From his mother, *érōs* receives precariousness and need, while from his father he inherits impetuousness and the desire for wisdom. We are therefore speaking about a "dubious" god (Rist 1995: 43), who, nevertheless, is the reason why we stretch out toward Good and Beauty so as to attain the happiness of the gods.

From this point of view it is understandable that any thinking that does not accept the possibility of a love that goes beyond *érōs* is nec-essarily condemned to *aporia*. Erotic love is incapable of giving itself that which is contained in the promise it bears. As Benedict XVI notes, this way of explaining the dynamics of *érōs* found its greatest commentator in Aristotle, who used *érōs* to explain how the unmoved mover of all reality attracts everything to it through love: "The divine power that Aristotle at the height of Greek philosophy sought to grasp through reflection is indeed for every being an object of desire and of love ... but in itself it lacks nothing and does not love: it is solely the object of love" (*DCE* 9).

The limits of this concept of erotic rationality are thus only too clear. A way of thinking that does not accept the possibility of a love that goes beyond *érōs* plunges irredeemably into internal contradic-tion. When the Stagrite defines good as that "which all desire" (*Eth.* I, 1:1094a3), he links it very closely with *érōs* as the beginning of move-ment. However, this statement does not solve the problem because *érōs*, which certainly explains the manner of moving and directing an action, does not lead man to the happiness promised or to his true plenitude.

To reach its perfection, *érōs* needs precisely that which its desire cannot produce: a gift (cf. Ratzinger 2002: 172). There must, there-fore, be openness to an initiative that comes from much farther back than a natural principle and the desire within urges; an openness that leads to a person who loved us first. Having reached this point, we are in a position to understand truly what the divine weight of *érōs* consists of, something that cannot be an intrinsic aspect of erotic love, but must rather be a bonding of the latter with the principle of perfection and can no longer be termed *érōs*.

Érōs, thus, is always awaiting a new kind of love that surpasses it. For this reason, every attempt to make *érōs* an absolute, as happened in the case of mythological divinization, implies a detraction from human dignity because it loses the support of the truth of love (cf. Lewis 2000: 16–17). Using the words of Nygren, whom the Pope echoes, we can affirm that any ascending movement in itself calls for a descending principle, in which is found perfection, taking into account that such descent is not an ontic fall, which would be incapable of explaining perfection, but a communication in goodness.

Amor Concupiscentiae and *Amor Benevolentiae*

In this sense, the pair *amor concupiscentiae—amor benevolentiae* that Benedict XVI cites in parallel with the binomial *érōs-agápē* (cf. DCE 7) allows us to appreciate in a clearer fashion the dynamic unity that exists between possessive love and oblative love and the centrality of the person and interpersonality in the construction of the act of love. In effect, with *amor concupiscentiae* we love the good of what we refer to, with *amor benevolentiae*, as a person. In this way we can understand *amor concupiscentiae* to be an imperfect love and a movement that is contained in *amor benevolentiae* (cf. *Scriptum* III, d. 27, q. 2, a. 1; d. 28, q. un., aa. 1–2; d. 29, q. un., a. 3).

At this point we should remember the paradox of *érōs* that was described earlier, that is, the fact that it is unable to give itself that which its desire is unable to produce: a gift. The same thing happens in possessiveness, which encounters its perfection precisely in the person it calls beloved, a person who must necessarily be "recognized" as a gift and who cannot be turned into an object (cf. Lacroix 1972: 43ff.).

We can therefore note the perspicacity of St. Thomas in his definition of love: "in hoc praecipue consistit amor, quod amans amato bonum velit" (*Contra Gent.*, l. 3, c. 90, 2657), which clearly brings out this fundamental characteristic of love, that of being a single act with two distinct objects: goodness and the beloved (ibid., l. 1, c. 91, 763). This statement implies the consideration of goodness present in the beloved through love, from an ontological perspective, which exceeds the triple Aristotelian division based on the subject's reasons of desirability (cf. *Eth.* II, 3: 1104 b). Thus the possible reduction of the person who is loved to a *bonum* appears (cf. Pérez-Soba 2002: 231–40) as well as a new horizon for understanding different ways of loving.

When a good exists in itself, as in the case of the person, we love it with *amor benevolentiae*, properly and truly, wanting the good for it; whereas, when it is a matter of a good that the beloved possesses, such as knowledge or health, we do not love it for its own sake, but for the sake of the beloved (cf. *Exp. Super libr. Dionys. de div. nom.*, c. 4, lec. 9, 404). This ontological distinction of *bonum* has an anthropological flavor in the loves of providence, conversion, and friendship, which are formed according to the ontological worth of the lovers (cf. ibid., 407).

Among the different ways of loving, friendship is a point of convergence since it is already prefigured in some way in the necessary reciprocity of movement between providence and conversion. Indeed, the Aeropagite's cosmological argument presents providence as an original love, which requires a converted response from its creatures (cf. *De Div. Nom.* IV, 10: PG 3, 708; IV, 13: PG 3, 712; IV, 15: PG 3, 714).

In this way, the dynamism of God's love (*agápē*) and that of human love (*érōs*) may be united, since, in order to achieve an ultimate aim through action, one has to submit to divine providence and the only movement that can make this submission possible is conversion, which is described by St. Thomas as being the fundamental act of freedom (cf. Bouillard 1941: 174ff.). Through the movement of free conversion, man opens himself up to God and prepares to become the object of a new divine intervention.

In this way, St. Thomas manages to separate the supernatural quality of *agápē* from the appetites of natural urges, placing it instead in the mutuality or reciprocity that is established between creation's love of friendship and the conversion of all beings to God, according to their capacity to love rightly.

The Revelation of a New Love: *Agápē*

Starting with the close link indicated by the encyclical between *érōs* and *agápē*, we have thought carefully about the interpersonal dynamism that moves it, pointing out that it is based on communication in goodness. At a later point, Benedict XVI invites us to penetrate the mysterious nature of the new love, which man can receive only as a gift.

To demonstrate the absolute novelty of this "descending" love, the Pope begins with the prayer of *Shema* (Deut 6:4), which contains an incomprehensible idea for Greek culture: creation. "There is only one God, the Creator of heaven and earth, who is thus the God of all. Two facts are significant about this statement: all other gods are not God, and the universe in which we live has its source in God and was created by him" (*DCE* 9).

The idea of creation conceals an original love (cf. Méndez 1990: 325) that is not born of desire for an already existent good but which consists precisely in a communication of that good. What does the encyclical mean, therefore, when it affirms that God's love may be qualified as *érōs* (cf. *DCE* 9)? In order to answer that question, we need to take into account the fact that the Pope was referring, not strictly to creative love, but to that elective, salvific love that led God to seal a covenant with the people of Israel. It is, therefore, a love that supposes human freedom and that implies a call to dialogue.

Moreover, with the reference to Pseudo-Dionysius (cf. *De Div. Nom.* IV, 12: PG 3, 709), Benedict XVI shows that it concerns an erotic love, totally transformed by *agápē*. We need, therefore, to take into account that, by identifying Platonic *érōs* with the *agápē* of the New Testament, the Areopagite is returning to a tradition that goes back to Origen (cf. *Comm. in Cant.*, prol., II, 20–25) but which attains a new perspective therein. If, in Origen, *érōs-agápē* is the movement of human spirit or soul toward the divine *logos* characteristic of the Platonic *érōs*, going from down to up, in Pseudo-Dionysius, instead, the essential characteristic, common to all *érōs*, is no longer an upward movement but an "ecstasy". That is to say, it is a movement with the capacity to go outside oneself and toward others who may be above or below or at the same level, with a movement of conversion, providence, or friendship (cf. Horn 1925: 278–89).

The Pope also refers to the descriptions of the divine *érōs* written by the prophets using the metaphors of betrothal and marriage, where God reveals his exclusive and eternal spousal love, thereby purifying pagan and even Jewish ideas about marriage (cf. *DCE* 11). In this way, the human experience of love assumes the value of a revelation, in which God makes his "new" love manifest, to which he calls us. Vatican Council II actually invites us to understand revelation as being a communication between persons in the framework of friendship (cf. *DV* 2). God resorts to an analogy with human love (*érōs*) to reveal his mysteries in such a way that they may be comprehensible to man and, at the same time, he shows and invites him to live a new love (*agápē*). For this reason we respond to revelation with faith, the personal act of accepting the communication of divine love.

The essence of this "new" love is the giving of oneself, "an ongoing exodus out of the closed inward-looking self towards its liberation through self-giving, and thus towards authentic self-discovery and indeed the discovery of God: 'Whosoever seeks to save his life will lose it . . .' (Lk 17:33)" (*DCE* 6). The preference for Luke's Gospel over and above other parallels for expressing the Christian paradox of the discovery of personal identity through the giving of oneself may be due to the fact that it is the reference text for *Gaudium et Spes* 24, where it states that man "cannot fully find himself except in sincere self-giving". In this way, we return to the idea discussed above concerning the value of divine revelation in human love.

Nevertheless, the giving, which allows us to know ourselves fully, is enfolded in a last gift from God. A special two-way flow is thereby established, both ascending and descending, as a result of the mutual involvement of desire and giving in a process of assimilation. To the extent that we give ourselves, we begin to resemble God, the source of every gift. This is explained by Benedict XVI by referring to Jacob's ladder (cf. Gen 28:12; Jn 1:51), in the interpretation of St. Gregory the Great, who sees in this biblical image the deep union that exists between divine contemplation and helping, in charity, to resolve our neighbors' problems (cf. *DCE* 7; *Regula Pastoralis* II, 5: *SCh* 381, 198).

All of this becomes evident in the mystery of the Eucharist, which perpetuates the "self-giving" of Jesus Christ on the Cross. The Eucharist, which intimately unites us with Jesus' surrender in his body and in his blood, at the same time also has a social character, since union with Christ also supposes union with all the others to whom he gives himself (cf. *DCE* 14). In Christ's Heart and in his eucharistic love, therefore, we have the ultimate source of love whose perfection lies in forgiveness and mercy.

When confronted with sin, God's merciful love appears to place itself in opposition to his justice, which would require punishment. In the Old Testament, the prophets used the metaphor of marriage to illustrate God's passionate love for his people, which leads him to turn against himself in the face of Israel's infidelity. This testimony, however, is no more than a preparation for the revelation of Christ's spousal love (*DCE* 10, 12), which makes the Fatherhood of God present to us and introduces us to the deepest mystery of the Trinity.

Conclusion

The first part of Benedict XVI's encyclical *Deus Caritas Est* makes it possible for us to understand the binomial *érōs-agápē* as two necessary moments in the unique dynamic of love that guides and illuminates the lives of men. Both throughout the history of mankind as in the course of our own personal lives, *érōs* appears as an irresistible experience that contains a promise of eternity that it cannot give to itself. It therefore remains a difficult-to-interpret phenomenon that reaches its peak of perfection in the moment of *agápē*, the essence of which is the giving of oneself. In this way, *érōs* is always waiting to be redeemed by the human *logos*, which shows it the truth of goodness as the only path for achieving its own complete fulfillment.

In the foregoing pages we have been able to show how possessive love and oblative love react with each other in the context of an interpersonal relationship, through communication in goodness. The human *érōs*, therefore, transfigured by *agápē*, has its source in an original love that leads the human *logos* to open itself up to faith and the revelation of a new love. This creative and descending love thus turns itself into a necessary element for the redemption of desire, which reaches its perfection in a movement of conversion.

The human experience of love, in the last analysis, acquires the value of divine revelation that enables man to understand himself and accede to the mystery of intra-trinitarian love. The ultimate source of this love, however, is to be found in the Heart of Christ. In the spousal and merciful love of Christ, in effect, God becomes our neighbor, and in him, love for our neighbor becomes love for God.

Bibliography

Bouillard, H. 1941. *Conversion et grâce chez S. Thomas d'Aquin*. Paris: Aubier.

D'Arcy, M. C. 1958. *La Double Nature de l'amour*. Paris: Aubier.

Dietz, D. 1976. *The Christian Meaning of Love: A Study of the Thought of Anders Nygren*. San Antonio, Tex.: Pontificia Universitas S. Thomae de Urbe.

Gilleman, G. 1950. "Erôs ou Ágape: Comment centrer la conscience chrétienne". *Nouvelle Revue Theologique* 72:3–26.

Gillon, L. B. 1946. "Genèse de la théorie thomiste de l'amour". *Revue Thomiste* 46:322–29.

Giuliodori, C. 2001. *Intelligenza teologica del maschile e del femminile: Problemi e prospettive nella rilettura di H. U. von Balthasar e P. Evdokimov*. Rome: Città Nuova.

Horn, G. 1925. "Amour et extase d'après Denys l'Aréopagite". *Revue d'Ascetique et mystique* 6:278–89.

Lacroix, J. 1972. *Le Personnalisme comme anti-idéologie*. Paris: Presses Universitaires de France.

Lewis, C. S. 2000. *Los cuatro amores*. Madrid: Rialp. [*The Four Loves*. New York: Harcourt, Brace, 1960.]

Melina, L. 1999. "Amore, desiderio ed azione". In *Domanda sul bene e domanda su Dio*, edited by L. Melina and J. Noriega, 91–108. Rome: PUL-Mursia.

Méndez, J. R. 1990. *El amor fundamento de la participación metafísica: Hermenéutica de la "Summa contra Gentiles"*. Buenos Aires: Ed. Sudamericana.

Mouroux, J. 1946. "Eros et Agape". *La Vie intellectuelle* 14:23–38.

Noriega, J. 2004. "Los ojos de la caridad". In *«Camminare nella luce»: Prospettive della teologia morale a partire da Veritatis Splendor*, edited by L. Melina and J. Noriega, 699–713. Rome: Lateran University Press.

_____. 2005. *El destino del eros: Perspectivas de moral sexual*. Madrid: Palabra.

Nussbaum, M. C. 1990. *Love's Knowledge: Essays on Philosophy and Literature*. New York and Oxford: Oxford University Press.

Nygren, A. 1962. *Érôs et Agapè: La Notion chrétienne de l'amour et ses transformations*. 3 vols. Paris: Aubier Montaigne. [*Agape and Eros*. Philadelphia: Westminster Press, 1953.]

Pérez-Soba, J. J. 2001. *«Amor es nombre de persona»: Estudio de la interpersonalidad en el amor en Santo Tomás de Aquino*. Rome: PUL-Mursia.

_____. 2002. "Il *bonum honestum* e la determinazione del bene della persona". In *Il bene e la persona nell'agire*, edited by L. Melina and J. J. Pérez-Soba, 231–40. Rome: Lateran University Press.

Pope, K. S., ed. 1980. *On Love and Loving: Psychological Perspectives on the Nature and Experience of Romantic Love*. San Francisco, Washington, and London: Jossey-Bass.

Ratzinger, J. 1996. *Introducción al Cristianismo*. Salamanca: Sígueme. [*Introduction to Christianity*. Translated by J. R. Foster. San Francisco: Ignatius Press, 2004.]

_____. 2002. *Dios y el mundo: Creer y vivir en nuestra época: una conversación con Peter Seewald*. Barcelona: Círculo de Lectores: Galaxia Gutenberg. [*God and the World: Believing and Living in Our Time: A Conversation with Peter Seewald*. Translated by Henry Taylor. San Francisco: Ignatius Press, 2002.]

Rist, J. M. 1995. *Eros e Psyche: Studi sulla filosofia di Platone, Plotino e Origene*. Milan: Vita e Pensiero. [*Eros and Psyche: Studies in Plato, Plotinus and Origen*. Toronto: University of Toronto Press, 1965.]

Robin, L. 1922. *La Théorie platonicienne de l'Amour*. Paris: Alcan.

Rougemont, D. de. 1972. *L'Amour et l'Occident*. Paris: Éditions 10/18. 1972. [*Love in the Western World*. Princeton, N.J.: Princeton University Press, 1983.]

_____. 1996. *Les Mythes de l'amour*. Paris: Albin Michel.

Scola, A. 1989. *Identidad y diferencia: La relación hombre-mujer*. Madrid: Encuentro.

Simonin, H. D. 1931. "Autour de la solution thomiste du problème de l'amour". *AHDLMA* 6:174–272.

_____. 1936. "La Lumière de l'amour: Essai sur la connaissance affective". *La Vie spirituelle (Supplément)* 46:65–72.

Solov'ëv, V. 1983. *Il significato dell'amore e altri scritti*. Milan: La Casa di Matriona. [*The Meaning of Love*. Herndon, Va.: Lindisfarne Books, 1985.]

Tomás de la Cruz. 1956. *El amor y su fundamento ontológico según Santo Tomás: Estudio previo a la teología de la caridad*. Rome: Pontificium Athenaeum Angelicum de Urbe.

West, M. L. 1987. "Eros". In *The Encyclopedia of Religion*, edited by M. Eliade, 5:148–49. New York and London: Macmillan and Collier Macmillan.

Zuanazzi, G. 1991. *Temi e simboli dell'eros*. Rome: Città Nuova Editrice.

The Covenantal Character of Love: Reflections on *Deus Caritas Est*

*David S. Crawford**

"The Newness of Biblical Faith"

"God is love, and he who abides in love abides in God, and God abides in him" (1 Jn 4:16). So begins Benedict XVI's first encyclical. With this irreducible core of revelation and the Christian faith, the Pope indicates the central theme of the encyclical: the character of divine and human love and, as he puts it, their "intrinsic link" (*DCE* 1). In developing this theme, *Deus Caritas Est* tells us that the "newness of biblical faith is shown chiefly in two elements" (*DCE* 8), each correlating in its own way with the interior meaning of love: "the Christian image of God and the resulting image of mankind and its destiny" (*DCE* 1; cf. *DCE* 8).

Certainly, one of the most remarkable passages in the encyclical occurs in the discussion of the first of these, the "new image of God" (*DCE* 9). There Benedict tells us that God's love can be characterized, following Pseudo-Dionysius, as simultaneously *érōs* and *agápē*. As the Pope succinctly puts it, "God's eros for man is also totally *agape*.... God is the absolute and ultimate source of all being; but this universal principle of creation—the *Logos*, primordial reason—is at the same time a lover with all the passion of a true love" (*DCE* 10). This "passionate" character of God's love seeks out man lost in the ambiguities and half-light of his sin. Where in this tangle of culpable ignorances,

---

*Assistant Professor of Moral Theology and Family Law, Pontifical John Paul II Institute for Studies on Marriage and Family at The Catholic University of America, Washington, D.C.

ambivalences, and obscure histories, ambiguous cultural and social structures, and confused and distorted actions is the real human being?
Thus God is himself a "seeker", and therefore his love is *érōs*.

Even more crucially, however, God's "heart recoils" from abandoning sinful man; his "compassion grows warm and tender" (*DCE*
10, quoting Hos 11:8). Our situation draws out God's mercy, which
in turn elicits a decisive "turn ... against himself" (*DCE* 10: *contra se
ipsum vertat Deum*; *DCE* 12: *contra se vertit Deus*), "his love against his
justice" (*DCE* 10). He shows himself to be wholly self-sacrificial even
in the penetration of his justice with a mercy that goes so far as the
agapic love of the Cross.

This brief commentary will consider this notion of God seeking
and bringing man back into the love that lies at the heart of his covenant. Along with St. John's lapidary proclamation that "God is love",
the notion of "covenant" forms an essential element of the faith. As
Joseph Ratzinger once put it, the idea of covenant constitutes the
"interior thread of Scripture itself"; it seems "somehow to sum up
conclusively the 'essence of Christianity'" (Ratzinger 1995: 635). Concretely, God's own "seeking" and this "turning" in love constitute the
basic structure of the Christian notion of "covenant". In a sense, this
movement describes its very heart.

And the second element, the new "image of man"? As Benedict
also emphasizes, the "newness of biblical faith" not only tells us about
God; it also tells us who we are. It discloses us to ourselves, precisely
in showing us the inner meaning of man's "primordial aspiration" for
God (*DCE* 10; cf. *GS* 22). Without in any way claiming to offer an
exhaustive discussion, this essay will address the consequences of God's
seeking us in his covenant for our understanding of the human love at
the heart of marriage, which is itself a "covenant" (*GS* 48; *CCC* 1601).

The New Image of God

As we have just seen, in Jesus Christ "it is God himself who goes in
search of ... a suffering and lost humanity."

> When Jesus speaks in his parables of the shepherd who goes after
> the lost sheep, of the woman who looks for the lost coin, of the

father who goes to meet and embrace his prodigal son, these are no mere words: they constitute an explanation of his very being and activity (*DCE* 12).

This would seem to constitute a revolutionary feature of Christian faith. While the Greek understanding of love (*érōs*) would highlight man's search for God through contemplation, the Christian God is the one who sets off in search of us. As Benedict tells us, the idea of *érōs* is that it represents this kind of searching love. But in searching out and finding us, in becoming one of us in Christ, God turns and faces himself as man. Certainly the possibility for this second moment is already given in the eternal reality of God-facing-God in the Persons of the Trinity. But now this turning and facing constitutes the center of history (*RH* 1; cf. Balthasar 1994), as the Son "becomes sin" and takes on the guilt of humanity, "so that in him we might become the righteousness of God" (2 Cor 5:21). In the words of the encyclical, God not only turns to face himself, he in fact "turns against himself" (*contra se ipsum vertat Deum*) for the sake of man. If God passionately seeks his lost creatures in his infinite *érōs*, God in Christ even takes onto his shoulders the world's sinful antagonism to God through the agapic love of the Cross. His divine *érōs* for man issues forth in divine *agápē*. God gives, between the Divine Persons of the Trinity, the response, the Yes on behalf of man, and man is confronted in Christ, like the prodigal son, with the justice and mercy of the Father.

The Bible uses nuptial terms to describe this finding and "turning". Our relationship with God is no longer that of simply "standing in God's presence" (*DCE* 13). Now it "becomes union with God through sharing in Jesus' self-gift, sharing in his body and blood" (*DCE* 13). Thus, the Eucharist also becomes crucial to the meaning of Christian love: "The Eucharist draws us into Jesus' act of self-oblation. More than just statically receiving the incarnate *Logos*, we enter into the very dynamic of his self-giving" (*DCE* 13). Moreover, union with Christ is also "union with all those to whom he gives himself" (*DCE* 14). We become one in the eucharistic-ecclesial body. Indeed, Benedict reminds us that *agápē* was also a name for the Eucharist itself: "there God's own *agape* comes to us bodily, in order to continue his work in us and through us" (*DCE* 14).

Christ's "becoming sin", far from leaving us passive or helpless in the face of God's action on our behalf, demands that our own love, our lives and actions, be fitted into and take the form of his own Yes to the Father. His love is therefore the source and meaning of all Christian love, and, against it, all love will finally be measured (*DCE* 11; cf. Balthasar 1983: 27). "Only by keeping in mind this Christological and sacramental basis can we correctly understand Jesus' teaching on love" (*DCE* 14).

Love's Turn in the Old Covenant

The drama of this searching and turning against himself is played out in the evolving understanding of God's covenant with his people, which begins in what appears to be the legalism of God's unilateral imposition of law and ends with the nuptial union of God and man in the Eucharist.

The series of covenantal stories in the Old Testament show an emerging awareness of the meaning of God's covenant with man. Creation itself constituted an original covenantal relationship (cf. Camino 2001: 218–19), one that entailed the relationship of man and woman as such in their mutual relation to God. There are also the covenants with Noah and David, and especially with Abraham. But particularly important is the covenantal relationship set up on Sinai, which is set forth in the form of laws. In an essay on the idea of covenant, Joseph Ratzinger argues that the covenant between Yahweh and his people at first was characterized by a lack of possible reciprocity due to God's utter transcendence. Thus, the translators of the Septuagint translate *b'rith* as *diathéke*, indicating the first meaning of covenant is God's decree. However, there is here a sense of the meaning of covenant as gift. If the covenant is unilateral in the sense that it is God's decree, it is nevertheless, at the same time, God's gift, giving definitive identity to his people (Ratzinger 1995: 637). The Israelites are the ones who have been chosen (this aspect of God's covenant is established in the Abrahamic covenant) and have been taught the living content of this belonging (the Mosaic covenant).

But how, Ratzinger asks, does the nuptial language of the prophets change our understanding of God's covenant with his people? Characterized in terms of marriage, infidelity to the covenant can be described as adultery. Certainly, according to the justice of the relationship, Israel deserved to be cast off as a faithless spouse, having broken the spousal covenant to her Lord. Instead, Yahweh turns aside his anger. But more fundamentally, the prophets' use of the nuptial analogy would seem to import into the idea of God's covenant with his people a kind of bilateral relationship. Certainly, the possibility of a breach under the Mosaic law allowed for the openness to a certain reciprocity. God gives the law, but his people are expected to follow the law in order to stay within the covenant. The relationship here, also, is one of love: "The history of the love-relationship between God and Israel consists, at the deepest level, in the fact that he gives her the *Torah*" (*DCE* 9).

But the prophetic use of nuptial language further develops this reciprocity. It introduces the additional element that God himself is implied in the relationship, insofar as it suggests that the relationship is no longer simply thought of in terms of lord and vassal. Rather, it becomes a kind of "love story" (Ratzinger 1995: 637). It implies God's own commitment and enduring fidelity in the face of faithlessness on the part of Israel. Thus, *Deus Caritas Est* reminds us of the passionate language used by the prophets:

> The Prophets, particularly Hosea and Ezekiel, described God's passion for his people using boldly erotic images. God's relationship with Israel is described using the metaphors of betrothal and marriage. (*DCE* 9)

It is in this light that the encyclical quotes Hosea 11:8–9:

> How can I give you up, O Ephraim! How can I hand you over, O Israel! . . . My heart recoils within me, my compassion grows warm and tender. I will not execute my fierce anger. I will not again destroy Ephraim; for I am God and not man, the Holy One in your midst. (*DCE* 10)

The Realism of the New Covenant

The moment of God "turning against himself", foreshadowed in the nuptial analogy offered by the prophets (*DCE* 10), takes on an extreme

realism in the New Covenant—*é kainé diathéke*—effected in the body
of Christ and his nuptial relationship with the Church. At the Last
Supper, we have a reenactment of the covenant in blood of the Old
Testament. There Moses sprinkles the altar, which substitutes for God,
and the people, "saying 'this is the blood of my covenant which the
Lord has made with you'" (Ratzinger 1995: 641, quoting Ex 24:8).
Christ pours out his own blood for the forgiveness of sins and for the
redemption of the world. According to this form of covenant stem-
ming from Sinai, the parties would enter into a pact or would admit
a stranger into a familial relation through a kind of legal fiction (Ratzinger 1995: 641–42).

By invoking this tradition, Christ is also radicalizing it. The covenant has become not only a fictitious or juridical kinship, but a
covenant written in the body of Christ himself, thus intensifying it
"to an overwhelming realism and simultaneously reveal[ing] a hith-
erto inconceivable depth.... For this sacramental communion of blood,
which has now become possible, unites the recipient with this bodily
man Jesus, and thus with his divine mystery, in a totally concrete and
even physical communion" (Ratzinger 1995: 642). In this way, man is
drawn out of himself, taken up into God's own "mode of being", and
divinized.

The reality of flesh and blood in the New Covenant is therefore
the reality of God's covenant with man brought to its deepest implications. As Benedict tells us, it is here that we find "love in its most
radical form". As he puts it, in "contemplating the pierced side of
Christ ... , we can understand the starting-point of this Encyclical
Letter: 'God is love'.... It is there that this truth can be contemplated. It is from there that our definition of love must begin" (*DCE* 12).

If God's *érōs* seeks out man, it does so in order to unite us with
God in the bodily realism of the New Covenant. In this sense, then,
God's seeking is simultaneous with his "turning against himself" out
of love and compassion for us. If God's turning is inherent in his mercy
for man, it is at the same time an attempt to uncover mankind itself.
Thus, Benedict reminds us that the union between God and man "is
no mere fusion, a sinking into the nameless ocean of the Divine; it is
a unity which creates love, a unity in which both God and man remain
themselves and yet become fully one" (*DCE* 10). Far from being a

loss of mankind, and far from being an acceptance of man's sins, it is a demand that we reemerge in love. It is a reaffirmation of our initial and inherent value. Not only does God seek union with us, he also seeks a recovery of our personal richness and irreplaceable goodness.

The New Image of Man

Now, the discussion of the kenotic character of God's love is preceded in the encyclical by a rather rich discussion of human love as such, particularly in relation to marriage. Indeed, the encyclical begins by telling us that the foundation of love, its "epitome" (*imago perfecta*), is the man-woman relationship, which seeks happiness in marriage. The love between man and woman would therefore seem to constitute a starting point for any understanding of love, a kind of *analogatum princeps* (cf. Scola 2005: 90). As Benedict puts it, this "exclusive and definitive love becomes the icon of the relationship between God and his people and vice versa" (*DCE* 11).

As the most complete example of human love, conjugal love is also at the center of natural human inclinations. It would seem to promise, as the encyclical emphasizes, a sort of complete happiness. The *Catechism* tells us that "conjugal love involves a totality, in which all the elements of the person enter—appeal of the body and instinct, power of feeling and affectivity, aspiration of the spirit and of will" (*CCC* 1643, quoting *FC* 13). Given their "derivative" character (*FC* 18), something similar may be said of the whole of family life and love. This very rich and subtle mélange of human instinct, attraction, desire, self-sacrifice, spiritual aspiration, rational and explicit "choice", is all part of—realized differently in each case, of course—the various familial loves. Man longs for the fruit of marriage, the child and more generally the family. The family constitutes the milieu in which a child naturally thrives and can attain a fullness of life. The child represents an affirmation of the parents' place in history and a perfecting gift from God, insofar as the child represents a link to the future and therefore also to past generations. Hence, the human search for love looks to personal fulfillment in the "good" of marriage and the child. For all of these reasons, this good is worthy as an object of human desire and a noble fulfillment of human nature and moral action.

When we consider conjugal love and its natural ordination toward procreation and the family, however, we realize that built into the very center of this natural institution is a demand for growth toward a self-giving, even self-sacrificial, love. This can be seen first of all in the fact that, as Benedict tells us, the love of man and woman necessarily seeks "definitiveness". Conjugal love "seeks to become definitive" in two senses: as exclusive and as eternal (*DCE* 6). As was already suggested by the discussion of the biblical covenant, monotheistic faith is closely associated with monogamous love and with love's irrevocability (*DCE* 11). Indeed, the classical properties of marriage—unity and indissolubility—represent exactly this understanding.

Certainly, the definitiveness described by these two properties entails a kind of totality. Conjugal love cannot therefore be simply one of the many wants and loves of life; it must rather be the one that gives meaning to all the others precisely because it is the one that entails the absolute gratuity and goodness of another. Because of this definitiveness, conjugal love constitutes all man has to give, since it entails the element of the whole of a person's freedom for self-bestowal, now and in the future.

This totality is directed in a way that compels us. Benedict puts this in terms of being "fulfilled" or even "perfected" (*DCE* 11: *perfectus*), drawing analogously on Aristophanes' speech concerning love in Plato's *Symposium*, in which the sexes seek to be "completed" (*completus*) in each other. The *érōs* of man and woman for each other is not the result of a punishment, nor are they seeking to reclaim a lost fusion into a single being, as in the account given by Plato's Aristophanes. Christianity, as Benedict points out, speaks instead in terms of a "communion with the opposite sex" (*DCE* 11). Nevertheless, Plato's text suggests something of the lack of "perfection" (*imperfectus*) experienced by Adam in searching among the animals for a "helper fit for him" (Gen 2:20). It also suggests the meaning of his rapturous declaration that "this at last is bone of my bones and flesh of my flesh" (Gen 2:23) upon awaking to the woman. Thus, man is "driven by nature to seek in another the part that can make him whole, the idea that only in communion with the opposite sex can he become 'complete'." From this "imperfection", Benedict draws two fundamental points: first, that "*eros* is somehow rooted in man's very nature;

Adam is a seeker who 'abandons his mother and father' in order to find woman; only together do the two represent complete humanity and become 'one flesh'" (*DCE* 11). Second, "from the standpoint of creation, *eros* directs man towards marriage, to a bond which is unique and definitive; thus, and only thus, does it fulfill its deepest purpose" (ibid.). It is only in the totality of the marital covenant that human love can be said to find its fullness.

As the Pope tells us, human * érōs* "tends to rise 'in ecstasy' towards the Divine, to lead us beyond ourselves; yet for this very reason it calls for a path of ascent, renunciation, purification and healing" (*DCE* 5). Indeed, the many "types" of love finally all deserve the name love (Lewis 1960: 1–9; cf. *DCE* 2; 8), because all of them, however tawdry they may often be, tacitly and despite themselves aim toward this central meaning. Thus, "God's way of loving becomes the measure of human love" (*DCE* 11).

Certainly, "love" is an analogous term, particularly when discussed in terms of the relationship between God's love and human love. God's *érōs* can in no way denote a "neediness" or "deficiency". Man's *érōs*, on the other hand, is precisely an expression of his dependency. Moreover, as we have seen, divine and guiltless love "turns God against himself" in response to the abuse of human freedom. Of course, God's guiltless love "turns" in the sense of an agapic outpouring that flows naturally from its *érōs*. The "turning" required for the maturation of human love, on the contrary, must first of all constitute a turn from its sinful self-absorption. Thus, as we saw, Hosea tells us that God's passionate refusal to cast off faithless Israel can only be because he is "God and not man". But even man's guilty love secretly longs for the "turn" that would bring it to the threshold of fair love. And, moreover, even an innocent human love would have to undergo some kind of "turn" in order to arrive at the fullness of love, in order to allow the other's necessary "difference" to stand out within the "unity" effected by love.

The Marital Covenant and Love's Turn

Not long after his election, Benedict said that: "to be able to say to someone: 'your life is good, even though I may not know your future', requires an authority and credibility superior to what individuals can assume on their own" (Benedict 2005). The pronouncement of the marriage vows is such a declaration of the goodness of the other's life; indeed, the ability to pledge oneself in marriage, in the sense implied by the marital covenant, implies the pronouncement that the spouse's life is worthy of a "leap of faith", a leap that entails the whole of life. Assuming the "definitive" character of conjugal love—its exclusive and eternal character—it is the pronouncement of a word that is in fact greater than the bride and bridegroom are capable of stating firmly on their own.

First, when we think about it for a moment, it is impossible for the bride and bridegroom to know precisely what is being pledged in marriage. Since they cannot know with any assurance or accuracy what the future holds, they cannot know the quality or quantity of what they are giving away or of what they are receiving. While marriage usually results in children and a family, this is certainly not guaranteed. Nor can the qualities or character of that family be accurately predicted. Thus, spouses-to-be cannot, strictly speaking, calculate, control, or even "choose" a particular or knowable goodness. Neither can marriage be thought of as a kind of "high-stakes gamble", according to which a bride and bridegroom could attach "odds", risking possible "failure" in order to arrive at what is thought to be more likely "success". The lifelong pledge of marriage—"for better or for worse, for richer, for poorer, in sickness and in health"—is a pledge to accept *in principle* the whole of life, of whatever "quality", not only as a possible risk but as an inherent aspect of the underlying goodness of this person and of the union. It is a declaration that even in poor conditions, even in conditions of sin, there is a basic goodness to the relation and to the other that cannot be lost.

The definitive character of conjugal love—the fact that it requires taking a stand with the entirety of one's life for and with another—therefore means that more is sought in marriage than can be summed up in the idea of fulfillment. "Fulfillment" as such, if taken without the further "turn" of love, suggests the subordination of some good to my flourishing. Indeed, this would seem to be implicit in the idea of a human searching love. However, the "definitiveness" of marriage suggests a submission of one's life to the goodness of the spouse and the marital union itself. The pledge is a declaration that my spouse's life, my own life, the lives of our children, and our conjugal and familial love are good no matter what happens. It is a pledge to stand by the side of the spouse no matter what the future holds. Conjugal love means a willingness to accept vulnerability analogous to God's acceptance of "vulnerability" in his Yes to the world, a Yes that resulted in the crucifixion of his only begotten Son. The definitiveness of marriage is set precisely against the vagaries of sin in this world. In this sense, then, conjugal love's definitiveness makes it a "redemptive" love that, even in its very beginning, tacitly both seeks and gives mercy (*DM* 6).

Because of the more-than-human capacity required to make this pronouncement fully, the capacity to enter into the covenant at the foundation of Christian marriage implies that the spouses' narrow freedom depends radically on God's all-encompassing and limitless freedom. Indeed, it is God's freedom that opens their freedom up, giving it eternal implications. Just as the humanity of Jesus is assumed into the Person of Christ, so too divine and conjugal love mutually dwell within each other—or, as the Council Fathers tell us, "Authentic married love is caught up into divine love ... and enriched by Christ's redeeming power" (*GS* 48). When Christ turns back to the Father, he enables the inner reality of the covenant of God with his people. His Yes to the Father is a giving over of his entire being on behalf of all mankind. But at the same time the personal freedom and love of each human person is also entailed in Christ's Yes. The freedom manifested in the *consensus matrimonialis* is therefore taken up and given its transcendent platform in faith in God's infinite freedom. As a response, and as a pledge, conjugal love necessarily entails not only the spouses' freedom and action, and not only the "invitation" to the spouses' marital and familial communion, but the reciprocity represented in their relationship to God.

Analogous to the "turning" of God's love in Christ, then, the searching of human *érōs* finally requires a kind of turning against itself and its initial understanding of the meaning of "desire" and "fulfillment". The turning, then, is the realization not only that here is one who is "fit for me", but also that I am "for" this other, that I must on that basis give myself "for" this other (Eph 5:25; *DCE* 7), in a reciprocal grant of mercy (cf. *DM 6*). "*Eros* is thus supremely ennobled, yet at the same time it is so purified as to become one with *agape*" (*DCE* 10).

The Eternity of Love

I would like to conclude by posing a basic question. "Love looks to the eternal", as Benedict tells us (*DCE* 6; cf. Balthasar 1983: 38–39; Scola 2005: 105). But the marital covenant, unlike that of God and man in Christ, will finally be transcended in the eschaton. Its root-edness in "this age" (Lk 20:34) will blossom into the virginal exis-tence of the coming kingdom: "For in the resurrection they neither marry nor are given in marriage" (Mt 22:30; see also, Mk 12:25 and Lk 20:34–36). At the wedding feast of the Lamb (Rev 19:7–8), all the saints will be married within the one Bride. Does this mean that the aspiration at the heart of conjugal love for the eternal is to be frus-trated precisely with respect to its essential characteristic—definitiveness? Does this "blossoming" leave room for the particularity of the indi-vidual marital covenant and its striving for the eternal?

Perhaps Pius XII offered one of the more suggestive responses to these questions:

> Far from destroying the bonds of human and supernatural love which are contracted in marriage, death can perfect them and strengthen them. It is true that legally, and on the plane of per-ceptible realities, the matrimonial institution does not exist any more, but that which constituted its soul, gave it strength and beauty—conjugal love with all its splendor and its eternal vows—lives on just as the spiritual and free beings live on who have pledged themselves to each other. (Pius XII 1957–58: 289)

Bibliography

Balthasar, Hans Urs von. 1983. *The Christian State of Life*. San Fran-cisco: Ignatius Press.

———. 1994. *A Theology of History*. San Francisco: Ignatius Press.

Benedict XVI. 2005. "Anthropological Foundation of the Family". Opening remarks to Ecclesial Congress of the Diocese of Rome, "Family and Christian Community: Formation of the Person and Transmission of the Faith", delivered at Basilica of St. John Lateran in Rome (June 6, 2005).

Caffarra, Carlo. 1984. "Marriage as a Reality of the Order of Creation and Marriage as a Sacrament". In *Contemporary Perspectives on Christian Marriage*, edited by Richard Malone and John Connery, 119–80. Loyola University Press.

Camino, J. Martínez. 2001. "'Through Whom All Things Were Made': Creation in Christ". *Communio International Catholic Review* 28 (Summer): 214–29.

Lewis, C. S. 1960. *The Four Loves*. New York: Harcourt Brace & Company.

McCarthy, Margaret H. 2005. "'Husbands, Love Your Wives as Your Own Bodies': Is Nuptial Love a Case of Love or Its Paradigm?" *Communio International Catholic Review* 32 (Summer): 260–94.

Pius XII. 1957–1958. "Christian Widowhood: An Address to the World of Family Organizations". *The Pope Speaks* 4 (Winter): 287–92.

Ratzinger, Joseph. 1986. "The Church's Teaching Authority—Faith—Morals". In *Principles of Christian Morality*. San Francisco: Ignatius Press.

———. 1995. "The New Covenant: A Theology of Covenant in the New Testament". Translated by Maria Shrady. *Communio International Catholic Review* 22 (Winter): 635–51.

———. 2003. *God Is Near Us: The Eucharist, the Heart of Life*. San Francisco: Ignatius Press.

Schmemann, Alexander. 1963. *For the Life of the World: Sacraments and Orthodoxy*. Crestwood, N.Y.: St. Vladimir's Seminary Press.

Scola, Angelo. 2005. *The Nuptial Mystery*. Grand Rapids, Mich.: Eerdmans.

Participating in His Gift:
The Eucharist

Nicola Reali*

Charity and Its Concept

At the heart of the encyclical *Deus Caritas Est* lies the explicit awareness that charity is an all-engaging dimension in the life of Christians
for the simple reason, if it can be so called, that God himself is love.
This elementary statement immediately provokes us to wonder why
then, as Christians, we find it so difficult to perceive the bond that
ties our Christianity to charity or, in other words, why we are so
reluctant to live in charity and to give charity. In Benedict XVI's encyclical the most truthful answer is also the simplest one: Perhaps it is
because we have been content with "giving charity". We have, that is,
considered charity simply as something that should make up for the
deficit in concreteness that we feel is part of both faith and worship. In
order words, we are almost resigned to the idea that, in the end, what
is offered to us in the liturgy, in which we participate, thanks to our
faith, is something that is however lacking in concreteness in the sense
that it apparently does not provide us with the social impetus that
alone can change the world by meeting people's real needs. And, finally,
behind this more or less latent objection lies the thought that in the
end the heritage of our faith must be validated through action, and, if
this does not happen, there is the risk that faith and worship will be
relegated to remaining purely abstract.

* Assistant Professor of Theology, Pontifical John Paul II Institute for Studies on Marriage and Family, Rome.

This is all motivated by the immediate transparency of action, that is, by the belief that action as such is immediately evident and, therefore, can be understood by all since everyone has the necessary intelligence. In other words, it is more and more widely felt that in the concreteness of action there is something that is universally valid, since—unlike faith and worship—it is apparently always and in all cases related to a concept or an idea whose value can be appreciated by all. The lack of concreteness in worship and faith, as opposed to countless other concepts, should therefore be countered through "charitable" action, almost as if this represented an experimental verification by which to make the truth of faith and worship credible for everyone.

Often we believe and take part in worship because, in spite of everything, we wish to believe that something that does not provide sufficient concrete criteria to establish itself might be true. This is often our reasoning, with a constant reference to the need for something concrete to place before our eyes so that this incontrovertible fact might legitimize the right of our faith to participate in universal knowledge. This is based on the irrefutable assumption that only something that can in fact be understood by all (because everyone has an adequate concept of it) can release our faith from the narrow cage of a worship that is unable to assert itself.

It is obvious that, in this case, only an action for which there is an adequate concept by which it can be placed within the space of humanity's universal heritage can assist the world's interest (but ours too) in Christianity. It is equally obvious that, deprived of an adequately universal concept, charitable action would loose some of its power. At the same time, I think that the extreme impertinence of such a belief is obvious. Benedict XVI's statement that "faith, worship and *ethos* are interwoven as a single reality which takes shape in our encounter with God's *agape*" (*DCE* 14) immediately dispels any possible confusion. This argument is strengthened by the consideration according to which the eucharistic dimension of this mutual permeation is accentuated. It is in worship itself and in the Eucharist that the source of all possible charitable action is to be found, since "'worship' itself, Eucharistic communion, includes the reality both of being loved and of loving others in turn" (*DCE* 14). It is, therefore, fair to say that charity does not make up for any lack of concreteness in worship and faith. On the

contrary, one might go so far as to say that we should not "give charity" to make up for the *deficit* in terms of the liturgy's concreteness but
rather to grasp its excess in comparison to the only shortage that may
exist: that of concepts.

The Self-Hermeneutics of the Logos

We must then, first of all, start by clarifying this, considering the way in
which reference has too often been made to the universal transparency
of the concepts by which charitable action should be viewed. In the eucharistic reality there are no "concepts" or "ideas", narrowly understood,
that can explain its dynamics, that is, the sacramental economy does
not represent an action as belonging to a preceding rationality that the
"concept" can interpret and explain. As Benedict XVI explains, "the
real novelty of the New Testament lies not so much in new ideas as in
the figure of Christ himself, who gives flesh and blood to those concepts" (*DCE* 12). Thus, the requirement that prompts clarification
can immediately be defined as a decision to come out of the narrow
scheme presented, to overturn the perspective radically. This is not a
definition, the comprehensive and complete pre-defined formula of
interpretation, or the absolute and atemporal a priori classification of
the value of the action, but rather an organized and all-inclusive look at
experience as it has become embodied in the evangelical text and in the
mysterious (but no less real) reality of the eucharistic sacrifice.

   This leads the Holy Father to focus on the extreme realism of Christ's
eucharistic gift, which represents the most immediate way of concretely indicating, *in re*, the way in which the entire dynamics of
Christian existence becomes freely involved in the event of God's Incarnation and, therefore, of the only reality of love. It is significant that
this is underlined in view not only of the statement of the "novelty of
Christ" but also by the assertion that Jesus' words and parables of Jesus
"constitute an explanation of his very being and activity" (*DCE* 12).
This is an indication that, behind the extreme simplicity of the words
themselves, hints directly at an essential element in the process orien-
tated at finding within the eucharistic mystery the vital point of unity
between worship, faith, and charity. If indeed it might seem demean-
ing to conceive the plausibility of Christian charity on the horizon of

a universal and abstract conceptuality that sets aside the uniqueness of the christological event, this is due to the fact that Christ's actions find their "explanation" only in the "explanation" that Jesus provided: it is the *logos* of the Logos that one must heed in order to gain an understanding of his work.

Such an affirmation should not be all that surprising, especially when the eucharistic mystery is being considered, since it is exactly that reality which makes the emphasis even more evident. In this regard, it suffices to recall the well-known eucharistic episode of the Emmaus disciples (Lk 24:13–25). On the road from Jerusalem to Emmaus, two disciples—or maybe it should be said, two former disciples of Jesus—were walking and talking to each other. They "were talking with each other"—as the Gospel says—"about all these things that had happened" (v. 14). That is, they discussed what had happened suddenly without any apparent reason and without a predictable cause. In short, they talked of the events that had concretely and irrefutably happened in Jerusalem during those days and that were, furthermore, known to everyone.

Their topic of conversation is, therefore, extremely specific ("all these things that had happened"). The facts were so concrete that it was not even necessary to recall them. So concrete—and therefore evident—that the two disciples, in a way that is even unintentionally comical, are surprised that someone might still not be aware of them. "Are you the only visitor to Jerusalem who does not know the things that have happened there in these days?" (v. 18). Know what? And, almost as if it were a judicial investigation, there follows the clearest possible answer: "'Concerning Jesus of Nazareth, who was a prophet mighty in deed and word before God and all the people. . . . Our chief priests and rulers . . . crucified him'" (vv. 19–20).

This is the fact, the incident, the event guaranteed by a factuality offered to everyone and so public that an entire city (and what a city!) could bear witness to it. It was an extremely concrete fact that everyone knew about and to which everyone could bear witness, but which—in spite of its extreme concreteness—no one was able to understand, no one was able to read, because no one possessed the key by which to penetrate it: "O foolish men, and slow of heart to believe" (v. 25)!

It may be worth dwelling upon these foolish disciples (it might be better to say men lacking intelligence), who in many ways could be our brothers. Indeed, like them we too walk along our paths being careful to fix our attention on concrete facts in the absolute certainty that what happens concretely is something that no one can doubt for the simple reason that everyone can understand its meaning. They are absolutely certain of what has happened and cannot even consider having suffered an illusion, because an entire city can confirm their intuition. The fact is clear, evident, and its interpretation is equally evident: Jesus is dead. One might deplore his death and be saddened by it, but it is universally known by all that no one can return from death. This cannot be questioned.

Thus it can be noted right from the start that what is lacking in Jesus' two former disciples is, not the factuality of the event that had happened, but the understanding of it. They have seen with their own eyes, and yet they have not understood. What is missing that could enable them to understand? Certainly not the concreteness of the action.

At this point something unexpected happens. Christ himself joins them ("Jesus himself drew near and went with them" v. 15), and—one imagines after a period of silence—Jesus starts talking to them. He listens to what they are saying (their *logoi* without *logos*), and, walking along the same road, he speaks to them (his *logos*). Yet, as the Gospel notes, "their eyes were kept from recognizing him" (v. 16). Let us ask: Why do they not recognize him? What concrete sign, what sensible perception do they not have by which to recognize him? None obviously, and yet they do not recognize him. Why, then, do they deny the evidence? Very probably not because the evidence is lacking but because this evidence denies and contradicts any understanding they might have of the fact. Indeed, maybe it would be better to say that it is because it denies and contradicts their pre-understanding of a concrete fact that took place before their very eyes. The absolute certainty that accompanies their interpretation of what has taken place shows their inability to read the event of Jesus' death, leaving them at the mercy of a cloud of prejudices. It is not that the two disciples do not wish to believe that it is Jesus: more simply they do not question their pre-understanding of the fact that death is death, and that is it.

Everything that is beyond this universally shared certainty must not even be taken into account and, consequently, must be excluded.

The bare factuality of what has happened before their eyes and of what is happening precisely at that moment is totally illegible solely on the basis of their pre-understanding, on the basis of the conceptuality that is universally accessible to everyone. It requires something more: "Jesus himself drew near ... and beginning with Moses and all the prophets, he interpreted to them in all the Scriptures the things concerning himself" (v. 15, 27). Only the self-hermeneutics of the Logos make all the *logoi* of the Scriptures accessible and make it possible to glimpse the fact that what happened in those days in Jerusalem is something that already possesses its "explanation" in the text of the Scriptures. However, this could only be "interpreted" by the One who is the protagonist of the Scriptures. Indeed, the two disciples already possess the right key by which to interpret the events that took place in those days. The understanding of the recent events is the point of arrival of Jesus of Nazareth's entire existence since he himself has proleptically announced its completion after three days (Lk 9:2). It has been revealed to them that love would prove to be stronger than the apparently absolute and tyrannical power of death and, almost as if this verbal announcement were not enough, the disciples have also received an initial confirmation of the truth of Christ's words: "Some women of our company amazed us.... They came back saying ... that he was alive" (Lk 24:22–23). Even "some of those who were with us" (v. 24) could confirm the accuracy of the testimony of the women because they "went to the tomb, and found it just as the women had said" (ibid.), but obviously not even this was enough. On the contrary, "these words seemed to them an idle tale" (v. 11).

"But him they did not see" (v. 24). The disciples' disbelief is as heavy, indeed, as the stone of the sepulcher. The words the disciples use to interpret the fact are indisputably the most obvious proof of how God's work in Christ remains totally inaccessible to humans if they do not abandon the practice of reading God's work based only on their pre-understandings. So, no one "sees anything" because no one looks at those facts as God looks at them; no one is willing to see in Jesus' Passion the highest revelation of God's charity. "'God is love'.... It is there [in Christ's pierced side] that this truth can be contemplated" (*DCE* 12).

Words and Actions

The action in this case, far from being presented as universally accessible, in that it can be referred to a concept known by all, acquires intelligibility (and therefore universality) in reference to the self-hermeneutics of the Word. It is in the *logos* of the Logos, as the "only exegete" (cf. Jn 1:18) of God, that the surpassing lesson of every exegesis and all hermeneutics is to be found. Luke's text says nothing of this exegesis, if not that it was aimed at making the disciples understand that "Was it not necessary that the Christ should suffer these things and enter into his glory?" (Lk 24:26). Only this "necessity"—impossible to understand at a human level—can reveal meaning in what happened, thus making it possible to find the "words" and the "concepts" suited to explaining what happened. When, finally, the logic (theo-logic) of events is revealed, everything becomes clear and what has until just a few moments before been dark is lit up, contributing to the surprise of finding themselves affected and moved: "Did not our hearts burn within us while he ... opened to us the Scriptures?" (v. 32).

This is thus the discovery of a new meaning, a new interpretation, a new *logos*, with the meaningful warning, however, that this fervor does not stem from human concepts nor does it come only from the "interpretation" of the Scriptures. The ultimate meaning of events appears, not in a word, but in an action: "He took the bread and blessed and broke it, and gave it to them" (v. 30).

The understanding of Scripture alone is not enough to reveal fully the meaning of Christ's story. That meaning comes to light and becomes intelligible only when its explanation is fulfilled in action; in short, when Scripture is not separate from the sacraments (*in primis* from the Eucharist). It is here that it perfectly "makes all men see ... the mystery hidden for ages in God" (Eph 3:9) that—in addition to opening the eyes of the disciples so that they "recognized him" (Lk 24:31)— reveals finally and definitively "the manifold wisdom of God" (Eph 3:10). In this sense, then, it is enlightening when Benedict XVI says that the eucharistic mystery identifies the fulfillment of mankind's aspiration to eternal wisdom: "The ancient world had dimly perceived that man's real food ... is ultimately the *Logos*, eternal wisdom: this same *Logos* now truly becomes food for us—as love" (*DCE* 13). And, indeed, the Logos of God's eternal wisdom, testified by the text of the Scripture, reaches each single person on the face of the earth of all times in the memorial of his Passion, death, and Resurrection, whereby we are nourished by his Body and his Blood.

After all, the whole economy of the Christian revelation involves an awareness of God's infinite indulgence that has come to man that he might truly take part in the fullness of the life that God has offered. This is a participation that inevitably always involves something new compared to human expectations and aspirations, so it is not so surprising if Benedict XVI celebrates the extraordinary originality of the eucharistic sacrament in relation to the human aspiration to take part in God's wisdom.

In the Eucharist, there is no attempt to transcribe with scrupulous and passionate fidelity the anthropological desire in terms of an action representing an otherwise unutterable *logos*. Rather, it is the offer of a wisdom that, presenting itself as something beyond any a priori conceptual understanding, defines at the same time the concrete form of its donation and, thus, of its participation in human existence. Proof of this lies in the fact that, in the cited episode in the Gospel, the only reaction provoked by the self-hermeneutics of the Word in the two disciples is the plea "stay with us" (Lk 24:29). "Stay with us" is what the Samaritans had asked for, and obtained, from Jesus (cf. Jn 4:40); what Christ had asked for, and obtained, from Zacchaeus (cf. Lk 19:5); but, also, what the disciples had denied Christ at Gethsemane (cf. Mt 26:38).

Indeed, this plea appears to be one of the most fortunate expressions by which we can humbly appeal for the gift of human wisdom. After the defeat to be suffered by our "concepts" and our "preunderstanding", there is nothing to be done other than beg him to stay with us, that the Logos give us his *logos*, his wisdom to interpret and understand what has happened and what no one is able to grasp, understand, or interpret. Once again, the episode in question converges in revealing that this gift is given, not simply in a word, but in the eucharistic action that reveals how for man there is only one alternative: "to have or not have his *logos* abiding in us" (cf. Jn 5:38; 1 Jn 2:14), to be nourished or not by the Logos itself (cf. *DCE* 13).

The Mystique of the Eucharist

"More than just statically receiving the incarnate *Logos*, we enter into the very dynamic of his self-giving" (*DCE* 13). Christ's action, which finally reveals the meaning of his existence, opens wide an unthinkable horizon for the two disciples, so that they not only recognize Jesus resurrected "in the breaking of the bread", but they too "rise again" (cf. Lk 24:33) and turn back toward Jerusalem to meet with the apostles. Here the disciples report what has happened to them. They "repeat the explanation" (cf. v. 35) they themselves have received (v. 27) and the action of the "breaking the bread" that has enabled them to recognize him. All this suddenly reveals once again the reality of Christ's Resurrection: "Jesus himself stood among them" (v. 36).

The link that must be suitably recognized between the episode with the disciples and the apparition to the apostles once again brings to the forefront the eucharistic action's character of revelation. By carrying out the "interpretation" of the Scriptures, we are always led to the certainty of resurrection that, significantly, appears always in contraposition to a presence of Christ seen, but not recognized. What "startles and frightens" (cf. Lk 24:37) the apostles is, indeed, what they were seeing or "supposed that they saw" (v. 37). Was it a ghost, a trick, an illusion? As to the more simple, more reasonable hypothesis (that it might actually be Jesus), it remains incredible, unthinkable; the only explanation that is inaccessible to their spirit. The obstacle, once again, lies in the inability to understand because of a *deficit* in adequate meanings or concepts to interpret the concreteness that was before their own eyes.

What hinders faith is therefore to be linked to a lack of concreteness that any action could fill. If anything, it is necessary to recognize that what is lacking are the concepts, the ideas, which prove to be inadequate for correctly interpreting facts. Thus, a scenario develops in which no "idea" can suit the christological action a priori, if not in the case of an extreme conceit on the part of anyone who might wish to enclose God's work in a conceptual system, with the consequence, however, of moving toward the same disappointment that distressed the souls of the Emmaus disciples. Nor would it be useful to refer to an excess of operativeness on the human part, almost as if this were the only way of making up for the shortage of concepts and ideas. Nothing can guarantee that mysterious but real participation in Christ's altruistic action if not his gift itself, the gift of his Logos, which in the sacramental action acquires all of its light and transparency. Faith and participation in worship thus emerge as the only act through which man can face the excess of concreteness and realism that belongs to God's work. After all, it is this excess of concreteness in "the figure of Christ himself, who gives flesh and blood to those concepts" (*DCE* 12) that is the most difficult thing to interpret and understand, and, it is worth repeating this, only another concrete figure in the shape of action can match it: the Eucharist.

It may even be said that man faces difficulties in tolerating the splendor that issues from the concreteness of God's work in Christ. It is a splendor that human eyes cannot look at without being blinded by so much light, almost as if the light, rather than illuminating, darkened the presence of God among us. We are thus called upon to see the in-visible and un-watchable splendor that issues from God's action. This situation would remain inexorably and tragically unfulfilled if God himself had not drawn closer to us. In giving his light, at the same time he has given the ability to see the invisible. We are not only the recipients of God's gift or, even less, his condition; rather, we appear like he who has always been involved in the self-manifestation of God, who by giving himself at the same time also gives the possibility of the anthropological acceptance. This possibility is the concrete form of the eucharistic action that, when read and interpreted as the extreme sign of divine charity, "opens the—*blinded*—eyes" (cf. Lk 24:31) of man. We suddenly and freely find ourselves able to see what any human effort would have failed even to catch a glimpse of: "the sacramental 'mysticism', grounded in God's condescension towards us, [that] operates at a radically different level and lifts us to far greater heights than anything that any human mystical elevation could ever accomplish" (*DCE* 13).

Johannine Foundations of the Church as the Family of God

*Michael Waldstein**

In his inaugural encyclical, *Deus Caritas Est*, Pope Benedict XVI follows Vatican II and his predecessor John Paul II in stressing the importance of the concept of the "family" for understanding the Church. "The Spirit is ... the energy which transforms the heart of the ecclesial community, so that it becomes a witness before the world to the love of the Father, who wishes to make humanity a single family in his Son" (*DCE* 19) (see, with further bibliography, Bechina 1998; Hellerman 2001).

In the dominant culture of Modernity, this paradigmatic role of the family, particularly the role of the father, has been called into question at its very roots. Before we turn to the Gospel of John, it is thus helpful to examine at least briefly one radical rejection of the category "family" and particularly of the category "father" in the name of the dignity and autonomy of the person.

Kant's Rejection of the Family Image

According to Kant, the government of a state must not intend the happiness of citizens, because this would cast those who govern in a role of father and the citizens in the role of sons. Such a paternal government, Kant argues, denies the personal dignity of citizens and deprives them of all their rights.

*President of the International Theological Institute for Studies on Marriage and the Family (ITI), Gaming, Austria (institute associated to the Pontifical John Paul II Institute for Studies on Marriage and Family).

If a government is built on the principle of benevolence similar
to that of a *father* toward his children, that is, a *paternal government*
(*imperium paternale*), in which subjects are treated like children
who have not yet come of age and who cannot distinguish what
is truly beneficial from what is harmful for them, [a government]
furthermore, in which subjects are forced to be passive, in order
to await the judgment of the head of state, how they *should* be
happy, and his sheer benevolence, whether he actually wills them
to be so: this is the greatest *despotism* imaginable (that is, a constitution that annuls the entire freedom of subjects and leaves
them without any rights). Not a *paternal*, but a *patriotic* government (*imperium non paternale, sed patrioticum*) is the only government conceivable for human beings who are capable of rights.
(Kant 1793b: 290–91)

The superlative in this text is astounding: *the greatest* despotism *imaginable*. What is the greatest despotism imaginable? A slave state in which
the head of state *does not intend* the good of citizens but rules them *for
his own* ends, considering them mere means to those ends? No, a state
under the benevolence of a father who *does* intend the good of the
citizens—this is superlative despotism.

This astounding superlative can be understood in light of Kant's
concept of autonomy according to which moral goodness and hence
human dignity consists in the radical self-movement of the will that
imposes its own universal law (the categorical imperative) on itself.
"The will is not simply subject to the law; it is subject in such a way
that it must also be considered *as self-legislative* and for this reason, as
the very first, subject to the law whose author it can consider itself to
be" (Kant 1785: 431). Human dignity consists in this self-legislative
power and self-movement of the human will and reason. If the state
were ordered to the happiness of its citizens, it would cast its citizens
in a role of dependence, that is, of sonship, under a benevolent father
to whose direction and judgment citizens would submit. Dependence,
however, is incompatible with human dignity as a dignity that resides
in autonomy.

Filial submission to a benevolent father destroys autonomy even
more radically than slavish submission to a violent master, because it
implies an interior and spiritual submission, not only an external

conformity in actions. A slave's heart can be his own; a true son's heart belongs to his father. The direct clash between Kant's teaching on autonomy and the Lord's Prayer is remarkable. If the Our Father is indeed the paradigmatic prayer of Christians, then the destruction of human dignity, that is, the heteronomy of sonship, lies at the very heart of Christianity.

In contrast to the state, a church, according to Kant, can rightly be understood as a family. While the state merely protects the rights of its citizens, a church is ordered to the moral improvement of its members. Yet, the family Kant has in mind seems to be defined as a real brotherhood without a real father.

> An ethical commonwealth, inasmuch as it is a church, that is, inasmuch as it is considered as a mere representative of a City of God, does not have a constitution whose principles resemble the constitution of a state. In a church, the constitution is neither monarchical (under a pope or patriarch), nor aristocratic (under bishops and prelates), nor democratic (as sectarian illuminati). It could best be compared to a domestic community (family) under a common, albeit invisible, moral Father, inasmuch as his holy Son, who knows his will and is at the same time related by blood to all its members, represents the Father's place in this community in order to make his will known to these members, who thus honor the Father in him and thereby enter into a voluntary, universal, and enduring union of hearts. (Kant 1793a: 102)

Although in this text he uses the category "family" for the church and speaks of God as Father and Jesus as the Son, Kant does not take away one iota from his radical personalism of autonomy. God is for him a postulate of practical reason. It is morally decent to act as if God existed, but one can neither affirm nor deny the existence of God on a theoretical level.

> To believe in him [God] morally and practically means ... acting in a manner *as if* such a rule of the world *were* real. (Kant 1796: 396, emphasis added)

> [The proof of the three practical postulates: the freedom of the will, the immortality of the soul, and the existence of God] is not a proof of the truth of these statements seen as theoretical

statements and, thus, not a proof of the objective existence of the objects corresponding to them ... , but one that has only subjective and practical validity, one whose instruction is sufficient to produce the effect of our acting *as if* we knew that these objects *were* real. (Kant 1804: 298, emphasis added)

Since one cannot say on the level of theoretical reason that God exists (or that he does not exist), one cannot say that he is (or is not) a Father in the sense intended by the Christian tradition, namely, as the real Creator who gives the real gift of real being and orders all things to their real end. Kant excludes real dependence and real obedience.

Just as Kant's personalism of radical autonomy is shielded against the real existence of God as Father, it is shielded from radical dependence of the Son. In fact, the true point of the doctrine of the divinity of the Son of God is the doctrine of the divinity of all human beings.

That which alone can make a world the object of divine decree and the end of creation is *Humanity* (rational being in general in the world) *in its full moral perfection*, from which happiness [that is, man's happiness] follows in the will of the Highest Being directly as from its supreme condition.—This man, who is alone pleasing to God ["This is my beloved Son in whom I am well pleased" (Mt 3:17)], "is in him from all eternity" ["The Word was with God" (Jn 1:1)]; the idea of man proceeds from God's being; man is not, therefore, a created thing but God's only begotten Son [Jn 1:18; 3:16–18], "the Word (the Fiat!) through which all other things are, and without whom nothing that is made would exist" [Jn 1:1–3] (since for him, that is, for a rational being in the world, as it can be thought according to its moral determination, everything was made ["All things were created through him and for him" (Col 1:16)]).—"He is the reflection of his glory" [Heb 1:3].—"In him God loved the world" [Jn 3:16], and only in him and through the adoption of his dispositions can we hope "to become children of God" [Jn 1:12]; and so on. (Kant 1793a: 60–61).

Kant's appeal to key trinitarian passages in Scripture can easily obscure the central point of his rational faith: he sees man, not as a creature, but as the absolute locus of all true meaning *from itself, a se*. The Son, that is, the man, is equal to the Father, but not born from the Father. The human personal self has no origin distinct from itself. Its autonomous self-movement is the highest value and the final purpose of all things.

> Concerning man (and thus every rational being in the world) as a moral being, one cannot ask further: For what end (*quem in finem*) does he exist? His existence has the highest purpose in itself. He can, as far as possible, subject the whole of nature to this purpose. At the least, he must not submit himself to any influence of nature contrary to this purpose.—Now if the beings of the world as beings that are contingent in their existence are in need of a highest cause that acts according to purpose, then man is the final purpose of creation. For, without man the chain of purposes subordinate to each other would not be explained in its entirety. It is only in man, and in man only as the subject of morality, that an unconditioned legislation concerning purposes can be found, which thus enables him alone to be a final purpose to which the whole of nature is teleologically subordinated. (Kant 1796: 435–36)

> While man is unholy enough, the *humanity* in his person must be holy to him. In all of creation, everything one might want and over which one has power can be used *as a mere means*. Only man himself and with him every rational creature is an *end in itself*. For, in virtue of the autonomy of his freedom, he is the subject of the moral law, which is holy. (Kant 1788: 435–36, cf. 5:131; see also Kant 1797: 434)

> The practical imperative is thus the following. Act in such a way that at all times you treat human nature in your own person as well as in the person of every other human being simultaneously as a purpose, never as a mere means. (Kant 1785: 429)

One can rightly call this view "personalism" because it sees man as the highest value to which all other values are subordinated. It is a radically anti-trinitarian personalism: all light is focused in the unrelated person, in the person's moral dignity understood as self-legislative autonomy. Man's glory is not a reflection of glory; rather, it stands absolutely in the autonomous self. Kant obliterates the relational character of trinitarian language (Father-Son, glory-reflection, and so on) in favor of this autonomous self, more precisely, in favor of each and every autonomous self, a series of juxtaposed selves that can enter into relation but are not defined in their very being by any relation.

"Anti-trinitarian" is not a philosophical category. One might therefore object to its use in this brief sketch of Kant's personalism. In response one can point out that Kant himself understood his philosophy as an affirmation of absolute autonomy in conscious encounter and contrast with Christian revelation. He is fully aware of trinitarian language and makes use of it. At the same time he undercuts it by proposing his philosophical religion of moral autonomy as the true subtext of the biblical text, as the enlightened philosophical religion that must eventually replace the ecclesial religion expressed in sacred books.

Roots of Personhood according to John

Kant's personalism has the great merit of raising the question of personhood on a level of reflection that goes to the very roots of personhood. His clear exaltation of autonomy as the root of the dignity of the person challenges Christian theology to give an account of personhood on a similarly radical level. When one examines the Gospel of John in light of this challenge, two words stand out as particularly important: *love* and *gift*.

Trinitarian Foundations

One can see these two words at work in the first extensive controversy between Jesus and the Judean authorities in Jerusalem. The controversy takes place after Jesus heals a lame man on the Sabbath (see Jn 5:1–15). The authorities "persecuted Jesus, because he did this on the sabbath" (5:16). Jesus' response to his adversaries is highly theological in a manner characteristic of the Gospel of John. "My Father is working still, and I am working" (5:17). This response seems to presuppose the doctrine attested in Jewish sources that God (and God alone) is not bound by the Sabbath command. He works even on the Sabbath to continue his life-giving providence over the world. The authorities conclude from Jesus' statement that he was "making himself equal with God" (5:18). On this basis, they resolve to inflict on him the most extreme form of punishment, death. Death corresponds to the gravity of the sin, because what is at issue is the very center of Israel's faith. "Hear, O Israel, the LORD our God is one LORD" (Deut 6:4).

Jesus responds in a long discourse (5:19–47) that articulates the new trinitarian understanding of God in continuity with Israel's profession of the oneness of God. Let us take a look at the first two verses of this discourse.

> Truly, truly, I say to you,
> the Son can do nothing of his own accord, but only what he sees
>   the Father doing;
> for whatever he does, that the Son does likewise.
> For the Father loves the Son, and shows him all that he himself
>   is doing. (Jn 5:19–20)

The statement "the Son can do nothing of his own accord" responds directly to the charge he was "making himself equal with God". Contrary to this charge, Jesus does not arrogate anything to himself; he is not setting himself up as a second God independent from and in competition with the Father; rather, he remains completely subordinate to the Father in all his activities. "The Son can do nothing of his own accord, but only what he sees the Father doing." To be a son is to have being and life from another. Thus Thomas Aquinas connects "the Son can do nothing of his own accord" with the begetting of the Only-Begotten.

> Christ, as the Divine Word, shows the origin of his power when
> he says: I cannot do anything of myself, in the way he said above,
> "the Son can do nothing of himself" (5:19). For his very doing
> and his power are his being (esse); but being (esse) in him is from
> another, that is, from his Father. And so, just as he is not of
> himself (a se), so of himself he cannot do anything: "I do noth-
> ing of myself" (below 8:28). (Thomas Aquinas, Super Ioannem,
> cap. 5, lect. 5, 794–98)

The next statement counterbalances the note of subordination contained in "the Son can do nothing of his own accord" by generalizing the claim to an exclusively divine activity made in 5:17: "For whatever [the Father] does, that the Son does likewise" (5:19). The prologue to John makes a similar statement about God's act of creation, which is shared by the Logos. "All things were made through him, and without him was not anything made that was made" (1:3). Yet, while the prologue refers only to the creative activity of the Logos in union with God ("through him"), 5:19 makes a more sweeping claim: there is no activity of the Father that is not also one of the Son.

Although there is a certain opposition between the two clauses, subordination and equality, they are closely tied together by a causal link. The all-encompassing equality of activity between the Father and the Son is the reason why the Son's activity is not independent and separate. He can do nothing of his own accord because (Greek: *gar*) whatever the Father does, that the Son does likewise. Nothing in the Father is closed to the Son: everything is open and communicated. Correspondingly, there is nothing emancipated and private in the Son over against the Father.

The immediately following clause pushes the causal line of thought one step farther (second *gar*): the reason for the comprehensive unity of activity between the Father and the Son is the love of the Father: "For [*gar*] the Father loves the Son, and shows him all that he himself is doing" (5:20). To bring out the order of objective foundation affirmed by 5:19–20, one can invert the steps: The Father's "love" (5:20) stands at the origin. It is a total or radical love and therefore a love in which the Father "shows" whatever he does to the Son. Due to this gift and its completeness, the operation of the Father and the Son forms an inseparable interrelated whole. Since their operation forms such a whole, Jesus does not act "of his own accord", contrary to the charge that he "makes" himself equal with God.

The category of gift is implicit in "showing". "Gift" is made explicit in 5:26 where Jesus says that the Father "grants" life to the Son. "For as the Father has life in himself, so he has *granted* the Son also to have life in himself." To have "life in himself" is the specifically divine way of having life in contrast to human beings who have "life in his name" (20:31).

How can the simultaneity of the subordination and the equality of the Son in 5:19 be understood? Do they not stand in tension with

each other? Does subordination not lead into Arianism, in which the
Son is the first and greatest of creatures? Does equality not lead into
Sabellianism, in which Father and Son are not distinct persons but
mere aspects of one and the same divinity? Verse 5:20 suggests a point
of unity from which both sides of the tension can be understood as
necessary and correlative, namely, the completeness of the gift made
by the Father. According to 5:20a, the Father loves the Son and therefore shows him *all* he does. Verse 5:26 continues one step deeper in
the same vein: The Father gives his own life to the Son, and this gift
is so complete that the Son has "life in himself"; cf. "All that the
Father has is mine" (16:15). "All mine are yours, and yours are mine"
(17:10). As a complete *gift* the Son's activity and life are subordinate to
the Father's activity and life; as a *complete* gift they are equal with the
Father's.

> One could also say, as Hilary does, that even according to the
> divine nature the Father is greater than the Son, yet the Son is
> not inferior to the Father, but equal. For the Father is not greater
> than the Son in power, eternity, and greatness, but by the author-
> ity of a giver or beginning. For the Father receives nothing from
> an other, but the Son, if I may put it in this way, receives his
> nature from the Father by an eternal generation. So, the Father is
> greater, because he gives, yet the Son is not inferior, but equal,
> because he receives all that the Father has: "God has given him
> the name that is above every name" (Phil 2:9). No less than the
> giver is he to whom one and the same being is given. (Thomas
> Aquinas, *Super Ioannem*, cap. 14, lect. 8, 1971)

Other passages in John describe the Father's love in a similar way.
"The Father *loves* the Son, and has *given* all things into his hand"
(3:35). "Father, I desire that they also, whom you have *given* me, may
be with me where I am, to behold my glory which you have *given* me
in your *love* for me before the foundation of the world" (17:24).

A first conclusion can be drawn from the evidence presented so
far. In the key discourse 5:19ff., which makes the step from the faith
of Israel ("Hear, O Israel, the Lord our God is one Lord") to the
revelation of the new and distinctively Christian understanding of God,
Jesus uses the conceptual pair "love" and "gift" to articulate the new

understanding. From the Father's radical love, a gift comes forth that is total and unreserved, the gift of the entire divine life and being. This gift shows how subordination and equality fit together. Since he receives himself from the Father's love as a complete *gift*, the Son is subordinate to the Father. Since he receives himself as a *complete* gift, the Son is equal to the Father. John Paul II calls the systematic account and application of this logic of love and gift "hermeneutics of the gift" (John Paul II 1997: 58, 66).

Sharing in Trinitarian Life

It remains to be shown how, according to John, the logic of love and gift extends from the Trinity into the community of Jesus' disciples. Two important passages spell out this extension: 13:34–35 and 17:20–23.

(17:20) I do not pray for these only, but also for those who believe in me through their word,	(22) The glory which you have given me I have given to them,	A new commandment I give to you,
(21) **THAT** [*hina*] they may all be one; even	**THAT** [*hina*] they may be one even	**THAT** [*hina*] you love one another; even
AS [*kathōs*] you, Father, are *in* me, and I *in* you,	**AS** [*kathōs*] we are one, (23) I *in* them and you *in* me,	**AS** [*kathōs*] I have loved you,
THAT [*hina*] they also may be *in* us, so	**THAT** [*hina*] they may become perfectly one, so	**THAT** [*hina*] you also love one another.
THAT [*hina*] the world may believe that you have sent me.	**THAT** [*hina*] the world may know that you sent me and have loved them even AS you have loved me.	By this all men will know that you are my disciples, if you have love for one another. (13:34–35)

These three panels follow the same pattern. After an introductory clause, all three have a sandwich formed by two final clauses with the conjunction *hina*: ("that", "so that", "in order that") surrounding a comparison introduced by *kathōs*: "as". The pattern concludes with another *hina* clause in 17:21 and 17:23, a main clause in 13:35, all three of which point to the effect: so that the world (or all) will know and believe.

The three panels point to three important dimensions of Christian life:

(1) the first is the dimension of the *future* in which the Father will realize unity (17:20–21): unity appears as a desired future result for which Jesus asks the Father;

(2) the second is the dimension of the *past* and *present* in which the gift of "glory" or grace has already been given by Jesus (17:22–23): here unity appears as an event or fact that has been and is taking place;

(3) the third is the dimension of *ethics*, of what should be done, summarized in the "new commandment" (13:34–35).

Each of these dimensions is essential for Christian life. A certain primacy of place, however, belongs to the second dimension. What is first is not hope for the future, and especially not ethics, but a past and present event.

> *We have come to believe in God's love*: in these words the Christian can express the fundamental decision of his life. Being Christian is not the result of an ethical choice or a lofty idea, but the encounter with an event, a person, which gives life a new horizon and a decisive direction. Saint John's Gospel describes that event in these words: "God so loved the world that he gave his only Son, that whoever believes in him should ... have eternal life" (3:16). (*DCE* 1)

The key element in Jesus' prayer is the trinitarian exemplar in which man is to participate. Thus St. Thomas writes about John 17:11 ("Keep them in your name ... that they may be one, even as we are one") as follows.

> They are preserved for this goal, namely, to be one. For, our entire perfection consists in the unity of the Spirit, "Take every care to preserve the unity of the Spirit by the peace that binds you together" (Eph 4:3). "How good and joyful it is when brothers dwell in unity!" (Ps 133:1).
>
> But he adds, "as we are one". There is a difficulty in this statement. They are one in essence; therefore we will also be one in essence. But this is not true.

Response: The perfection of each being is nothing other than a participation in the divine likeness. For we are good to the degree in which we are made like God. Our unity, therefore, is perfective precisely in the degree to which it participates in the divine unity.

Now, there is a twofold unity in God, namely, the unity of nature (cf. "The Father and I are one" [Jn 10:30]) and the unity of love in the Father and the Son which is the unity of the Spirit. Both of these are in us, not in equality of rank, but by a certain likeness. For the Father and the Son are numerically of one nature, but we are one in nature according to our kind. Again, they are one by a love that is not derived from the gift of someone else but that proceeds from them. For the Father and the Son love each other by the Holy Spirit, but we by a love in which we participate as something derived from a higher source [that is, the Holy Spirit]. (Thomas Aquinas, *Super Ioannem*, cap. 17, lect. 3, 2214)

The deepest roots of the Christian conception of personhood lie here. As St. Thomas puts it, "Our entire perfection consists in the unity of the Spirit ... which is the unity of love between the Father and the Son." While for Kant the dignity and perfection of the person lies in the autonomy of self-caused moral willing, for the Gospel of John (as interpreted by St. Thomas) it lies in the unity of love between the Father and the Son, which is the unity of the Spirit. Sharing in the divine likeness in exactly this respect constitutes the deepest meaning of being a human person.

The Church as the Family of God according to Vatican II

John Paul II sees the increasing awareness of sharing in the trinitarian likeness as the main thrust of Vatican II. In his book on Vatican II, *Sources of Renewal*, Wojtyła sets himself the task of outlining the implementation of Vatican II in a manner that corresponds to the actual intentions of the Council. The original guiding question of Vatican II, he argues, was, *Ecclesia, quid dicis de te ipsa?* Church, what do you say about yourself? (Wojtyła 1980: 420) "The People of God"—this is the Council's answer, Wojtyła claims (Wojtyła 1980: 112–54). The way both the question and the answer "People of God" must be under-stood, Wojtyła adds, is pastoral. How can the Church *grow in her aware-ness and life* as the People of God? Although the question is in the first place a question about the Church as a *social* organism, the growth of the Church's awareness must take place in the life of the individual *persons* that constitute her. It must take place in their lived experience of personal subjectivity.

What is the content of the notion the "People of God" that should be received in the experience of personal subjectivity, according to Wojtyła? In his retreat for Paul VI, at the highpoint of the retreat, the beginning of the seventh talk, he writes,

> Let us turn our thoughts to God who is gift and the source of all giving. The fathers of the second Vatican Council were con-vinced that the complex reality of the Church cannot be ade-quately expressed in societal terms alone, even when the society constituted by the Church is called the "People of God". In order properly to describe this reality and appreciate its underlying sig-nificance it is necessary to return to the dimension of mystery, that is to the dimension of the most Holy Trinity. That is why the Constitution *Lumen gentium* starts with an introductory account of the divine economy of salvation, which ultimately is a trini-tarian economy (cf. *Lumen gentium*, nn. 2–4). . . . Love, an uncre-ated gift, is part of the inner mystery of God and is the very nucleus of theology. (Wojtyła 1977: 53 and 55)

What is to be received from Vatican II in the lived experience of the believer is thus the mystery of the Trinity as a mystery of love and of gift that gives its deepest form to the society called "Church". There are two texts of Vatican II to which John Paul II returns again and again, because he finds in them in miniature this core heritage of Vatican II.

> The truth is that only in the mystery of the incarnate Word does the mystery of man take on light. For Adam, the first man, was a figure of Him Who was to come, namely Christ the Lord. Christ, the final Adam, by the revelation of the mystery of the Father and His love, fully reveals man to man himself and makes his supreme calling clear. (*GS* 22, 1)

Indeed, the Lord Jesus, when He prayed to the Father, "that all may be one ... as we are one" (Jn 17:21–22), opened up vistas closed to human reason, for He implied a certain likeness between the union of the divine Persons, and the unity of God's sons in truth and charity. This likeness reveals that man, who is the only creature on earth which God willed for itself, cannot fully find himself except through a sincere gift of himself (cf. Lk 17:33). (GS 24, 3)

Both of these key texts have a rich trinitarian content on which all other details depend. In *Gaudium et Spes* 22, 1, the revelation of the mystery of the Father and his love fully reveals man to himself and makes his supreme calling clear. In *Gaudium et Spes* 24, 3, the likeness between the union of the Divine Persons and the union of human beings shows that man can only find himself in a sincere gift of self. There is a close connection between the two main results affirmed by these texts: "reveals man to man himself" and "man fully finds himself." These two formulations seem to aim at one and the same thing: for man to be fully revealed to himself and to find himself seem identical, though "be revealed" may have a more cognitive character, "find" a more comprehensive existential one.

This close connection suggests a similarly close connection between the causes or conditions that lead to such revelation and finding, namely, on the one hand, the revelation of the mystery of the Father and his love and, on the other, the sincere gift of self. The union between the Divine Persons proceeds, according to John, from the love of the Father, who is the source of the Son's life. The union between human beings is to be shaped in accord with this prior divine union. In view of this fact, one would expect fatherhood to play a central role in human life, particularly in the life of the Church. One would expect not only divine fatherhood, but human fatherhood in many analogical forms. From a Kantian point of view, which identifies personal dignity with individual autonomy, this pervasive presence of the family image in general and of fatherhood in particular will necessarily come under suspicion as a way of enslaving the weak and serving the interests of the powerful. Yet, Christians are bound by the example of Christ, who did not come to be served, but to serve.

A bishop, since he is sent by the Father [that is, God] to govern his family, must keep before his eyes the example of the Good Shepherd, who came not to be ministered unto but to minister, and to lay down his life for his sheep. (LG 27:3)

In this text it is quite clear that the bishop is father in the sense that he represents the true, divine Father of the family. He does not have the source of his authority within himself. He can only exercise his fatherhood according to the example of Christ's unreserved gift of his life.

In this perspective one could unfold the texts of Vatican II that speak about the Church as the family of God (for example, LG 28, 32, 51; Christus Dominus 16; Unitatis Redintegratio 2; see Bechina, 1998: 22–228). A single norm runs through all these texts, namely, the "new commandment" articulated in the Gospel of John, which is linked as a golden chain with the mystery of the Father's love: "Love one another; even as I have loved you" (13:34). "As the Father has loved me, so have I loved you" (15:9). Love and gift, rooted in the trinitarian exemplar, above all in the Father, are the basic defining elements of the Christian understanding of the person. Gaudium et Spes 24, 3, formulates a principle of human dignity very similar to Kant's personalist norm. Kant says, "Act in such a way that at all times you treat human nature in your own person as well as in the person of every other human being simultaneously as a purpose, never as a mere means" (Kant 1785: 429). Vatican II says, "Man ... is the only creature on earth which God willed for itself" (GS 24, 3). The crucial difference lies in what Vatican II adds. "Man, who is the only creature on earth which God willed for itself, *cannot fully find himself except through a sincere gift of himself* (cf. Lk 17:33)."

Bibliography

Bechina, F. 1998. *Die Kirche als "Familie Gottes": Die Stellung dieses theologischen Konzeptes im Zweiten Vatikanischen Konzil und in den Bischofssynoden von 1974 bis 1994 im Hinblick auf eine "Familia-Dei-Ekklesiologie".* Rome: Editrice Pontificia Università Gregoriana.

Hellerman, J. H. 2001. *The Ancient Church as Family: Early Christian Communities and Surrogate Kinship.* Minneapolis, Minn.: Fortress Press.

John Paul II. 1997. *The Theology of the Body*. Boston: Pauline Books and Media.

Kant, Immanuel. 1785. *Grundlegung zur Metaphysik der Sitten* [*Groundwork of the Metaphysics of Morals*]. Akademieausgabe 4:385–464.

———. 1788. *Kritik der praktischen Vernunft* [*Critique of Practical Reason*]. Akademieausgabe 5:1–163.

———. 1793a. *Die Religion innerhalb der Grenzen der bloßen Vernunft* [*Religion within the Bounds of Reason Alone*]. Akademieausgabe 6:1–202.

———. 1793b. *Über den Gemeinspruch: Das mag in der Theorie richtig sein, taugt aber nicht für die Praxis* [*On the Common Saying: This May Be Right in Theory, but It Is No Good in Practice*]. Akademieausgabe 8:273–314.

———. 1796. *Von einem neuerdings erhobenen vornehmen Ton in der Philosophie* [*On a Recently Assumed Noble Tone in Philosophy*]. Akademieausgabe 8:387–406.

———. 1797. *Die Metaphysik der Sitten* [*Metaphysics of Morals*]. Akademieausgabe 6:203–493.

———. 1804. *Preisschrift über die Fortschritte der Metaphysik: Von dem, was seit der Leibniz-Wolffischen Epoche in Ansehung des Objektes der Metaphysik, d. i. ihres Endzweckes, ausgerichtet worden?* [*What Are the Real Advances Made by Metaphysics in Germany since the Time of Leibniz and Wolff?*]. Akademieausgabe 20:253–332.

Wojtyła. K. 1977. *Sign of Contradiction*. New York: Seabury Press.

———. 1980. *Sources of Renewal: The Implementation of the Second Vatican Council*. San Francisco: Harper & Row.

To Love as God Loves: Marriage

*Gilfredo Marengo**

> Ah, Torvald, the most wonderful thing of all
> would have to happen.... Both you and I
> would have to be so changed that ... oh,
> Torvald, I don't believe any longer in
> wonderful things happening, ... that our life
> together would be a real wedlock. Goodbye.

These words, as sharp as a knife blade, conclude Henrik Ibsen's celebrated drama *A Doll's House* (London: Faber and Faber, 1996) and can serve as a suggestive introduction to help us in reading the encyclical's teaching and reflection on the reality of Christian marriage. The human and the cultural conditions in which Ibsen wrote were profoundly rooted in his time (1879), but it is not difficult to find in his genius echoes of the dramatic questioning about the reality of love and marriage, a questioning that is present in the heart of all people and which, no doubt, is a privileged interlocutor of the author of *Deus Caritas Est.*

Nora's words seem to allude to the expectation of a certain marvelous and wonderful reality that can bring the love between man and woman to its fullness but which—as Torvald still naively does not seem to understand—is out of the reach of human beings and their good will. The fruit of this miracle has a name, *marriage*, at once heralded and yet believed impossible, wherefore the last word can only be a heartrending, desperate "Goodbye!"

---

*Professor of Theological Anthropology, Pontifical John Paul II Institute for Studies on Marriage and Family, Rome.

Seeking to enter as closely as possible into the mind of the encyclical's author, we can then ask whether, by his suspicion of what is new and distinct about the Christian understanding of love (*DCE* 3), contemporary man does not resentfully admit that he is unable to hope for the fulfillment of love's marvelous promise and for the possibility that it might become true in everyone's life.

Before discussing the merits of Benedict XVI's reflections on this theme, it is worth recalling a well-known book on the historical and cultural evolution of the experience of *éros* and marriage, a volume that for decades has been the standard for those studying these issues. It is the famous treatise on *Love in the Western World* by the Swiss philosopher Denis de Rougemont (Princeton, N.J.: Princeton University Press, 1983; original French: Paris: Plon, 1939), which, seeking to answer the same Nietzschean provocation as the one mentioned in the encyclical, concludes by opposing *éros* to *agápē*. It understands the latter, as it is given in marriage, as that which avenges itself on *éros* by rescuing it (cf. p. 311). It is remarkable how with its a priori negative interpretation of *éros*, the Swiss scholar's broad and complex discourse concludes with an evaluation of *agápē* that, even if formally correct, inevitably gives in to the equivocal idea of *agápē* as being something that "limits" or softens the erotic impetus ("marriage is the tomb of wild love", B. Croce), and that consequently—and paradoxically—renders still more acute the desperate expectation of a miracle, which Ibsen knew so well how to evoke.

We recall these tensions, which are dramatically present in everyone's life, in order to outline the general topic of Benedict XVI's text and also in order to show its novelty and fruitfulness by way of contrast. What the encyclical has to say about love and marriage is framed by two concise and dense affirmations. In the first part of this *inclusio*, we read that "love between man and woman, where body and soul are inseparably joined and human beings glimpse an apparently irresistible promise of happiness, ... would seem to be the very epitome of love; all other kinds of love immediately seem to fade in comparison" (*DCE* 2). At the end of a brief anthropological sketch, the encyclical then continues, saying that "this close connection between eros and marriage in the Bible has practically no equivalent in extra-biblical literature" (*DCE* 11).

A first glance at the text suggests a general consideration: love between man and woman, which in its most complete form involves all the dimensions of their humanity (according to the traditional teaching of the unity of body and soul), is the unsurpassable and original level of the very reality of love. Unless we understand this reality, we will be unable to understand the other forms of love. And, as biblical revelation teaches us, this love is *érōs* in its close connection with marriage. Thus, the encyclical suggests nuptial love as the starting point for our reflection on love, holding fast to the erotic connotation which it receives from our daily experience and from the Word of God.

Notwithstanding the risk of a possible oversimplification, this can be seen as a potential key to reading the Holy Father's sober but recurring suggestions concerning marriage itself. Even though the theologian Joseph Ratzinger has already given his specific attention to this topic, it would be incorrect to read the encyclical as a text intending to offer an explicit treatment of the sacrament of marriage as such. Rather, it seems that the subject matter of marriage is presented here in order to serve the fundamental preoccupation of the text, namely, to explain and render more intelligible a succinct understanding of love in the inseparable unity of *érōs* and *agápē*. Marriage, therefore, is presented as the place where human love is revealed. This fact merits being highlighted in order to draw attention to its particular novelty and to gather some useful suggestions from it, above all of a methodological character.

Even though the encyclical makes only sparing use of footnotes, in its very tone the text reveals all the richness of John Paul II's Magisterium on human love and marriage. Most naturally and without crisis of continuity, the present pope proceeds in the lines traced out by his predecessor. Moreover, this first magisterial act of Benedict XVI seems to reveals a particular approach that one cannot help noticing. Like any acute observer of our times, the present pontiff has certainly noticed that the specific character of marriage is seriously put into question today by the most diverse cultural, social, and political viewpoints. The encyclical, however, remarks on these problems only discretely and seems to aim directly at a positive proposal. This fact has not escaped various commentators, and, in the context of theological reflection, it is not without significance. In other words, it is a matter of recognizing that in order to fight adequately the contention about the *humanum* (John Paul II)—a contention from which love and marriage can emerge as the victorious protagonists or as the most precious victims—it is not enough to defend values and principles. Rather, one has to focus on what is truly at stake: the very possibility for man to live the love that has been given to him by his Creator and that is revealed in Christian marriage in a particular way.

The encyclical, therefore, seems to aim at guiding Christians and all men of goodwill to rediscover the *mirabilia Dei* contained in human and divine love so as to help them to discover that God's marvels are not only "in heaven ... [or] beyond the sea.... The word is very near you; it is in your mouth and in your heart, so that you can do it" (Deut 30:12–14). It is important to note a twofold positive attitude that emerges here: the human heart possesses a passionate confidence, and there is the enduring certainty that in its novelty the Christian message will demonstrate its appeal and its capacity to attract and fulfill the expectations of this same heart. In addition, this insistence on the fascination and the promise of happiness offered by the Christian faith is precisely one of the dominant themes of the first year of Benedict XVI's Magisterium, starting with his homily at the inaugural Mass of his Pontificate:

> If we let Christ into our lives, we lose nothing, nothing, absolutely nothing of what makes life free, beautiful and great. No! Only in this friendship are the doors of life opened wide. Only in this friendship is the great potential of human existence truly revealed. Only in this friendship do we experience beauty and liberation. And so, today, with great strength and great conviction, on the basis of long personal experience of life, I say to you, dear young people: Do not be afraid of Christ! He takes nothing away, and he gives you everything. When we give ourselves to him, we receive a hundredfold in return. Yes, open, open wide the doors to Christ—and you will find true life. (24 April 2005)

Returning to the reading of the encyclical's text, we will now focus our attention on the passage of the document that is most pertinent to the reality of marriage:

Two aspects of this are important. First, *eros* is somehow rooted in man's very nature; Adam is a seeker, who "abandons his mother and father" in order to find woman; only together do the two represent complete humanity and become "one flesh". The second aspect is equally important. From the standpoint of creation, *eros* directs man towards marriage, to a bond which is unique and definitive; thus, and only thus, does it fulfill its deepest purpose. Corresponding to the image of a monotheistic God is monogamous marriage. Marriage based on exclusive and definitive love becomes the icon of the relationship between God and his people and vice versa. God's way of loving becomes the measure of human love. This close connection between *eros* and marriage in the Bible has practically no equivalent in extra-biblical literature. (*DCE* 11)

This section serves as the conclusion of an anthropological reflection that is part of a twofold movement, the first part of which discusses "the newness of biblical faith" that proposes a "new image of God" (*DCE* 8–10); the second part then turns to the "image of man" (*DCE* 11). These two parts are intrinsically connected, and it is worth drawing attention to an element that, although occurring in the first part dealing with the image of God, sums up the central and characteristic point of the anthropological section.

We are referring to a thesis proposed by Pseudo-Dionysius that marvelously holds together the affirmations of divine love as *érōs* and as *agápē* (*DCE* 9). The logic of the argument of the Dionysian text illuminates and highlights another consideration of the encyclical as it observes that "man cannot live by oblative, descending love alone. He cannot always give, he must also receive. Anyone who wishes to give love must also receive love as a gift" (*DCE* 7). Drawing from the rich biblical witness and above all from the prophetic and sapiential literature, Benedict XVI seems intent on showing the particular "humanity" of the love of God who is "at the same time a lover with all the passion of a true love" (*DCE* 10).

Reflections on human love can be naturally rooted in this fertile theological ground, manifesting their most attractive fruits. Two basic ideas are presented here: first, there is the reality of *érōs*, which evokes the original fact of Christian anthropology, namely, the understanding of man as created in the image of God, in the duality of sexual distinction as male and female (Gen 1:27); second, it follows from these reflections that the presence of *érōs* in the experience of every human subject reveals man's original ordination to marriage (Gen 2:23–24).

In line with these reflections, the encyclical firmly maintains the profound unity, without confusion, of *érōs* and *agápē*: in fact, for the papal document love in its complete form as found in marriage does not bracket the *ecstatic* impulse specific to *érōs*. While there is a need for purification and a path to be traveled, married love is presented as the authentic fulfillment of *érōs* itself:

> It is part of love's growth towards higher levels and inward purification that it now seeks to become definitive, and it does so in a twofold sense: both in the sense of exclusivity (this particular person alone) and in the sense of being "for ever". Love embraces the whole of existence in each of its dimensions, including the dimension of time. It could hardly be otherwise, since its promise looks towards its definitive goal: love looks to the eternal. Love is indeed "ecstasy", not in the sense of a moment of intoxication, but rather as a journey, an ongoing exodus out of the closed inward-looking self towards its liberation through self-giving, and thus towards authentic self-discovery and indeed the discovery of God. (*DCE* 6)

What determines this authentic fulfillment is clearly indicated by the dimension of time and historicity, that is, what *érōs* desires as such is meant to last in the future. Benedict XVI's suggestion appears precious and provocative for anthropological and theological reflection, insofar as it discretely proposes the necessity of showing the way in which the Christian faith can help man in the somewhat paradoxical task of temporal loving, of hoping, and of committing himself to a *forever* in an experience that, due to its original intensity, seems bound to wear out and to exist entirely in the moment. In fact, however, the Christian faith can help us to confront our human inability to "guarantee" the act of our freedom in a dimension (the future) that does not yet belong to us.

One could say that the idea of temporality plays a twofold role in the encyclical: first, it appears as the element that urges the experience of the erotic not to close itself in on the "ecstatic moment"; second, it is precisely by providing *érōs* with the possibility of a history that Christianity allows for the event of *agápē*—and thus for the fulfillment of human love—to occur.

In this context it is worthwhile mentioning how the encyclical evokes the irreducible historicity of the Christian event. Thus, with great precision it affirms, "being Christian is not the result of an ethical choice or a lofty idea, but the encounter with an event, a person, which gives life a new horizon and a decisive direction" (*DCE* 1). The closeness or—still better perhaps—the inherent naturalness between the loving rapport and the relationship between man and Christ is indicated by the use of terms such as "encounter", "event", and "person", which immediately remind us of the fundamental way in which, prior to every subsequent determination, everyone knows what it means to love or to fall in love. Thus, it can be suggested that the encyclical invites us to look at Christian marriage as the factor that is capable of bestowing time and history on human love.

It is well-known that romantic culture and sensibility—which go well beyond the historical period called Romanticism—have dedicated great energies to investigating and narrating the experience of love, particularly in the form of the novel. Likewise well-attested is the fact that this sensibility is much more interested in the variations of fortune characteristic of the beginnings of a love story (what could be called the "time of being in love"). Attending to these facts, we arrive at a surprising conclusion: in the most acute and, humanly speaking, most involving a priori expressions of love understood as a somewhat mystical, complete fusion of the lovers, the lovers' tragic end seems to be a prerequisite. From the archetypes of Tristan and Isolde and Romeo and Juliet to the great tradition of nineteenth-century melodrama, the most passionate love stories inevitably end with the death of the protagonists. Unable to perceive how the perfect form of love, understood as fusion, can occur in time and, above all, convinced of the impossibility of its duration, the romantic artist calls on death to intervene and sanction this impossibility dramaturgically. Death enters as a negative *deus ex machina!*

Another interpretative current is characterized by the famous final provisions of many narrations ("and they lived happily ever after").

Interestingly, however, the content of this story of happiness and contentment does not appear to be interesting. It is suggested only at the end of a narration, but never narrated or investigated; the true love story is prior! This sensibility, which merits much deeper reflections and analyses, finds a unique counterpoint in the novelty of the Christian revelation about love and marriage, a counterpoint that the encyclical evokes with the notions of *"definitiveness, exclusivity, eternity"*. It is certainly not the Pope's intention to develop organically the teaching of these points, which, in synthesis, represent the adequate terms for understanding the fullness of the sacramental reality of matrimony.

In any case, the encyclical should be read as an invitation to follow the still largely undeveloped path of a type of theological research for which the suggestion of an intrinsic connection between the anthropological and the sacramental moment appears as a methodological point of no return. It is, however, impossible not to notice some signs that indicate the encyclical's objective interest in this regard. In the first place, there is the topic of the analogy between biblical monotheism and marriage in its revealed form (*DCE* 11).

As the encyclical develops its reflections, this affirmation indeed seems central. The document takes up Old Testament revelation, which, as it recalls (*DCE* 10), makes abundant use of the nuptial metaphor in order to speak of the relationship between God and his people. At the same time, Benedict XVI uses this metaphor to indicate that the nuptial form of God's love for Israel is "the measure of human love" (*DCE* 11). Given the strict connection between the Old and the New Testament, this interpretation of the scriptural data anticipates what will be the center of St. Paul's teaching on marriage: "Husbands, love your wives, as Christ loved the Church and gave himself up for her" (Eph 5:25). From this perspective the reference to Old Testament monotheism as illustrative of the singular uniqueness and definitiveness of marriage seems to suggest two converging perspectives.

First, one can say that the Pontiff aims at underlining the novelty of the biblical revelation of creation and of a single God, seeing in this context the adequate framework for discovering the truth of human love. The broader context into which this part of Benedict XVI's encyclical is inserted is the fruitful ground laid by John Paul II's famous catecheses on human love, above all where they develop a completely

original reading of the Genesis accounts of creation. The other great
theme of Wojtyła's, the *communio personarum*, shines through in the
further development of the encyclical dedicated to the Christ-like form
of human love (*DCE* 17).

What the encyclical has to say in conclusion of its christological
reflections merits our particular attention: "The 'commandment' of
love is only possible because it is more than a requirement. Love can
be 'commanded' because it has first been given" (*DCE* 14). The
privileged place given to the notions of "gift" and "giving", in comparison to the concepts of "commandments" (obligations) and "*requirements*", is a truly thought-provoking suggestion and opens an abundant
path for further reflection.

In the short space of this essay it is only possible to hint briefly at
the possibilities for further elaboration of some of the ideas contained
in this text. First of all, we must keep in mind that for the encyclical
the dynamic movement of *érōs* does not unfold "naturally" as a simple
process; rather, there is a break of continuity. In other words, by itself
desire is not enough for the path of human freedom to arrive at the
fulfilled experience of love. Human freedom is made to love and is
called to recognize that to be truly free and loving, it must be liberated.

From this perspective, the novelty brought by Jesus Christ can
never be understood as a simple course correction or, still less, as the
emergence of a series of ethical requirements that simply have the
purpose of restraining the humanly incontrollable impulse of love and
of erotic passion and bringing them to a good end. In this line, to the
extent to which they are part of "true" love *quo talis*, the "requirements" of Christian marriage (fidelity, indissolubility, fruitfulness) find
their foundation in the logic of God's gift. In fact, to say that love
must first of all be given allows us to highlight some important factors.

To start with, on the anthropological level, a certain emphasis on
the necessity of the absolutely gratuitous and oblative character of love
that is sometimes present in Christian sentiment finds a corrective. In
this regard the encyclical clarifies that "man cannot live by oblative,
descending love alone. He cannot always give, he must also receive.
Anyone who wishes to give love must also receive love as a gift. Certainly, as the Lord tells us, one can become a source from which rivers
of living water flow (cf. Jn 7:37–38). Yet to become such a source,

one must constantly drink anew from the original source, which is Jesus Christ, from whose pierced heart flows the love of God (cf. Jn 19:34)" (*DCE* 7). Christ, therefore, is the source of love, the one who gives love. In this way the document invites us to recognize the primacy of the Father's initiative in Christ, the principle of every authentic realization of love among human beings (cf. 1 Jn 4:12).

Acknowledging the primacy of the love of God who loves us first becomes concrete for us in the "contact with the visible manifestations of God's love [that] can awaken within us a feeling of joy born of the experience of being loved" (*DCE* 17), but, as Benedict XVI points out, this surprising joy is not meant to remain an initial spark, fragile as every other sentiment. Again, the text of the encyclical reveals its strong attention to the historicity of human existence, guiding the reader to consider the ways in which this initial experience can become the source of the history of human love. First of all, the encyclical affirms that the experience of being loved involves all the faculties and potentialities of the subject, tending to unify them in an act, that is, the act of love, which by itself is all-engaging.

Secondly, appreciating once more the insuperable historical dimension of human existence, the document advises us that "this process is always open-ended; love is never 'finished' and complete; throughout life, it changes and matures and thus remains faithful to itself" (ibid.). The pretense, at times ingenuous, of a love that is perfect once and for all is the dramatic sign of the human desire for a fullness that can be experienced in the here and now. At the same time, it marks our proneness to the subtle temptation of freeing ourselves from the effort, labor, and toil involved in undertaking and walking the road of our fulfillment every day, embracing most profoundly our quality of being *homo viator*. In contrast to this pretense, the encyclical offers the perspective of a real fulfillment of love, a fulfillment that is not hindered by the continuous transformations through which love passes and that do not contradict its initial momentum but rather progressively reveal its face.

Embraced by these two coordinates, that is, the totality of all human faculties involved in the particular *imperfection* of time, the experience of being loved offers man the possibility of discovering who he truly is, "based on the realization that God is in fact more deeply present to me than I am to myself" (ibid.). In recognizing himself in love, man finds himself, since he can know his good only in the experience of love; only if he discovers that his path leads him to the goal in which "self-abandonment to God increases and God becomes our joy" (ibid.). This *joy* will conclude the path of the history of love, just as it has begun it, which almost suggests that love is sufficient in itself, that it possesses the *logos* of its own occurrence, development, persistence, and fulfillment in human life.

The more one reflects about human love thus understood, the more one sees that it postulates, precisely insofar as it is truly human, the horizon of transcendence. The more one looks at love, the more one discovers the face of God who is Love. The better that human love is understood, the more it reveals its "divine" pedigree, and, vice versa, the more that God's love is understood—in all its complexity— the more it appears to us to be "surprisingly human".

In this way the sacrament of matrimony is revealed as that reality of salvation which enables us to experience how our existence can be profoundly transformed by the grace of Christ. In this sacrament the progressive assimilation to his Humanity and to his Love occur in a context and in ways that are immediately perceptible to every human being, so that it can truly be a place that is uniquely privileged, a place where everyone experiences that "only in the mystery of the incarnate Word does the mystery of man take on light" (*GS* 22).

The author of *A Doll's House* cited in the beginning is said to have envisioned his drama *Brand* (Oxford: Oxford University Press, 1972) in St. Peter's Basilica in Rome in 1866. In conclusion we entrust to the words of the impelling finale of this theatrical work the task of evoking the dramatic tension that we hope to have highlighted in *Deus Caritas Est*, a dramatic tension that permeates the encyclical dynamically. There is the tormenting, excruciating cry of mankind, to which God's paternal tenderness responds with the embrace of love, freely given and thus and only thus attainable in the existence of every human being:

Brand: Answer me, God, in the jaws of death: / is there no salvation for the Will of Man? / No small measure of salvation? A Voice: He is *Deus caritatis!*

The Harmony of Love:
"Idem velle atque idem nolle"

*Donna Lynn Orsuto**

Introduction

The central message of Christianity, on which Benedict XVI's first encyclical focuses, is expressed in 1 John 4:16, "God is love, and he who abides in love abides in God, and God abides in him." The Pope points out that Christian life is more than an ethical choice or the embrace of an ideal. It is an encounter with the person and event of Jesus Christ, who opens new horizons in one's life. The ethical command—and it is a command—to love God and neighbor as oneself is, at its root, a response to God's love that has been lavished upon us in Jesus Christ. This is the source of the love we share with others.

In reflecting upon the nature of Christian love, Benedict XVI reminds us in the first part of the encyclical that it is "not merely a sentiment. Sentiments come and go. A sentiment can be a marvelous first spark, but it is not the fullness of love." Mature love engages the whole person. It is not only a "feeling of joy born of the experience of being loved" but also an encounter that "engages our will and our intellect". Love's purification is a process that occurs over time and is always "open-ended". Though it changes and matures over time, it is never "finished" or complete (*Deus Caritas Est* 17).

* Assistant Professor of Spirituality, Pontifical John Paul II Institute for Studies on Marriage and Family, Rome. Assistant Professor of Theology and Lay Spirituality, Pontifical Gregorian University, Rome.

Idem Velle atque Idem Nolle: A Classical Definition of Friendship

It is in this context that Benedict XVI quotes Sallust (Gaius Sallustius Crispus), who, in his *De coniuratione Catilinae*, writes, "idem velle atque idem nolle." A Roman historian and politician (86–34 B.C.), Sallust, in his *Catilinarian Conspiracy* (62 B.C.), describes how the enigmatic Roman politician Catiline (108–62 B.C.), when addressing his troops and fellow conspirators, notes that the union brought about through their reciprocal bond of friendship is so great that whatever advantages or evils affect one also affect the other. Furthermore, their friendship means that they have the same desires and aversions. The full quotation on the lips of Catiline is: "Idem velle atque idem nolle, ea demum firma amicitia est", which can be translated as: "To like and to dislike the same thing, this is indeed true friendship" (Sallust, *De coniuratione Catilinae* 20, 4). Sallust's saying gradually evolved into a classical definition of friendship that was used by a number of Christian writers. For example, variants of this proverb occur in Cassian (*Confer.* 16, 1) and Ambrose (*De Fide* 4, 74) (cf. Carmichael 2004: 228). Twelfth-century Cistercian abbot Aelred of Rievaulx also quotes Sallust in *De spirituali amicitia* and notes that "to like and to dislike the same thing" is one of the "laws of friendship". St. Thomas Aquinas also links "idem velle et idem nolle" to friendship when he attributes the Sallust saying to Cicero (Marcus Tullius). The Angelic Doctor writes that "it is reckoned a sign of friendship if people 'make choice of the same things' (*Ethic.* ix, 4), and Tullius says (*De Amicitia*) that friends 'like and dislike the same things'" (*STh* II–II 29, 3). In paragraph 17 of *Deus Caritas Est*, Benedict XVI quotes the first part of Sallust's proverbial saying, "idem velle atque idem nolle", but leaves out the second, "ea demum firma amicitia est".

Philía and Agápē

This omission brings up an interesting question about the encyclical: Where is friendship mentioned? The answer is that the word occurs twice, both times in paragraph 3. The first instance is where the three Greek words for love are explained, *érōs*, *philía* (the love of friendship) and *agápē*. The second is when Benedict XVI goes on to suggest that "the term *philia*, the love of friendship . . . is used with added depth of meaning in Saint John's Gospel in order to express the relationship between Jesus and his disciples. The tendency to avoid the word *eros*, together with the new vision of love expressed through the word *agape*, clearly point to something new and distinct about the Christian understanding of love" (*DCE* 3).

Though *philía* seems to be eclipsed by *agápē* in the encyclical in general and though it is not mentioned explicitly in the Sallust quotation as used by Benedict XVI in paragraph 17, it is certainly implied. This is evident because the same quotation from Sallust occurs in the homily of the *Missa Pro Eligendo Romano Pontefice*, where (the then) Cardinal Ratzinger focuses on the theme of friendship with Christ. Just after the homily, many press releases accented what he said about the "dictatorship of relativism". The fact is, though, that "relativism" is mentioned only twice, whereas the theme of friendship occurs eighteen times. It is reasonable to conclude that in the twenty-nine paragraphs that make up this homily, friendship emerges as a key theme. What Cardinal Ratzinger proposed in his last homily before being elected pope with regard to the theme of friendship with Christ gives insight into what Benedict XVI means in his first encyclical when he quotes Sallust.

Benedict XVI and Christian Friendship

In his homily, the comments about friendship are woven around the Johannine passage where Jesus says, "No longer do I call you servants . . . ; but I have called you friends" (Jn 15:15). Even though one may at times feel like a useless servant (cf. Lk 17:10), Cardinal Ratzinger continues,

> Yet, in spite of this, the Lord calls us friends, he makes us his friends, he gives us his friendship. The Lord gives friendship a dual definition. There are no secrets between friends: Christ tells us all that he hears from the Father; he gives us his full trust and with trust, also knowledge. He reveals his face and his heart to us. He shows us the tenderness he feels for us, his passionate love that goes even as far as the folly of the Cross. He entrusts himself to us, he gives us the power to speak in his name: "this is my

body ...", "I forgive you ...". He entrusts his Body, the Church, to us. (Ratzinger 2005)

So the first point is that Christ made us his friends and shares with us what he hears from the Father. The second element of friendship with Jesus involves a "communion of wills". It is here that Cardinal Ratzinger, in quoting Sallust while rounding it off with a profoundly Christian reflection on Jesus' call to us, makes a specific reference to friendship,

> For the Romans "*Idem velle—idem nolle*" [same desires, same dislikes] was also the definition of friendship. "You are my friends if you do what I command you" (Jn 15:14). Friendship with Christ coincides with the third request of the *Our Father:* "Thy will be done on earth as it is in heaven." At his hour in the Garden of Gethsemane, Jesus transformed our rebellious human will into a will conformed and united with the divine will. He suffered the whole drama of our autonomy—and precisely by placing our will in God's hands, he gives us true freedom: "Not as I will, but as you will" (Mt 26:39). (Ratzinger 2005)

This friendship with Christ which is none other than a harmony of wills, *idem velle—idem nolle*, is both gift and responsibility. We receive it as gift because Christ, through his death and Resurrection, brings about this transformation through our redemption. It is also our responsibility to respond to the gift by using our free will to know and love Jesus more. As this happens, we progressively experience greater freedom and joy in our lives. As the future pope said:

> Our redemption is brought about in this communion of wills: being friends of Jesus, to become friends of God. The more we love Jesus, the more we know him, the more our true freedom develops and our joy in being redeemed flourishes. Thank you, Jesus, for your friendship! (Ratzinger 2005)

Friendship with Christ, a Recurring Theme in Benedict XVI's Early Pontificate

In many of the early texts of Benedict XVI's pontificate, friendship is a recurring theme. Specifically, he emphasizes the centrality of friendship with the person of Jesus Christ. To the clergy of Rome, he explains that this implies being "nourished by personal encounter with Christ" (Benedict XVI 2005a). With disarming simplicity, the theme of friendship with Christ again emerges in his catechetical dialogue with young Roman first communicants. In responding to their questions, he reminds them in numerous ways that their first communion is the beginning of a "lifelong friendship with Jesus, the beginning of a journey together because in walking with Jesus we do well and life becomes good" (Benedict XVI 2005b). The young people gathered for World Youth Day in Cologne, addressed as "dear friends" by Benedict XVI, hear the words that were part of his first homily as pope:

> If we let Christ into our lives, we lose nothing, nothing, absolutely nothing of what makes life free, beautiful and great. No! Only in this friendship are the doors of life opened wide. Only in this friendship is the great potential of human existence truly revealed. Only in this friendship do we experience beauty and liberation. (Benedict XVI 2005d)

From Friendship with Christ to Friendship without Frontiers

As one comes to know and love God, gradually one comes to know and love what God loves. Thus the bonds of friendship with God enable one to form profound friendships with others. Some of the early addresses of the new pontiff seem to suggest that this has been the experience of Benedict XVI himself. For example, in the first visit to his homeland for World Youth Day in August 2006, the Pope mentions the different cardinals of Cologne in the context of a "chain of friendships (that) was never broken". He speaks of Cardinal Frings as one who gave him "his full confidence from the very first, making an authentically fatherly friendship with me". With Cardinal Höffner, he also had a "deep and lively friendship". He notes that "Cardinal Meisner has also been my friend for a very long time." This friendship is the reason why he feels "at home" in Cologne (Benedict XVI 2005f).

Friendship extends to other Christians, for example, in his address at the ecumenical meeting at the Archbishop's House, he mentions his "long ... and ... cordial friendship" with Roger Schutz, who had just died. The theme of friendship also occurs three times in his address to the Jewish Representatives whom he met in Cologne. There he repeats twice that "the Catholic Church is committed—I reaffirm this again today—to tolerance, respect, friendship and peace between all peoples, cultures and religions." Furthermore he states that he wishes "to reaffirm that I intend to continue with great vigor on the path towards improved relations and friendship with the Jewish People, following the decisive lead given by Pope John Paul II [cf. *Address to the Delegation of the International Jewish Committee on Interreligious Consultations*, 9 June 2005]" (Benedict XVI 2005g). Finally, he reminds the "dear and esteemed Muslim friends" gathered in Cologne that, during his meeting with the delegates of Churches and Christian Communities and with representatives of the various religious traditions, he affirmed that "the Church wants to continue building bridges of friendship with the followers of all religions, in order to seek the true good of every person and of society as a whole [*L'Osservatore Romano*, 25 April 2005, 4]" (Benedict XVI 2005e).

An essential part of the Christian message is that God's love knows know bounds. It moves us beyond ourselves, beyond our small circle of friends to reach out to others. As we experience the love of God manifest through friendship with Jesus, it gradually leads to a friendship without frontiers. Though Benedict XVI does not quote St. Thomas Aquinas, there is a passage from the *Summa theologiae* that explains how the experience of friendship with God spills over to all those whom God loves.

> Friendship extends to . . . someone in respect of another, as, when a man has friendship for a certain person, for his sake he loves all belonging to him, be they children, servants, or connected with him in any way. Indeed so much do we love our friends, that for their sake we love all who belong to them, even if they hurt or hate us; so that, in this way, the friendship of charity extends even to our enemies, whom we love out of charity in relation to God, to Whom the friendship of charity is chiefly directed. (*STh* II–II, 23, 1 ad 2)

Since all humanity is loved by God, as we enter into friendship with God, which is possible only because of God's grace poured into our hearts through the Holy Spirit, we begin to love all those whom God loves. In other words, it is only natural that, as we experience God's friendship, we love "those who are connected with him in any way". This is one dimension of the harmony of wills.

A Growing Communion of Will and Thought

The encyclical *Deus Caritas Est* is not explicitly about friendship. At the same time, Benedict XVI does mention that love is a single reality, though it has many and varied manifestations, and so implicitly it touches on this theme. Reflecting on friendship in the Holy Father's early sermons sheds light on how love is understood in this encyclical. It is clear that a major theme of the encyclical is to rehabilitate *éros* and show that in fact, if it is purified and healed, it becomes "a certain foretaste of the pinnacle of our existence, of the beatitude for which our whole being yearns" (*DCE* 4).

This purification of love begins with an experience of God's love breaking into one's life and broadening one's horizons. One way of describing this is to say that it is an experience of "being in love". As the Jesuit philosopher and theologian Bernard Lonergan (1904–1984) says, "Such being in love has its antecedents, its causes, its conditions, its occasions. But once it has blossomed forth and as long as it lasts, it takes over. It is the first principle. From it flow one's desires and fears, one's joys and sorrows, one's discernment of values, one's decisions and deeds" (Lonergan 1971: 105). Lonergan explains that "being in love with God, as experienced, is being in love in an unrestricted fashion. All love is self-surrender, but being in love with God is being in love without limits or qualifications or conditions or reservations" (ibid., 105–6).

This encyclical is about the blossoming forth of love. It is not merely about "being in love" but about "staying in love", about letting love be purified and matured so that gradually one lives in harmony with the Beloved. It means allowing Christ's way of being and acting to penetrate one's will and intellect. In the words of Benedict XVI:

> The love-story between God and man consists in the very fact
> that this communion of wills increases in a communion of thought

and sentiment, and thus our will and God's will increasingly coincide: God's will is no longer for me an alien will, something imposed on me from without by the commandments, but it is now my own will, based on the realization that God is in fact more deeply present to me than I am to myself. Then self-abandonment to God increases and God becomes our joy (cf. Ps 73 [72]23–28). (*DCE* 17)

Practical Implications: On the Road to Jericho

In light of this short reflection on friendship, the harmony of wills, and *Deus Caritas Est*, one might ask how the experience of God's love impacts our Christian responsibility to exercise charity toward others. The simple answer is that we are invited to love and to care for those whom God loves, especially the most vulnerable and weak. A more profound response, perhaps at the heart of this encyclical, is that having experienced God's gracious love (and one might add, genuine friendship with Jesus), we are gradually drawn to love all that he loves. Reflecting on the double spiritual meaning of the Good Samaritan parable (Lk 10:25–37) might shed light on the dynamic at work.

In Jesus' time, the thirteen-mile downhill journey from Jerusalem to Jericho through a desert wasteland was not only difficult, it was also dangerous. The perils of the journey are well known and the reaction of the priest and Levite are not surprising. In reflecting on this parable, we all too quickly (and rightly) see in the Good Samaritan an example of what we as Christians are called to be. Like Blessed Mother Teresa of Calcutta, whom John Paul II described as "an icon of the Good Samaritan", we are each invited in our own way to reach out to those in need. As Benedict XVI notes in his encyclical, "The Christian's program—the program of the Good Samaritan, the program of Jesus—is 'a heart which sees'. This heart sees where love is needed and acts accordingly" (*DCE* 31b).

There is another interpretation of the parable that is also important. Spiritual writers from St. Augustine to Luther remind us that we are like the wounded man on the road to Jericho. Each of us has experienced the loving care of the Good Samaritan, who has bandaged our wounds and poured healing oil on them. The inn is sometimes seen as an image of the Church where we are gradually healed through the sacraments of what holds us back from fully entering into and sharing that love with others. The Good Samaritan is Jesus himself, who manifests to us the compassion of Father. The lifelong process of purification and transformation has begun in baptism, but, as Pope Benedict XVI notes, this growth in love is a journey, an "ongoing exodus out of the closed inward-looking self towards its liberation through self-giving" (*DCE* 6).

Precisely because we have been lovingly ministered to by the Good Samaritan, it will gradually become normative that we stop along the way to help those in need, for between God and us there will gradually be a harmony of wills. It will become natural because as our love of God is purified and transformed, it will expand to include those whom he loves.

In the Redemptoris Chapel found in the Vatican's Apostolic Palace, there is a striking mosaic of the Good Samaritan. As Marko Rupnik notes, "The Samaritan has the same face as the wounded man.... Christ is the Good Samaritan who has come to heal us. We can only love after having been loved. At the same time, the Word is valid for us, 'whatever you did for one of these least brothers of mine, you did for me' (Mt 25:40)" (Rupnik 1999: 295). In a way, it is because Christ heals us through his loving gaze that we are able to reach out in love to others, to see Christ in others. Love is the key: God's love revealed in Jesus, given freely, and now shared with those whom we meet on our journey from Jerusalem to Jericho.

Bibliography

Aelred of Rievaulx. 1997. *Spiritual Friendship*. Kalamazoo: Cistercian Publications.

Benedict XVI. 2005a. *Address* to the Clergy of Rome, May 13.

_____. 2005b. Catechetical Meeting with Children Who Had Received First Communion during the Year. October 15.

_____. 2005c. Ecumenical Meeting at the Archbishopric of Cologne. *Address*. August 19.

_____. 2005d. Mass ... for the Beginning of the Petrine Ministry of the Bishop of Rome. *Homily*. April 24.

————. 2005e. Meeting with Representatives of Some Muslim Communities. *Address*. August 20.

————. 2005f. Visit to the Cathedral of Cologne. *Greetings*. August 18.

————. 2005g. Visit to the Synagogue of Cologne. *Greetings*. August 19.

Carmichael, L. 2004. *Friendship. Interpreting Christian Love*. London: T&T Clark.

Lonergan, B. 1971. *Method in Theology*. Toronto: University of Toronto Press for the Lonergan Research Institute.

Ratzinger, Joseph Cardinal. 2005. "Homily by the Cardinal Who Became Pope: Mass for the Election of the Roman Pontiff: Monday, 18 April". *L'Osservatore Romano*, no. 16: 3.

Rupnik, M. I. 1999. "Descrizione delle Illustrazioni". In *La Cappella "Redemptoris Mater"*, edited by M. Apa, O. Clément, and C. Valenziano. Vatican City.

Sallust. 1971. *War with Catiline, War with Jugurtha, Selection from the Histories. Doubtful Works*. Translated by J. C. Rolfe. Loeb Classical Library, vol. 116. Cambridge, Mass.: Harvard.

The Spark of Sentiment and the Fullness of Love

José Noriega*

> In the gradual unfolding of this encounter, it is clearly revealed
> that love is not merely a sentiment.
> Sentiments come and go.
> A sentiment can be a marvelous first spark,
> but it is not the fullness of love.
> —*DCE* 17

The Rediscovery of Sentiment and Its Ambiguity

What is the value of sentiment in human life? The symbolic universe
of the experience of love in the West is conditioned, in large part, by
the identification of love with passion and sentiment. The first identification appears in medieval chivalry literature, where love is seen as
an unappeased tension toward an impossible ideal, whose theological
stamp comes from the dualism of the Cathars (Rougemont 1983). The
second identification takes place in Romanticism, which, in opposition to the "dream" of rationalism that has overcome the emotional
realm, tries to defend the role that sentiment plays in authentic human
life: the unifying principle of conduct in these identifications is no
longer reason but sentiment.

Both intentions were crystallized into the current symbolic image
of love and were assumed under diverse cultural manifestations. They

*Assistant Professor of Special Moral Theology, Pontifical John Paul II Institute for
Studies on Marriage and Family, Rome.

influence the current experience of love in which a new reduction is made: that of love to sex.

In this cultural context, the ambiguity of all discourse that speaks of love, and especially of sentiment, becomes understandable. A danger of misinterpretation exists that might short-circuit the very teaching of the Church. Because the words that are transmitted are received in a different register, such misunderstanding leads to an entirely different melody. One means to speak of "love", that is, of interpersonal relationship, of self-giving, of intimacy, of reciprocity, of irrevocability, of faithfulness. The message people receive, however, is understood as mere sentiment, affection, emotion. We can identify the theme of this melody with an implicit narcissism that upsets people's experiences and makes them incapable of truly building their own lives. Herein lies the radical ambiguity of how the West lives the experience of love.

The feeling of love would be that joyful instant in which its protagonist experiences the richness of the living flow. But it is an experience that dies as soon as it is enjoyed: the moment dazzles but is incapable of illuminating a person's entire life. Our enamored one is faced with the great enemy, the real ghost of love, time, which strikes at the roots of love, since it prevents the assurance that the current experience will continue to be felt into the future. The spark of sentiment then seems to languish and be extinguished in the nostalgia of its brilliance, focusing on the instant being lived, with a hope that does not extend farther than the satisfactions that can be found. Today, the verses that Horace spoke to Leuconoë sound in a new way:

Ask not—we cannot know—
what end the gods have set for you, for me; . . .
How much better to endure whatever comes,
whether Jupiter grants us additional winters or whether this is our last. . . .
Be wise, strain the wine;
and since life is brief, prune back far-reaching hopes!
Even while we speak, envious time has passed:
pluck the day, putting as little trust as possible in tomorrow!

Horace Ode I–XI

The person living at the beginning of this millennium is an emotional subject who has lost the vital horizon of sentiment and is therefore seized by a terrible mania, that of demanding at all cost to relive experiences so that the spark might continue shining. The reduction of love to sentiment carries with it an intimist withdrawal in which everything is prized according to the emotional intensity it offers.

In such a situation, would it not be better to use other categories? Should we abandon the way of love and sentiment? Pope Benedict in his first encyclical, however, takes another path, in which he highlights its role in human life, emphasizing the intrinsic unity of love. If we stop speaking of love because of the danger of being misunderstood, would our contemporaries understand us? Or even worse, would there not be the danger of distorting the Christian message, making human experience inexplicable and the Gospel irrelevant?

Undoubtedly, the experience of love possesses a sentimental dimension, since its protagonist becomes aware of what is happening and enjoys it, becoming engrossed in it. The question is not to dispense with this dimension but rather to let it speak in all its grandeur. Is not the spark that all love ignites capable of illuminating the destiny of an entire life? Does the spark that all love entails not bear within it an essential truth about ourselves? Does the spark of sentiment not need the fullness of love?

The Revelation of Love: The Destiny of Life

Every experience of love takes place within an encounter. It is not simply something that can be arrived at from nature itself, although it is possible only because of nature. We are vulnerable to one another because our nature is made that way, sensitive to others' different and complementary values. The loving encounter implies a newness in life at both a sentimental level as well as, and more importantly, at an ontological level. That is, it is an event that transforms and enriches us.

When we encounter another in love, we experience a newness of life and realize the impossibility of reducing the event to its conscious elements or, even less, to elements of our choosing. The experience of love encloses a mystery that is revealed to us with the passing of time. Before we have chosen anything, we feel loved and loving. Sentiment implies being aware, at a cognitive level, of something that has happened in us.

There is a variety in the richness of sentiments: not all fall into the same category. The feeling of discomfort from a toothache has a neuro-physiological cause as does the feeling of vitality that one gets from a sunny spring day: this is why they are sentiments that can be evoked by simulating their cause. However, the feeling of happiness experienced in the face of reconciliation with a parent is not one that is explainable on a merely neurophysiological level; neither is the sentiment of fear in the face of a serious illness. Here, rather, we are confronted with sentiments motivated by the meaning of reconciliation or illness. Happiness, sadness, fear, hope, and love are meaningful because their sense is not found in them but rather in their response to another reality of which they become signs and to which we feel greatly attracted. These are sentiments that move us to act because they dispose us toward something and implicate our freedom (Von Hildebrand 1997, chap. 2). This is why it is necessary to know how to interpret their meaning. It is here that we encounter one of the greatest difficulties, given the intensity with which sentiments present themselves.

The interpretation of sentiments has two decisive criteria: first, the intentionality that they entail and, second, the way that the end they lead us to implies freedom, since there are sentiments that simply move us to feel while others move us to act. This is how we can ask ourselves where the sentiment is leading: Is it to an affair? To a fuller way of loving? In this way, sentiments reveal themselves as new ways of relating to and interacting with persons. In sentiment, a promise of plenitude is announced that expresses the same quality as one's desire. Sentiment becomes a principle that moves one to want (Angelini 1994: 86–89), to exercise freedom. In sentiment lies hidden a promise of fullness, not just to feel, but above all to build: "Love promises infinity, eternity—a reality far greater and totally other than our everyday existence" (DCE 5).

In light of this intentional dimension that brings our freedom into play, we can see that there are true sentiments and false sentiments, not because some are more or less intense, but because some allow the possibility of realizing the fullness they promise while others make this realization impossible. All sentiment, being a response to a good that affects us, implies an original experience whose content is not posited by the person living it but rather is given in the way in which the person is capable of welcoming a personal reality (Scola 2003). The experience of love in itself calls for a verification of its content, a judgment of the sentiment itself (Botturi 2004).

In this way we can appreciate how the sentiment of love and the desire that arises from it contain, not simply the desire for pleasure or satisfaction, but above all the desire for happiness, for fullness. This desire cannot be satisfied by a simple technique or a fleeting emotional state because it is directed to a plenitude in the way of desiring. Sentiments thus occupy a role of "mediation" between the *bios* and the *logos*, offering an entire field of motivation for conduct (Ricoeur 1967: 122–202). In the love between a man and a woman, "human beings glimpse an apparently irresistible promise of happiness" (*DCE* 2).

Interpreting the meaning of an affective experience, then, is equivalent to situating the concrete and contingent experience within the context of a life considered in its entirety. Its meaning lies in the nexus that is established with the fullness that promises, with the ultimate truth of humanity, the ideal ego of each person as he was conceived by God, prefigured in the loving sentiment. This is how love allows us to recognize the absolute worth of each person (Solov'ëv 1950).

It is thus revealed that the experience of love opens a space within man: between that-which-is and that-which-can-become, between what has been received and what is promised. Love thus inaugurates a path in life, a path toward a promised plenitude: a promise, however, that is just that. The task lies in achieving this fullness. In this way, love generates hope. If, in the reduction of love to sentiment, hope becomes impossible, it is conversely understood that the true experience of love is capable of being transformed into hope and thus of motivating all of life. It is in light of hope that the true essence of love becomes visible, saving it from a reduction to feeling (Ratzinger 1991: 47–48).

There are encounters so dense—such as the encounter with the Person of Christ—that they give "life a new horizon and a decisive direction" (*DCE* 1). Man is also vulnerable to God and can, because of that, be affected by him when drawing near to him. In this encounter Christ reveals the promise of ultimate fullness in which all love attains its meaning and equilibrium.

Sentiment is a marvelous spark that ignites in an encounter and in whose light appears the destiny of a life (Noriega 2005: 19–89).

The Ontological Foundation: The Unity of the Loving Subject

Is this way of understanding sentiment not excessive, in that it is inhabited by a truth that refers to the final realization of a person? In the end, "sentiments come and go." Is this not attributing more to the loving sentiment than it actually contains? Is this not projecting onto it rational content that is foreign to it? The difficulty appears in all its radicality in the Freudian interpretation of sexual impulse: if impulsive energy can create inner conflicts, the solution would be to channel it into higher, more creative, socially esteemed ends. The response to possible impulsive chaos would be the sublimation of that impulse. The limitation of this interpretation lies, not in the value of the impulsive dimension of love, but rather in not appreciating that there is an *inner logos* to the impulse by which man is oriented toward the world or, more, to a way of relating that implies a new perfection in man. Such an impulse cannot be reduced to a mere equilibrium of forces: the experience of love has made possible a newness whose meaning is the most perfect unity possible (Lear 1998: 142–55).

Where is the foundation of this *inner logos* found? Simply stated, it is found in the unity of the loving subject. "This is due first and foremost to the fact that man is a being made up of body and soul. Man is truly himself when his body and soul are intimately united. . . . Yet it is neither the spirit alone nor the body alone that loves: it is man, the person, a unified creature composed of body and soul, who loves" (*DCE* 5). It is in virtue of the ontological unity of man that the body itself and the passions and sentiments it makes possible are something properly human.

Because of the unity of body and soul that exists in man, the corporal dimensions of existence have a truly human meaning. The body is capable of expressing the person, inaugurating an enormously meaningful language: the language of the body (John Paul II). Thus, sensible knowing implies intellectual knowing, and in sensibly perceiving, a person "knows". In the same way, sentiment in itself implies a spiritual dimension by which the person, with his sentiments, is capable of perceiving the final intentionality of his sentiment and thus of knowing its meaning. Sentiments are permeated by intelligence (Nussbaum).

The Path of Unification and the Fullness of Love

Now, this ontological foundation in virtue of which man acts in the unity of body and soul requires an adequate equivalent in the dynamic process of conduct. It is of vital importance to notice that it is not enough to be "capable" of carrying out certain actions; one must be "prepared" for them: it is one thing to be capable of playing the piano like Mozart or of running a marathon and another thing to be effectively prepared for doing so. Capability is determined by one's nature, while preparation is determined by the subjects themselves. Our freedom, being rooted in corporality, requires a habitual tendency not only to be effective but most of all to find its suitable course.

If the experience of love has opened a path to the person and shown the possibility of fullness, the person must still take this path and actualize that plenitude. This cannot be done without a maturation of sentiments and desires, precisely since each person has been created a child, inexpert, and lacking perfection (St. Irenaeus), and because each person holds within the divisive forces that are the fruit of original sin. In many occasions, the experience of sentiments presents itself as chaotic and conflict-ridden. Between that-which-is and that-which-we-are-called-to-become is a gap that must be filled with freedom and training.

On this path toward the announced plenitude, "we have also seen that the way to attain this goal is not simply by submitting to instinct" (*DCE* 5). Separated from the *logos* that animates the person from within *érōs*, one becomes lost and winds up being destroyed in focusing on the intoxication of a happiness understood as mere pleasure. This fact is far from implying the negativity of *érōs*, since it does not cancel its original openness to the promise of plenitude but rather shows how it is necessary to be saved from such danger and to mature. "True, *eros* tends to rise 'in ecstasy' towards the Divine, to lead us beyond ourselves; yet for this very reason it calls for a path of ascent, renunciation, purification and healing" (*DCE* 5). It opens a path for human desire, a "process of purification and maturation by which *eros* comes fully into its own, becomes love in the full meaning of the word. It is characteristic of mature love that it calls into play all man's potentialities; it engages the whole man, so to speak" (*DCE* 17).

How can we understand this "process of maturation" that *érōs*, human desire, goes through? We find some indications in the pontifical document: "Love now becomes concern and care for the other. No longer is it self-seeking, a sinking in the intoxication of happiness; instead it seeks the good of the beloved: it becomes renunciation, and it is ready, and even willing, for sacrifice" (*DCE* 6).

Love is now faced with a reality that will measure its own quality: the good of the other, the good of the beloved (Melina 2001). Love will now be valued not so much for the intensity of the sentiment that it generates as for its capacity to seek the true good of the beloved. In this way love involves intelligence in its movement, which will carry a decisive weight in seeing the good that the beloved desires and in the will to want it and not just to feel it. This inclusion of love, intelligence, and will is what will allow love to become the principle of action (Aquinas *STh* I–II, 28, 6), that is, to move one to certain conduct, to action. The mediation of the good becomes essential in the experience of love (Pérez-Soba 2001).

In this way it is possible to understand that it is a love that embraces the fullness of existence and all its dimensions, including time as well; that is, it embraces the whole person. Or, said in another way, the promise that love offers gives the call to an integration of all the dimensions that the experience of love entails (Wojtyła 1981). In this integration there is an order that makes the effective realization of the experience of love possible. This "order of love" is what St. Augustine knows as virtue. Now it can be spoken of as a mature love. "Love is indeed 'ecstasy', not in the sense of a moment of intoxication, but rather as a journey, an ongoing exodus out of the closed inward-looking self towards its liberation through self-giving, and thus towards authentic self-discovery and indeed the discovery of God" (*DCE* 6). In this way, the maturation of love allows *érōs* not to be left prisoner to the concrete good that seduces it and opens it to the fullness it indicates; that is, in the desire of pleasure it looks for an authentic happiness. This is what the virtue of chastity is all about.

The origin of this maturation of love is found in the love that one receives. God transmits divine love in authentic human love. "God does not demand of us a feeling which we ourselves are incapable of producing. He loves us, he makes us see and experience his love, and since he has 'loved us first', love can also blossom as a response within us" (*DCE* 17).

The maturity of love refers to an essential fact: love can grow, just as friendship can mature. Certainly, "sentiments come and go", but the love in that coming and going of sentiments grows, matures. The very experience and witness of so many people show how love can come to be a singular harmony, not just with others, but also with God, in such a way that its desire is decisively qualified.

Sentiment and the Moral Life

Communion of will comes to mean sentiment itself (cf. *DCE* 18). If before we saw how sentiment was initially illuminated and how it moved, now it appears that desiring the authentic good in accordance with others and with God has an influence on sentiment itself. What kind of influence? Among others the Pope emphasizes the unity of gaze: "Then I learn to look on this other person, not simply with my eyes and my feelings, but from the perspective of Jesus Christ. His friend is my friend" (*DCE* 18).

A path to understanding this affirmation is to see the cognitive value that sentiments have in the moral life. They are what allow us to recognize the people we love and the goods suitable to friendship. Thanks to friendship, the good of the beloved is interiorly rooted in the loving subject. To see and to feel in the same way is possible by a maturation of affect in such a way that one can properly respond, discovering the true good and not just the apparent good. It is here, between the appearance of an illusion and the truth of fullness, that the drama of sentiment is found. This distinction is determined, not by a merely rational form, but rather by the connaturality of the true good that is the fruit of an integrated love. That is how one can notice when sentiment is complete; it is like good taste that allows one to appreciate not only the food that is good but that which is excellent (Caldera). For that reason, the maturation of sentiment helps us not only to act well but, above all, to react well when faced with the values that seduce us.

Coming to desire the same thing as the Lord in regard to the love he has given us makes it possible to see and feel as the Lord himself and to react well. The encounter with Christ begins to transform sentiment, giving it a new flavor (Larrú 2004: 162–72). In this way a new heart is born that has a very unique feature; it is a "heart which sees" (DCE 31b), which is capable of seeing what friendship is truly built of and, especially, of seeing the necessity of love in what persons encounter.

The opposite occurs in an "ethical blindness" (DCE 28a) that prohibits practical reason from illuminating the concrete field of human action. This blindness has its origin in a problem of the heart, in one that gives prevalence to interests and power, preventing the recognition of what is just and good to do.

The Eyes of Charity: "Si Vides Caritatem, Trinitatem Vides"

The Holy Spirit is the protagonist of this harmony between Christ and the faithful: "The Spirit, in fact, is that interior power which harmonizes their hearts with Christ's heart and moves them to love their brethren as Christ loved them" (DCE 19). The service of charity that the faithful carry out is thus transformed into the pathway for seeing the mystery of God that, for others, occurred with the life of Christ and his handing over on the Cross.

If the mystery of God in itself could blind man with its brilliance, because his eyes are not accustomed to such light, it nevertheless opens a unique path in love that unites men to one another and to God, since God is charity, and whoever abides in charity abides in God. What we see when we love is not just an image but the reality of charity itself, within which is enclosed the divine mystery (Granados 2002). With this the Pope is recovering the path of love pointed out by St. Augustine in De Trinitate. It is essential to understand that in the same love that God gives to man and with which man loves his neighbor and God, the pathway to God opens to him, not as an instrumental route that might as well be done without, but rather as a path in which the point of arrival is already encountered.

Man has the privileged path of love to gain access to the mystery of God. Following the course of love implies remaining in charity or heading toward it, if it is not yet mastered. This tension between *érōs* and *agápē*, and its corresponding unity, is what permits the Pope to apply the Augustinian reflection to all of love. In human love is found divine love, the Holy Spirit, and it is thus that human eyes are not dazzled by divine brilliance, since they are already accustomed to the mystery in love. Perhaps modern man rejects a certain image of God, thinking that he does not love God because he does not know him yet. Nevertheless, in the mystery of human love that he lives, if it is lived in the fullness it entails, he is drawing closer to God because God has drawn nearer to him.

In this way, love is changed into the path to knowing God. There is no true knowledge that does not put love into play or, even more, that is not born of love. This is also the path of wisdom that, in St. Thomas' thought, begins from the gift of the Spirit and is made possible thanks to an innate knowledge of God (*STh* II–II, 45, 2). This knowledge will become the axis of the Christian's entire moral labor because it allows him to direct his conduct toward God and to experience him in his actions (Noriega 2000: 514–48).

Conclusion

Sentiment is a marvelous spark that brightens the darkness and allows us to see the beauty of destiny. It is certainly true that it comes and goes. It can, however, mature and be integrated into the light that reveals it: even more, into the light of what it has given us, because every experience of love supposes the joyful event that transforms and enriches its protagonists. If the identification of love with passion and sentiment makes it impossible for love to be transformed into hope, thus putting the subject in movement and allowing the spark to languish and go out, the purification and maturation of sentiment makes it possible to be integrated into a love of personal devotion.

A truth is already hidden in sentiment itself: the truth of its origin and its destiny. The ambiguity with which it is lived means, not that it should be eliminated, but rather that man should be helped to live the fullness that it embraces, that is, so that it can mature into authentic love. It is in this love that a path to the mystery of God will be opened.

"The actual feeling of love is merely a stimulus suggesting to us that we can and must recreate the wholeness of the human being. Every time that this sacred spark is lit in the human heart, all the groaning and travailing creation waits for the first manifestation of the glory of the sons of God" (Solov'ëv 1985: 166).

Bibliography

Angelini, Giuseppe. 1994. *Le virtù e la fede*. Milan: Glossa.

Botturi, Francesco. 2004. "Etica degli affetti?" In *Affetti e legami*, edited by Francesco Botturi and Carmelo Vigna, 37–64. Anuario di Etica 1.

Caldera, Rafael Tomás. 1980. *Le Jugement par inclination chez saint Thomas d'Aquin*. Paris: Vrin.

Granados, José. 2002. "*Vides Trinitatem si caritatem vides*: Vía del amor y Espíritu Santo en el *De Trinitate* de san Agustín". *Revista Agustiniana* 43:23–61.

Larrú, Juan. 2004. *Cristo en la acción humana según los Comentarios al Nuevo Testamento de Santo Tomás de Aquino*. Rome: LUP.

Lear, Jonathan. 1998. *Love and Its Place in Nature: A Philosophical Interpretation of Freudian Psychoanalysis*. New Haven: Yale University Press.

Melina, Livio. 2001. *Cristo e il dinamismo dell'agire: Linee di rinnovamento della Teologia Morale Fondamentale*. Rome: PUL-Mursia.

Noriega, José. 2000. "*Guiados por el Espíritu*": El Espíritu Santo y el conocimiento moral en Tomás de Aquino. Rome: PUL-Mursia.

———. 2005. *El Destino del Eros: Perspectivas de moral sexual*. Madrid: Palabra.

Nussbaum, Martha C. 2001. *Upheavals of Thought: The Intelligence of the Emotions*. Cambridge, Mass.: Cambridge University Press.

Pérez-Soba, Juan José. 2001. "*Amor es nombre de persona*": Estudio de la interpersonalidad en el amor en Santo Tomás de Aquino. Rome: PUL-Mursia.

Ratzinger, Joseph. 1991. *To Look on Christ: Exercises in Faith, Hope, and Love*. New York: Crossroad.

Ricoeur, Paul. 1967. "Affective Fragility". Chap. 4, 122–202, of *Fallible Man: Philosophy of the Will*. Chicago: Henry Regnery.

Rougemont, Denis de. 1983. *Love in the Western World*. Princeton, N.J.: Princeton University Press.

Scola, Angelo. 2003. *L'esperienza elementare: Per capire la vena profonda del pensiero di Giovanni Paolo II*. Turin: Marietti.

Solov'ëv, Vladimir. 1950. "The Meaning of Love". In *A Solovyov Anthology*, 150–79. London: William Clowes and Sons.

Von Hildebrand, Dietrich. 1997. *El corazón: Análisis de la afectividad humana*. Madrid: Palabra. [*The Heart: An analysis of human and divine affectivity*. Chicago: Franciscan Herald Press, 1977.]

Wojtyła, Karol. 1981. *Love and Responsibility*. New York: Farrar, Straus and Giroux.

Love of God and Love of Neighbor

*Juan-José Pérez-Soba**

Introduction

"On this basis, then, the essence of the love of God and neighbor as described in the Bible is shown to be the center of Christian existence, the result of faith" (Benedict XVI 2006a). With these words Benedict XVI teaches the importance of what, in fact, constitutes the heart of his encyclical. It was absolutely necessary to deal with this question in order to clarify the basic elements of the role of love in the Christian life. The unity of the parts of the encyclical, highlighted from the beginning (*DCE* 1), is brought together precisely in this question, which has been the object of one of the most important ecclesial debates since the 1960s and which still affects how the Church and her mission in the world are understood.

The way of confronting this question is the subject of the entire encyclical and, on this point, is situated in continuity with *Veritatis splendor.* That is, in light of the existing dualisms in the ideological system of certain lines of thought claiming to be post-Christian, an adequate study of the Christian experience leads us to perceive a dynamic unity that is much richer inasmuch as it is the truth of man. In this case, it deals with a unity between the love of God and the love of one's neighbor that belongs to the essence of the Gospel and that emphasizes a unique Christian particularity. The earlier unity between

---

* Assistant Professor of Moral Theology, Pontifical John Paul II Institute for Studies on Marriage and Family, Spanish session. Professor of Fundamental Moral Theology, Facultad de Teología San Dámaso, Madrid.

érōs and *agápē* (*DCE* 3–8) and the later one between justice and charity (*DCE* 26–29) are based on this unity.

The Gospel Revelation: Newness in Continuity

Any attempt to clarify the relation between love of God and love of neighbor has to take into consideration the evangelical revelation of the commandment to love. It is the only way to avoid considering love as an abstraction, that is to say, from the standpoint of an ambiguous image of God or man. However, it is essential to begin by clarifying this God-man relation in order to tackle the question of love in all its forcefulness. The encyclical starts with this very question. It indicates how Jesus Christ united the two commandments that the People of Israel knew concerning love (*DCE* 1). On the one hand, there is the imperative to love God above all else (Deut 6:4–5), to indicate that the Covenant implied a total response to the preferential love of God. So far as love of neighbor is concerned, it appears in the code of holiness (Lev 19:18) in a slightly more ambiguous way, although it is part of the response to divine love that the Covenant upholds (Coda 1996). Despite the difference between the importance attached to the two commandments, significant links already existed between the two in Jewish tradition. Love of neighbor is already expressed in the text as a continuation of the holiness of God. It is yet another duty that the People of Israel have toward divine providence (cf. *DCE* 9). It is an aspect that far exceeds the Aristotelian interpretation of a god that does not love the world and does not become involved with its contingencies. The union between love of neighbor and the providence of God is one of the main arguments in the second part of the encyclical and is inserted in this manner in the first divine revelation.

The Gospel parallel to which the encyclical grants special emphasis in this first part is that of Mark 12:29–31, where, in what is more a sapiential dialogue than a discussion, it more strongly asserts that this is a single commandment with two expressions. This is the conclusion at which Benedict XVI arrives in his explanation (cf. *DCE* 1 and 14), and this unity is what sustains the entire argument.

The constitutive unity of love for God and neighbor is demonstrated by all of Christian tradition. Its most detailed explanation is to be found in the answer to the Scholastic question: "How is it that the difference between the two beloved objects (God and neighbor) does not divide the virtue of charity?" The reason is that both are loved with the same love, although in different ways (*STh* II–II, 23, 5, and 25, 1). There is therefore the implication that the difference in content lies in a dynamic unity. This constitutes the hermeneutics of love that is present throughout the encyclical.

The unity of these commandments here does not only have a sense of sensibility characterized by the admiring answer of the scribe, but rather it is Christ who invites a deeper meaning in saying: "You are not far from the kingdom of God" (Mk 12:34). With this affirmation he places love in a surprising relationship to the kingdom, and its acceptance is mysteriously united to the practice of this commandment. With this, a Christ-centered meaning of this relationship is privileged since it is Christ himself who indissolubly unites the love of God and of neighbor as a New Covenant. Thus it is through a neighbor, a person, through Christ, that we can arrive at the love of the living God. The infinite distance between God and man that prevented friendship is thus overcome. As St. Thomas explains it: "The notion of being a neighbor is preserved both in him who gives favors and in him who receives, but not that whoever gives favors is a neighbor since it is required among neighbors that there be a sharing in some order. Therefore God, although he gives favors, cannot be said to be our neighbor; but Christ inasmuch as he is man, is called our neighbor according as he gives favors to us" (Aquinas, *Questio Disputata de Caritate* 1, 7 ad 18).

The fullness of God's love is revealed to us through human love, which then follows the same intention as Christ's love, who loves us *propter nos* ("for our sake", as we say in the Creed), in response to the love of the Father. In this manner Christ identifies with man in his need to be loved. This is the reason for the importance of the passage from Matthew 25 throughout the encyclical (*DCE* 15, 31, 40, and 42), showing in an eschatological sense the ultimate commandment of charity in the surprising way in which Christ identifies with the needy and in the response that has to be given when the needy person asks for charity. In this way love of neighbor is, in a special way, love of Christ as well as the coming of the kingdom, "that they may see your good works and give glory to your Father who is in heaven" (Mt 5:16).

The Good Samaritan (Ratzinger 1991: 100–105)

The foregoing reflection is continued in narrative form in the parable of the Good Samaritan (*DCE* 15 and 31), which is basically the key to understanding the term "neighbor" within the Christian revelation and which, naturally, has pride of place in the encyclical since it serves as an introduction to the part that deals explicitly with the love of God and neighbor. The reference to neighbor in the parable achieves an astonishing universality, all the more important because it is not neutral, directed indifferently toward all men. In this story, with characteristic force, it includes conquering the enmity and also, in this case, the religious hatred that existed between Jews and Samaritans—the most virulent kind of hatred (Eph 2:14). In other words, it is a way of affirming the principle of love that in no way excludes any man. However, this universality is based in addition upon a very special first moment, when any trace of indifference is directly overcome. On the one hand, it starts, not from a formal principle, but from a concrete necessity that must be answered (*DCE* 31a) and that has as a correlate a very concrete affective movement. Thus the Good Samaritan is "moved with compassion" (Lk 10:33), an affective movement that breaks through the indifference shown by the priest and the Levite. A primary action of God is thus expressed that sustains love for one's neighbor and confers an active meaning on the role—the neighbor is not the one in need but "the one who showed mercy on him" (Lk 10:37). The moral requirement contained within the entire story is not just to offer help in a time of need; rather, the story points to the more fundamental requisite of "being a neighbor to others" (Pinckaers 1992: 66), of approaching another in the unique closeness that is born of mercy, and of avoiding all diversionary tactics that prevent us from seeing the other or that distance us from the other, preventing us from having human contact with the person in need.

The christological meaning of this story that was brought out by the Church Fathers shines new light on the entire text. Christ is the one who saw the half-dead, mistreated person who was not sufficiently cared for by the others, and Christ is the one who drew near to redeem him, delivering him to the Church until he returns. It is

Christ himself who, with his action of "being a neighbor" to another, reveals the Father's mercy. The priority of grace and the process of christological identification that frames the story give a new horizon to the command, full of the beauty of a divine love and the demand for a human answer.

In this story, love attains a unique operative value that far surpasses any attempt to reduce it to a feeling that makes us feel good about ourselves. In light of the theoretical explanation that the scribe was seeking about how to define who was a neighbor in order to "justify" himself, that is, to get to justice through the words themselves, Christ's answer "go and do likewise" (Lk 10:37) sounds astonishing. The man learns to love loving. There is no need for a recipe; he must only respond to the inner revelation, which is the Holy Spirit. The Holy Spirit has a directive role. The active feeling of grace that is produced in the merciful heart moved by the Holy Spirit is the inner teacher of love that must be attended to in order to arrive at God's justification. The commandment here is uncovered at its deepest root as a gift, the answer to a first divine love (cf. *DCE* 1) that in its loving communication wants to reach the concrete persons in need to meet them in their need; "the love of God is not idle" (Gregory the Great, *XL Homiliarum In Evang.*, l. 2, h. 30, 2).

The Universality of Love, Revelation of Divine Love

The parable of the Good Samaritan shines a specific light upon one of the strongest accusations against the central role of love in human existence. It is that of those who say that love cannot be universal because it is based on an affectivity that is always preferential and that would lead to the exclusion of particular people. Love should endure an earlier justice that could indeed account for its universality in the rights and dignity of the person, both of which would be threatened by love were it to be left to its own devices and not dependent on a greater force.

That is to say, in this question one of the most topical aspects of love is debated: the relationship between charity and justice, which the encyclical treats in its social aspect and which will be the subject of later commentary.

There is a current school of thought that, interpreting divine love based on the requirement of universality and announcement of divine justice as pronounced by prophets, preferred to define love of neighbor as a dispassionate, purely egalitarian view of the person, outside any affective tie that could be a sign of preference. This school of thought called itself "equal regard" and liked to define itself as the divine *agápē* in the following way: "The look is toward every single human being in existence, setting him apart from all the special traits and actions, etc., that distinguish individual personalities from each other" (Outka 1977: 9).

Benedict XVI, presenting *agápē* as a true divine revelation, does so through very different characteristics, pointing out the preferential aspect of this love, a unique "elective" love (*DCE* 9) that he truly considers personal, that is, worthy of persons, in that it reveals their true dignity. This must have found its roots in creation, which, as an act of love, is a loving choice of persons, in which each one is deeply loved as he is. It is not so much an egalitarian love as it is comprehensive of all the personal differences in the richness of a love of communion that enriches all and that has in God a universal extension.

The true divine universality made manifest in creation that attains a new value in the forgiveness offered to man in redemption (*DCE* 10) is thus attained. Each man can say that the Son of God has "given himself for me" (Gal 2:20). The revelation of divine love that even reaches to one's enemies, who are not separate from divine providence but are more the recipients of the offer of a forgiveness that can convert them into friends, is based in this universality.

Current Disputes

In spite of the clarity and the richness that revelation offers us, this theme of the relationship between the love of God and love of one's neighbor has been one of the most debated points of twentieth-century theology since the Second World War. It is certain that the sincere acceptance of revealed love makes it impossible to separate one from the other; however, the question is focused, not on this point, but on assigning priorities in its exercise and integrating the demand of love for God in the case of an unbeliever. Perhaps a person who does not believe in God is not capable of love, of true love? Is love for one's neighbor not primary, then, as a necessary means to love for God? If this primacy is accepted, would not some of the Church's pastoral preferences have to change? Apart from a love of neighbor, what sense would there be in worship of God or in a life dedicated to contemplation but affectively unconnected to helping the person in need? How is it that the celebration of the Eucharist does not lead to a more fervent love of neighbor? These questions received very different answers during the seventies, when different trends were being propounded, especially with regard to how pastoral activities should be conceived.

To speak of priorities signifies getting involved with difficult questions that affect the very activity of the Church as such and have led to serious confrontations that are very difficult to resolve. What comes first for the Church, religious practice or devotion to the needs of one's neighbor? How do these preferences affect the Church as such?

According to a rationally formal interpretation of charity as understood by the Neoscholastics, the charitable love of neighbor is *propter Deum*, that is to say, we would love God in our neighbor, and not the neighbor "for his own sake". This manner of expression is strange, as it is not God's way of loving; as the Second Vatican Council says in *Gaudium et Spes* 24, man is the only creature on earth that God has loved for itself.

However, we come to the opposite stance, that of presenting love of neighbor as the first necessary step to be able, later, to reach a love of God. Liberation theology, heir to German political theology, has made this interpretation of charity its own. Thus the general context of the problem can be posed as follows:

Historically speaking, we are in a cultural situation where two mental attitudes oppose each other:

• one mentality, called traditional, puts the accent on the union with God from which a certain human action in the world can be inferred; however, this comes at the cost of recognizing all the implications of human autonomy, and

• a predominant mentality, which appears secular, that insists on human social autonomy; this considers union with God as a confirmation of the Christian compromise in the world but has

the tendency to lose sight of Christian specificity. (Van Caster
1973: 292ff.)

The Pope echoes these issues and with great skill reveals the characteristic core of each one. He looks at it from the point of view mentioned earlier, which leads him to ask: "How can we live it?" and
which focuses on the two principal issues: How can we love a God
whom we do not see, and how can we be commanded to love, an
imperative that only acquires any meaning when, and only when, it
refers to "our neighbor"? He insists upon it again in presenting the
encyclical in the magazine *Famiglia Cristiana* when he says: "I have
only wanted to respond to a couple of very concrete questions about
Christian life. The first question is the following: *Is it truly possible to
love God?* And again: can love be imposed from the outside?" Or, in
the encyclical (*DCE* 16): "Can we love God without seeing him?
And can love be commanded?" In these two questions lies the crux of
the theme of love of God and love of neighbor to which we must
respond.

The Two Areas of Reference: Knowledge of God and Recognition of Neighbor

It is important to point out that this deals with two distinct problems,
although they are intrinsically united in human life. The first is about
a way of knowing God and is essential in order to clarify the way God
reveals himself throughout history of mankind. In this revelation there
is no substitute for love. It is here that the term *agápē* in all its novelty
has its rightful place, which has moved in the history of theology
toward the concept of charitable love.

The problem of love of neighbor, however, is different, consisting
in knowing how to determine that it is an obligation and not spontaneous, something that could not be demanded were love not felt.
From this arises the question of the possibility of loving our enemies
or those who have no direct relationship to us.

Any requirement to love one's neighbor runs the risk of relativ-
ization. This is due to the difficulty of determining what exactly is
meant, in the light of the plurality of neighbors and immense number

of needs. Moreover, this requirement springs from a link with them wherein the love of God does not appear, as it would seem an unnecessary requirement for truly loving another person.

In this way, without man losing his quest for God, the problem of knowing the love of God would appear to become subordinate to the possibility of loving one's neighbor first.

In the light of this difficulty, Rahner put forward a fundamental proposal by way of solution, a fundamental axiom on love: "Our fundamental thesis of the specific reciprocal identity of love of God and love of neighbor" (Rahner 1967: 280).

The problem with this affirmation, in principle so incisive, is that then an act of love toward a neighbor would be enough to make one a Christian, even if one explicitly denied the love of God, that is to say, the theory that he himself defined as the existence of "anonymous Christians". Because of the psychological primacy of love of neighbor, to do many things for him would appear de facto to make the explicit love of God something extra that does not add anything significant, except to make explicit something that was already to be found in human love.

There can be no denying the secularizing effects of this way of presenting love, to the extent that it considers an implicit love of God valid, which would be very difficult to qualify as a truly personal love. Afterward, time revealed the consequences only too clearly in the spreading confusion between charity and philanthropy, which the encyclical strives to overcome (DCE 31) (Pope 1994).

In this sense, the encyclical follows precisely the opposite path. In the first place, it strongly affirms the explicit demand of a love of God. In the second place, it connects the real discovery of the personal value of love to the revelation of God as a person by means of an exclusive, everlasting love (DCE 9–11).

The love of neighbor acquires originality in that it is incapable of explaining its own source. The existence of an originating love is what gives human love a new universal horizon. It is because of this that he can affirm more than once in the second part that there is a specifically Christian way of loving one's neighbor.

If Benedict XVI distances himself from the thesis of Rahner with these affirmations, he still does not make completely clear how the two kinds of love are actually united in the human act, although he does offer an essential indication to find the way.

Dynamic Unity

As happens throughout the entire encyclical, revealing a deep under-standing of the phenomenon of love, the answer is not found in a harmony between ideas but rather in perceiving the dynamic internal unity that marks a specific logic of love, which is most important in this case.

The opposition between the two foregoing views depends, in the final analysis, upon a psychologist's perception of love: Call love of God every action where God is presented as the objective end and, therefore, love of neighbor where the end is a human being. In this way an act of love is either for a neighbor or for God; it cannot be an act of love toward both at one and the same time, although it can be for one and then the other in turn. This is a dialectical way of think-ing similar to that concerning the descending movement of *agápē* and the ascending one of *érōs* that appeared to be incompatible.

Basically it is the same way that Lutheranism reformulated love of neighbor, since, for the reformer, charity did not change a person's corrupt heart. Its value lay rather in being a pure sign of the divine *agápē* with which God loves us and a source of external providence for everybody else. Thus, our charity would have nothing to do with our love of God, who would himself be involved in the dynamics of *érōs*. It is this merely symbolic interpretation of love of neighbor that began the secularized consideration of a separate, not to say even oppos-ing, charitable love of neighbor as compared to love of God.

In this manner of understanding love, the initiative lies totally with the person who loves. It is he who with complete freedom chooses the one to love, in which case the decision could be presented as making himself worthier in a situation where he would have to love either God or his neighbor first.

Faced with such a limited interpretation, it is necessary to find another path. We have to base ourselves in a deeper analysis of love that can reveal its internal dynamic in order to avoid the reference to mere self-awareness that ignores the total worth of the affective moment

of love. That is, if we start from the affective moment, it is evident
that all human love, at its origin, is *always a response* to an offered love.
It is thus that the first moment of its internal dynamic must be considered in order to be able to, from there, consider the role that each
loved one plays. This is the perspective of the encyclical when it says:
"[God] loves us, he makes us see and experience his love, and since
he has 'loved us first', love can also blossom as a response within us"
(*DCE* 17). This argument is already anticipated at the beginning of
the encyclical: "Since God has first loved us (cf. 1 Jn 4:10), love is
now no longer a mere 'command'; it is the response to the gift of love
with which God draws near to us" (*DCE* 1).

The immediate conclusion drawn from this consideration is a primacy in the way God asks for the response of love on the part of man:
"[God] did not only offer us his love; he was the first to live out this
love, and he knocks at the door of our hearts in so many ways, seeking
to stir up our love in response" (*Famiglia Cristiana*). For this reason, when
looking at love, not from the perspective of our way of loving, but rather
from how first the beloved loves us, the two loves cannot be precisely
parallel because the way God offers us his love is very distinct from how
the neighbor offers it. The neighbor always does so through mediation,
that is, through the good that he communicates to his neighbor together
with the lover and which the latter has to perceive in order to be able
to consider it true love. On the other hand, God's love is the only one
that directly penetrates man because it is immediate, intimate, and tran-
scendental in a manner that completely surpasses love of neighbor. As
the encyclical explained earlier, it was morally necessary to reveal that
God loves us in a personal and concrete way so that then man could
discover the union that exists between love and the human being
(*DCE* 6–8). God is the teacher of love who makes possible any other
kind of love worthy of a human being.

The importance of this process can be seen in the encyclical to
the extent that the way in which God reveals love to us shows that
there exists an "explicit" love of God, since faith is a response to an
explicit call in the form of a communication of love. That is the meaning of the words used by Christ to introduce love in the context of a
definitive revelation: "I have called you friends, for all that I have heard
from my Father I have made known to you" (Jn 15:15).

Therefore, the manner of determining the dynamic unity of both loves is due to the primacy of the impulse to *give* in love, the origin and purpose of which are divine. The gift is always to be found in a reciprocal relationship of giving and receiving that is necessary to understand the origin and purpose of love. The end of a gift is not to give something, but rather, above all, it has the goal of reaching an identity of persons as the "gift of self". This is why, since the good is based in a creative love that measures the good not just for its pleasing aspect, love is primarily a communication capable of communicating itself according to the noted medieval aphorism: *bonum communicativum sui*. In loving, persons are consequently situated within a communicative current of the good that precedes them, which obeys a divine intention and of which they are, in the first place, recipients. It is only through this reception that they can, at the same time, give. This is how the encyclical presents it at the beginning, in a direct manner: "I wish ... to speak of the love which God lavishes upon us and which we in turn must share with others" (*DCE* 1).

A communicative dynamic, then, is the deepest reason for the unity of the two parts of the encyclical. By mentioning communication, the encyclical signals the unifying thread of the second part in a way that integrates the great contributions of the first. The end of this communication is found in the Eucharist (*DCE* 13–14, 17, 21–22), which thus acts as origin of a unique communion with God and with others.

The difficulty encountered, then, lies in coming to know the richness of the primary gift of God, which, precisely because of its immediacy, is not evident. Here is where it must be confirmed in the love of neighbor that is born as an inner impulse of the Holy Spirit, uncreated charity. This is why the question that directs the subject of the possibility of the love of God is precisely one of coming to know him as a living God, not as an idea or as the content of just another religious tradition (*DCE* 16).

We can then conclude that *a phenomenological primacy of love of neighbor* exists, since the neighbor is the first beloved to be consciously perceived, but at the same time there is a *dynamic primacy of love of God* that sustains all love of charity for one's neighbor as the gift and instinct of the Holy Spirit.

This is why love of neighbor must be distinguished from a love of charity for the same person, since they have different affective principles that it is wise not to confuse. The definitive union between the two resides in one of the subjects that the encyclical does not develop: friendship. However, we find a valuable indication of it in the commentary presented to *Famiglia cristiana* as the response to the second of the questions directed at love of neighbor: "*Can we truly love our 'neighbor' who is unfamiliar to us or whom we may even dislike?*" "Yes, we can, if we are friends of God. We can if we are friends of Christ, and so it becomes ever more clear that he has loved us and still loves us, although we frequently turn away from him and live according to other standards."

Universality is here centered on supporting the intention of the love of Christ, that is to say, on a love so true for him (cf. Ratzinger 1991: 86) that he transforms us inside by giving us a new principle of love—charity.

Light for Action

The dynamic aspect of the love of charity impels us to respond to the definitive commandment Jesus makes in regard to one's neighbor: "Go and do likewise" (Lk 10:37). The insistence of the entire second part of the encyclical on the purifying aspect of reason and the motivation of charity in the social sphere (*DCE* 28–29) is sustained in this specific dynamism of love whose full revelation is produced in the building of a true communion between persons.

So it is that we perceive the effective primacy of trinitarian Love, which comes before any human love and supports it and opens up an unexpected horizon for all manner of human communion. It is a structural primacy, not one that is directly discerned. Rather, only through his actions does the person become aware of the affective gifts he receives. This happens in the case of human affections: usually it is only when he himself becomes a father that a man becomes truly aware of the love he received from his parents. This is because filial love, the first love, provides the basis for our subjectivity and does not have the impact of novelty upon it as frequently happens in the process of falling in love. Thus the reception of filial love is mainly through the development of the person who grows by being educated and trained in his capacities.

Communication of divine love is similar: it is a true basis for human love, the truth of which can only be discovered in the degree to which man is capable of developing all its implications. Thus love of neighbor is the way in which man verifies his response to divine love, the way in which he can speak of a *living God*.

Ordo amoris (STh II–II, 26)

The integration of the two loves of man and God is brought about in a double scope of intensity and efficiency. There are people to whom we are especially close, and we have a moral duty to grow in our love for them. On the other hand, we need to know how to respond effectively to certain extraneous needs. The two criteria are different and can lead to different preferences in different circumstances. The urgent need to look after someone who is wounded can make other things that could be done secondary, for example, spending time with one's wife, but this does not mean that a man loves the wounded person more than his wife.

The way to find the link between these different preferences is what in Christian tradition, after Origen, is called *ordo amoris*. This order establishes a criterion that allows us to bring harmony to both the affections and actions we use in building our lives.

In the encyclical there is no direct reference to this question, but there is an indication of the impossibility of presenting a human love that is only a "pure giving". Love must also be "received" in order to build a life (*DCE* 7). The way in which the two distinct areas of life relate to one another in the configuration of a personal life is now the fundamental criterion for ordering this love.

The encyclical also speaks of the possibility of a love that overcomes immediate affects to specify the appearance of a divine affect that will even allow a love of one's enemies, the greatest expression of a heart that is renewed by charity. This order is summed up by Origen as: "Here now is an example of [love's] order and its measure. In loving God there is no measure to observe, no limit, save only that you ought to give Him as much as you have got. For in Christ Jesus

God is to be loved with the whole heart, and the whole soul, and the whole strength. So in this there is no measure. But for the love of one's neighbour there is a certain measure: *Thou shalt love thy neighbour as thyself,* Scripture says" (Origen 1957: 188).

As is natural, the primacy in this order lies in the love of God that is prior to any other love and that, because of its incomparable intensity, asks for an answer beyond compare. Only he is owed a love "with all your heart, and with all your soul, and with all your might" (Deut 6:5). The *Shema* is thus the first way in which God reveals his nearness to man in a *personal relationship,* a love of adoration due only to him without which it is impossible to speak properly of the *rectitude* of the human heart. It is the way love is; it is at the same time an impetus for human action and the way of determining the destiny of man.

This primacy has as its specific point of reference the Person of Christ, by way of response to his invitation to "come and follow me", based on Christ's gaze, which is a look of love, and the new commandment in which mutual ecclesial love is now based on the first gift, the offering of Christ that comes about on the Cross. From then on to be a follower is combined with an absolute preference for Christ at the affective level (Mt 10:39): "He who loves father or mother more than me is not worthy of me; and he who loves son or daughter more than me is not worthy of me" (Mt 10:37).

In this flow of communication, which already has its own valuation of good, "Holy Scripture uses a very wise and profound way to describe love of neighbor: 'to love as you love yourself'. It does not demand any fantastic and unreal heroism.... True love is fair: where it is leading us is to love oneself as one of the members of Christ's body. Oneself like the others.... Only if God exists, only if he becomes the center of my life, is this 'love my neighbor as myself' possible. But if he exists, if he becomes my center, then it is also possible to reach this inward freedom of love" (Ratzinger 1991: 103–4). In this way a later order is established of the places where we live the following levels of communion: the Church, family, work, society are its most significant elements.

It is only then that we truly respond to the communication of the charity that makes up the authentic "communion of saints" and of which the Eucharist is the earthly foretaste since "it makes us a 'we' which transcends our divisions and makes us one, until in the end God is 'all in all' (1 Cor 15:28)" (*DCE* 18).

Bibliography

Balthasar, Hans Urs von. 1971. "Die Liebe zu Jesus Christus". In *Klarstellungen zur Prüfung der Geister*, 46–52. Freiburg im Breisgau: Herder. ["Our Love of Jesus Christ". In *Elucidations*, 69–79. San Francisco: Ignatius Press, 1998.]

Benedict XVI. 2006a. "Charity Exceeds Philanthropy by 'Showing Christ'". Address of His Holiness Benedict XVI to the Participants at the Meeting Promoted by the Pontifical Council "Cor Unum", January 23. *L'Osservatore Romano*, no. 5 (February 1, 2006): 4.

Coda, Piero. 1996. *El agape como gracia y libertad: En la raíz de la teología y praxis de los cristianos*. Rome: Ciudad Nueva.

De Jong, Jan. 1974. *A New Commandment: The Unity of Love of Neighbor and Love of God in Recent Theology*. Hales Corners, Wisc.: Priests of the Sacred Heart.

Noriega, José. 2005. "*Ordo amoris e ordo rationis*". In *Limiti alla responsabilità? Amore e giustizia*, edited by Livio Melina and Daniel Granada, 187–205. Rome: Lateran University Press.

Origen. 1957. *The Song of Songs: Commentary and Homilies*. Westminster, Md.: Newman Press.

Outka, Gene. 1977. *Agape: An Ethical Analysis*. New Haven, Conn.: Yale University Press.

Pérez-Soba, Juan-José. 2001. "Presencia, encuentro y comunión". In *La plenitud del obrar cristiano. Dinámica de la acción y perspectiva teológica de la moral*, edited by Livio Melina, José Noriega, and Juan-José Pérez-Soba, 345–77. Madrid: Palabra.

Pinckaers, Servais. 1992. *El Evangelio y la moral*. Barcelona: EIUNSA.

Pope, Stephen J. 1994. *The Evolution of Altruism and the Ordering of Love*. Washington, D.C.: Georgetown University Press.

Rahner, Karl. 1971. "Reflections on the Unity of the Love of Neighbour and the Love of God". In *Theological Investigations* 6: 231–49. London: Darton, Longman, & Todd.

Ratzinger, Joseph. 1991. "What Shall I Do to Inherit Eternal Life? (Homily on Lk 10:25–37)." In *To Look on Christ: Exercises in Faith, Hope, and Love*, 100–105. New York: Crossroad.

———. 1993. *The Meaning of Christian Brotherhood*. San Francisco: Ignatius Press.

Schockenhoff, Eberhard. 2002. "The Theological Virtue of Charity (IIa IIae, qq. 23–46)". In *The Ethics of Aquinas*, edited by Stephen J. Pope, 244–58. Washington, D.C.: Georgetown University Press.

Van Caster, Marcel. 1973. "Aimer Dieu en aimant les hommes". *Lumen vitae* 28: 292–316.

Charity and Philanthropy

*Sergio Belardinelli**

Deus caritas est. In this way, ancient and ever new, Benedict XVI's first encyclical reproposes the "unprecedented realism" (*DCE* 12) of the figure of Jesus Christ, his gift of love, which, precisely insofar as it is a "gift", can also become a "commandment" (*DCE* 14), something that commits us to become like him, to look at the world with his eyes. In this way, love—a concept almost worn-out by the superficial and reductive uses made of it by the culture of our times—all of a sudden regains "flesh and blood"; it regains a measure that raises it well beyond sentimentalism, sexual attraction, or philanthropy and thus becomes the key that "calls into play all man's potentialities; it engages the whole man, so to speak" (*DCE* 17). *Érōs* and *agápē* together: this is the love to which we are called as individual believers and as Christian community. Faith in Jesus Christ and in the Eucharist, a faith that is living and alive, is not possible apart from the commandment of the love of God and neighbor. With admirable cogency Benedict XVI says that this

> twofold commandment of love ... , and [the] grounding [of] the whole life of faith on this central precept, is not simply a matter of morality—something that could exist apart from and alongside faith in Christ and its sacramental re-actualization. Faith, worship and *ethos* are interwoven as a single reality which takes shape in our encounter with God's *agape*. Here the usual contraposition between worship and ethics simply falls apart.

*Assistant Professor of Sociology, Pontifical John Paul II Institute for Studies on Marriage and Family, Rome. Professor of Sociology of the Cultural Processes, University of Bologna.

"Worship" itself, Eucharistic communion, includes the reality both
of being loved and of loving others in turn. A Eucharist which
does not pass over into the concrete practice of love is intrinsically fragmented. (*DCE* 14)

Different commentators have already spoken of a "programmatic" encyclical. And in some ways it certainly is programmatic, somewhat like
Redemptor hominis was for John Paul II's great Magisterium. However,
in both cases we are dealing with a program that is *sui generis*. The
encyclical does not simply give a list of themes but rather opens up
horizons that are very likely to animate everything that will come
thereafter. And I do not think it out of place to imagine that Benedict
XVI proposed the commandment of love, "the necessary interplay
between love of God and love of neighbor" (*DCE* 18), as the true
litmus test of Christian life, both on the level of individual life and on
the level of the ecclesial community. In short, the encyclical strongly
recommends a topic that is destined to have a notable impact not only
on the Church, but also on today's culture. *Deus caritas est:* here the
face of God is revealed, which Benedict XVI, through the Church,
invites us to contemplate. "For the Church, charity is not a kind of
welfare activity which could equally well be left to others, but is a
part of her nature, an indispensable expression of her very being"
(*DCE* 25a).

Starting from this theological premise, I would like to dwell on
two aspects of the encyclical that I find particularly significant: the
"specific profile" of charitable activity as such and the relationship in
which this activity stands to the diverse forms of social assistance and
humanitarian activity that can be found in today's society.

Charity as a Task

"The entire activity of the Church is an expression of a love that
seeks the integral good of man: it seeks his evangelization through
Word and Sacrament, an undertaking that is often heroic in the way it
is acted out in history; and it seeks to promote man in the various
arenas of life and human activity" (*DCE* 19). It is therefore inevitable
that such a love also affects the realm of politics in general and the

realm of justice in particular. In this regard, having stressed the principle of the autonomy of the so-called temporal sphere, Benedict XVI
does not fail also to reaffirm that the two spheres, faith and politics,
Church and State, are "always interrelated". Countering those who,
misunderstanding the rightful autonomy of the temporal order, would
like to separate clearly faith from politics and reduce the former to a
purely private affair, the encyclical recalls that there is a point where
"politics and faith meet" (*DCE* 28). This point is constituted by the
very nature of the human being. Human nature is the more rational,
the more faith and reason illuminate each other reciprocally instead of
opposing each other antithetically; human nature is the more rational,
the more reason, especially when confronting crucial questions, such
as justice, remains truly open, allowing itself to "be purified" by the
faith. Starting from this point, faith illuminates politics about the sense
of true justice, protecting it from the danger of submitting to power as
an end in itself and of giving in to the temptation of being self-
sufficient, by which an autonomous, liberal, and democratic politics is
turned into its contrary (Belardinelli 1999). Benedict XVI reminds us,
"The Church cannot and must not take upon herself the political
battle to bring about the most just society possible. She cannot and
must not replace the State. Yet at the same time she cannot and must
not remain on the sidelines in the fight for justice. She has to play her
part through rational argument, and she has to reawaken the spiritual
energy without which justice, which always demands sacrifice, cannot
prevail and prosper" (*DCE* 28a).

A recurring theme in the reflections of Joseph Cardinal Ratzinger
resonates in this reference to the "spiritual energy" that is indispensable for a politics at the service of justice but which cannot be brought
about by politics itself. In the words of Wolfgang Böckenförde, an
author certainly known to him, we can say that the liberal constitu-
tional state lives on presuppositions that it cannot itself guarantee (Böckenförde 1967). The proper functioning of liberal democratic institutions
and the knowledge of their limits require a political culture and a
moral conscience that are difficult to maintain when their religious
presuppositions, their "spiritual energies", so to speak, are forgotten.
In the midst of the democratic dialectics inspired by the majority principle, these "spiritual energies" alone are capable of keeping alive the

sense of something that is unconditionally valid. "The question of what is unconditionally good and what is unconditionally bad cannot be evaded if there is to be an order of freedom worthy of man" (Ratzinger 2002; p. 24). This same argumentative structure, asserting something without which politics risks becoming closed in on itself, is thus reproduced in the encyclical. In a certain sense, though recognizing the importance of discourse about justice, Benedict XVI reminds us of the fact that this discourse is not self-sufficient, urging us to look farther and not to forget that even the most just society cannot eliminate pain, sickness, solitude, death. "Love—*caritas*—will always prove necessary, even in the most just society. There is no ordering of the State so just that it can eliminate the need for a service of love. Whoever wants to eliminate love is preparing to eliminate man as such" (*DCE* 28b).

Modern politics, in fact, does not seem very open to this kind of argumentation. For the most part, its anthropological presuppositions are materialistic and individualistic, at one time tending to reduce the human to the social and at another time leaning toward separating the two realms neatly and aprioristically. Therefore, these presuppositions are incapable of accounting for man's essential relationality and transcendence, that is, for the fact that man is someone who essentially exists in relationships (in relationship with God, with the world, with others) and who can never be reduced to the mere social or biological conditions of his existence. In the end, the typically modern tendency to reduce the complex dialectics of society to a dialectics between the State and the citizen can be attributed to this deficient anthropology. However, after the tragedy of totalitarian regimes, there are a number of indications that seem to suggest that the anthropological question is regaining center stage. Firstly, there is the phenomenon of globalization and the crisis of the Western model of the welfare state, which, on the national and international level, render the problem of justice ever more dramatic. Furthermore, there is the cultural crisis of our liberal democracies, which are wedged between individualistic fragmentation and the growing hegemony of a technological culture. Individualism makes the perception of a common ethos ever more difficult, while the hegemony of technology transforms every desire into a "right". But finally, there is also John Paul II's truly powerful Magisterium. To my mind, all this serves as the context in which to read the anthropology of love proposed to us by Benedict XVI's encyclical.

Man is not made to be alone; to be happy he needs to love and be loved. He need others, who, precisely for that reason, do not just represent the "limit" of his freedom, or, worse still, his "hell"—according to a well-known expression by Jean Paul Sartre—but rather the condition of his happiness. Naturally, man also needs justice, but still more he needs love. Aristotle, too, must have had in mind something along these lines when in his *Nicomachean Ethics* he recommends governors certainly to cultivate justice, but most of all to keep an eye on friendship: "When men are friends they have no need of justice, while when they are just they need friendship as well." On this point, Benedict XVI's argument seems to follow and enrich Aristotle's. The State cannot compensate the essential fallenness of human life; if it were to take on everything, precisely for that reason it would become man's worst enemy. The encyclical very beautifully reminds us,

> There will always be suffering which cries out for consolation and help. There will always be loneliness. There will always be situations of material need where help in the form of concrete love of neighbor is indispensable. The State which would provide everything, absorbing everything into itself, would ultimately become a mere bureaucracy incapable of guaranteeing the very thing which the suffering person—every person—needs: namely, loving personal concern. We do not need a State which regulates and controls everything, but a State which, in accordance with the principle of subsidiarity, generously acknowledges and supports initiatives arising from the different social forces and combines spontaneity with closeness to those in need. (*DCE* 28)

Thus, with regard to the proper relationship between the State and the "different social forces", that is, between the State and civil society, Benedict XVI affirms the centrality of the principle of subsidiarity, along the lines by now firmly established by the Magisterium of the Church. He then turns to the Church herself and continues in this way: "The Church is one of those living forces: she is alive with the love enkindled by the Spirit of Christ. This love does not simply offer people material help, but refreshment and care for their souls, something which often is even more necessary than material support" (*DCE* 28). In this way, we have arrived at the *opus proprium* of the Church, defined in terms of charity and distinct from simple social assistance and philanthropy, but also ready to promote practical collaboration with every initiative that contributes to confronting the needs of man. This point certainly merits some deeper consideration, especially given the ongoing debate between those who would like to reduce the Church to an agency of social solidarity and those who instead would like to alienate her altogether from the concrete needs of the world's poor.

Charitable Activity and Humanitarian Activity

In paragraph no. 30 of the encyclical, there is a significant "word of gratitude and appreciation" on the part of the Pope to all who, in and outside the Church, work for the promotion of human dignity. An appreciation is expressed to the Church's charitable activities and to those of the individual faithful, to those of the State and to those of "humanitarian associations" and "volunteer work", to initiatives of "other Churches" and to those of "numerous organizations for charitable or philanthropic purposes"; all these are appreciated as encouraging signs of a growing solidarity among the peoples, as a sign that "love of neighbor is inscribed by the Creator in man's very nature", and that, proclaimed by Jesus Christ, love of neighbor has "spread well beyond the frontiers of the Christian faith" (*DCE* 31). Thus the Church unreservedly recognizes the value of what is being done on the personal, associative, national, and international level to alleviate human need and suffering. We cannot remain deaf to the misery, the pain, and the loneliness of our neighbor; how much less can the Church do so. Indeed, Benedict XVI explicitly evokes the parable of the Good Samaritan as the "program of Jesus" and thus as the true model of the Church's solicitude for man. At the same time, however, the encyclical expresses the Pope's concern that the Church's charity "does not become just another form of social assistance" (*DCE* 31). This seems to be a very important aspect, particularly in light of the appreciation for general humanitarian and philanthropic activity expressed in the previous lines. Therefore, we will seek to determine what to Benedict XVI's mind are "the essential elements of Christian and ecclesial charity" (*DCE* 31).

A first premise is that, "following the example given in the parable of the Good Samaritan, Christian charity is first of all the simple response to immediate needs and specific situations: feeding the hungry, clothing the naked, caring for and healing the sick, visiting those in prison, etc." (*DCE* 31a). Thus, the encyclical proposes as first "essential element" of Christian charity the "professional competence" of those practicing it, that is, "they should be properly trained in what to do and how to do it" (ibid.) and also possess certain organizational skills. But professionalism by itself is not enough. "We are dealing with human beings, and human beings always need something more than technically proper care. They need humanity. They need heartfelt concern" (ibid.). From this follows the second and more important constitutive element of Christian charity: the "formation of the heart" (ibid.), that is, interiorizing Christ in a way that enables us to become like him as far as possible, even to becoming one with him. A heart formed on the model of Christ is a heart for which love of neighbor is no longer "a commandment imposed, so to speak, from without, but a consequence deriving from their faith, a faith which becomes active through love" (ibid. 31).

Precisely because its model is represented by Jesus Christ and is born of faith, Christian charity—and here is the third "essential element"—"must be independent of parties and ideologies" (*DCE* 31b). Benedict XVI is well familiar with the historical events of the last two centuries and with the influence exercised by political ideologies, such as Marxism, which have discredited charitable works because they considered these works to serve the conservation of the *status quo* and thus to obstruct the full unfolding of the revolutionary dialectics. The Pope also knows well that many political parties are tempted to instrumentalize the Church's charitable works to their own advantage in order to present themselves as the party of the good. It is precisely for this reason that he emphatically asserts the specific nature of the Church's charity, insisting that it must not become "another form of social assistance" (*DCE* 31). For the same reason, he insists with as much force on the fourth "essential element" of Christian charity: the Church's charity "cannot be used as a means of engaging in what is nowadays considered proselytism" (*DCE* 31c). Benedict XVI reminds us very beautifully that:

> Love is free; it is not practiced as a way of achieving other ends.... Those who practice charity in the Church's name will never seek to impose the Church's faith upon others. They realize that a pure and generous love is the best witness to the God in whom we believe and by whom we are driven to love. A Christian knows ... that God is love ... and that God's presence is felt at the very time when the only thing we do is to love. He knows ... that disdain for love is disdain for God and man alike; it is an attempt to do without God. Consequently, the best defense of God and man consists precisely in love. It is the responsibility of the Church's charitable organizations to reinforce this awareness in their members, so that by their activity—as well as their words, their silence, their example—they may be credible witnesses to Christ. (*DCE* 31)

If, as we have seen, not even justice can take the place of this love that expresses the essence of God and the salvation of man, if not even justice can pretend to express exhaustively the sense of *caritas*, how much less can simple philanthropy do so. Certainly both justice and philanthropy are good things. But both can be instrumentalized; both can become a pretense, a means to serve ulterior motives that often go unacknowledged, or they can even become the occasion for turning against the world with destructive virulence, a world considered guilty of having produced an unacceptable evil, with regard to which one refuses to do even the good possible here and now, in expectation of a future greater good that will heal all wounds. From this point of view, Dostoevsky's *The Devils* perhaps most clearly documents how desire for universal justice and philanthropy, transformed into an ideology, can conceal a radical rejection of the real world and thus become an element of destruction and despotism. It is, therefore, no minor merit of Benedict XVI's first encyclical to remind us that only the love of God allows us truly to love other human beings, the world, and ourselves and to see the good side of everything that exists despite its deformations.

Hegelian philosophy sought to explain the sense of this universal goodness by means of the concept of "conciliation" (*Versöhnung*), a continuous work exercised by the Spirit. It is perhaps not exaggerated to maintain that a great part of modern philosophy is a vain search for a functional equivalent to what the love of God is able to offer *ontologically, even prior to what it can offer ethically*, namely, a guarantee of the goodness of being. To my mind Charles Taylor has shown this in a convincing way (Taylor 1993), just as Friedrich Nietzsche, with his desperate lucidity, has shown its destructive and disquieting traits. In the end, the modern efforts of building a more just society, constructed by persons able to acknowledge each other reciprocally "as if God did not exist", have been revealed a failure. Communism and nazism, as Augusto Del Noce saw clearly, were not just "horrific faults against culture" but also, and perhaps above all, "faults of culture", which, seeking emancipation from its Christian tradition, in the end found itself in the hands of barbarism (Del Noce 1978). To speak with Nietzsche, though in a sense contrary to his, it seems that we truly had to experience the destruction of Christian values, that we had to experience nihilism, in order to understand to the very depth "the value of these values" (Nietzsche 1995: 8). In many cases the great modern ideals of autonomy and individual liberty, severed from any metaphysical order, or—if we want—from any order of love, have revealed themselves as man's basic will to exceed and go beyond himself (cf. Nietzsche's *Übermensch*). Yet, following the great masters of suspicion (Marx, Nietzsche, Freud, and many others) and their pretense of unmasking the lies hidden behind the ethical and cognitive "limits" that human reason encounters on its way, we have bit by bit impoverished reason and destroyed the very sense of reality. There is no longer any common world to serve as a house for all, nor are there other human beings any longer. We only have to think of Husserl's Fifth *Cartesian Meditation* and the difficulties that Husserl's "I" encounters in accounting for the reality of another "I". However, when we no longer possess solid reasons for attributing to the recipients of our benevolence the same unconditional value as we attribute to ourselves, benevolence itself can become destructive for those exercising it and humiliating for those receiving it. This is in line with what Joseph Cardinal Ratzinger wrote at the end of the 1980s: "Pure universalism, general philanthropy, remains empty, while the distinct and determinate choice of this unique person (Christ) bestows the world and other persons on me anew and me to them" (Ratzinger 1989: 73). Today, Benedict XVI writes, "Practical activity will always be insufficient unless it visibly expresses a love for man, a love nourished by an encounter with Christ. My deep personal sharing in the needs and sufferings of others becomes a sharing of my very self with them: if my gift is not to prove a source of humiliation, I must give to others not only something that is my own, but my very self; I must be personally present in my gift" (*DCE* 34).

Charity as Antidote to the Dehumanization of Society

Reading these words in a culture like ours, which is permeated by many anxieties and yet obstinate in confronting the many challenges it faces "as if God did not exit", one has the spontaneous sensation of gratitude and hope. For instance, the recent developments in the sphere of biotechnology eloquently show how desires passed off as rights or a philanthropy that has become blind to what is truly human risk sparking off processes that turn against man. Furthermore, when we read pronouncements such as those by the German philosopher Marc Jongen, who, in the title of his article published in *Die Zeit* in 2003, claims that man is nothing but "his own experiment", or such as those by Peter Sloterdijk, another German philosopher, who, again in *Die Zeit* in 1999, salutes the new biotechnologies as finally enabling us to fulfill our dream of giving life to beings superior to man, then this means that we are effectively turning down a bad road. In principle, this road no longer knows any limits to the unfolding of a purely functionalist logic, behind which looms heavily the cynical statement by Niklas Luhmann, certainly one of the most important sociologists of the last century, "Man is no longer the measure of society" (Luhmann 1990: 354).

Obviously this is not the place to go into more detail on these things; however, I do think that Luhmann's functionalism represents the most disquieting metaphor of a certain modern "I", a person who seeks emancipation from all ties only to find himself cast out of society and roaming in its "environment". For Luhmann the unfortunate phenomenon of the growing alienation between the "social" and the "human" is simply the sign of a growing functionalization of social systems, which become more and more differentiated and which function ever more on the basis of their own functional code, that is, as if the individual did not exist. In some way, what Luhmann seems to imply is the following: the modern subject is born from the specific will to emancipation from all social ties; human liberty and autonomy are incompatible with any form of conditioning; today's modern subjects have fulfilled their dream; they have finally become themselves; they have left society; they have become self-referential (Belardinelli 2004). In a word, man is no longer "the measure of society".

It is necessary to say with Benedict XVI that "man can indeed enter into union with God" (*DCE* 10). This union is indissoluble. When we reason "as if God did not exist", it is not surprising that we finally end up reasoning "as if man did not exist". And the functionalism now governing our society is perhaps the most eloquent proof of this. Today, we are effectively following Emile Durkheim, certainly one of the fathers of functionalism, in subordinating morality to the requirements of social life, thus sidelining the very sense of unconditional value and obligation. To say it in the words of the French sociologist, our morality has become "flexible": "There is nothing indefinitely and unconditionally good" (Durkheim 1969: 76). Our morality has become a function of the requirements of social life. In principle, therefore, even the killing of an innocent can become legitimate, as long as one succeeds in demonstrating that such a course of action is good for society, something that could always be done rather easily. Functionalism, in effect, does not know any limits. According to whatever may be convenient at any given time, it posits some values for reference, proportioning all others to them. Insofar as what matters primarily is producing merchandise at the lowest costs possible, functionalism is no longer concerned with the almost inhumane conditions in which production takes place in China, for instance. To give another example, if it is a matter of lowering the demographic level of a given population, functionalism by itself does not exclude recourse to forced sterilization, as in fact often happens today. Finally, if it is a question of satisfying the desire for motherhood or fatherhood, functionalism is indifferent to the moral consequences of the technique used, because the only thing that matters is the result. It is possible to continue giving similar examples (Belardinelli 2002).

Thus, I believe that it has never been as important as it is today to emphasize the sense of the "unconditional" both in individual and social life. In an ever more functionalized society, which tends to expel what is human from social life, the need for an anthropology that knows how to give a full account of the incommensurable dignity of every man goes hand in hand with the obligation to realize more humane living conditions and greater justice on the earth that we share with our fellow men. "Every man is a thought of God", Joseph Cardinal Ratzinger wrote a few years ago (Ratzinger 2001: 67). As we have seen, *Deus Caritas Est* indicates to us the ancient and ever new way of faith in the living God, the "unprecedented realism" of the person of Jesus Christ. It does so with the conviction that "from God's standpoint", that is, from the standpoint of a God who is love, reason can be liberated "from its blind spots" and therefore be helped "to be ever more fully itself" (*DCE* 28a) and to discover "the unbreakable bond between love of God and love of neighbor" (*DCE* 16).

"Purification of reason" and "attention of the heart": these seem to be the privileged pillars upon which Benedict XVI wants to base the Church's every action.

Bibliography

Belardinelli, S. 1999. *La comunità liberale: La libertà, il bene comune e la religione nelle società complesse.* Rome: Studium.

———. 2002. *La normalità e l'eccezione: Il ritorno della natura nella cultura contemporanea.* Catanzaro: Rubbettino.

———. 2004. "Ascesa e rovina del soggetto moderno. Il caso Luhmann". In Gruppo SPE, *Verso una sociologia della persona,* pp. 36–46. Milan: Franco Angeli.

Böckenförde, W. 1967. "Die Entstehung des Staates als Vorgang der Säkularisation". In *Säkularisation und Utopie: Ebracher Studien. Ernst Forsthoff zum 65. Geburtstag.* Stuttgart.

Del Noce, A. 1978. *Il suicidio della rivoluzione.* Milan: Rusconi.

Durkheim, E. 1969. *Le regole del metodo sociologico.* Milan: Comunità. [*Rules of Sociological Method.* New York: Free Press, 1982.]

Luhmann, N. 1990. *Sistemi sociali*. Bologna: Il Mulino. [*Social Systems*. Stanford: Stanford University Press, 1995.]

Nietzsche, F. 1995. *Genealogia della morale*. Milan: Adelphi. [*The Genealogy of Morals*. Mineola, N.Y.: Dover Publications, 2003.]

Ratzinger, J. 1989. *Guardare Cristo: Esercizi di fede, speranza e carità*. Milan: Jaca Book. [*The Yes of Jesus Christ: Spiritual Exercises in Faith, Hope and Love*. New York: Crossroad, 2005.]

———. 2001. *Dio e il mondo: Essere cristiani nel nuovo millennio*. Milan: Edizioni San Paolo. [*God and the World: Believing and Living in Our Time: A Conversation with Peter Seewald*. San Francisco: Ignatius Press, 2002.]

———. 2002. *Le religioni mondiali e la domanda di verità: Intervista a Joseph Ratzinger*. In *Il Monoteismo*. Milan: Mondadori.

Taylor, C. 1993. *Radici dell'io: La costruzione dell'identità moderna*. Milan: Feltrinelli. [*Sources of the Self. The Making of the Modern Identity*. Cambridge: Cambridge University Press, 1989.]

Charity and the Common Good

Lorenza Gattamorta *

Introduction

The title of this contribution suggests a twofold consideration that, in light of the encyclical *Deus Caritas Est*, could be summarized as follows: Charity means sharing a good; since this good consists, first of all, in the fact that God has given man his own nature, which is love, charity cannot be reduced to what the Church defines as "common good", although, indirectly, it generates common good. Starting from this premise, it will be shown that practicing charity, as giving and sharing God's love for man, is a mission that is intrinsic to the Church, while the achievement of the common good is primarily (but not exclusively) the task of politics, which recognizes and values contributions coming from other social entities according to the principle of subsidiarity. In light of the encyclical, both the role of the Church in practicing charity and the responsibility of politics and society toward the common good will be considered, as well as the relationship between these two aspects.

Church and Charity

In the encyclical *Deus Caritas Est* (*DCE* 17–18), Benedict XVI resumes a theme upon which he has reflected on various occasions as a theologian. In Greek antiquity, god was considered to be a pure and unmov-

* Assistant Professor of Social Doctrine, Pontifical John Paul II Institute for Studies on Marriage and Family, Rome. Professor of Sociology of the Cultural Processes, Facoltà di Scienze Politiche "Roberto Ruffilli", University of Bologna.

able spirit, existing in blessed solitude far away from human events and incapable of experiencing emotions. It is to this vision that the "great act of love" of the Christian God is opposed. The Christian God "identifies himself with us right to the extent of sharing bodily life—and thereby identifies us with himself and draws us into his love" (Ratzinger 2002: 197). Christianity is the message that states how God has given man, above all other things, his own nature, which consists in a love that is both exclusive and diffusive at the same time: through the choice of some, it strives to communicate itself to all (Ratzinger 2005: 82–94).

Benedict XVI shows that, together with the proclamation of God's word and the celebration of the sacraments, the ministry of charity is one of three duties through which the nature of the Church expresses itself and—precisely because it is an indispensable expression of the Church's essence—the Church's *caritas* cannot be considered to be "a kind of welfare activity" (*DCE* 25). However, when charity defines a type of relationship that establishes itself inside the community of believers (*DCE* 20), it tends to extend itself also to those who are beyond the frontiers of the Church (*DCE* 25). Ratzinger held to a similar point in his study of the fundamental elements of Christian brotherhood (1960), where he affirmed charity as an intrinsic claim of the faith, manifesting itself concurrently in the favor of all (Ratzinger 2005: 94–105). Christians practice charity above all among themselves, living out God's love for the Church and in the Church (cf. Ratzinger 1971: 141–70), but at the same time are responsible for all people whom they encounter through mission, *agápē*, and suffering.

In a similar way to John Paul II in the encyclical *Redemptoris Missio* (1990) on the mission of the Church, Benedict XVI senses the need to reaffirm the peculiarity of the Church's charitable activity in the present historical situation (*DCE* 31). The Church cannot become one among the many social assistance organizations if she does not want to become one of their, more or less ancillary, variables. To maintain the particularity that belongs to her, it is necessary to turn to the essence of Christian charity, which may be divided into three elements.

First, charity originates from an attempt to *answer a need* that, in certain circumstances, presents itself as an immediate necessity. This notion implies that the forms of organization that Christian charity sometimes assumes do not stem merely from the desire to make plans and projects, as can happen in the case of political and/or social welfare activities. The origin of Christian charity consists, not in an answer to directives of a political or administrative nature that come from the outside, but rather in an attempt to answer a need that is encountered. This attempt is much different from the pure universalism or the abstract philanthropical challenge of certain initiatives that, by addressing millions of persons, risk forgetting individual persons in their particularity (Ratzinger 1991; concerning this subject, see also Finkielkraut 2002). In this way, "the concept of 'neighbor' is now universalized, yet it remains concrete" (*DCE* 15).

Secondly, charitable Christian activity must be *independent from organized parties and ideology*. Two important documents from the Congregation for the Doctrine of the Faith, while Ratzinger was its head, were dedicated to the temptation toward ideology, which is always strong for social Christian organizations: *Libertatis Nuntius: Instruction on Certain Aspects of the Theology of Liberation* (1984) and *Libertatis Conscientia: Instruction on Christian Freedom and Liberation* (1986).

Thirdly, the practice of Christian charity has as its origin and outcome a *gratuitous love* that, seeking the integral good of persons, unites evangelization and the promotion of humanity (*DCE* 19). Christian love between man and woman, and analogously, love in its social dimension—understood as *caritas*—defines an act of gratuitous affirmation of the other person's being. The person who loves, even before thinking of self, acts because of the loved one and discovers only thereafter that in this way his own existence has become more complete. "By saying 'yes' to another, to 'you,' I receive myself made new and can now in a new way say 'yes' to myself thanks to you" (Ratzinger 1991: 84). The insistence upon the gratuity of Christian love is particularly relevant, considering how gratuity comes to have a central role in contemporary societies. This change of horizons regarding the theme of "gift" has been subject to research in philosophy (Marion 2002) as well as in social sciences (see, for example, the MAUSS or Anti-Utilitaristic Movement in the Social Sciences, which, originating in France and mostly active in the 1970s and 1980s, has among its principal exponents Caillé 2000 and Godbout 1998).

Common Good and Subsidiarity

Benedict XVI feels the need to "define more accurately" the relationship between the necessary commitment to justice (and the common good) and the ministry of charity (*DCE* 28) by reaffirming the traditional distinction between what belongs to Caesar and what belongs to God. This distinction, though always precarious in the history of religious and political institutes, corresponds to the nature of Christianity. The mission of the Church has an essentially transcendent objective that cannot be translated within a purely secular horizon, while at the same time politics and the State lose the sacred qualities that were attributed to them in many ancient societies. The encyclical does not focus so much on the cultural or juridical aspects of the distinction between Church and politics as have other documents on the social doctrine of the Church. Rather, it favors actual social aspects, stating that a more just society "must be the achievement of politics, not of the Church" (*DCE* 28a).

The responsibility of politics toward justice and the common good has been a topic of social Christian doctrine on various occasions. The *Catechism of the Catholic Church* (*CCC* 1905–12) reminds us of three essential elements that constitute the common good: *respect of the human person*, *social well-being*, and *peace* in justice and security. *Mater et Magistra* considers to be the common good "all those social conditions which favor the full development of human personality" (*MM* 65). *Pacem in Terris* brings to mind the importance of personal and social liberty, reaffirming that "the whole *raison d'être* of public authority is to safeguard the interests of the community. Its sovereign duty is to recognize the noble realm of freedom and protect its rights" (*PT* 104). In an analogous way, the conciliar document *Gaudium et Spes* defines the common good as "the sum of those conditions of social life which allow social groups and their individual members relatively thorough and ready access to their own fulfillment" (*GS* 26).

In the above-mentioned definitions, the personalistic foundation of the concept of the common good, proper to the social doctrine of the Church and of social Christian thinking, is evident. It was no coincidence, therefore, that Pierpaolo Donati, in his study on social doctrine, talked about the human person as "the good of the common goods"

(Donati 1997: 98) and as "subject and goal of the common goods" (ibid., 60). So, echoing what already had been affirmed by John XXIII, "individual human beings are the foundation, the cause and the end of every social institution" (*MM* 219). In *Love and Responsibility*, Wojtyła defines the common good as being not only the external end to which persons tend, but also the end that unites persons from the inside: "The bond of a *common good* ... does not mean merely that we both seek a common good; it also unites the persons involved internally, and so constitutes the essential core round which any love must grow" (Wojtyła 1993: 28). In *The Acting Person*, Wojtyła again dedicates some pages to the teleological and personalistic concept of the common good:

> To identify the common good, however, with the goal of common acting by a group of people is manifestly a cursory and superficial simplification.... The *goal* of common acting, when understood in a purely objective and "material" way, though it includes some elements of the common good and has reference to it, can never fully and completely constitute it.... It is impossible to define the common good without simultaneously taking into account the subjective moment, that is, the moment of acting in relation to the acting persons.... We can conceive of the common good as being the goal of acting only in that double—subjective *and* objective—sense. Its subjective sense is strictly related to participation as a property of the acting person. (Wojtyła 1979: 338)

In the contemporary philosophical and social sciences as well, various attempts are being made to review, through a personalistic lens, philosophical anthropology (cf. Taylor 1989; Spaemann 1996), the goods that men produce and divide within social relationships (cf. Archer 2000; Donati and Terenzi 2005) and cultural-symbolical spheres (cf. Gattamorta 2005; Belardinelli and Allodi 2006). In different ways, all of these contemporary lines of thought try to exceed both modern individualism and collectivism, maintaining that, as Buber states: "Individualism sees man only in relation to himself, but collectivism does not see *man* at all, it sees only 'society.' In the former, man's face is distorted, but in the latter it is masked" (Buber 1990: 119).

Another significant passage in the encyclical suggests that the pursuit of justice must be the fundamental end of the State, even if a social order in which each and everyone shares in common goods can only be guaranteed by the principle of subsidiarity (*DCE* 26). Before *Deus Caritas Est*, social doctrine on many occasions had reflected upon the principle of subsidiarity, which may be considered the fulcrum of a correct relationship between the State and the social activities promoted by subjects of civil society, as is also shown by recent studies in the social sciences (Belardinelli 2005). The most important documents on social doctrine worthy of mention include Pius XI's *Quadragesimo Anno* (80–81), John XXIII's *Pacem in Terris* (74), *Gaudium et Spes* (75), Paul VI's *Populorum Progressio*, John Paul II's *Familiaris Consortio* (45), and the instruction of the Congregation for the Doctrine of the Faith *Liberatis Conscientia* (74).

The principle of subsidiarity, related to the tasks of politics and of the State toward the common good, was also insisted upon by the encyclical *Centesimus Annus* (*CA*), which highlights the limits and degeneration of a social State that forgets this important principle. In that case, John Paul II called to mind the extension of the State's level of intervention in social justice, which in a certain fashion provided a new configuration of what now may be called the *welfare state*. This development should be considered positive, since it witnesses the attempt to answer most adequately the needs brought forth by industrial society, offering remedies to forms of poverty that are incompatible with the dignity of the human person. However, in the development of welfare states, undeserved incursions in the area of intervention were also to be found, causing grave criticism. The switch from a "welfare state" to the innate degeneration in the model of a "social assistance state" derives from an erroneous understanding of the proper tasks of the State.

In present-day societies, the importance of the principle of subsidiarity needs to be reaffirmed:

> A community of a higher order should not interfere in the internal life of a community of a lower order, depriving the latter of its functions, but rather should support it in case of need and help to coordinate its activity with the activities of the rest of society, always with a view to the common good. By intervening directly and depriving society of its responsibility, the Social Assistance State leads to a loss of human energies and an inordinate increase of public agencies, which are dominated more by bureaucratic ways of thinking

than by concern for serving their clients, and which are accompanied by an enormous increase in spending. In fact, it would appear that needs are best understood and satisfied by people who are closest to them and who act as neighbors to those in need. It should be added that certain kinds of demands often call for a response which is not simply material but which is capable of perceiving the deeper human need. (*CA* 48)

Applying the principle of subsidiarity, the efforts of lay people in society, together with the charity directly practiced by the Church, are instances that indirectly or directly contribute to the *common good*, without overlooking how the construction of a just social and civic order "as a political task ... cannot be the Church's immediate responsibility" (*DCE* 28a).

Church and Politics

In light of what has been said up to here, the encyclical also offers a significant contribution reflecting the nature of the relationships between Church and politics. Above all, it reaffirms that the Christian view on politics excludes every type of utopianism: "Love—*caritas*—will always prove necessary, even in the most just society. There is no ordering of the State so just that it can eliminate the need for a service of love. Whoever wants to eliminate love is preparing to eliminate man as such" (*DCE* 28b). From this affirmation, it may be deduced that some people, as T. S. Eliot poetically would say, pursue an alienating utopia when they "constantly try to escape / from the darkness outside and within / by dreaming of systems so perfect that no one will need to be good" (Eliot, "The Rock", VI, 21–23), since the duty to build a more just society will never be definitively fulfilled, and much less will the "service of love" ever be made superfluous.

Ratzinger had already reflected on this theme on various occasions, remembering that politics, if it wants to maintain a certain level of rationality and not be attracted to old or new political myths, should preserve the sobriety of the one who tries to realize what is possible: "But in truth political morality consists precisely of resisting the seductive temptation of the big words by which humanity and its opportunities are gambled away. It is not the adventurous moralism that wants itself to do God's work that is moral, but the honesty that accepts the standards of man and in them does the work of man" (Ratzinger 1988: 149). As the tradition of Christian and Augustinian political realism teaches, by which Ratzinger was always inspired as a theologian, the city of God can never be transformed into the city of man:

> For Augustine, the element of Christian novelty is preserved: his doctrine of the two *civitates* does not try to make the State ecclesiastical or to make the Church State-like but, in the middle of the regulations of this world—that will always be of this world— wants the new power of the faith to be present in the unity of men in the body of Christ, as an element of transformation whose ultimate form will be created by God himself when history shall come to its fulfillment. (Ratzinger 1973: 105; on Augustinian realism, the study *Christian Realism and Political Problems*, published in 1953 by the Protestant thinker Reinhold Niebuhr, remains relevant)

In conformity with other interventions by the Magisterium of the Church regarding social issues, the encyclical affirms now more than ever that there is no need for a State that controls and dominates everything. Rather, a State should be able to recognize and sustain the initiatives that arise from the various active social forces (including the Church), always in light of the principle of subsidiarity. Whoever is more motivated and closer to those who are in situations of need will be able to work more efficiently and respectfully toward human dignity in all of its aspects—not only in material aspects, but also in those more particularly human and relational aspects.

It is evident that talking about a distinction between Church and politics—between the Christian practice of charity by the Church and services to persons recognized as subjects of the civil society and of the State—does not mean talking about reciprocal distrust or, even worse, hostility. In the past, as well as today, there have been and still are forms of cooperation between agencies of the State and the Church that turn out to be fruitful (*DCE* 30). Particularly, ecclesiastical initiatives that are transparent and faithful to their witness of the Gospel may also serve as points of reference and as inspiration for works of solidarity originating in civil society. This encyclical serves as a reminder, in fact, that the greatest benefit the Church brings to the common good and to the construction of a more human society consists in pursuing her own mission of evangelization without having as a priority the task of responding to the social needs presenting themselves from time to time.

Consequently, one may say that the Church contributes *indirectly* to the common good by practicing charity as well as by her social doctrine. The encyclical states that faith "by its specific nature is an encounter with the living God.... But it is also a purifying force for reason itself" (*DCE* 28a). And indeed, as it has been correctly seen, the particular hermeneutics of social doctrine have a religious foundation, which has also been revealed, but it nevertheless is still able to bring forth a rational knowledge that has a base *in re* (Donati 1997: 30). In this sense, the social doctrine of the Church does not intend to provide a series of prefabricated responses to the problems that social life imposes on man. Social doctrine cannot be considered one ideology among others; it cannot be used for special interests; and it also cannot be considered (cf. Schindler 1996) a third way between socialism and liberalism, as some people have erroneously tried to sustain.

From an epistemological point of view, as is shown for example in *Sollicitudo rei socialis*, social doctrine has a peculiarity that makes it different from every other ideology, for it "constitutes a category of its own", being "the accurate formulation of the results of a careful reflection on the complex realities of human existence, in society and in the international order, in the light of faith and of the Church's tradition. Its main aim is to *interpret* these realities ... to guide Christian behavior" (*SRS* 41). It is for this reason that social doctrine does not provide a series of preconceived solutions to man's problems but rather tries to clarify and bring to mind the ultimate principles that allow for a definition of human and social problems by going to their roots. One of these ultimate principles is the desire to love and to be loved, which animates—more or less consciously—a great part of human life, exerting influence on some changes that occur within society.

Bibliography

Archer, M. S. 2000. *Being Human: The Problem of Agency*. Cambridge: Cambridge University Press.

Belardinelli, S., ed. 2005. *Welfare Community e sussidiarietà*. Milan: Egea.

Belardinelli, S., and L. Allodi, eds. 2006. *Sociologia della cultura*. Milan: Franco Angeli.

Boltanski, L. 1990. *L'Amour et la justice comme compétences: Trois essais de sociologie de l'action*. Paris: Métailié.

Buber, M. 1990. *Il problema dell'uomo*. Turin: Leumann. [*Between Man and Man*. New York: Macmillan, 1965.]

Caillé, A. 2000. *Anthropologie du don: Le tiers paradigme*. Paris: Desclée de Brouwer.

Chalmeta, G. 2000. *La giustizia politica in Tommaso d'Aquino: Un'interpretazione di bene comune politico*. Rome: Armando.

Donati, P. 1997. *Pensiero sociale cristiano e società post-moderna*. Rome: Ave.

Donati, P., and P. Terenzi, eds. 2005. *Invito alla sociologia relazionale*. Milan: Franco Angeli.

Finkielkraut, A. 2002. *L'Imparfait du présent*. Paris: Gallimard.

Gattamorta, L. 2005. *Teorie del simbolo: Studio sulla sociologia fenomenologica*. Milan: Franco Angeli.

Godbout, J. T. 1998. *The World of the Gift*. London: McGill-Queen's University Press.

Laubier P. de. 1980. *La Pensée sociale de l'Église catholique: Un Idéal historique de Léon XIII à Jean Paul II*. Paris: Albatros.

Marion, J.-L. 2002. *Being Given: Toward a Phenomenology of Givenness*. Stanford: Stanford University Press.

Melina, L., and D. Granada. 2005. *Limiti alla responsabilità? Amore e giustizia*. Rome: Lateran University Press.

Niebuhr, R. 1953. *Christian Realism and Political Problems*. New York: Scribner.

Pieper, J. 1974. *About Love*. Chicago: Franciscan Herald Press.

Pontifical Council for Justice and Peace. 2005. *Compendium of the Social Doctrine of the Church*. Washington, D.C.: USCCB Publishing.

Ratzinger, J. 1971. *Popolo e casa di Dio in Sant'Agostino*. Milan: Jaca Book.

————. 1973. *L'unità delle nazioni: Una visione dei padri della Chiesa.* Brescia: Morcelliana.

————. 1988. *Church, Ecumenism, and Politics: New Essays in Ecclesiology.* New York: Crossroad.

————. 1991. *To Look on Christ: Exercises in Faith, Hope and Love.* New York: Crossroad.

————. 2002. *God and the World. Believing and Living in Our Time: A Conversation with Peter Seewald.* San Francisco: Ignatius Press.

————. 2005. *La fraternità cristiana.* Brescia: Editrice Queriniana. [*The Meaning of Christian Brotherhood.* San Francisco: Ignatius Press, 1993.]

Schindler, D. L. 1996. *Heart of the World, Center of the Church: Communio Ecclesiology, Liberalism, and Liberation.* Grand Rapids, Mich.: Eerdmans.

Spaemann, R. 1996. *Personen: Versuche über den Unterschied zwischen «etwas» und «jemand».* Stuttgart: Klett-Cotta.

Spiazzi, R., ed. 1992. *Enciclopedia del pensiero sociale cristiano.* Bologna: ESD.

Taylor, C. 1989. *Sources of the Self: The Making of the Modern Identity.* Cambridge: Cambridge University Press.

Wojtyła, K. 1979. *The Acting Person.* Dordrecht: Reidel.

————. 1993. *Love and Responsibility.* San Francisco: Ignatius Press.

Justice and Charity in *Deus Caritas Est*

Carl A. Anderson*

Introduction

Pope Benedict XVI explores the relationship between justice and charity in sections 26–29 of his inaugural encyclical, *Deus Caritas Est*. The first of the four sections presents objections to charity in the name of justice. The second deals with the Church's response as she developed a social doctrine, beginning with Leo XIII and culminating in the *Compendium of the Social Doctrine of the Church*. Next, Pope Benedict considers the Church's teaching on justice and charity and their compatibility. Finally, the conclusions drawn from the previous three sections are laid out.

There are important anthropological and theological components that this encyclical draws upon in order to make its case to a world that has changed dramatically in its values and culture during the past century, particularly in recent decades. Sections 26–29 speak directly to many of the confusions of our so-called "postmodern" world, but, in order to transmit this message effectively, it is important to trace the genesis of this line of thought in terms of Pope Benedict, Pope John Paul II, and the documents of the Second Vatican Council.

That the link between justice and charity should make up an important portion of Pope Benedict XVI's first encyclical is not surprising. The connection between the two has been debated over the past century, and Joseph Cardinal Ratzinger has often been an important

*Vice-President of the Pontifical John Paul II Institute for Studies on Marriage and Family at The Catholic University of America, Washington, D.C., and Supreme Knight of the Knights of Columbus.

participant in that conversation. Critical to the debate have been the definition of the human person and the criteria used to determine what is just. Therefore, one must look to the anthropological foundations of the encyclical, to its precursors in the writings of our present pope and his predecessors, and to the canon of Catholic social teaching, all of which are cited by Pope Benedict in this section (*DCE* 27).

Justice and Charity before *Deus Caritas Est*

Nearly two decades ago, in March 1986, the heading *Justice and Charity* was considered in the *Instruction on Christian Freedom and Liberation*:

> Evangelical love, and the vocation to be children of God to which all are called, have as a consequence the direct and imperative requirement of respect for all human beings in their rights to life and to dignity. There is no gap between love of neighbor and desire for justice. To contrast the two is to distort both love and justice. Indeed, the meaning of mercy completes the meaning of justice by preventing justice from shutting itself up within the circle of revenge. The evil inequities and oppression of every kind which afflict millions of men and women today openly contradict Christ's Gospel and cannot leave the conscience of any Christian indifferent. The Church, in her docility to the Spirit, goes forward faithfully along the paths to authentic liberation. Her members are aware of their failings and their delays in this quest. But a vast number of Christians, from the time of the Apostles onwards, have committed their powers and their lives to liberation from every form of oppression and to the promotion of human dignity. The experience of the saints and the example of so many works of service to one's neighbor are an incentive and a beacon for the liberating undertakings that are needed today. (*ICFL* 57)

In many ways, the *Instruction* prefigures the discussion of justice and charity in *Deus Caritas Est*. For instance, the document notes that "to contrast the two is to distort both love and justice." Today, in the twilight of Marxism and liberation theology, Pope Benedict XVI revisited the nexus between these two principles. "Love—*caritas*—will always prove necessary, even in the most just society. There is no ordering of the State so just that it can eliminate the need for a service of love. Whoever wants to eliminate love is preparing to eliminate man as such" (*DCE* 28b).

To eliminate charity is to eliminate man. In order to understand such a powerful statement, we must look to Pope Benedict's definition of man. The "vocation to love" includes the necessity (or the vocation) to share that love with others in order to be fully human.

Just weeks before he was elected pope, Cardinal Ratzinger provided a key to interpreting the relationship between justice and charity. In a homily given on the fortieth anniversary of *Gaudium et Spes*, he noted that the pastoral constitution sought to address "the significance of the Christian contribution to the improvement of human welfare, through works of mercy and justice, within the overall mission of the Church" (Ratzinger 2005: 2). Cardinal Ratzinger went on to lay out the aspects of love required by the Christian, noting:

> Classical theology, as we know, understands the virtue of justice as composed of two elements which for Christians cannot be separated; justice is the firm will to render to God what is owed to God, and to our neighbor what is owed to him; indeed, justice toward God is what we call the "virtue of religion"; justice toward other human beings is the fundamental attitude that respects the other as a person created by God.

> We should not be surprised if the attitudes toward Jesus that we find in the Gospel continue today in attitudes toward his Church.

> It is certainly true that today, when the Church commits herself to works of justice on a human level (and there are few institutions in the world which accomplish what the Catholic Church accomplishes for the poor and disadvantaged), the world praises the Church.

Responding to the criticisms of the Church claiming that charity gets in the way of justice, Cardinal Ratzinger made specific reference to the criticisms leveled against the Church when her work for justice does not meet the world's definition:

> When the Church's work for justice touches on issues and problems which the world no longer sees as bound up with human

dignity, like protecting the right to life of every human being from conception to natural death, or when the Church confesses that justice also includes our responsibilities toward God himself, then the world not infrequently reaches for the stones mentioned in our Gospel today.

Whatever the world may think, his conclusion is simple:

> As Christians we must constantly be reminded that the call of justice is not something which can be reduced to the categories of this world. And this is the beauty of the Pastoral Constitution *Gaudium et Spes*, evident in the very structure of the Council's text; only when we Christians grasp our vocation, as having been created in the image of God and believing that "the form of this world is passing away ... [and] that God is preparing a new dwelling and a new earth, in which justice dwells" (GS 39) can we address the urgent social problems of our time from a truly Christian perspective.

An Adequate Anthropology

These considerations of the proper role of justice and charity are critical to understanding Pope Benedict XVI's discussion of justice and charity in *Deus Caritas Est*, precisely because an understanding of the anthropology in *Gaudium et Spes* is necessary to understand justice and charity in recent Catholic thought and in *Deus Caritas Est*, specifically. To understand the importance of charity as a complement to justice requires a proper comprehension of man. Such a definition is contained paragraph 22 of *Gaudium et Spes*, which states:

> The truth is that only in the mystery of the incarnate Word does the mystery of man take on light. For Adam, the first man, was a figure of Him Who was to come, namely Christ the Lord. Christ, the final Adam, by the revelation of the mystery of the Father and His love, fully reveals man to man himself and makes his supreme calling clear. It is not surprising, then, that in Him all the aforementioned truths find their root and attain their crown. (GS 22)

The paragraph goes on to call each person to follow the example of Jesus to live in love:

As an innocent lamb He merited for us life by the free shedding of His own blood. In Him God reconciled us to Himself and among ourselves; from bondage to the devil and sin He delivered us, so that each one of us can say with the Apostle: The Son of God "loved me and gave Himself up for me" (Gal 2:20). By suffering for us He not only provided us with an example for our imitation, He blazed a trail, and if we follow it, life and death are made holy and take on a new meaning.

The Christian man, conformed to the likeness of that Son Who is the firstborn of many brothers, received "the first-fruits of the Spirit" (Rom 8:23) by which he becomes capable of discharging the new law of love.

Therein lies the key to understanding our vocation to love and the need to be charitable in order to be fully human, no matter how just a society in which we may live. Man must discharge the law of love, which means, not only loving God, but loving our neighbor as ourselves. It is impossible to take anthropological insight to heart without understanding that conforming ourselves to the law of love necessitates charity. In the *Instruction* we are reminded that: "Fraternal love is the touchstone of love of God: 'He who does not love his brother whom he has seen cannot love God whom he has not seen' (1 Jn 4:20)" (*ICFL* 56).

Furthermore, the *Compendium*, which Pope Benedict cites in this section of *Deus Caritas Est*, provides a similar analysis of man's need to love, even where there is justice: "Love presupposes and transcends justice, which 'must find its fulfillment in charity'" (Pontifical Council for Justice and Peace 2005: 206). It is not only that charity must be done for the benefit of the poor, but also that the opportunity to perform works of charity must exist for the giver to understand God fully and to follow Christ in discharging the law of love.

Justice and Charity: Essential and Inseparable

"Strive first for the kingdom of heaven and its justice, and all these things will be given to you as well" (Mt 6:33). In this command, Christ reveals the intimate relationship between charity and justice.

Clearly there is a justice that belongs to God and his kingdom. Indeed, God is the source of all justice. Justice means rendering what is properly due to another. We creatures owe to God gratitude, adoration, and thanksgiving. This is his due, his *right*, in virtue of who he is as God, the Creator and source of all being.

There is, as well, a justice owed to our neighbor: "Justice toward men disposes one to respect the rights of each and to establish in human relationships the harmony that promotes equity with regard to persons and to the common good" (*CCC* 1807).

Justice immediately suggests a life of relationship in which we give the other what is due, that which can be rightly expected from us. Each individual person, made in the image of God, is called to live, as does God himself, in a community of life and love. As there is a justice owed to God, there is also a justice owed to family, to the civil government, to friends, to country, and to the Church. Just as all virtue begets a life of human flourishing, the virtue of justice is ordered to the flourishing of the common good. Vatican II offers clear direction when it states that: "Every social group must take account of the needs and legitimate aspirations of other groups, and even of the general welfare of the entire human family" (*GS 26*). Justice is about how we live with others—other persons and other communities—to achieve a family of love.

Much as we can speak of God's justice toward himself, there is a justice in his calling us to act with charity toward his other creatures, our neighbors. This is the reality that is at the heart of the Church. "The Spirit is also the energy which transforms the heart of the ecclesial community, so that it becomes a witness before the world to the love of the Father, who wishes to make humanity a single family in his Son" (*DCE* 19). God commands that we love our neighbor, not with a charity from within ourselves, but with that love that flows between Father, Son, and Holy Spirit and that comes to us from the pierced side of his only begotten Son. By drinking from the side of Christ in the life of the Church, the Christian finds the strength to love those who are as of yet unknown, unwanted, or unloved.

It is God's justice that demands that the Christian take on the responsibility for loving, in very practical ways, all of God's people, even beyond the limits of the community of the Christian faithful. Because God loves so perfectly those whom he has made, his determination to save them from sin and death is seen in his sending of his Son. As the Son draws those whom the Father loves to his side, this divine charity is such that it imparts the ability to return God's love. We can now love God with his own love, Jesus Christ, who is love incarnate. This becomes the justice that guides the life of every Christian in the practice of charity toward God and neighbor.

Justice and Charity after *Gaudium et Spes*

John Paul II made repeated reference to *Gaudium et Spes* as providing the anthropology needed to fully understand the human need to love, beginning with his first encyclical, *Redemptor Hominis*. Shortly after the Second Vatican Council, Father Joseph Ratzinger wrote the following regarding *Gaudium et Spes*:

> We are probably justified in saying that here for the first time in an official document of the magisterium, a new type of completely Christocentric theology appears. On the basis of Christ this dares to present theology as anthropology and only becomes radically theological by including man in discourse about God by way of Christ, thus manifesting the deepest unity of theology. The generally theologically reserved text of the Pastoral Constitution here attains very lofty heights and points the way to theological reflection in our present situation. (Ratzinger 1989)

From this foundation came the call of Pope John Paul II in *Familiaris Consortio* to a "vocation to love" (*FC* 1), a call echoed by the *Compendium*'s call for a "civilization of love" (Pontifical Council for Justice and Peace 2005: 580).

With such an anthropology and understanding of the dignity of man, an important question taken up by this section of *Deus Caritas Est* concerns the proper role of the Church in relation to the role of the state. To understand fully Pope Benedict's answer we must look more broadly to his thoughts on the subject. Writing in 1982, Cardinal Ratzinger wrote: "In the long run, neither embrace nor ghetto can solve for Christians the problem of the modern world" (Ratzinger 1987: 391). Pope Benedict in *Deus Caritas Est* takes care to navigate the waters between ghetto and embrace.

In dealing with the issue of how Catholicism can help create justice without venturing into those realms that are rightly Caesar's, Pope Benedict notes that the problem of what is justice "is one of practical reason". He continues: "but if reason is to be exercised properly, it must undergo constant purification, since it can never be completely free of the danger of a certain ethical blindness caused by the dazzling effect of power and special interests" (*DCE* 28a).

It is here, Pope Benedict tells us, that "politics and faith meet", for faith provides a "purifying force" for the exercise of reason. "Its aim is simply to help purify reason and to contribute, here and now, to the acknowledgment and attainment of what is just" (*DCE* 28a). In this way, Pope Benedict presents a means of avoiding both the ghetto and the embrace. The Church is most certainly not to withdraw from the world as if she has nothing to say; nor is she to try to mold herself in the image and likeness of the world. Rather, she is to provide a public witness for the common good without seeking temporal power. At the same time, she should provide an example and examination of conscience for the world.

Tracey Rowland has argued that *Gaudium et Spes* did not have a fully developed sense of culture or of what *modern* meant in a cultural sense. Indeed, it is interesting to note, with Rowland, that *huius temporis*, "of this time", becomes the *modern world* in the English translation of *Gaudium et Spes*, despite the fact that such wording is fraught with cultural and philosophical meaning that goes beyond a simple denotation of time (Rowland 2003: 18).

The proper dialogue between culture and the Church was considered by the International Theological Commission. The Commission wrote the following "statement of principle":

In the "last times" inaugurated at Pentecost, the risen Christ, Alpha and Omega, enters into the history of peoples: from that moment, the sense of history and thus of culture is unsealed and the Holy Spirit reveals it by actualizing and communicating it to all. The Church is the sacrament of this revelation and its communication. It recenters every culture into which Christ is received, placing it in the axis of the "world which is coming" and restores the union broken by the "prince of this world." Culture is thus eschatologically situated; it tends toward its completion in Christ, but it cannot be saved except by associating itself with the repudiation of evil. (International Theological Commission 1989: 800–807)

Such a definition of culture fits well with *Deus Caritas Est*'s call—in the section on justice and charity—for the Church to purify reason and motivate culture toward just ends, its eschatological purpose.

Throughout the history of the Church many have heeded the call to love and actively to improve the lives of those around them. One such example of long-standing Catholic tradition of justice and charity can be found in St. Augustine. As St. Augustine wrote on charity in the *City of God*:

In the Earthly City, princes are as much mastered by the lust for mastery as the nations which they subdue are by them; in the Heavenly, all serve one another in charity, rulers by their counsel, and subjects by their obedience. The one city loves its own strength as displayed in its mighty men; the other says to its God, "I will love Thee, O Lord, my strength." (Augustine, *De Civitate Dei*, 14, 28)

Still, much has changed over the past several decades, and, since the time of *Gaudium et Spes*, the changes have seemed to accelerate. The modern world is now considered by many to be the "postmodern" world. In *Salt of the Earth*, Cardinal Ratzinger argued that pronouncements on "the end of modernity" and the rise of "postmodernity" were "hasty classifications" (Ratzinger 1997: 281). Nevertheless, while cautioning that such terms were fundamentally "Western", he conceded that "a revolution is taking place that is bringing something different from the four or five hundred years of modernity lying behind us" (ibid.).

It is up to us, according to Cardinal Ratzinger, to guide what comes next "so that this newer time, too, which replaces the one that until now has been new, but is already beginning to grow old, will remain a time of man and of God" (Ratzinger 1997: 282).

Conclusion

In our contemporary age, an age that has seen worldwide disillusionment with various aspects of modernity, we have been provided with a new opportunity. We have an opportunity to witness to the world in the midst of its anthropological vacuum. Such a witness must begin with the renewal of Christian categories—not the least of which are to be found in an authentic understanding of our concepts of justice and charity.

Even before his election as pope, the need for man to return to love was a common theme of Joseph Ratzinger: "The true drama of history", he said in *Salt of the Earth*, "can ultimately be reduced to this formula: Yes or no to love" (Ratzinger 1997: 283).

Bibliography

Cessario, R. 2002. *The Virtues, or the Examined Life*. London and New York: Continuum.

International Theological Commission. 1989. "Faith and Inculturation". *Origins*, 18, 47 (1989): 800–807.

MacIntyre, A. 1998. *Whose Justice? Which Rationality?* London: Duckworth.

Pieper, J. 1965. *The Four Cardinal Virtues*. Notre Dame: University of Notre Dame Press.

Pinckaers, S. 1995. *The Sources of Christian Ethics*. Washington, D.C.: Catholic University of America Press.

Pontifical Council for Justice and Peace. 2005. *Compendium of the Social Doctrine of the Church*. Washington, D.C.: USCCB Publishing.

Ratzinger, J. 1987. *Principles of Catholic Theology: Building Stones for a Fundamental Theology*. San Francisco: Ignatius Press.

———. 1989. "Dignity of the Human Person". In *Commentary on the Documents of Vatican II*, edited by Herbert Vorgrimler. New York: Herder and Herder.

———. 1997. *Salt of the Earth*. San Francisco: Ignatius Press.

_____. 2005. "Heeding the Universal Call to Justice for All": Fortieth Anniversary of Gaudium et Spes: Homily of Cardinal Ratzinger. March 18. *L'Osservatore Romano* 13 (March 30, 2005): 2.

Rowland, T. 2003. *Culture and the Thomist Tradition after Vatican II.* New York: Routledge.

Wadell, P. 1989. *Friendship and the Moral Life.* Notre Dame: University of Notre Dame Press.

Charity and the Formation of the Heart

Maria Luisa di Pietro*

A "Heart Which Sees"

"The Christian's program", we read in the encyclical *Deus Caritas Est*, "is 'a heart which sees'. This heart sees where love is needed and acts accordingly" (*DCE* 31b). "A heart which sees" is the program and objective to be attained in the "formation of the heart". Benedict XVI includes this among the priorities that distinguish those who work for the Church's charitable organizations as "they dedicate themselves to others with heartfelt concern, enabling them to experience the richness of their humanity. Consequently, in addition to their necessary professional training, these charity workers need a 'formation of the heart'" (*DCE* 31a).

"A heart which sees" rather than a "heart which feels" because, even if human sentiments were stable, deep, and enduring affective states, they are not sufficient to describe the entire experience of love: "The sentiments come and go. A sentiment can be a marvelous first spark, but it is not the fullness of love" (*DCE* 17).

It is "a heart which sees" because it knows how to recognize its own "history" (the vertical dimension of charity) and how to recognize the other (the horizontal dimension of charity). In fact, from the moment when charity becomes an experience of love and of gift, it can no longer be experienced without an awareness of the origin of one's own "history", that is, of the awareness that our love is born of

---
*Assistant Professor of Bioethics and the Family, Pontifical John Paul II Institute for Studies on Marriage and Family, Rome. Associate Professor of Bioethics, Università Cattolica del Sacro Cuore, Rome.

a Love that precedes us, of the Love with which God has "first loved us" and continues to love us (*DCE* 17). The first great act of love is to be called into existence from nothingness. This is the origin of human "history", and man is the only creature capable of responding to his Creator with the language of this awareness. The heart then becomes capable of seeing the other, of looking upon the other person "not only with my eyes and my feelings, but from the perspective of Jesus Christ" (*DCE* 18).

Knowing (*conoscere*) in order to recognize (*ri-conoscere*) are two inseparable moments, so much so that, "if I have no contact whatsoever with God in my life, then I cannot see in the other anything more than the other, and I am incapable of seeing in him the image of God. But if in my life I fail completely to heed others, solely out of a desire to be 'devout' and to perform my 'religious duties', then my relationship with God will also grow arid" (*DCE* 18).

On the other hand, the eclipse of the sense of God is essentially the eclipse of the sense of man. Recalling the words of John Paul II in his encyclical *Evangelium Vitae*, "when the sense of God is lost, there is the tendency to lose the sense of man, of his dignity and his life" (*EV* 21). "The eclipse of the sense of God and of man inevitably leads to a *practical materialism*, which breeds individualism, utilitarianism and hedonism. . . . The values of *being* are replaced by those of *having*" (*EV* 23). As a result, not only is man unable to recognize either himself or those like him as the Other, he also—in not recognizing the presence of God—lives as if he were god. This "leads people to think that they can control life and death by taking the decisions about them into their own hands. What really happens in this case is that the individual is overcome and crushed by a death deprived of any prospect of meaning or hope" (*EV* 15). Hence, the loss of the sense of the Fatherhood of God leads to the loss of the sense of fraternity with all men.

A heart which does "not see" must be illuminated in order to be able to search for "what is pleasing to the Lord [and] take no part in the unfruitful works of darkness" (Eph 5:10-11). A heart that is so illuminated can perceive God's presence, as "God does not demand of us a feeling which we ourselves are incapable of producing. He loves us, he makes us *see* and experience his love, and since he has 'loved us first', love can also blossom as a response within us" (*DCE* 17; italics added).

Forming the Heart

If "a heart which sees" is the program of the Christian and the objective to be attained, what method does its authentic formation employ? The formation of the heart must be considered integral to the formation of the person, that is, from the moment in which "the human heart is made to the measure of the divine.... Other things may occupy it but can never satisfy it. It must be listened to, known, and educated gradually, with patience and love on the part of the educators" (Gnocchi 1998: 12). In order to individualize the method of formation, it is necessary to have the dual dimensions of charity present: vertical and horizontal.

a. Formation in the Vertical Sense: The Experience of God's love. Man is created in God's image and, as such, is created for love. "God is love (1 Jn 4:8)", we read in the apostolic exhortation *Familiaris Consortio*, "and in Himself He lives a mystery of personal loving communion. Creating [them] in His own image ... , God inscribed in the humanity of man and woman the vocation, and thus the capacity and responsibility, of love and communion. Love is therefore the fundamental and innate vocation of every human being" (*FC* 11).

This disposition to love is, therefore, inherent in man, and in knowing the love that "can be 'commanded' because it has first been given" (*DCE* 14), we discover that charity is not only the expansion of one's own being toward the other, but above all the acceptance of God's love. Once the relationship between love of God and love of neighbor is established, it will encourage and accentuate every gesture and attention devoted to the other.

Formation in the vertical sense needs to avail itself, first of all, of its "midwiving" labor, or rather of that capacity of bringing to life that which is inherent in the human person: in this case, the fact that "humanity is loved by God", as John Paul II wrote in the apostolic exhortation *Christifideles laici* (*CL* 34). Therefore, this means, on the one hand, cultivating as an existential choice and a way of life that which most deeply characterizes the human being and, on the other hand, communicating the truth of God's love and presenting Christ as the model and principle of charity while at the same time witnessing to the love that needs to inspire the lives of those who follow him.

In fact, the discovery of God is possible only "by means of a message that is appropriated, explicitly announced, and witnessed" through which "man is able to discover the profound reality that awaits him for his existence" (Schepens 1998: 265). Perhaps it is for this reason that the witness of the saints is a central theme of the encyclical. "The saints—consider the example of Blessed Teresa of Calcutta—constantly renewed their capacity for love of neighbor from their encounter with the Eucharistic Lord, and conversely this encounter acquired its realism and depth in their service to others. Love of God and love of neighbor are thus inseparable, they form a single commandment" (*DCE* 18). And again, "the figures of saints such as Francis of Assisi, Ignatius of Loyola, John of God, Camillus of Lellis, Vincent de Paul, Louise de Marillac, Giuseppe B. Cottolengo, John Bosco, Luigi Orione, Teresa of Calcutta, to name but a few—stand out as lasting models of social charity for all people of good will. The saints are the true bearers of light within history, for they are men and women of faith, hope and love" (*DCE* 40).

The theme of witness has also been the object of Benedict XVI's previous reflections. "One need only think of such figures as St. Benedict, St. Francis of Assisi, St. Teresa of Avila, St. Ignatius of Loyola, St. Charles Borromeo, the founders of nineteenth-century religious orders who inspired and guided the social movement, or the saints of our own day—Maximilian Kolbe, Edith Stein, Mother Teresa, Padre Pio. In contemplating these figures we learn what it means 'to adore' and what it means to live according to the measure of the Child of Bethlehem, by the measure of Jesus Christ and of God himself" (Benedict XVI 2005c).

The discovery of the God of love not only bears evidence of the inherent human disposition to love but is itself the formative experience of Love. In fact, the person who discovers the existence of God not so much as a "support" in times of need but as a value in himself is like someone who moves from love as a response to a need to love as a welcoming of the other and the reciprocity of relation. In both cases, the capacity to shift one's center away from oneself permits one to live the fruitfulness of love for God and for others.

> "Where do I find standards to live by, what are the criteria that govern responsible cooperation in building the present and the future of our world? On whom can I rely? To whom shall I entrust myself? Where is the One who can offer me the response capable of satisfying my heart's deepest desires?" The fact that we ask questions like these means that we realize our journey is not over until we meet the One who has the power to establish that universal Kingdom of justice and peace to which all people aspire, but which they are unable to build by themselves. (Benedict XVI 2005a)

The *ethos* most adequate for formation in the vertical sense is undoubtedly the family: "In this atmosphere of prayer and of awareness of the presence and paternity of God, the truth of faith and morals will be taught, comprised of and penetrated with reverence, the word of God will be read and experienced with love" (Pontificio Consiglio per la Famiglia 1995: 63). The entire Christian community, however, must hear this commitment in a way that gives it priority, favoring the fullness of existential experiences so that they may be able to connect faith with the realities of the world. "He who has learned to see and to understand the divine depths of reality will probably also be able to listen to the original word and be innovative in expressing the religious message regarding God" (Schepens 1998: 268).

b. Formation in the Horizontal Sense: The Experience of the Other

If the act of charity in a human person does not proceed from an interior habit assisted by natural potency but from the movements of the Holy Spirit, we find before us a dual position: either the act of charity is not voluntary, which is impossible since in fact it is the same as to love and, in a certain way, to will, or it is nothing more than a natural faculty, and this is heresy. It is therefore necessary that there be in us a certain created habit of charity, a habit which is the formal principle of our act of dilection. This necessity does not exclude the fact that the Holy Spirit,

which is uncreated charity, is made present in the person to provide charity, created to move the soul in the act of love in the
way in which God moves all agents to those operations to which
their form is already inclined. (Thomas Aquinas, *Quaest. Disput.
De Caritate* a.1 c)

The discovery of the love of God opens us up to the love of neighbor.
Formation in the vertical sense must, of necessity, intersect with formation in the horizontal sense in order that one can become capable
of recognizing, of receiving, and of accompanying.

Lastly, we should especially mention the great parable of the Last
Judgment (cf. Mt 25:31–46), in which love becomes the criterion for the definitive decision about a human life's worth or
lack thereof. Jesus identifies himself with those in need, with the
hungry, the thirsty, the stranger, the naked, the sick and those in
prison. "As you did it to one of the least of these my brethren,
you did it to me" (Mt 25:40). Love of God and love of neighbor
have become one: in the least of the brethren we find Jesus himself, and in Jesus we find God. (*DCE* 15)

An emblematic example of love of neighbor exists in the parable of
the Good Samaritan, as well as perhaps some clarification regarding the aim of formation of the heart. The first clarification deals
with the concept of "neighbor". "Until that time, the concept of 'neighbor' was understood as referring essentially to one's countrymen and
to foreigners who had settled in the land of Israel; in other words, to
the closely-knit community of a single country or people. This limit
is now abolished. Anyone who needs me, and whom I can help, is my
neighbor. The concept of 'neighbor' is now universalized, yet it remains
concrete" (*DCE* 15).

The Good Samaritan takes care of the other who is a complete
stranger from a cultural, social, and religious point of view, simply
because in him he recognizes a person in need. The Good Samaritan
is therefore "good", not a priori, but inasmuch as he was capable of
recognizing in the other his shared belonging to humanity and his
shared dignity. Such recognition renders love possible, surpassing all
creeds and all cultures, and makes the complete stranger our neighbor.

The second clarification regarding the concept of neighbor is that "despite being extended to all mankind, it is not reduced to a generic, abstract and undemanding expression of love, but calls for my own practical commitment here and now" (*DCE* 15). The Good Samaritan is concerned and stoops to serve his neighbor as if to indicate the way we must follow if we are to help those in need (Rocchetta 2000: 221–25).

Moving forward from his initial recognition of the other, the Good Samaritan harbors, not simple pity for the other, but compassion, a compassion that allows him to go out from himself to be with the one who suffers. Compassion does not leave one indifferent or insensible to another person's suffering but beckons one to solidarity with the suffering person. John Paul II writes that this solidarity "is not a feeling of vague compassion or shallow distress at the misfortunes of so many people, both near and far. On the contrary, it is a firm and persevering determination to commit oneself to the common good; that is to say to the good of all and of each individual, because we are all really responsible for all" (*SRS* 38). Compassion born of this recognizing and stimulated by love "creates" the neighbor.

Love of neighbor, therefore, is born of this recognition from within an interpersonal relationship, from free choice, and from the desire of openness to the other. Thus emerges the targets of formation in the horizontal sense: affectivity (relationship with the other), moral feeling (free acceptance), and solidarity (openness to the other).

"A Heart in Systole and Diastole"

Affectivity is the human capacity to feel emotions, sentiments, and passions and to be in a given mood in relation to subjective or objective situations (Centro Studi Filosofici di Gallarate 1979: 88–89). Or, in the understanding of affective love, it is the "faculty to respond to values, including sexual values, of the person in all his complexity" (Wojtyła 1978: 99). The unifying element is the wide-ranging reactions that we are able to display when faced with some stimulus, whether it comes from within or from outside our own reality (from God, experiences of relationship, the environment, socio-cultural stimuli, and so on), and which always lead us to interior modifications and action before the person or thing that caused such worries.

On the other hand, the term "affectivity" derives from the Latin *afficere*, meaning "to influence", "to produce a modification in the body or soul", "to strike", a dual and uninterrupted movement, of "systole" (union with the object of one's attraction, an exchange of being) and of "diastole" (to go out of one's self). This movement is truly exemplified by interpersonal relations (Padovese 2004: 46–49).

Keeping in mind the relational aspect of affectivity, we are able to distinguish four steps in the development of affectivity (Cesari and Di Pietro 1996): (1) The capacity to engage in positive relationships with all; (2) the capacity to initiate friendly relations; (3) friendship; (4) the capacity for love of one spouse or for all, according to one's state in life (conjugal or virginal). The development of affectivity also augments sensitivity in the vertical dimension of formation by facilitating the interiorization of the Word of God that enables one to live it out as a personal message.

For an adequate formation of affectivity, it is first of all essential to have a familiar condition that is characterized by a strong affective charge given by natural ties between the members. In itself, this is not educational, but it becomes so over time in response to the intention and the commitment that the parents are able to express (Santelli Beccegato 1985).

If planned from the earliest age, a person's affective equilibrium as well as interior well-being will be developed day by day. Such education should not be reserved only for the important decisions of life but should instead take place in every moment in the way we live and give witness daily. This is the reason for the need to grow up in a family that is present and influential, that practices and is able to keep up satisfying relationships. It is also necessary to be part of a group of equals with whom to experience sincere, authentic, and profound feelings of friendship; to sustain the challenge of knowing how to live one's own duties and tasks in an independent and reliable manner; to develop self-knowledge, autonomy, self-acceptance, self-worth, and self-esteem; and to develop the capacity for understanding, integration, adaptation, and the control of one's own impulses.

If the affective development of the individual is to be harmonious, if self–control has been learned as well as the ability to love parents and siblings, to enjoy the friendship of companions and the esteem of teachers, then a horizon that expands beyond one's individual world toward the consideration of one's obligations to others can be hoped for.

"A Heart at the Crossroads"

What is characteristic of affectivity is its capacity for contemplation and openness to recognizing the total good of the person, which appear in strict connection with moral feelings.

> If morality is considered as a coordination of values and is comparable to a logical grouping, then we would need to admit that interpersonal feelings have a place as a species of operation. At first glance it seems that the affective life is of a purely intuitive order and that its spontaneity excludes all that would resemble an operation of the intellect. In reality this romantic idea is true only in early infancy, a time in which impulsivity impedes every constant direction of thought as with the sentiments. Little by little, as these are organized, we see develop, in reverse, regulators of which the will forms the final equilibrium. It is the will, therefore, which is the true affective equivalent to the operations of reason. However, the will is a function that appears very late, and its real function is linked to the autonomous moral sentiments. This is why we have waited until this stage to mention it. (Piaget 1967: 66–67)

Formation of affectivity needs, therefore, to accompany the formation of moral feelings with the following objectives: to define precisely the reasons for which we, if we are to realize our own human essence, need to act in one way and not another; to help individuals acquire an awareness of their own actions and responsibilities as well as essential tools such as the criteria for judgment and criteria for motivation, so that they may work out a synthesis between freedom and responsibility; to offer sound objective criteria and clear understanding for action.

The goal, therefore, of the formation of moral feelings is an education for freedom, or, better said, for the responsible management of freedom, in order to have a complete adherence to that truth which, written into the nature and essence of all persons, reveals to them their form, meaning, and destiny (Giammancheri and Peretti 1977).

> No less critical in the formation of conscience is the recovery of the necessary link between freedom and truth. . . . It is therefore essential that man should acknowledge his inherent condition as a creature to whom God has granted being and life as a gift and a duty. Only by admitting his innate dependence can man live and use his freedom to the full, and at the same time respect the life and freedom of every other person. (*EV* 96)

In other words, this involves helping all persons attain moral freedom in such a way that they may be freely able to adhere to the "law of being" and to be determined by the good to such a degree that they are unable to choose the bad: "It is like finding ourselves at a crossroads: which direction do we take? The one prompted by the passions or the one indicated by the star which shines in your conscience? The Magi heard the answer '*In Bethlehem of Judea; for so it is written by the prophet*' (Mt 2:5), and, enlightened by these words, they chose to press forward to the very end" (Benedict XVI 2005a).

The formation of moral feelings needs to consider both the sphere of values as well as that of virtues, understood as *habitus*, "dispositions", "habits", or "predispositions": on the two different planes that intersect, the natural one of moral or cardinal virtues (prudence, justice, fortitude, and temperance), and the supernatural one of infused or theological virtues (faith, hope, and charity). This is because "man is not an angelic reality but is intimately structured in a way composed of body and soul. The virtues, therefore, need to regulate the entire being of the person, transforming not only the intellect and the will, but also permeating the sensible, passionate, and affective horizons. For this reason the virtues are not limited to the realm of the spirit but must invade one's whole being" (Ravasi 2005: 22).

In fact, if the formation of moral feelings is to help persons construct their own identity, to acquire values considered important for declaring to self and others one's own being, to ensure the capacity to

resist destructive forces from within and without, to guarantee a coher-
ent and lasting interior unity, then a selective control of values is neither easy nor sufficient without at the same time the acquisition of
those values. The person is formed in succeeding to construct a filter
through which to verify and to evaluate which things to accept and
which to reject. In other words, when that person is able to respond
to the question "what kind of person should I be?" The commitment,
then, must be one that helps the person to grow in virtue, or rather,
to acquire a permanent attitude for doing good and doing it well. The
habitus of acting virtuously, far from being a sort of passive, unconscious repetition of gestures, presents itself as the ability decisively and
dutifully to orient one's freedom toward true values.

"A Heart that Loves"

Since we receive the same Lord and he gathers us together and
draws us into himself, we ourselves are one. This must be evident in our lives. . . . It must be seen in our commitment to our
neighbors, both those close at hand and those physically far away,
whom we nevertheless consider to be close. Today, there are many
forms of volunteer assistance, models of mutual service, of which
our society has urgent need. (Benedict XVI 2005b)

Formation in the vertical sense and formation in the horizontal sense,
therefore, find their point of intersection in the God who gives us his
own Body and Blood in the Eucharist: the discovery that God loves us
and makes us "one" in himself opens us up to the necessities of the other.

Acceptance, accompaniment, and solidarity are some of the ways
of calling that charity which leads us to share, not with a selective
attitude, but with real participation, the joys and sufferings of others.
In this case as well, the formative challenge is strong, which calls once
more for participation regarding the entirety of the person.

Formation in solidarity with those who are alone, who suffer, who
need to be listened to, considered, and touched ("If there is among
you a poor man, one of your brethren, . . . you shall not harden your
heart or shut your hand"; Deut 15:7), also requires formation in the
sacredness of life: man is not the absolute master of himself, of his

own body, or of his own spirit. Human life is a good that is not only personal, but also social, and which the community needs to defend. The life of every person is a good because, from the view of charity, our neighbor does not have ethnicity, race, or age. "Let brotherly love [*philadelphia*] continue. Do not neglect hospitality [*philoxenia*]" (Heb 13:1–2). Human life is a good that cannot be left at the mercy of some "false" freedom, the epi-phenomenon of desperation, loneliness, and abandonment. Think, for example, of the recourse to abortion or the request for euthanasia.

Formation in solidarity is also entrusted, first of all, to the family, even if its commitment extends to educational agencies. In other words, it is about consulting the Samaritan spirit of the Christian community, of taking up the burden of fragile and difficult situations. The growth in volunteers and organizations dedicated to the care of the disabled are examples of the concrete decision to orient oneself to truth, to authenticity, and to the service of charity.

A "Mature Heart"

Having a mature heart thus means:

–Forming the heart to overcome selfishness, impatience, arrogance, envy, and to assume altruism, patience, reflection, and disinterestedness, with charity as a guide and a goal.
–Forming the heart to reach the fullness—the maturity—of Christian life and being, in the words of St. Paul, "so that we may no longer be children, tossed back and forth and carried about with every wind of doctrine, by the cunning of men, by their craftiness in deceitful wiles" (Eph 4:14).
–Forming the heart and mind to be capable not only to respond to immediate need with solicitude and professional competence, but also to bear in mind that the persons who stand before us "need humanity. They need heartfelt concern" (*DCE* 31a).
–Forming the heart not only of those who work in the Church's charitable institutions, but also of those who, in their profession, come in contact with the needy and the suffering, especially health-care workers.

—Forming the heart to put oneself at the service of life because "as you did it to one of the least of these my brethren, you did it to me" (Mt 25:40).

Bibliography

Benedict XVI. 2005a. Celebration Welcoming the Young People. *Address*. Cologne-Poller Wiesen, August 18.

———. 2005b. Eucharistic Celebration. *Homily*. Cologne-Marienfeld. August 21.

———. 2005c. Youth Vigil. *Address*. Cologne-Marienfeld. August 20.

Centro Studi Filosofici di Gallarate. 1979. *Enciclopedia filosofica*. Rome: EPIDEM. 1:88–89.

Cesari, G., and M. L. Di Pietro. 1996. *L'educazione della sessualità*. Brescia: La Scuola.

Giammancheri, E., and M. Peretti, eds. 1977. *L'educazione morale*. Brescia: La Scuola.

Gnocchi, C. 1998. *Educazione del cuore*. Milan: Ancora.

Padovese, L. 2004. *Affettività (voce)*. In *Enciclopedia di Bioetica e Sessuologia*, edited by G. Russo, pp. 46–49. Leumann (Turin): Elledici—CIC Edizioni Internazionali.

Piaget, J. 1967. *Psicologia e sviluppo mentale del bambino*. Milan: Giulio Einaudi Editore.

Pontificio Consiglio per la Famiglia. 1995. *Sessualità umana: Orientamenti educativi in famiglia*. December 8.

Ravasi, G. 2005. *Ritorno alle virtù: La scoperta di uno stile di vita*. Milan: Mondadori.

Rocchetta, C. 2000. *Teologia della tenerezza*. Bologna: EDB.

Santelli Beccegato, L. 1985. *L'educazione affettiva e sessuale*. In *Vogliamo educare i nostri figli*, edited by N. Galli, pp. 245–53, 316–22. Milan: Vita e Pensiero.

Schepens, J. 1998. *Cristiani impegnati nell'educazione in una società post-cristiana*. In *Donna e umanizzazione della cultura alle soglie del terzo millenio: La via dell'educazione*, ed. Piera Cavaglià et al., pp. 242–72. Rome: LAS.

Wojtyła, K. 1978. *Amore e responsabilità*. Turin: Marietti. [*Love and Responsibility*, San Francisco: Ignatius Press, 1993.]

Abbreviations

CA   John Paul II, encyclical *Centesimus Annus*, May 1, 1991

CC   Pius XI, encyclical *Casti Connubii*, December 31, 1930

CCC   *Catechism of the Catholic Church*, 2nd ed. Libreria Editrice Vaticana, 1997

CEP   Benedict XVI, "Charity Exceeds Philanthropy by 'Showing Christ'", Address to the Participants at the Meeting Promoted by the Pontifical Council "Cor Unum", January 23, 2006

CL   John Paul II, apostolic exhortation *Christifideles Laici*, December 30, 1988

DCE   Benedict XVI, encyclical *Deus Caritas Est*, December 25, 2005

DM   John Paul II, encyclical *Dives et Misericordia*, November 30, 1980

DV   Vatican Council II, Dogmatic Constitution on Divine Revelation *Dei Verbum*, November 18, 1965

EV   John Paul II, encyclical *Evangelium Vitae*, March 25, 1995

FC   John Paul II, apostolic exhortation *Familiaris Consortio*, November 22, 1981

FR   John Paul II, encyclical *Fides et Ratio*, September 15, 1998

GS   Vatican Council II, Pastoral Constitution on the Church in the Modern World, *Gaudium et Spes*, December 7, 1965

HA   Pius XII, encyclical *Haurietis Aquas*, May 15, 1956

HV   Paul VI, encyclical *Humanae Vitae*, July 25, 1968

ICFL   Congregation for the Doctrine of the Faith, *Instruction on Christian Freedom and Liberation, Libertatis Conscientia*, March 22, 1986

PG   J. P. Migne, *Patrologia Graeca*

PL   J. P. Migne, *Patrologia Latina*

RH   John Paul II, encyclical *Redemptor Hominis*, March 4, 1979

SCh   Sources chrétiennes (Paris: 1942–)

SRS   John Paul II, encyclical *Sollicitudo Rei Socialis*, December 30, 1987

STh   Thomas Aquinas, *Summa Theologiae*

TSZ   Friedrich Nietzsche, *Thus Spoke Zarathustra*

VS   John Paul II, encyclical *Veritatis Splendor*, August 6, 1993